Clean Code with C#

Refactor your legacy C# code base and improve application
performance using best practices

Jason Alls

BIRMINGHAM—MUMBAI

Clean Code with C#

Copyright © 2023 Packt Publishing

Associate Group Product Manager: Kunal Sawant

Book Project Manager: Prajakta Naik

Senior Editor: Ruvika Rao

Technical Editor: Vidhisha Patidar

Copy Editor: Safis Editing

Indexer: Tejal Daruwale Soni

Production Designer: Alishon Mendonca

DevRel Marketing Coordinators: Shrinidhi Manoharan and Sonia Chauhan

Business Development Executive: Kriti Sharma

First published: July 2020
Second edition: December 2023

Production reference: 1141223

Published by Packt Publishing Ltd.
Grosvenor House
11 St Paul's Square
Birmingham
B3 1RB, UK.

ISBN 978-1-83763-519-1

www.packtpub.com

To my parents, for supporting me throughout my life and career. To all the people in the world of software that have made my career possible, and who have employed me, trained me, and worked alongside me. You have been instrumental in helping me to get to where I am today.

I thank you all.

– Jason Alls

Contributors

About the author

Jason Alls has been programming for over 21 years using Microsoft technologies. Working with an Australasian company, he started his career developing call center management reporting software used by global clients including telecom providers, banks, airlines, and the police. He then moved on to develop GIS marketing applications and worked in the banking sector performing data migrations between Oracle and SQL Server. Certified as an MCAD in C# since 2005, he has been involved in the development of various desktop, web, and mobile applications.

I would like to thank my parents for always being there, and supporting me throughout my life and career. Career-wise, I would like to thank all the people in the world of computing who have made my career possible. Especially those who have employed me, trained me, and worked alongside me. You have helped me to get to where I am today.

A special thank you to all the staff at Packt Publishing who provided me with the opportunity to write this book, and who assisted me in improving the content. It has been an eye-opening experience and a pleasant one. It is your hard work and dedication to the book-writing process that enables computer programmers like me to become accomplished authors. This book would not be what it is without your valuable input.

About the reviewers

Vladica Ognjanovic, CEO of MVP-Soft based in the USA and Serbia, holds a Bachelor's in Computer Science from the University of Niš. With over two decades in the tech industry, Vladica has mastered IT management, software development, and database design. He's led various enterprise projects, including custom ERP solutions, price tracking systems, IoT solutions, demonstrating strong skills in web, desktop, and database technologies. Known for innovative problem-solving, Vladica excels in team leadership and client engagement, making significant contributions to software development and project management.

Omprakash Pandey, has been working with industry experts and helping SW consultants from last 20 years. His SW expertise ranges from Microsoft 365, Power Platform, Security Solutions, JEE technologies, .Net and Cloud expertise. He has been working on areas of Azure Infrastructure, Azure Development using C#, Azure Architecting. He has also delivered consulting assignments and developed products for SharePoint custom solutions using .Net. Organizing resources and ensuring project completion in right time DevOps has been the key transformation agent for the same. He is also expert in Azure DevOps solution.

Since it first computer, a Commodore Vic20, **Gian Maria** was interested in everything regarding Computer Programming. Its passion range from low level (Assembly) to project management. He worked with Microsoft .NET technologies since very first beta as a passionate Visual Basic .NET then C# software architect/developer. He has strong experience in DevOps methodologies and techniques, covering all aspect from managing Requirements to effectively manage code with Git to automatic Deployment on premise and on cloud resources. Always curious about new technologies he lives and work in Italy as an independent consultant.

Jegadeesan Ponnusamy worked in the software industry for more than 16 years. He has a master's degree in software engineering from the Birla Institute of Technology & Science, Pilani. He received gold medal, Sri Hiren D. Barucha Memorial award for his excellence in academic and other recognitions for his work in his career. He currently lives in Voorhees, New Jersey with his wife and two daughters.

Table of Contents

3

Classes, Objects, and Data Structures   53

4

Writing Clean Functions   97

5

Exception Handling   131

6

Unit Testing   165

7

Designing and Developing APIs   191

8

Addressing Cross-Cutting Concerns   227

9

AOP with PostSharp   251

12

Functional Programming   333

13

Cross-Platform Application Development with MAUI   367

14

Microservices   395

Assessments   431

Preface

Welcome to *Clean Code in C#*. You will learn how to identify problematic code that, while it compiles, does not lend itself to readability, maintainability, and extensibility. You will also learn about various tools and patterns, along with ways to refactor code to make it clean.

Who this book is for

This book is aimed at computer programmers with a good grasp of the C# programming language who would like guidance on identifying problematic code and writing clean code in C#. Primarily, the reader base will range from graduate to mid-level programmers, but even senior programmers may find this book valuable.

What this book covers

Chapter 1, Coding Standards and Principles in C#, contrasts some good code with some bad code. As you read through this chapter, you will come to understand why you need coding standards, principles, methodologies, and code conventions. You will learn about modularity and the KISS, YAGNI, DRY, SOLID, and Occam's razor design guidelines.

Chapter 2, Code Review – Process and Importance, takes you through the code review process and provides reasons for its importance. In this chapter, you are guided through the process of preparing code for review, leading a code review, knowing what to review, knowing when to send code for review, and how to provide and respond to review feedback.

Chapter 3, Classes, Objects, and Data Structures, covers the broad topics of class organization, documentation comments, cohesion, coupling, the Law of Demeter, and immutable objects and data structures. By the end of the chapter, you will be able to write code that is well organized and only has a single responsibility, provide users of the code with relevant documentation, and make the code extensible.

Chapter 4, Writing Clean Functions, helps you to understand functional programming, how to keep methods small, and how to avoid code duplication and multiple parameters. By the time you finish this chapter, you will be able to describe functional programming, write functional code, avoid writing code with more than two parameters, write immutable data objects and structures, keep your methods small, and write code that adheres to the single responsibility principle.

Chapter 5, Exception Handling, covers checked and unchecked exceptions, and `NullPointerEx-ception`, and how to avoid them as well as covering, business rule exceptions, providing meaningful data, and building your own custom exceptions.

Chapter 6, Unit Testing, takes you through using the **Behavior-Driven Development (BDD)** software methodology using `SpecFlow`, and **Test-Driven Development** (TDD) using `MSTest` and `NUnit`. You will learn how to write mock (fake) objects using `Moq`, and how to use the TDD software methodology to write tests that fail, make the tests pass, and then refactor the code once it passes.

Chapter 7, Designing and Developing APIs, helps you to understand what an API is, and covers API proxies, API design guidelines, API design using RAML, and Swagger API development. In this chapter, you will design a language-agnostic API in RAML and develop it in C#, and you will document your API using Swagger.

Chapter 8, Addressing Cross-Cutting Concerns, introduces you to using PostSharp to address cross-cutting concerns using aspects and attributes that form the basis of aspect-oriented development. You will also learn how to use proxies and decorators.

Chapter 9, AOP with PostSharp, explores using PostSharp to implement **Aspect-Oriented Programming** (**AOP**). With our AOP framework, we will learn how to manage common functionalities such as exception handling, logging, security, and transactions within our applications. But before that, let's put your brain to work to see what you have learned.

Chapter 10, Using Tools to Improve Code Quality, exposes you to various tools that will assist you in writing quality code and improving the quality of existing code. You'll gain exposure to code metrics and code analysis, quick actions, the JetBrains tools called **dotTrace Profiler** and **Resharper**, and **Telerik JustDecompile**.

Chapter 11, Refactoring C# Code, is the first of two chapters that take you through different types of problematic code and show you how to modify it to be clean code that is easy to read, maintain, and extend. Code problems are listed alphabetically through each chapter. Here, you will cover such topics as class dependencies, code that can't be modified, collections, and combinatorial explosion.

Chapter 12, Functional Programming, provides a detailed look at functional programming. You will learn the difference between imperative and functional programming. Then you will learn about delegates, anonymous methods, and lambda expressions Next, you move on to the topics of asynchronous functional programming, recursion, and then finally, pattern matching.

Chapter 13, Cross-platform development with MAUI, delves into building applications with .NET MAUI. You will learn the differences between the older `Xamarin.Forms` and the newer MAUI, including using UI controls using the MVVM pattern, data binding, access device resources, data access accessing remote microservices and Azure Functions, dependency injection, and styling.

Chapter 14, Microservices, looks at developing microservices using Azure Functions.

To get the most out of this book

Software/hardware covered in the book	Requirements
Visual Studio 2019	Windows 10, macOS
Atom	Windows 10, macOS, Linux: `https://atom.io/`
Azure resources	Azure subscription: `https://azure.microsoft.com/en-gb/`
Azure Key Vault	Azure subscription: `https://azure.microsoft.com/en-gb/`
The Morningstar API	Obtain your own API key from `https://rapidapi.com/integraatio/api/morningstar1`
Postman	Windows 10, macOS, Linux: `https://www.postman.com/`

It will be useful to have these in place before you start reading and working your way through the chapters.

If you are using the digital version of this book, we advise you to type the code yourself or access the code from the book's GitHub repository (a link is available in the next section). Doing so will help you avoid any potential errors related to the copying and pasting of code.

You should have basic experience using Visual Studio 2019 Community Edition or higher, and basic C# programming skills, including writing console applications. Many examples will be in the form of C# console applications. The main project use ASP.NET. It will help if you are capable of writing ASP.NET websites using the framework and core. However, don't worry – you will be guided through the steps that you need to go through.

Download the example code files

You can download the example code files for this book from GitHub at `https://github.com/PacktPublishing/Clean-Code-with-CSharp-Second-Edition/tree/main`. If there's an update to the code, it will be updated in the GitHub repository.

We also have other code bundles from our rich catalog of books and videos available at `https://github.com/PacktPublishing/`. Check them out!

Conventions used

There are a number of text conventions used throughout this book.

`Code in text`: Indicates code words in text, database table names, folder names, filenames, file extensions, pathnames, dummy URLs, user input, and Twitter handles. Here is an example: "The `InMemoryRepository` class implements the `GetApiKey()` method of `IRepository`. This returns a dictionary of API keys. These keys will be stored in our_apiKeys dictionary member variable"

A block of code is set as follows:

```
using CH10_DividendCalendar.Security.Authentication;
using System.Threading.Tasks;

namespace CH10_DividendCalendar.Repository {
    public interface IRepository
    {
        Task<ApiKey> GetApiKey(string providedApiKey);
    }
}
```

Any command-line input or output is written as follows:

```
az group create --name "<YourResourceGroupName>" --location "East US"
```

Bold: Indicates a new term, an important word, or words that you see onscreen. For instance, words in menus or dialog boxes appear in **bold**. Here is an example: "To create the app service, right-click the project you created and select **Publish** from the menu."

> **Tips or important notes**
> Appear like this.

Get in touch

Feedback from our readers is always welcome.

General feedback: If you have questions about any aspect of this book, email us at customercare@ packtpub.com and mention the book title in the subject of your message.

Errata: Although we have taken every care to ensure the accuracy of our content, mistakes do happen. If you have found a mistake in this book, we would be grateful if you would report this to us. Please visit www.packtpub.com/support/errata and fill in the form.

Piracy: If you come across any illegal copies of our works in any form on the internet, we would be grateful if you would provide us with the location address or website name. Please contact us at copyright@packt.com with a link to the material.

If you are interested in becoming an author: If there is a topic that you have expertise in and you are interested in either writing or contributing to a book, please visit authors.packtpub.com.

Share Your Thoughts

Once you've read *Clean Code with C#*, we'd love to hear your thoughts! Scan the QR code below to go straight to the Amazon review page for this book and share your feedback.

https://packt.link/r/1837635196

Your review is important to us and the tech community and will help us make sure we're delivering excellent quality content.

Download a free PDF copy of this book

Thanks for purchasing this book!

Do you like to read on the go but are unable to carry your print books everywhere?

Is your eBook purchase not compatible with the device of your choice?

Don't worry, now with every Packt book you get a DRM-free PDF version of that book at no cost.

Read anywhere, any place, on any device. Search, copy, and paste code from your favorite technical books directly into your application.

The perks don't stop there, you can get exclusive access to discounts, newsletters, and great free content in your inbox daily

Follow these simple steps to get the benefits:

1. Scan the QR code or visit the link below

https://packt.link/free-ebook/9781837635191

2. Submit your proof of purchase
3. That's it! We'll send your free PDF and other benefits to your email directly

1
Coding Standards and Principles in C#

The primary goal of coding standards and principles in C# is for programmers to become better at their craft by programming code that is more performant and easier to maintain. In this chapter, we will look at some examples of good code contrasted with examples of bad code. This will lead nicely into discussing why we need coding standards, principles, and methodologies. As we delve into coding standards, we will consider conventions for naming, commenting, and formatting source code, including classes, methods, and variables.

A big program can be rather unwieldy to understand and maintain. For programming teams, getting to know the code and what it does can be a daunting prospect, and they can find it hard to work together on such projects. Because of this, we will look at how to use modularity to break programs down into smaller modules that all work together to produce a fully functioning solution that is also fully testable, can be worked on by multiple teams simultaneously, and is much easier to read, understand, and document. And we'll finish this chapter by looking at some programming design guidelines.

The following topics will be covered in this chapter:

- The need for coding standards, principles, and methodologies
- Naming conventions and methods
- Comments and formatting
- Modularity
- KISS
- YAGNI
- DRY
- SOLID
- Occam's razor

After reading this chapter, you will be able to do the following:

- Understand how good code positively impacts projects
- Understand why bad code negatively impacts projects.
- Understand how coding standards improve code and how to enforce them
- Understand how coding principles enhance software quality
- Understand how methodologies aid the development of clean code
- Implement coding standards
- Choose solutions with the least assumptions

We'll now look at the technical requirements that you will need as you work through this book.

Technical requirements

To work on the code in this book, you will need to download and install the latest version of Visual Studio Community Edition. The IDE can be downloaded from `https://visualstudio.microsoft.com`.

> **Note**
> There are no code samples for this chapter.

Good code versus bad code

Both good and bad code compile. There are reasons why code is labeled good code and bad code, as shown in the following comparison table:

Good Code	Bad Code
Proper indentation	Improper indentation
Meaningful comments	Comments that state the obvious
API documentation comments	Comments that excuse bad code and commented-out lines of code
Proper organization using namespaces	Improper organization using namespaces
Good naming conventions	Bad naming conventions
Classes that do one thing	Classes that do multiple things
Methods that do a single thing	Methods that do multiple things
Methods with less than 10 lines, and preferably no more than 4	Methods with more than 10 lines of code

Methods with no more than two parameters	Methods with more than two parameters
Proper use of exceptions	Using exceptions to control program flow
Readable code	Code that is difficult to read
Code that is loosely coupled	Code that is tightly couples
High cohesion	Low cohesion
Objects are cleanly disposed of	Objects are left hanging around
Avoidance of the `Finalize` method	Use of the `Finalize` method
The right level of abstraction	Over-engineering
Use of regions in larger classes	Lack of regions in larger classes
Encapsulation and information hiding	Directly exposing information
Object-orientated code	Spaghetti code
Design patterns	Design anti-patterns

Table 1.1: Good code versus bad code

This table contains an extensive list of what makes code good, and what makes code bad. As you work on your code and review your peer's code, try and maintain as much of this list in your head as you can. It will come in handy for ensuring you have the right, good, clean code and can identify bad code and refactor it.

We will now look at the need for coding standards, principles, and software methodologies.

The need for coding standards, principles, and methodologies

As a C# programmer, coding standards, principles, and methodologies are important for several reasons:

- **Consistency**: Coding standards, principles, and methodologies help ensure consistency across a code base. By following these guidelines, developers can ensure that their code is written in a similar style and adheres to the same best practices, making it easier for other developers to understand, modify, and maintain the code.

- **Quality**: Coding standards, principles, and methodologies promote the use of best practices that improve code quality, such as error handling, documentation, and modular design. Following these guidelines can help reduce bugs, improve performance, and make the code more maintainable over time.

- **Collaboration**: When a team of developers is working on a project, everyone must be on the same page. Coding standards, principles, and methodologies can help ensure that everyone is working toward the same goals and following the same guidelines, making it easier to collaborate and avoid conflicts.

- **Efficiency**: Following coding standards, principles, and methodologies can help improve efficiency by promoting the use of reusable code, modular design, and other best practices. This can reduce development time and make it easier to modify and maintain the code base over time.

- **Professionalism**: Following coding standards, principles, and methodologies is a hallmark of professionalism in the software development industry. It shows that you are committed to producing high-quality code that is easy to understand, maintain, and extend.

Overall, coding standards, principles, and methodologies are important for ensuring that software is of high quality, easy to maintain, and produced professionally and efficiently. By following these guidelines, C# programmers can improve their code, work more effectively with their team, and build better software.

Coding standards

Coding standards are a set of guidelines and best practices that are used by C# programmers to write high-quality, maintainable, and readable code. These standards help promote consistency across the code base and make it easier for developers to understand, modify, and maintain each other's code. Here are some key components of coding standards for C# programmers:

- **Naming conventions**: C# programmers typically use consistent and meaningful names for variables, methods, classes, and other programming elements. This makes it easier to understand the purpose of each element and promotes code readability.

- **Code formatting**: C# programmers typically use consistent formatting styles for their code, including indentation, line breaks, and spacing. This makes it easier to read and understand the code, especially when working with code that spans multiple lines.

- **Error handling**: C# programmers typically use consistent error-handling practices, including try-catch blocks, error messages, and logging. This helps to improve the reliability and maintainability of the code and makes it easier to diagnose and fix errors.

- **Code reuse**: C# programmers typically use inheritance, polymorphism, and other object-oriented programming principles to promote code reuse. This helps reduce duplication of code and makes it easier to maintain and modify the code base.

- **Code documentation**: C# programmers typically use XML comments and other forms of documentation to describe the purpose and behavior of their code. This helps make the code base more understandable and maintainable, especially for developers who are new to the project.

- **Code reviews**: C# programmers typically conduct code reviews to ensure that the code meets the coding standards and other best practices. This helps improve the quality of the code and promotes consistency across the code base.

By following coding standards, C# programmers can write code that is easy to read, understand, and maintain, which helps reduce errors and improve the overall quality of the software.

Coding principles

Coding principles, also known as software development principles or programming principles, are a set of guidelines or best practices that software developers use to write high-quality, efficient, and maintainable code. These principles are designed to help developers write code that is easy to understand, modify, and debug, and that meets the requirements of the project or application.

There are many different coding principles, each with a focus and set of guidelines. Some common coding principles include the following:

- **SOLID principles**: A set of five principles that focus on object-oriented design and programming, including the Single Responsibility Principle, Open/Closed Principle, Liskov Substitution Principle, Interface Segregation Principle, and Dependency Inversion Principle.

- **KISS principle**: Keep It Simple, Stupid. This principle emphasizes the importance of simplicity in software design and suggests that simple solutions are often the best solutions.

- **DRY principle**: Don't Repeat Yourself. This principle suggests that code should not be duplicated or repeated unnecessarily and that developers should strive to write reusable and modular code.

- **YAGNI principle**: You Ain't Gonna Need It. This principle suggests that developers should only implement features or functionality that are necessary for the current requirements and should avoid over-engineering or adding unnecessary complexity to the code.

- **Modularity principle**: This principle emphasizes the importance of breaking down a software system into smaller, self-contained modules or components.

By following these coding principles and others like them, software developers can write code that is easier to understand, maintain, and modify, and that meets the needs of the project or application.

Coding conventions

Coding conventions are a set of guidelines and rules that a C# programmer follows when writing code. These conventions help ensure that the code is consistent, readable, and maintainable, regardless of who wrote it. Here are some common coding conventions for C# programmers:

- **Naming conventions**: C# programmers typically use PascalCase for class names and method names, and camelCase for variable names. Constants are usually written in ALL_CAPS.

- **Indentation and braces**: C# programmers typically use four spaces for indentation and place opening braces on the same line as the statement that opens the block. Closing braces are typically placed on a new line.

- **Comments**: C# programmers typically use XML comments to document their code, including descriptions of classes, methods, and parameters.

- **Code formatting**: C# programmers typically use a consistent formatting style for their code, including spacing, line breaks, and indentation.

- **Error handling**: C# programmers typically use try-catch blocks to handle exceptions and avoid using exceptions for control flow.

- **Code reuse**: C# programmers typically use inheritance and interfaces to promote code reuse and avoid duplicating code.

- **Coding standards**: C# programmers typically follow coding standards established by their team or organization, which may include guidelines for naming, indentation, comments, and other coding conventions.

By following these coding conventions and others like them, C# programmers can write code that is consistent, readable, and maintainable, which can help reduce errors, improve productivity, and make it easier for other programmers to work with their code.

Microsoft coding conventions adoption

The Microsoft coding guidelines for C# programmers, also known as the .NET Framework Design Guidelines, were developed by Microsoft to provide a set of best practices for developing high-quality, reliable, and maintainable code. The guidelines cover a wide range of topics, including naming conventions, code formatting, error handling, performance, and security.

The adoption of the Microsoft coding guidelines has been widespread among C# programmers, especially those who develop applications for the Microsoft .NET Framework. These guidelines have become a de facto standard for C# programming, and many third-party tools and libraries have been developed to support their use.

These guidelines are regularly updated to reflect changes in the C# language, the .NET Framework, and best practices in software development. They are freely available online and are used by many organizations as a basis for their coding standards.

Overall, the adoption of the Microsoft coding guidelines has helped improve the quality and reliability of C# code and has made it easier for developers to write, read, and maintain code written by others.

Modularity

As a C# software developer, it is important to understand the modularity coding principle, which is a software design principle that emphasizes the importance of breaking down a software system into smaller, self-contained modules or components.

The modularity principle is based on the idea that complex systems can be easier to understand, maintain, and modify if they are broken down into smaller, more manageable parts. Each module should have a clear responsibility or purpose and should interact with other modules through well-defined interfaces.

To apply the modularity principle in C# programming, developers should design their software systems as a collection of self-contained modules or components. Each module should have a clearly defined purpose and a well-defined interface for interacting with other modules. This can help reduce the complexity of the system as developers can focus on designing and implementing individual modules without having to worry about the entire system.

By following the modularity principle, C# developers can create more maintainable and efficient code. They can also improve the scalability and flexibility of the system, as modules can be added or removed as needed without this affecting the entire system.

However, it is important to note that modularity can also introduce additional complexity and overhead, especially if the interfaces between modules are not well-designed or if the system is not properly tested. C# developers should still ensure that their modules are designed to work together seamlessly and that the overall system meets the requirements and is easy to understand and maintain.

SOLID

SOLID coding principles are a set of guidelines for writing clean, maintainable, and scalable code. The SOLID principles are as follows:

- **Single Responsibility Principle (SRP)**: This principle states that each class or module should have only one responsibility or reason to change. This means that a class should do one thing and do it well. By keeping classes focused on a single responsibility, it becomes easier to test, maintain, and extend them.

- **Open-Closed Principle (OCP)**: This principle states that classes should be open for extension but closed for modification. This means that you should be able to extend the behavior of a class without modifying its source code. By using abstractions and interfaces, you can create flexible and extensible code that can be adapted to new requirements without breaking existing functionality.

- **Liskov Substitution Principle (LSP)**: This principle states that a subclass should be substitutable for its base class. This means that you should be able to use a subclass wherever its base class is used without introducing errors or unexpected behavior. By following this principle, you can create code that is more modular, reusable, and extensible.

- **Interface Segregation Principle (ISP)**: This principle states that classes should not be forced to depend on interfaces they do not use. This means that interfaces should be designed with a single responsibility and clients should only depend on the interfaces that they need. By following this principle, you can create code that is more flexible and easier to maintain.

- **Dependency Inversion Principle (DIP)**: This principle states that high-level modules should not depend on low-level modules, but both should depend on abstractions. This means that the design of the system should be based on abstractions, not concrete implementations. By using dependency injection, you can create code that is more modular, testable, and extensible.

By following the SOLID principles, C# developers can write code that is more modular, maintainable, and extensible. These principles can help reduce the complexity of the code and make it easier to add new features, fix bugs, and refactor the code. The SOLID principles are widely adopted in the software development industry and are an essential part of creating high-quality software.

Keep It Simple Stupid (KISS)

The KISS coding principle is a problem-solving principle that suggests that simplicity should be a key goal in software design.

The KISS principle is based on the idea that simple solutions are often easier to understand, maintain, and modify than complex solutions. It emphasizes the importance of avoiding unnecessary complexity and keeping code as straightforward as possible.

To apply the KISS principle in C# programming, developers should strive to write code that is easy to understand and maintain. They should avoid over-engineering solutions and focus on writing code that meets the requirements in the simplest way possible. This includes using clear and concise variable names, commenting on code where necessary, and avoiding unnecessary abstractions and design patterns.

By following the KISS principle, C# developers can create more maintainable and efficient code. They can also reduce the time and effort required for development, testing, and debugging, as simple code is easier to understand and modify.

However, it is important to note that the KISS principle should not be used as an excuse to write code that is too simplistic or lacks the necessary features or functionality. C# developers should still ensure that their code meets the requirements and is flexible enough to accommodate future changes. The KISS principle should be used as a guideline to help simplify the problem-solving process, rather than as a strict rule.

You Ain't Gonna Need It (YAGNI)

The YAGNI coding principle is a software development principle that encourages developers to avoid adding functionality or code until it is needed.

The YAGNI principle is based on the idea that adding unnecessary code or features can increase the complexity of the system and make it harder to understand and maintain. It can also lead to wasted time and effort as features that are never used still require development, testing, and debugging.

To follow the YAGNI principle, C# developers should focus on implementing only the features and functionality that are required to meet the current requirements. They should avoid adding additional code or features in anticipation of future requirements, as these requirements may never materialize or may change significantly over time.

By following the YAGNI principle, C# developers can create more maintainable and efficient code. They can also reduce the time and effort required for development, testing, and debugging, as they are only working on the features and functionality that are needed.

However, it is important to note that the YAGNI principle should not be followed blindly. C# developers should still consider the long-term goals and requirements of the system, and make sure that the code they write is flexible and scalable enough to accommodate future changes. The YAGNI principle should be used as a guideline, rather than a hard-and-fast rule.

Don't Repeat Yourself (DRY)

The DRY coding principle is a software development principle that aims to reduce duplication of code. The DRY principle states that every piece of knowledge or logic should have a single, unambiguous, authoritative representation within a system.

The DRY principle is based on the idea that duplicated code is more difficult to maintain and can lead to inconsistencies and errors in the system. Duplication of code can also increase the complexity of the system and make it harder to understand and modify.

To follow the DRY principle, C# developers should strive to identify and eliminate duplication of code. This can be achieved by creating reusable code components such as functions, classes, or libraries, and using them wherever possible. Code duplication can also be eliminated by using inheritance and polymorphism, which allow for code to be shared across different parts of the system.

Following the DRY principle can help C# developers create more maintainable, scalable, and efficient code. It can also reduce the time and effort required for debugging and fixing errors in the system. By avoiding duplication of code, C# developers can focus on creating new features and functionality, rather than re-implementing existing code.

Occam's razor

The Occam's razor coding principle is a problem-solving principle that suggests that the simplest solution is often the best solution.

This principle is based on the idea that unnecessary complexity should be avoided when solving problems as it can lead to confusion, errors, and inefficiencies. Instead, the simplest solution that meets the requirements should be chosen.

To apply the Occam's razor principle in C# programming, developers should strive to write code that is clear, concise, and easy to understand. They should avoid adding unnecessary complexity or over-engineering solutions and focus on writing code that meets the requirements in the simplest way possible.

By following the Occam's razor principle, C# developers can create more maintainable and efficient code. They can also reduce the time and effort required for development, testing, and debugging, as simple code is easier to understand and modify.

However, it is important to note that the Occam's razor principle should not be used as a justification for writing code that is too simplistic or lacks the necessary features or functionality. C# developers should still ensure that their code meets the requirements and is flexible enough to accommodate future changes. The Occam's razor principle should be used as a guideline to help simplify the problem-solving process, rather than as a strict rule.

Coding methodologies

Coding methodologies break down the process of developing software into several predefined phases. Each phase will have several steps associated with it. Different developers and development teams will have coding methodologies that they follow. The main aim of coding methodologies is to streamline the process from the initial concept, through the coding phase, to the deployment and maintenance phases.

Some examples of C# coding methodologies include agile, test-driven development, behavior-driven development, and domain-driven design. Let's summarize each of these methodologies.

Agile

The Agile methodology is an iterative and incremental approach to software development that emphasizes flexibility and collaboration between team members. As a C# software developer, you can implement the Agile methodology in your development process to deliver high-quality software products faster and with greater flexibility.

Here are some of the key concepts and principles of the Agile methodology:

- **Iterative development**: In the Agile methodology, development is divided into small, incremental cycles called iterations. Each iteration typically lasts between 1-4 weeks and involves developing a working software increment that is then reviewed by the team and stakeholders.

- **Customer collaboration**: The Agile methodology emphasizes close collaboration between the development team and the customer or end user. This helps ensure that the software meets the customer's needs and is delivered on time and within budget.

- **Self-organizing teams**: Agile teams are typically self-organizing, with each team member taking on a specific role and contributing to the development process. This approach encourages teamwork and collaboration and enables the team to respond quickly to changing requirements.

- **Continuous improvement**: The Agile methodology places a strong emphasis on continuous improvement. This means that the team is constantly looking for ways to improve the development process, including the tools, techniques, and practices they use.

- **Adaptability**: The Agile methodology is designed to be adaptable to changing requirements and circumstances. This means that the team can quickly respond to changes in the project scope or requirements and adjust their approach accordingly.

To implement the Agile methodology in your development process, you can start by breaking down the project into smaller, more manageable tasks and setting up a regular schedule for iterative development. You can also work closely with the customer or end user to ensure that the software meets their needs and is delivered on time and within budget.

Overall, the Agile methodology can help you deliver high-quality software products faster and with greater flexibility, making it a valuable approach for C# software developers.

Scrum

Scrum is an agile software development methodology that is used to manage and control complex projects. It is based on an iterative and incremental approach, where the project is broken down into small, manageable chunks called sprints. Each sprint typically lasts between 2 and 4 weeks and consists of a series of tasks that need to be completed by the team.

The Scrum methodology is designed to be flexible and adaptable to changing requirements, with a focus on delivering a high-quality product that meets the needs of the customer. The key roles in the Scrum methodology are as follows:

- **Product owner**: Responsible for defining the product vision and prioritizing the backlog of features and requirements
- **Scrum master**: Responsible for facilitating the team and ensuring that they follow the Scrum methodology
- **Development team**: Responsible for designing, developing, and testing the product

The Scrum methodology also includes several key practices:

- **Sprint planning**: This is where the team decides what work they will complete in the upcoming sprint
- **Daily Scrum**: A short meeting where the team discusses progress, obstacles, and plans for the day
- **Sprint review**: A meeting where the team demonstrates the completed work to stakeholders and receives feedback
- **Sprint retrospective**: A meeting where the team reflects on the previous sprint and identifies areas for improvement

The Scrum methodology is often used in software development projects but can also be applied to other types of projects. Its emphasis on collaboration, communication, and continuous improvement makes it a popular choice for teams looking to deliver high-quality products in a timely and efficient manner.

Kanban

Kanban is a popular software development methodology that emphasizes continuous delivery, flexibility, and collaboration. It originated in Japanese manufacturing but has since been adapted to fit the needs of software development teams.

At its core, Kanban is a visual system for managing work. It is based on the concept of a "kanban board," which is essentially a visual representation of the work that needs to be done, the work that is currently in progress, and the work that has been completed. The board is typically divided into columns that represent different stages of the development process, such as "to-do," "in progress," and "done."

The Kanban methodology emphasizes a few key principles:

- **Visualize the workflow**: The kanban board provides a visual representation of the work that needs to be done, making it easier for team members to understand what needs to be accomplished and what stage each task is at.

- **Limit work in progress**: Kanban emphasizes limiting the amount of work that is in progress at any one time. This helps prevent bottlenecks and ensures that team members can focus on their current tasks.

- **Manage the flow**: By visualizing the workflow and limiting work in progress, teams can more easily manage the flow of work and ensure that tasks are completed in a timely and efficient manner.

- **Make process policies explicit**: Kanban encourages teams to make their process policies explicit and to continually evaluate and improve those policies as needed.

- **Implement feedback loops**: Finally, Kanban emphasizes the importance of implementing feedback loops to help teams continually improve their processes and deliver better results over time.

Overall, the Kanban methodology is a flexible and adaptable approach to software development that emphasizes collaboration, continuous delivery, and process improvement. It can be an effective way to manage complex development projects and ensure that teams can work efficiently and effectively.

Lean

Lean software development is a methodology that draws on principles and practices from the Lean manufacturing philosophy developed by Toyota. It focuses on maximizing value while minimizing waste, and it emphasizes collaboration, continuous improvement, and customer focus.

At its core, Lean software development is based on seven principles:

- **Eliminate waste**: Lean emphasizes the importance of identifying and eliminating waste in the development process. This includes things such as unnecessary features, defects, delays, and overproduction.

- **Amplify learning**: The Lean methodology encourages teams to continuously learn from their work and use that learning to improve their processes and outcomes.

- **Decide as late as possible**: The Lean approach emphasizes making decisions as late in the development process as possible to gather more information and make better-informed decisions.

- **Deliver as fast as possible**: Lean encourages teams to deliver work as quickly as possible to get feedback from users and customers and incorporate that feedback into the development process.

- **Empower the team**: Lean teams are empowered to make decisions and take ownership of the development process, rather than being micromanaged by a hierarchy of managers.

- **Build quality in**: The Lean methodology emphasizes the importance of building quality into the development process from the beginning, rather than relying on testing and bug-fixing later in the process.

- **See the whole**: Finally, Lean emphasizes the importance of seeing the big picture and understanding how all of the different parts of the development process fit together.

Overall, the Lean software development methodology focuses on delivering value to customers as quickly and efficiently as possible, while minimizing waste and continuously improving processes. It is a collaborative and customer-focused approach that can help teams deliver better outcomes and more successful products.

Crystal

The Crystal methodology is a family of agile software development methodologies that vary in size, complexity, and criticality. It was developed by Alistair Cockburn in the late 1990s and is based on the principles of agility, teamwork, and communication.

The Crystal methodology places a strong emphasis on the human aspect of software development, with an emphasis on collaboration and communication between team members. It is designed to be flexible and adaptable, with teams encouraged to tailor the methodology so that it meets the specific needs of their project.

The Crystal methodology is based on several core principles, including the following:

- **Individuals and interactions over processes and tools**: The focus is on communication and collaboration between team members, rather than relying solely on processes and tools

- **Working software over comprehensive documentation**: The goal is to develop working software that meets user needs, rather than spending excessive amounts of time on documentation

- **Customer collaboration over contract negotiation**: The customer is considered an active participant in the development process, with their needs and expectations being taken into account throughout the project

- **Responding to change over following a plan**: The methodology is designed to be flexible and adaptable, with changes in requirements and priorities being accommodated throughout the project

The Crystal methodology is based on several core practices, including these:

- **Teamwork**: The methodology emphasizes the importance of teamwork and collaboration, with team members encouraged to work together to achieve common goals

- **Incremental delivery**: The methodology emphasizes the importance of delivering software in small, incremental releases

- **Continuous integration**: The methodology encourages frequent integration of code to minimize conflicts and ensure that the software remains stable and functional

- **Reflective improvement**: The methodology encourages team members to reflect on their performance and make continuous improvements to their processes and practices

The Crystal methodology is well suited for small to medium-sized projects with changing requirements and high levels of complexity. It is particularly useful in situations where there is a need for flexibility, adaptability, and close collaboration between team members. However, the Crystal methodology may not be suitable for large, complex projects with well-defined requirements and limited flexibility.

Six Sigma

Six Sigma is a data-driven methodology for process improvement that originated in the manufacturing industry and has been adapted for software development. The goal of Six Sigma is to reduce variability and defects in a process by identifying and eliminating the root causes of errors and improving quality.

The Six Sigma methodology follows a structured approach known as DMAIC, which stands for Define, Measure, Analyze, Improve, and Control. Here is a brief overview of each phase:

- **Define**: In the Define phase, the team defines the problem they are trying to solve and establishes goals and objectives for the project. This involves gathering data and conducting a thorough analysis of the current process.

- **Measure**: In the Measure phase, the team establishes a baseline for the current process and measures **key performance indicators** (**KPIs**) to identify areas of improvement. This involves gathering data, analyzing it, and creating a measurement plan.

- **Analyze**: In the Analyze phase, the team analyzes the data collected in the previous phase to identify the root causes of defects and variability in the process. This may involve using statistical tools and techniques to identify patterns and correlations in the data.

- **Improve**: In the Improve phase, the team develops and implements solutions to address the root causes of defects and variability identified in the Analyze phase. This may involve testing and validating the proposed solutions to ensure they are effective.

- **Control**: In the Control phase, the team establishes control plans and processes to ensure that the improvements made in the Improve phase are sustained over time. This involves developing monitoring and feedback mechanisms to ensure that the process remains stable and efficient.

Overall, the Six Sigma methodology focuses on using data and statistical analysis to identify and eliminate the root causes of defects and variability in a process. By following the DMAIC process, software development teams can identify areas of improvement, develop effective solutions, and ensure that the improvements are sustained over time. This can lead to improved quality, increased efficiency, and greater customer satisfaction.

Extreme Programming (XP)

Extreme Programming (**XP**) is an Agile software development methodology that emphasizes continuous testing, pair programming, and frequent releases. The goal of XP is to enable faster and more efficient software development through a series of practices that promote collaboration, communication, and feedback.

At its core, XP is based on five key values:

- **Communication**: XP emphasizes communication between team members, with a focus on face-to-face communication over written documentation
- **Simplicity**: XP emphasizes keeping things simple and avoiding unnecessary complexity
- **Feedback**: XP emphasizes the importance of feedback throughout the software development process, including frequent testing and customer feedback
- **Courage**: XP emphasizes the importance of taking risks and making bold decisions, with a focus on continuous improvement and experimentation
- **Respect**: XP emphasizes respect for all team members, with a focus on creating a supportive and collaborative environment

XP also includes several specific practices designed to support these values, including the following:

- **Test-driven development** (**TDD**): A practice in which developers write automated tests for their code before writing the code itself
- **Pair programming**: A practice in which two developers work together at a single computer, with one person writing code and the other providing feedback and suggestions
- **Continuous integration**: A practice in which code changes are integrated into a shared repository and tested automatically
- **Refactoring**: A practice in which developers improve the design of existing code to make it more maintainable and easier to understand
- **Small releases**: A practice in which software is released in small, frequent increments, rather than in large, infrequent releases

Overall, the XP methodology is focused on enabling faster, more efficient, and higher-quality software development through a series of practices that promote collaboration, communication, and feedback. By emphasizing simplicity, courage, and respect, XP can help teams build better software products while also improving the development process itself.

DevOps

DevOps is a software development methodology that emphasizes collaboration between development and operations teams to streamline the software development and deployment process. The goal of DevOps is to enable faster and more frequent releases, higher-quality software, and greater efficiency and agility in the software development process.

At its core, DevOps is based on three key principles:

- **Culture**: DevOps emphasizes a culture of collaboration, trust, and continuous learning and improvement. This involves breaking down silos between development and operations teams and promoting cross-functional collaboration.

- **Automation**: DevOps emphasizes the use of automation tools and technologies to streamline the software development and deployment process. This includes tools for continuous integration, continuous delivery, and continuous testing, as well as infrastructure automation tools such as configuration management and **Infrastructure as Code** (**IaC**).

- **Measurement**: DevOps emphasizes the use of metrics and data to measure the performance of the software development and deployment process and identify areas for improvement. This involves establishing KPIs and using monitoring and analytics tools to track progress and identify trends.

Overall, the DevOps methodology focuses on enabling faster, more frequent, and higher-quality software releases through collaboration, automation, and measurement. By breaking down silos between development and operations teams and promoting a culture of collaboration and continuous improvement, DevOps can help organizations deliver software more efficiently and effectively, while also improving the quality and reliability of their software products.

Feature-driven development (FDD)

FDD is a software development methodology that emphasizes the iterative and incremental delivery of features. It is a lightweight, client-centric, and scalable agile approach that was first introduced by Jeff De Luca and Peter Coad in the late 1990s.

FDD is based on a five-step process:

1. **Develop the overall model**: The first step involves developing an overall model of the project. This includes identifying the features, developing a domain model, and creating a feature list.

2. **Build a feature list**: In this step, the features identified in the first step are broken down into smaller, more manageable tasks. These tasks are then prioritized based on their importance to the client.

3. **Plan by feature**: The third step involves planning the development of each feature. This includes creating a design for each feature, estimating the time required to develop it, and identifying any dependencies.

4. **Design by feature**: In this step, the design for each feature is created. This includes identifying the classes and objects required, creating sequence diagrams, and identifying any design patterns that may be required.

5. **Build by feature**: The final step involves building the features. This includes writing the code, testing the feature, and integrating it with the rest of the system.

FDD places a strong emphasis on teamwork and collaboration, with each team member assigned a specific role. These roles include a Chief Architect, Development Manager, Chief Programmer, Domain Expert, and Feature Team Members.

One of the key benefits of FDD is its focus on delivering features in small, incremental releases. This allows clients to see progress early on in the development process and provide feedback that can be incorporated into future releases.

FDD is well suited for large, complex projects that require a structured approach to development. However, it may not be suitable for smaller, less complex projects where a more flexible approach may be required.

Test-driven development (TDD)

TDD is a software development methodology that focuses on writing automated tests before writing the actual code. As a C# software developer, you can use TDD to create high-quality, bug-free software that meets the requirements of the client.

Here are the basic steps of TDD:

1. **Write a test**: The first step in TDD is to write a test that defines the desired behavior of the code. The test should be written in a testing framework such as NUnit, xUnit, or MSTest. The test should initially fail since there is no code to satisfy the test.

2. **Write the minimum code**: The next step is to write the minimum code required to pass the test. This code should be written in small increments and should only include the necessary functionality to pass the test.

3. **Refactor**: Once the test passes, you can refactor the code to improve its design and structure. Refactoring can help simplify the code, remove duplication, and improve performance.

4. **Repeat**: Finally, you can write another test and repeat the process of writing the minimum code required to pass the test, refactoring, and writing additional tests.

Here are the benefits of TDD:

- **Helps ensure that the code meets the requirements**: By writing tests before writing code, TDD ensures that the code satisfies the requirements of the client.

- **Facilitates continuous integration and delivery**: Since TDD produces a suite of automated tests, it facilitates continuous integration and delivery. This helps reduce the risk of introducing bugs into the code base and helps ensure that the software is always in a releasable state.

- **Reduces debugging time**: By catching bugs early in the development process, TDD helps reduce debugging time and costs.

- **Improves code quality**: By emphasizing writing clean, testable code, TDD helps improve code quality and maintainability.

Overall, TDD is a valuable methodology for C# software developers who want to create high-quality, bug-free software that meets the requirements of the client.

Behavior-driven development (BDD)

BDD is a software development methodology that emphasizes collaboration between developers, testers, and business stakeholders to ensure that software meets the requirements of the business. As a C# software developer, you can use BDD to create software that is aligned with the business needs.

Here are the basic steps of BDD:

1. **Define business requirements**: The first step in BDD is to define the business requirements for the software application. This involves working closely with business stakeholders to understand their needs and requirements.

2. **Define behaviors**: Once the business requirements have been defined, the next step is to define the behaviors of the software application. Behaviors are defined using a structured language such as Gherkin, which allows business stakeholders, developers, and testers to collaborate on a shared understanding of the requirements.

3. **Create automated tests**: Once the behaviors have been defined, the next step is to create automated tests that validate those behaviors. These tests are created using a testing framework such as SpecFlow, which integrates with C# and allows developers to write tests in a readable and understandable way.

4. **Write the code**: Once the tests have been created, the next step is to write the code that implements the behaviors. This code should be written in C# and should focus on satisfying the business requirements and passing the automated tests.

5. **Refactor and repeat**: Once the code has been written and tested, the next step is to refactor the code to improve its design and structure. This process should be repeated as necessary to ensure that the software meets the business requirements and passes the automated tests.

Here are the benefits of BDD:

- **Improved collaboration**: BDD emphasizes collaboration between developers, testers, and business stakeholders, which can help improve the quality of the software application and reduce development time and costs.

- **Increased visibility**: BDD provides increased visibility into the requirements and behaviors of the software application, which can help ensure that the software meets the needs of the business.

- **Reduced bugs**: BDD helps catch bugs early in the development process, which can help reduce debugging time and costs.

- **A better understanding of the requirements**: BDD helps ensure that developers have a clear understanding of the requirements of the business, which can help reduce the risk of building software that does not meet the needs of the business.

Overall, BDD is a valuable methodology for C# software developers who want to create software that meets the requirements of the business and is aligned with the needs of the stakeholders. By defining behaviors using a structured language and creating automated tests, developers can ensure that the software meets the business requirements and passes the tests.

Domain-driven design (DDD)

DDD is a software development methodology that focuses on understanding the domain of the software application and building a model of that domain that can be used to guide the development process. As a C# software developer, you can use DDD to create software that is closely aligned with the needs of the business or organization.

Here are the basic steps of DDD:

1. **Define the domain**: The first step in DDD is to define the domain of the software application. This involves working closely with the business or organization to understand its needs, requirements, and processes.

2. **Build the domain model**: Once the domain has been defined, the next step is to build a model of that domain that can be used to guide the development process. The domain model is a representation of the key concepts, entities, and relationships in the domain.

3. **Refine the domain model**: As development progresses, the domain model may need to be refined and updated based on new information or changes in the business or organization.

4. **Build the application**: Once the domain model has been established, the next step is to build the application using the model as a guide. This involves writing code in C# and using frameworks and libraries such as Entity Framework, ASP.NET, and others.

5. **Test and refine**: Once the application has been built, it should be thoroughly tested to ensure that it meets the requirements of the business or organization. The domain model and application code should be refined and updated as necessary based on testing feedback.

Here are the benefits of DDD:

- **Better alignment with business needs**: DDD helps ensure that the software application is closely aligned with the needs of the business or organization. By building a model of the domain, developers can better understand the requirements and processes of the business.

- **Improved software quality**: By focusing on the domain and building a model of that domain, DDD can help improve the quality of the software application.

- **Reduced development time and cost**: By better understanding the domain and building a model of that domain, DDD can help reduce development time and costs.

- **Facilitates teamwork and collaboration**: DDD emphasizes teamwork and collaboration between developers, business analysts, and other stakeholders, which can help improve the quality of the software application and reduce development time and costs.

Overall, DDD is a valuable methodology for C# software developers who want to create software that is closely aligned with the needs of the business or organization. By building a model of the domain, developers can better understand the requirements and processes of the business and build high-quality software that meets those needs.

Rapid Application Development (RAD)

Rapid Application Development (**RAD**) is a software development methodology that emphasizes rapid prototyping and iterative development. It was first introduced in the 1980s as a response to the traditional waterfall model, which was seen as too slow and inflexible for the rapidly changing business environment.

RAD is based on four key principles:

- **Active user involvement**: RAD emphasizes the importance of involving end users in the development process. This helps ensure that the system being developed meets their needs and expectations.

- **Iterative development**: RAD breaks down the development process into a series of iterative cycles. Each cycle involves building a small part of the system and then getting feedback from users before moving on to the next cycle.

- **Prototyping**: RAD uses prototyping as a means of quickly developing and testing system features. Prototypes are used to refine requirements and ensure that the system being developed meets user needs.

- **Timeboxing**: RAD places a strong emphasis on meeting deadlines. The development process is divided into a series of timeboxes, with each timebox having a specific set of deliverables and a fixed deadline.

RAD follows a five-step process:

1. **Requirements planning**: The first step involves identifying user requirements and defining the scope of the project.

2. **User design**: In this step, users and developers work together to create a prototype of the system. This prototype is used to refine requirements and ensure that the system meets user needs.

3. **Construction**: The construction phase involves developing the system based on the prototype and feedback from users.

4. **Testing**: In this step, the system is tested to ensure that it meets user requirements and is free of defects.

5. **Deployment**: The final step involves deploying the system and making it available to end users.

RAD is well suited for projects with tight deadlines and a need for rapid development. It is particularly useful in situations where user requirements are unclear or may change frequently. However, RAD may not be suitable for large, complex projects that require a more structured approach to development.

The Spiral Model

The Spiral Model is a software development methodology that combines elements of both iterative and waterfall models. It was first proposed by Barry Boehm in 1988 and is based on the idea of continuous risk management throughout the software development process.

The Spiral Model follows a series of iterative cycles, each of which involves four main phases:

- **Planning**: In the planning phase, the objectives of the iteration are defined, along with the resources, constraints, and risks associated with the development process. This phase also involves defining the system requirements and determining the feasibility of the project.

- **Risk analysis**: In the risk analysis phase, potential risks and uncertainties are identified, along with their impact on the project. Risk analysis is a continuous process throughout the software development life cycle, with risks being re-evaluated at each iteration.

- **Engineering**: In the engineering phase, the software is designed, coded, and tested. This phase also involves verifying and validating the software to ensure that it meets the requirements and standards of the project.

- **Evaluation**: In the evaluation phase, the software is evaluated by stakeholders to determine whether it meets their needs and expectations. Feedback from stakeholders is then used to refine the objectives and requirements of the next iteration.

The Spiral Model places a strong emphasis on risk management, with risks being identified and addressed at each stage of the development process. This allows for early detection and resolution of potential issues, which can help minimize project delays and costs.

The Spiral Model is well suited for large, complex projects with changing requirements and high levels of risk. It is particularly useful in situations where there is a need for constant feedback and adaptation throughout the software development process. However, the Spiral Model may not be suitable for small, simple projects with well-defined requirements and limited risks.

Summary

In this chapter, you were introduced to good code and bad code and, hopefully, you now understand why good code matters.

In software development, bad code refers to poorly written and structured code that is difficult to maintain, understand, and modify. In contrast, good code is well-written, structured, and maintainable, making it easier to understand and modify over time. To ensure that code is of high quality, software development teams often use coding standards, which define a set of rules and guidelines for writing code.

In addition to coding standards, software development also relies on principles and methodologies to guide the development process. Principles such as SOLID and DRY are used to ensure that code is maintainable and scalable over time.

Different software development methodologies such as Agile, Scrum, Waterfall, Spiral, RAD, and FDD offer different approaches to the software development process, each with its strengths and weaknesses. Agile methodologies, for example, prioritize flexibility and collaboration, while Waterfall methodologies prioritize strict planning and a linear development process.

In summary, writing good code is essential for creating maintainable and scalable software applications. Software development teams use coding standards, principles, and methodologies to ensure that code is of high quality and meets the needs of the project. By adhering to these standards and following proven methodologies, software developers can create software applications that are reliable, efficient, and easy to maintain over time.

In the next chapter, we will be looking at peer code reviews. They can be unpleasant at times, but peer code reviews help keep programmers in check by making sure they are adhering to the company's coding standards and guidelines.

Questions

1. What is bad code?
2. What is good code?
3. What are some common signs of bad code?
4. What are some common coding standards?
5. What are some coding principles?
6. What is agile software development?
7. What is **test-driven development** (TDD)?
8. What is refactoring?

Further reading

Here is a list of books on coding standards, principles, and methodologies, along with summaries of each:

- *Clean Code: A Handbook of Agile Software Craftsmanship*, by Robert C. Martin: This book provides a comprehensive guide to writing clean, maintainable code using best practices and principles of software craftsmanship.

- *Code Complete: A Practical Handbook of Software Construction*, by Steve McConnell: This book covers software development best practices and techniques, including code construction, debugging, testing, and maintenance.

- *The Pragmatic Programmer: From Journeyman to Master*, by Andrew Hunt and David Thomas: This book offers practical advice for improving code quality, productivity, and professionalism, and covers topics such as code organization, testing, and refactoring.

- *Design Patterns: Elements of Reusable Object-Oriented Software*, by Erich Gamma, Richard Helm, Ralph Johnson, and John Vlissides: This book covers design patterns, which are reusable solutions to common programming problems.

- *Refactoring: Improving the Design of Existing Code*, by Martin Fowler: This book provides a guide to refactoring, which is the process of improving the design of existing code without changing its external behavior.

- *Domain-Driven Design: Tackling Complexity in the Heart of Software*, by Eric Evans: This book covers DDD, which is an approach to software development that emphasizes understanding and modeling the domain of the problem being solved.

- *Test-Driven Development: By Example*, by Kent Beck: This book covers TDD, which is a software development approach that involves writing tests before writing the code to be tested.

- *Agile Estimating and Planning*, by Mike Cohn: This book covers agile project management, including techniques for estimating and planning software development projects.

- *Extreme Programming Explained: Embrace Change*, by Kent Beck: This book covers extreme programming, which is an agile software development methodology that emphasizes continuous improvement, customer involvement, and rapid feedback.

- *Patterns of Enterprise Application Architecture*, by Martin Fowler: This book covers patterns for designing and building enterprise applications, including patterns for data access, business logic, and user interface design.

- *Adaptive Code: Agile coding with design patterns and SOLID principles, Second Edition*, by Gary McLean Hall: This book provides practical guidance on how to write adaptive code using agile development methodologies, design patterns, and SOLID principles. It covers topics such as TDD, refactoring, and continuous integration and delivery.

- *Hands-On Design Patterns with C# and .NET Core*, by Jeffrey Chilberto and Gaurav Aroraa: This book provides a hands-on approach to learning design patterns using C# and .NET Core. It covers common design patterns such as creational, structural, and behavioral patterns, and provides practical examples and code snippets to demonstrate their use.

- *Building Maintainable Software, C# Edition*, by Rob van der Leek, Pascal van Eck, Gijs Wijnholds, Sylvan Rigal, and Joost Visser: This book provides guidance on how to write maintainable software using best practices and design patterns. It covers topics such as code quality, refactoring, and automated testing, and provides practical examples and case studies to demonstrate its principles.

These books are widely regarded as some of the best resources on coding standards, principles, and methodologies, and cover a wide range of topics and approaches to software development.

2

Code Review – Process and Importance

The primary motivation behind any code review is to improve the overall quality of the code. Code quality is very important. This almost goes without saying, especially if your code is part of a team project or is accessible to others, such as open-source developers and customers through escrow agreements.

If every developer were free to code as they pleased, you would end up with the same kind of code written in so many ways, and ultimately, the code would become an unwieldy mess. That is why it is important to have a coding standards policy that outlines the company's coding practices and code review procedures that are to be followed.

When code reviews are carried out, colleagues will review the code of other colleagues. Colleagues will understand that it is only human to make mistakes. They will check the code for mistakes, such as code that breaks the company's code of coding conduct, and any code that, while syntactically correct, can be improved upon to make it more readable, more maintainable, or more performant.

Therefore, in this chapter, we will cover the following topics to understand the code review process in detail:

- A brief introduction to GitHub
- The code review process
- Preparing code for review
- Leading a code review
- Knowing what to review
- Knowing when to send for code review
- Providing and responding to review feedback

> **Note**
>
> For the *Preparing code for review* and *Knowing when to send code for review* sections, we will be talking from the point of view of the **programmer**. For the *Leading a code review* and *Knowing what to review* sections, we will be talking from the point of view of the **code reviewer**. However, concerning the *Providing and responding to review feedback* section, we will cover the viewpoints of both the **programmer** and the **code reviewer**.

The learning objectives for this chapter are for you to be able to do the following:

- Understand GitHub and its potential use in the code review process
- Understand code reviews and why they are good
- Partake in code reviews
- Provide constructive criticism
- Respond positively to constructive criticism

Before we dive deep into these topics, let's understand the general code review process.

A brief introduction to GitHub

This section covers a brief introduction to programmers and developers who are new to GitHub and never used it since this chapter focuses on the use of GitHub for performing code reviews.

GitHub is a powerful platform that revolutionizes the way developers collaborate on projects. Whether you're a seasoned programmer or just starting your coding journey, GitHub provides a centralized hub for version control, collaboration, and code sharing. This introduction aims to guide beginners through the fundamentals of GitHub and provide resources to help you embark on your journey to becoming a proficient GitHub user.

What is GitHub?

GitHub is a web-based platform built around Git, a distributed version control system. In simpler terms, it helps you manage and track changes to your code. GitHub extends Git's functionality by providing a user-friendly interface and collaborative features, making it an essential tool for individual developers and large-scale teams alike.

Here are its key concepts:

- **Repositories**: These are containers for your project. A repository, or "repo," holds all the files, history, and documentation related to your project.
- **Commits**: Each change you make to your project is captured in a commit. Commits help you track the progress of your project and can be accompanied by messages to describe the changes.

- **Branches**: Branches allow you to work on different versions of your project simultaneously. You can experiment with new features or fix bugs without affecting the main project until you're ready to merge your changes.

- **Pull Requests**: When you've made changes in a branch and are ready to merge them into the main project, you create a pull request. This allows others to review your changes before they are incorporated.

GitHub's use within the code review process

GitHub plays a crucial role in the code review process, facilitating collaboration and maintaining code quality within a development team. Here's an overview of how GitHub is used in the code review process:

1. **Pull requests (PRs)**:

   - Developers typically create a branch for a new feature or bug fix. Once the changes have been implemented, they initiate a pull request.

   - A pull request is a proposal to merge the changes from one branch into another (often from a feature branch into the main branch).

   - PRs encapsulate the changes made, providing an overview of the additions, modifications, and deletions.

2. **Reviewers**:

   - In a collaborative environment, code reviews involve one or more reviewers who examine the changes proposed in a pull request.

   - Reviewers may include peers, team leads, or anyone with expertise in the code base. Their role is to ensure code quality, adherence to coding standards, and the correctness of the implementation.

3. **Discussion and feedback**:

   - GitHub's interface allows reviewers to comment on specific lines of code. This feature facilitates detailed discussions about the proposed changes.

   - Reviewers can suggest improvements, request clarifications, or point out potential issues directly within the context of the code.

4. **Continuous integration (CI)**:

   - Many development teams integrate CI tools (such as Jenkins, Travis CI, or GitHub Actions) with GitHub.

   - CI automatically builds and tests code changes whenever a pull request is opened or updated. This ensures that proposed changes don't break existing functionality and helps maintain a stable code base.

5. **Status checks**:

   • GitHub allows integration with various status checks, including automated tests, code style checks, and other custom checks defined by the development team.

   • Pull requests can only be merged if all defined status checks pass. This ensures that the proposed changes meet the project's quality standards.

6. **Iterative improvements**:

   • Code reviews often involve multiple iterations. Developers can make additional commits to the same branch in response to feedback and then update the pull request.

   • The iterative process continues until the changes are approved and meet the team's standards.

7. **Merge and deployment**:

   • Once the code review process is complete, and the changes are approved, the pull request can be merged into the target branch (for example, main or master)

   • Merging triggers further actions, such as deployment to staging or production environments, depending on the team's release process

8. **History and documentation**:

   • GitHub maintains a detailed history of all changes made through pull requests. This historical record is invaluable for understanding the evolution of the code base and tracking who contributed to specific features or fixes.

By leveraging GitHub's features for pull requests, code review, and integrations with CI tools, development teams can streamline their workflows, catch potential issues early in the development process, and maintain high-quality code bases. This collaborative approach promotes knowledge sharing, code consistency, and overall team efficiency.

Resources for learning

To learn more about using GitHub, coding best practices, and using software methodologies to manage your projects, you can use the following resources:

• **GitHub Learning Lab**: GitHub provides an interactive learning experience through *Learning Lab* (`https://github.com/apps/github-learning-lab`). This platform offers hands-on courses on Git, GitHub, and other related topics.

• **GitHub Guides**: *GitHub Guides* (`https://guides.github.com/`) covers a wide range of topics, from the basics of GitHub to more advanced workflows. The guides are well-structured and easy to follow.

- **YouTube tutorials**: Numerous tutorials on YouTube cater to GitHub beginners. Channels such as *The Net Ninja* and *Traversy Media* provide step-by-step guides for using GitHub.

- **Documentation**: GitHub's official documentation (`https://docs.github.com/en`) is a valuable resource. It covers everything from the basics to advanced topics, providing in-depth explanations and examples.

- **Interactive Git tutorial**: If you're new to Git, try the *tryGit* (*https://try.github.io/*) interactive tutorial. It's a hands-on way to learn the basics of Git right in your browser.

- **C# coding standards and best practices**: Dofactory has a good web page (`https://dofactory.com/csharp-coding-standards`) that provides C# coding standards and best practices with C# code.

- **C# design patterns**: Dofactory provides an excellent online resource (`https://dofactory.com/net/design-patterns`) that covers the **gang-of-four (GoF)** software design patterns with detailed explanations, UML diagrams, and source code.

- **Agile software development methodologies and how to apply them**: The Code Project article at `https://www.codeproject.com/articles/604417/agile-software-development-methodologies-and-how-t` takes you on a journey from the Waterfall method through to the modern Scrum methodology and is an interesting article on choosing the right project management methodology for managing your software projects.

- **Code Project**: Code Project (`https://www.codeproject.com/`) is a good place to search for articles, tutorials, and code examples, as well as search for software implementation guidance on topics such as YAGNI, DRY, SOLID, and the **software development life cycle (SDLC)**.

GitHub is an indispensable tool for modern software development, fostering collaboration, version control, and efficient project management. By familiarizing yourself with its key concepts and exploring the recommended resources, you'll be well on your way to mastering GitHub and enhancing your development workflow.

The code review process

The normal procedure for carrying out a code review is to make sure your code compiles and meets the requirements set. It should also pass all unit tests and end-to-end tests. Once you are confident that you can compile, test, and run your code successfully, it is checked into the current working branch. Once checked in, you must issue a pull request.

A peer reviewer will then review your code and share comments and feedback. If your code passes the code review, your code review is completed, and you can merge your working branch into the main trunk. Otherwise, the peer review will be rejected, and you will be required to review your work and address the issues raised in the comments provided by your reviewer.

The following diagram shows the peer code review process:

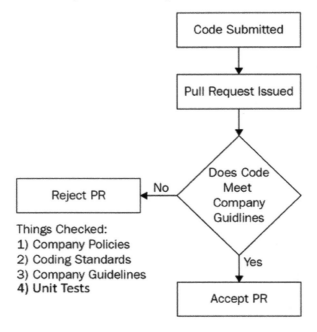

Figure 2.1: The code review process

In the following sections, you are going to read about the code review process in detail. We'll start by looking at preparing code for review.

Preparing code for review

Preparing for a code review can be a royal pain at times, but it does work for better overall code that is easy to read and maintain. It is a worthwhile practice that teams of developers should carry out as a standard coding procedure. This is an important step in the code review process as perfecting this step can save you considerable time and energy in performing the review.

> **Note**
>
> When working on a piece of code, you can create a draft PR. Your colleagues can then review the code without having to approve it. This is a good way to receive early feedback as you progress through the development or maintenance of the code. If your coding practices are in the process of being adopted, it is a good way to ensure those new practices are being followed. Once your work is ready for final submission and approval, you can publish your draft pull request. You can learn more about draft PRs on the GitHub website: `https://github.blog/2019-02-14-introducing-draft-pull-requests/`.

Here are some standard points to keep in mind when preparing your code for review:

- **Always keep the code review in mind**: When beginning any programming, you should have the code review in mind. So, keep your code small. If possible, limit your code to one feature, and always follow the coding standards.

- **Remember YAGNI**: As you code, make sure to only add code that is necessary to meet the requirement or feature you are working on. If you don't need it yet, then don't code it. Only add code when it is needed and not before.

- **Check for duplicate code**: If your code must be object-oriented and be DRY and SOLID, then review your code to see whether it contains any procedural or duplicate code. Should it do so, take the time to refactor it so that it is object-oriented, DRY, and SOLID.

- **Use static analyzers**: Static code analyzers that have been configured to enforce your company's best practices will check your code and highlight any issues that are encountered. Make sure that you do not ignore information and warnings. These could cause you issues further down the line.

- **Make sure that all your tests pass, even if your code builds**: If your code builds but you have failing tests, then deal immediately with what's causing those tests to fail. Then, when the tests pass as expected, you can move on. It is important to make sure that all unit tests pass and that end-to-end testing passes all tests. It is important that all testing is complete and gets the green light since releasing code that works but was a test fail could result in some very unhappy customers when the code goes to production.

> **Note**
>
> Most importantly, only check your code when you are confident that your code satisfies business requirements, adheres to coding standards, and passes all tests. If you check your code as part of a CI pipeline, and your code fails the build, then you will need to address the areas of concern raised by the CI pipeline. When you can check in your code and the CI pipeline gives the green light, then you can issue a pull request.

If you're new to software development and may not know what CI/CD pipelines are, we will briefly describe them before we go any further.

CI, **continuous delivery (CD)**, and **continuous deployment (CD)** are three software development practices that focus on improving the speed, quality, and reliability of software development processes. While these terms are sometimes used interchangeably, they represent different stages of a software delivery pipeline:

- **Continuous integration (CI)**: CI is the practice of frequently merging code changes from developers into a shared repository, followed by building and testing the code automatically. The goal of CI is to identify and fix issues as early as possible in the development process to prevent the accumulation of bugs and technical debt. With CI, developers can integrate their code changes into a shared repository multiple times a day, ensuring that the code is always in a releasable state.

- **Continuous delivery (CD)**: Continuous delivery is an extension of CI that focuses on automating the release of software to production. It is the practice of always keeping the code base in a releasable state and deploying it to production frequently, usually via an automated pipeline. With continuous delivery, developers can continuously deliver new features, bug fixes, and improvements to users in a fast and efficient manner.

- **Continuous deployment (CD)**: Continuous deployment is the most advanced stage of the software delivery pipeline and is where every change that passes through CI/CD is automatically deployed to production without any manual intervention. This process is only suitable for organizations that have a high degree of automation, test coverage, and confidence in their code base. Continuous deployment enables organizations to release features and updates to users in real-time, with little to no downtime.

In summary, CI ensures that the code base is always working, continuous delivery automates the release process, and continuous deployment takes automation one step further by deploying code changes to production automatically.

Leading a code review

When leading code reviews, it is important to have the right people present. The people who will attend the peer code review will be agreed upon with the project manager. The programmer(s) responsible for submitting the code for review will be present at the code review unless they work remotely. In the case of remote working, the reviewer will review the code and either accept the pull request, decline the pull request, or send the developer some questions to be answered before taking any further action.

A suitable lead for a code review should possess the following skills and knowledge:

- **Be a technical authority**: The person leading the code review should be a technical authority who understands the company's coding guidelines and software development methodologies. It is also important that they have a good overall understanding of the software under review. The person doing the code review should also be a master in the technology in which the code is written.

- **Have good soft skills**: As the leader of the code review, the person must be a warm and encouraging individual who can provide constructive feedback and not be overly critical. The person reviewing the programmer's code must have good soft skills so that there is no conflict between the reviewer and the person whose code is being reviewed.

In my experience, peer code reviews are always carried out on pull requests in the source control tool being used by the team. A programmer will submit the code to source control and then issue a pull request. The peer code reviewer will then review the code in the pull request. Constructive feedback will be provided in the form of comments that will be attached to the pull request. If there are problems with the pull request, then the reviewer will reject the change request and comment on specific issues that need to be addressed by the programmer. If the code review is successful, then the reviewer may add a comment providing positive feedback, merge the pull request, and close it.

Programmers will need to note any comments made by the reviewer and take them on board. If the code needs to be resubmitted, then the programmer will need to ensure that all the reviewer's comments have been addressed before resubmitting.

It is a good idea to keep code reviews short and not review too many lines at any one time.

Since a code review normally starts with a pull request, we will look at issuing a pull request, followed by responding to a pull request.

Issuing a pull request

In source control, a pull request is a mechanism for submitting proposed changes to the code base to the main branch or repository. It is a request to merge changes made in one branch of a repository into another branch, usually the main branch.

The process typically involves a developer creating a new branch from the main branch, making changes to the code in the new branch, and then submitting a pull request to merge the changes into the main branch. The pull request includes information about the changes made, the reasons for making them, and any related issues or tickets.

Once the pull request has been submitted, other developers can review the proposed changes, suggest modifications, or approve the changes for merging into the main branch. The code changes are typically reviewed for quality, compatibility, and compliance with any coding standards or best practices before they are merged into the main branch.

To issue a pull request, all you must do (once you've checked your code in or pushed it) is click on the **Pull requests** tab of your source control. There will then be a button you can click on – **New pull request**. This will add your pull request to a queue, where it will be picked up by the relevant reviewers.

> **Information**
>
> We will be focusing on using GitHub for version control. If you have never used GitHub before or are new to version control with GitHub, you can learn more about GitHub at GitHub Skills: `https://skills.github.com/`.

GitHub is a web-based platform that provides a collaborative environment for developers to store, manage, and share their code repositories. It is a cloud-based source control system that enables teams to work together on projects and manage the changes that are made to the code base over time.

GitHub allows developers to create and manage their own Git repositories, which can be either public or private. Developers can then use Git commands to push code changes to their repositories and track the history of changes made to the code base over time. Other developers can then clone or fork the repository to access the code and contribute to the project.

GitHub provides a range of features and tools to support collaboration, including issue tracking, pull requests, code reviews, and project management tools. These features enable teams to work together more efficiently, resolve issues quickly, and maintain high standards of code quality.

In addition to its core functionality as a version control system, GitHub has become a hub for open-source software development, with millions of open-source projects hosted on the platform. It also provides a marketplace for third-party integrations and tools, making it a valuable resource for developers looking to streamline their development workflows.

The following screenshots show the process of requesting and fulfilling a pull request via GitHub.

On your GitHub project page, click on the **Pull requests** tab:

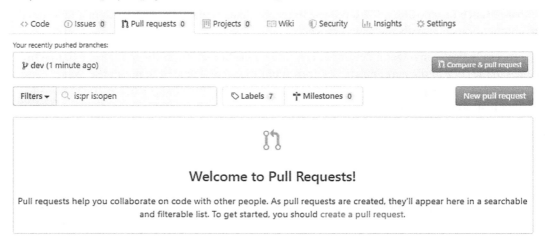

Figure 2.2: The Pull requests tab

Then, click on the **New pull request** button. This will display the **Comparing changes** page:

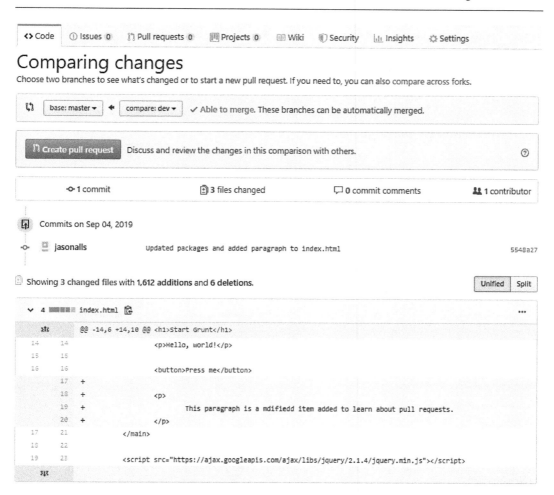

Figure 2.3: The Comparing changes page

If you are happy, then click on the **Create pull request** button to start the pull request. You will be presented with the **Open a pull request** screen:

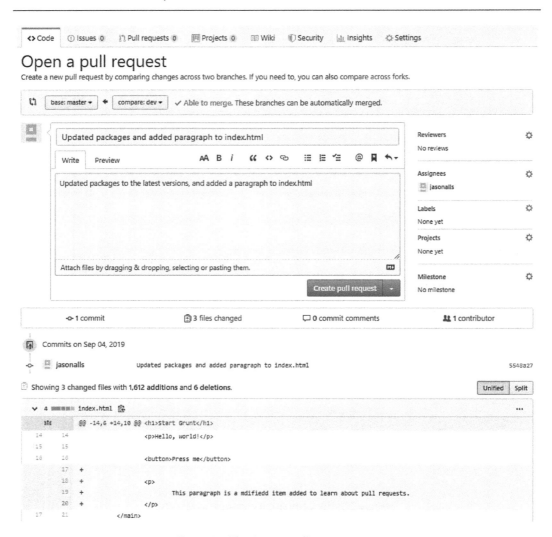

Figure 2.4: The Open a pull request page

Write your comment regarding the pull request. Provide all the necessary information for the code reviewer, but keep it brief and to the point. Useful comments include those that identify what changes have been made. Modify the **Reviewers**, **Assignees**, **Labels**, **Projects**, and **Milestones** fields as necessary. Then, once you are happy with the pull request details, click on the **Create pull request** button to create the pull request. Your code will now be ready to be reviewed by your peers.

> **Code conflict**
>
> In GitHub, code conflict resolution refers to the process of resolving conflicts that arise when two or more developers make changes to the same code file or lines of code in a Git repository. Code conflicts can occur when two or more developers modify the same piece of code in different ways, or when one developer modifies a code file while another deletes it.
>
> When a code conflict occurs, GitHub will highlight the conflicting lines of code in the code file and notify the developers who made the conflicting changes. The developers can then use the GitHub web interface or a Git client to review the changes and resolve the conflict.

There are several ways to resolve code conflicts in GitHub:

- **Merge**: Developers can merge their changes if they have made non-conflicting changes to different parts of the code. This involves reviewing the changes and manually merging the code changes.

- **Rebase**: Developers can use the `git rebase` command to apply their changes on top of the changes made by another developer. This involves rebasing their changes on top of the changes made by the other developer and resolving any conflicts that arise.

- **Manual resolution**: If the changes made by the developers conflict with each other, developers may need to manually resolve the conflicts by reviewing the changes and deciding which changes to keep and which to discard.

GitHub provides a range of tools to help developers resolve code conflicts, including visual diff tools, merge tools, and conflict resolution workflows. Code conflict resolution in GitHub aims to ensure that the code base is kept up to date, that conflicts are resolved efficiently, and that code quality is maintained.

Responding to a pull request

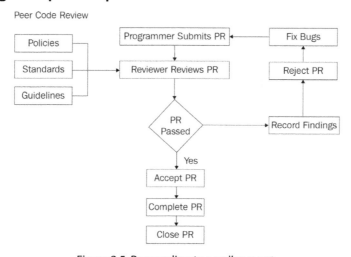

Figure 2.5: Responding to a pull request

Since the reviewer is responsible for reviewing pull requests before merging branches, we would do well to look at responding to pull requests:

1. Start by cloning a copy of the code under review.

2. Review the comments and changes in the pull request.

3. Check that there are no conflicts with the base branch. If there are, then you will have to reject the pull request with the necessary comments.

   Otherwise, you can review the changes, make sure the code builds without errors, and make sure there are no compilation warnings. At this stage, you will also look out for code smells and any potential bugs. *Code smell* is a term that's used in software development to describe common signs of poor code design or implementation that can lead to code that is difficult to understand, maintain, or extend.

   They are not necessarily errors, but rather indicators that the code could be improved. You will also check that the tests build, run, are correct, and provide good test coverage of the feature to be merged. Make any comments necessary and reject the pull request unless you are satisfied. When satisfied, you can add your comments and merge the pull request by clicking on the **Merge pull request** button, as shown here:

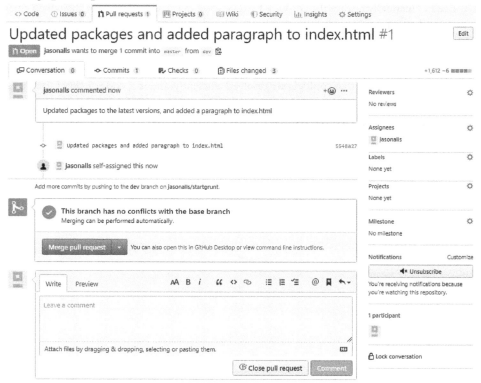

Figure 2.6: Merging pull requests

4. Now, confirm the merge by entering a comment and clicking on the **Confirm merge** button:

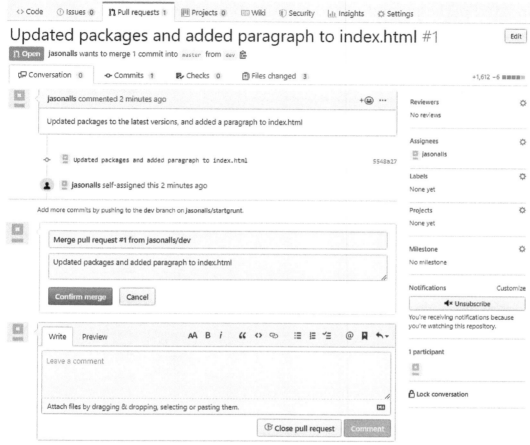

Figure 2.7: Confirming the merge

5. Once the pull request has been merged and the pull request has been closed, the branch can be deleted by clicking on the **Delete branch** button, as can be seen in the following screenshot:

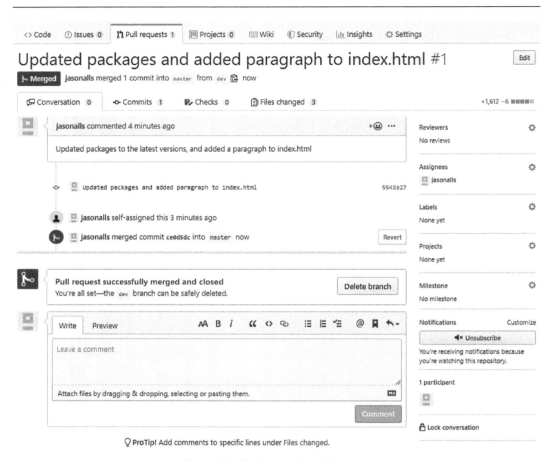

Figure 2.8: The Delete branch button

In the previous section, you saw how the reviewee raises a pull request to have their code peer-reviewed before it is merged. In this section, you saw how to review a pull request and complete it as part of a code review. Now, we will look at the negative and positive feedback that affects reviewees.

Effects of feedback on reviewees

When performing a code review of your peer's code, you must also consider the fact that feedback can be positive or negative. Negative feedback does not provide specific details about the problem. The reviewer focuses on the reviewee and not on the problem. Suggestions for improving the code are not offered to the reviewee by the reviewer, and the reviewer's feedback is aimed at hurting the reviewee.

Such negative feedback received by the reviewee offends them. This has a negative impact and can cause them to start doubting themselves. A lack of motivation then develops within the reviewee, and this can negatively impact the team, as work is not done on time or to the required level. The bad feelings between the reviewer and the reviewee will also be felt by the team, and an oppressive atmosphere that negatively impacts everyone on the team can ensue. This can lead to other colleagues becoming demotivated, and the overall project can end up suffering as a result.

In the end, it gets to the point where the reviewee has had enough and leaves for a new position somewhere else to get away from it all. The project then suffers time-wise and even financially, as time and money will need to be spent on finding a replacement. Whoever is found to fill the position must be trained in the system and the working procedures and guidelines. The following diagram shows negative feedback from the reviewer toward the reviewee:

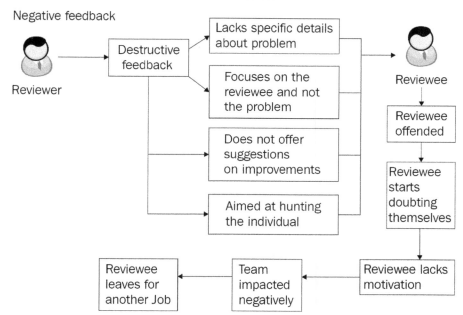

Figure 2.9: The negative feedback process

Conversely, positive feedback from the reviewer to the reviewee has the opposite effect. When the reviewer provides positive feedback to the reviewee, they focus on the problem and not on the person. They explain why the code they've submitted is not good, along with the problems it can cause. The reviewer will then suggest to the reviewee ways in which the code can be improved. The feedback provided by the reviewer is only given to improve the quality of the code submitted by the reviewee.

When the reviewee receives the positive (constructive) feedback, they respond positively. They take on board the reviewer's comments and respond appropriately by answering any questions and asking any relevant questions themselves. After this, the code is then updated based on the reviewer's feedback. The amended code is then resubmitted for review and acceptance. This has a positive impact on the team as the atmosphere remains a positive one, and work is done on time and to the required quality. The following diagram shows the results of positive feedback on the reviewee from the reviewer:

Positive feedback

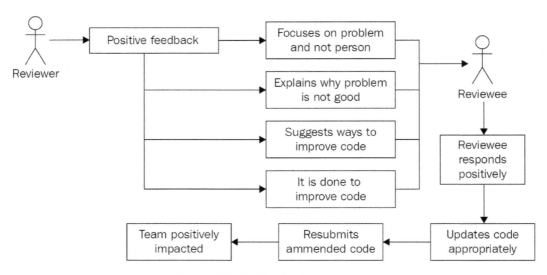

Figure 2.10: Positive feedback process

The point to remember is that your feedback can be constructive or destructive. Your aim as a reviewer is to be constructive and not destructive. A happy team is a productive team. A demoralized team is not productive and is damaging to the project. So, always strive to maintain a happy team through positive feedback.

A technique for positive criticism is the feedback sandwich technique. You start with praise on the good points, then you provide constructive criticism, and then you finish with further praise. This technique can be very useful if you have members on the team who don't react well to any form of criticism. Your soft skills in dealing with people are just as important as your software skills in delivering quality code. Don't forget that!

We will now move on and look at what we should review.

Knowing what to review

Different aspects of code must be considered when you're reviewing it. Primarily, the code being reviewed should only be the code that was modified by the programmer and submitted for review. That's why you should aim to make small submissions often. Small amounts of code are much easier to review and comment on.

Let's look at the different aspects a code reviewer should assess for a complete and thorough review.

The company's coding guidelines and business requirement(s)

All code being reviewed should be checked against the company's coding guidelines and the business requirement(s) the code is addressing. All new code should adhere to the latest coding standards and best practices employed by the company.

There are different types of business requirements. These requirements include those of the business and the user/stakeholder as well as functional and implementation requirements. Regardless of the type of requirement the code is addressing, it must be fully checked for correctness in meeting requirements.

For example, if the user/stakeholder requirement states that *as a user, I want to add a new customer account*, does the code under review meet all the conditions set out in this requirement? If the company's coding guidelines stipulate that all code must include unit tests that test the normal flow and exceptional cases, then have all the required tests been implemented? If the answer to any of these questions is *no*, then the new code added by the developer fails and is sent back to be corrected.

Naming conventions

The code should be checked to see whether the naming conventions have been followed for the various code constructs, such as classes, interfaces, member variables, local variables, enumerations, and methods. Nobody likes cryptic names that are hard to decipher, especially if the code base is large.

Here are a couple of questions that a reviewer should ask:

- Are the names long enough to be human-readable and understandable?
- Are they meaningful concerning the intent of the code, but short enough to not irritate other programmers?

As the reviewer, you must be able to read the code and understand it. If the code is difficult to read and understand, then it needs to be refactored before being merged.

Formatting

Formatting goes a long way to making code easy to understand. Namespaces, braces, and indentation should be employed according to the guidelines, and the start and end of code blocks should be easily identifiable.

Again, here is a set of questions a reviewer should consider asking in their review:

- Is code to be indented using spaces or tabs?
- Has the correct amount of white space been employed?
- Are there any lines of code that are too long that should be spread over multiple lines?
- What about line breaks? Do the line breaks adhere to the rules laid out in the coding standards?

- Following the style guidelines, is there only one statement per line? Is there only one declaration per line?

- Are continuation lines correctly indented using one tab stop?

- Are methods separated by one line?

- Are multiple clauses that make up a single expression separated by parentheses?

- Are classes and methods clean and small, and do they only do the work they are meant to do?

- Do you see anything that stands out that, even if it compiles and works in isolation, could cause bugs when integrated into the system?

Testing

Tests must be understandable and cover a good subset of use cases. They must cover the normal paths of execution and exceptional use cases. When it comes to testing the code, the reviewer should check for the following:

- Has the programmer provided tests for all the code?

- Is there any untested code?

- Do all the tests work?

- Do any of the tests fail?

Let's see how the process works:

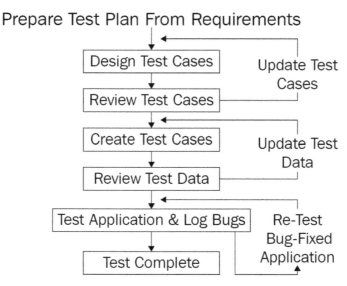

Figure 2.11: Test plan process flow

Untested code has the potential to raise unexpected exceptions during testing and production. But just as bad as code that is not tested are tests that are not correct. This can lead to bugs that are hard to diagnose, can be annoying for the customer, and make more work for you further down the line. Bugs are technical debt and are looked upon negatively by the business. And so, as part of the process of developing code, you need to ensure you have proper unit and end-to-end tests, and that the inputs and outputs of those tests are correct.

Moreover, you may have written the code, but others may have to read it as they maintain and extend the project. It is always a good idea to provide some documentation for your colleagues.

Now, concerning the customer, how are they going to know where your features are and how to use them? Good documentation that is user-friendly is a good idea. And remember, not all your users may be technically savvy. So, cater to the less technical person who may need handholding, but do it without being patronizing.

As a technical authority reviewing the code, do you detect any code smells that may become a problem? If so, then you must flag, comment, and reject the pull request and get the programmer to resubmit their work.

As a reviewer, you should check that those exceptions are not used to control the program flow and that any errors that are raised have meaningful messages that are helpful to developers and to the customers who will receive them.

Documentation

Documentation is vital to the success of a software project. You need enough documentation to enable a full understanding of the system so that it makes extending and maintaining the existing software easier and less error-prone. Good documentation makes it easier to on-board new software developers and help them get up and running faster. Here are some things to ask when reviewing the documentation for a project:

- Is there adequate documentation of the code, including comments, documentation comments, tests, and customer product documentation?

- Is the code well documented to aid with maintenance and support as well as adding new product extensions?

Architectural guidelines and design patterns

When performing an architectural review of a C# project, you should be looking at the overall structure of the application and ensuring that it adheres to best practices and is scalable, maintainable, and has good performance. You should also ensure that the architecture supports the current and future requirements of the project.

Here are some questions you should ask yourself during the review:

1. Is the application using a layered architecture, such as the **Model-View-Controller (MVC)** pattern or the **Model-View-ViewModel (MVVM)** pattern?

2. Are the layers of the application properly separated, and are there clear boundaries between them?

3. Are there any circular dependencies between components or modules in the application?

4. Are the interfaces between components or modules well-defined and easy to understand?

5. Are there any potential performance bottlenecks, such as slow database queries or inefficient algorithms?

6. Are there any security vulnerabilities in the application, such as injection attacks or **cross-site scripting (XSS)** attacks?

7. Is the code organized and structured in a way that makes it easy to maintain and understand?

8. Are there any anti-patterns or bad coding practices in the application?

9. Are there any unnecessary dependencies or components that could be removed to simplify the architecture?

10. Does the architecture allow for easy testing and debugging of the application?

11. Is the code adhering to SOLID principles and other design patterns to ensure code quality and extensibility?

12. Are there any performance issues or bottlenecks that could be improved, such as network latency, database connection pooling, or caching?

13. Is the application following a consistent naming convention and code style to ensure that it's easy to read and maintain by other developers?

14. Are there any dependencies or third-party libraries that are being used, and are they being properly managed and updated?

15. Is the architecture taking advantage of modern C# features, such as async/await and LINQ, to improve code readability and performance?

16. Is the application following any industry standards or best practices, such as OWASP guidelines for web security or Microsoft's .NET Core design guidelines?

17. Are there any opportunities to improve the code's organization and structure, such as grouping related code into namespaces or creating separate projects for different components of the application?

18. Are there any potential issues with deploying and scaling the application, such as difficulties with load balancing or scaling horizontally?

19. Are there any opportunities to introduce design patterns or architectural improvements to reduce complexity and improve maintainability?

20. Is there a clear separation of concerns between the different components and layers of the application, such as separating data access logic from business logic and presentation logic?

By addressing these questions during an architectural review, you can ensure that the C# application is well-designed, easy to maintain, and meets the requirements of its intended use case. This can lead to a more efficient development process, fewer bugs and issues, and improved user satisfaction.

Performance and security

Other things that may need to be considered include performance and security:

- How well does the code perform?

- Are there any bottlenecks that need to be addressed?

- Is the code programmed in such a way that it protects against SQL injection attacks and **denial-of-service (DoS)** attacks?

- Is code properly validated to keep the data clean so that only valid data gets stored in the database?

- Have you checked the user interface, documentation, and error messages for spelling mistakes?

- Have you encountered any magic numbers or hard-coded values?

- Is the configuration data correct?

- Have any secrets accidentally been checked in?

A comprehensive code review will encompass all the preceding aspects and their respective review parameters. But let's find out when it is the right time to even be performing a code review.

Knowing when to send code for review

In general, it's a good idea to send code for a code review whenever you have made significant changes or additions to the code base. This can help ensure that the code is well-designed, adheres to coding standards, and is free of bugs or other issues.

Here are some specific situations where you might want to send code for a code review:

1. **When you have completed a new feature or functionality**: If you have added a new feature or made a significant change to an existing feature, it's a good idea to send the code for review. This can help ensure that the feature works as intended and meets the requirements of the project.

2. **When you have made changes to core functionality**: If you have made changes to the core functionality of the application, such as the database or authentication system, it's important to get the code reviewed to ensure that the changes are well-designed and don't introduce any security vulnerabilities or other issues.

3. **When you have refactored or optimized code**: If you have made changes to the code to improve performance or make it more maintainable, it's a good idea to send the code for review to ensure that the changes are well-designed and don't introduce any new bugs or issues.

4. **When you are unsure about a particular piece of code**: If you are unsure about the best way to implement a particular piece of functionality or if you are not sure if a particular piece of code adheres to best practices or coding standards, it's a good idea to get the code reviewed by a more experienced developer.

5. **When there is a requirement for code review in your development process**: If your team or organization requires code review as part of the development process, you should send the code for review whenever you have made changes to the code base.

In general, it's a good idea to send code for review early and often, to catch issues early in the development process. Code review can help ensure that the code is well-designed, easy to maintain, and meets the requirements of the project.

Providing and responding to review feedback

It is worth remembering that code reviews are aimed at the overall quality of code in keeping with the company's guidelines. Therefore, feedback should be constructive and not used as an excuse to put down or embarrass a colleague. Similarly, reviewer feedback should not be taken personally and responses to the reviewer should focus on suitable action and explanation.

The following diagram shows the process of issuing a PR, performing a code review, and either accepting or rejecting the PR:

Peer Code Review

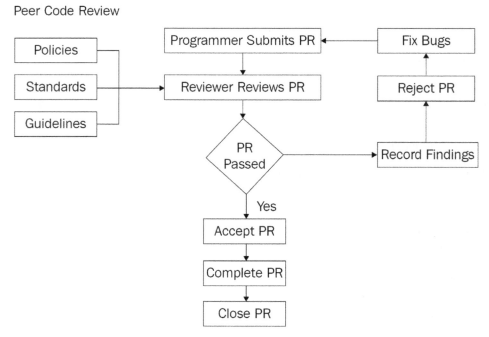

Figure 2.12: The peer code review process

Providing feedback as a reviewer

As the peer code reviewer, you will be responsible for understanding the requirements and making sure the code meets them. So, look for the answers to these questions:

- Are you able to read and understand the code?

- Can you see any potential bugs?

- Have any trade-offs been made?

- If so, why were the trade-offs made?

- Do the trade-offs incur any technical debt that will need to be factored into the project further down the line?

Once your review is complete, you will have three categories of feedback to choose from: positive, optional, and critical. With **positive feedback**, you can provide commendations on what the programmer has done well. This is a good way to bolster morale. **Optional feedback** can be very useful in helping computer programmers hone their programming skills in line with the company guidelines, and they can work to improve the overall well-being of the software being developed.

Finally, we have **critical feedback**. This is necessary for any problems that have been identified and must be addressed before the code can be accepted and passed on to the QA department. Your critical comments must address the specific issue being raised with valid reasons to support the feedback.

Responding to feedback as a reviewee

As the reviewee programmer, you must effectively communicate the background of your code to your reviewer. While you are waiting for your code to be reviewed, you must not make any further changes to it.

As you can guess, you will receive either positive, optional, or critical feedback from the reviewer. The positive feedback works to boost your confidence in the project as well as your morale. Build upon it and continue with your good practices. You may choose to act upon optional feedback, but it's always a good idea to talk it through with your reviewer.

For critical feedback, you must take it seriously and act upon it as this feedback is imperative for the very success of the project. You must handle critical feedback politely and professionally. Don't allow yourself to be offended by any comments from your reviewer; they are not meant to be personal.

As soon as you receive your reviewer's feedback, act upon it, and make sure that you discuss it with them as necessary.

Summary

In this chapter, we discussed the importance of performing code reviews and the complete process of getting code ready for review and responding to reviewer comments as the programmer, along with how to lead a code review and what to look for when performing a review as the code reviewer. There are two roles in a peer code review. These are the reviewer and the reviewee. The reviewer is the person performing the code review, and the reviewee is the person whose code is being reviewed.

You have also seen how you, as a reviewer, can categorize your feedback and why soft skills are important when providing feedback to fellow programmers. And as a reviewee whose code is being scrutinized, you have seen how important it is to build upon positive and optional feedback and how important it is to act upon critical feedback.

By now, you should have a good understanding of why it is important to conduct regular code reviews, and why they should be done before the code is passed on to the QA department. Peer code reviews do take time and can be uncomfortable for both the reviewer and reviewee. But in the long run, they work toward a high-quality product that is easy to extend and maintain, and they lead to better code reuse as well.

In the next chapter, we will look at how to write clean classes, objects, and data structures. We will discuss how to organize our classes effectively and ensure they only have one responsibility. We will also cover commenting on classes to help with documentation. Additionally, we'll look at designing for change, the Law of Demeter, cohesion, and coupling. We'll also cover concepts such as immutable objects, hiding data, and exposing methods in objects. Finally, we'll explore data structures.

Questions

Answer the following questions to test your knowledge of this chapter:

1. What are the two roles involved in a peer code review?
2. Who agrees on the people who will be involved in the peer code review?
3. How can you save your reviewer time and effort before requesting a peer code review?
4. When reviewing code, what kinds of things must you look out for?
5. What are the three categories of feedback?
6. As a developer, what are the things you should consider while developing a software application?

Further reading

To learn more about the topics that were covered in this chapter, take a look at the following resources:

- `https://docs.microsoft.com/en-us/visualstudio/code-quality/?view=vs-2019`: This documentation by Microsoft provides information on the different tools available to help you analyze and improve the quality and maintainability of your code

- `https://en.wikipedia.org/wiki/Code_review`: There are many useful links on this page to further your knowledge of code reviews and their value to your business

- `https://springframework.guru/gang-of-four-design-patterns/`: The Gang-of-Four design patterns book

- `https://www.packtpub.com/application-development/net-design-patterns`: *.NET Design Patterns*, by Praseed Pai and Shine Xavier

- `https://help.github.com/en`: GitHub's help page

- `https://dofactory.com/net/design-patterns`: *C# Design Patterns with Quick Examples (dofactory.com)*

3

Classes, Objects, and Data Structures

This chapter will provide an in-depth exploration of key concepts in C# **object-oriented programming (OOP)**. We will examine the importance of effective organization, formatting, and commenting when working with classes. Additionally, we will delve into the Law of Demeter and how it can be used to create clean and maintainable code. The chapter will also cover immutable objects and data structures, exploring the interfaces and classes in the `System.Collections.Immutable` namespace. Through these discussions, you will gain practical insights and skills that can help you write better code, organize your work more efficiently, and become a more proficient C# developer.

We will cover the following topics in this chapter:

- Organizing classes using namespaces
- Formatting and commenting on classes
- Writing clean C# objects and data structures that follow the Law of Demeter
- Immutable objects and data structures, and the interfaces and classes in the `System. Collections.Immutable` namespace

This is what we will learn:

- How to effectively organize classes using namespaces
- How to write classes with a single responsibility, leading to smaller and more meaningful classes
- How to write comments that can aid in generating documentation for APIs
- How to write programs that are easy to modify and extend, thanks to high cohesion and low coupling
- How to apply the Law of Demeter to write and use immutable data structures

First, let's review the technical requirements for working through this chapter.

Technical requirements

You will need a recent version of Visual Studio Community Edition to follow along. You can access the source code for this chapter on GitHub at `https://github.com/PacktPublishing/Clean-Code-with-CSharp-Second-Edition/tree/main/CH03`.

The code is contained in a single solution with folders for specific topics. The Core folder holds demonstration classes that demonstrate namespaces and class grouping, with classes only doing what they are supposed to. The other folders demonstrate cohesion, coupling, dependency injection, designing for change, encapsulation, using immutable objects and data structures, inversion of control, and the Law of Demeter.

Organizing classes

You will notice that the hallmark of a clean project is that it will have well-organized classes and that folders will be used to group classes that belong together. Furthermore, the classes in the folders will be enclosed within namespaces that match the assembly name and folder structure.

Each interface, class, struct, and enum should have its own source file in the correct namespace. Source files should be logically grouped in the appropriate folders and the namespaces for the source files should match the assembly name and folder structure. The following screenshot demonstrates a clean folder and file structure for a WPF project:

Figure 3.1: Clean folder structure

Figure 3.1 displays the file and folder structure for a Visual Studio C# solution that is clean in its organization. Folders are named correctly, and only classes with the relevant functionality are placed in those folders. This makes code easier to locate and maintain as developers will intuitively be able to locate the classes they are looking for. For instance, if the developer needed to find and work on the SQL Server-related classes, they would navigate to **Data** | **Relational** | `SqlServer`. There are three SQL Server-related classes in the `SqlServer` folder: `SqlServerDataExecutor`, `SqlServerDataReader`, and `SqlServerDataSource`.

> **Note**
>
> It is a bad idea to have more than one interface, class, struct, or enum in an actual source file. The reason for this is that it can make locating items difficult, despite the fact that we have IntelliSense to assist us. Intellisense is provided by IDEs such as Visual Studio and Visual Code.

When thinking about your namespaces, it is a good idea to follow the Pascal casing with a sequence of company name, product name, technology name, and then plural names for components separated by spaces. See the following for an example:

```
CH3.Product.Wpf.Feature.Subnamespace {} // Product, technology and
feature specific.
```

The reason for starting with the company name is that it helps to avoid namespace clashes. So, if Microsoft and `FakeCompany` both have a namespace called `System`, which `System` namespace you want to use can be differentiated by the company name. Naming classes too generically can also cause namespace clashes. And so, when naming a namespace, it is best to be specific. For example, if you have some WPF extensions, you would place them in the namespace called `FakeCompany.WpfUtilities`.

Next, any items of code that can be reused in multiple projects are best placed in separate assemblies that can be accessed by multiple projects:

```
CH3.Wpf.Feature.Subnamespace {} /* Technology and feature specific.
Can be used across multiple products. */
```

When using tests in your code, such as when doing **test-driven development** (TDD), it is always best to keep your test classes in separate assemblies. Test assemblies should always be given the name of the assembly they are testing with the namespace `Tests` appended to the end of the assembly name:

```
CH3.Core.Feature
CH3.Core.Feature.Tests
```

You should avoid putting tests for different assemblies in the same test assembly as each other for small to medium-sized solutions. Always try to keep them separate. However, if you have large solutions with many projects, you can group tests together. For example, when performing DDD, you can group tests by the bounded context such as `Dms.Engine`, `Dms.Shared`, `Dms.Projection`, `Dms.`

`Process`, and `Dms.Tests`. So, instead of having a separate test library for a bounded context, you would have a single one for all bounded contexts to avoid solution project overload. Large solutions with many projects can be hard to read and manage, and so from a human perspective, combining tests can be a simple way to reduce the solution project count. Test assemblies should be separated based on the type of test (unit, integration, functional, and so on).

In addition, the namespace and type should not use the same name as this can produce compiler conflicts. To summarize, here are the rules to keep in mind when organizing classes:

- Use Pascal casing with a sequence of company name, product name, technology name, and plural names for components separated by spaces

- Place reusable items of code in separate assemblies

- Don't use the same name for the namespace and type

- Don't pluralize company and product names and acronyms

- Split solutions into multiple projects depending on how the assemblies are to be deployed and distributed

- Remember what assemblies do (following the **single responsibility principle (SRP)**?

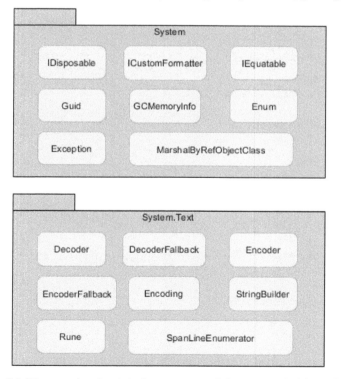

Figure 3.2: Diagram showing interface, struct, and class names inside packages

Figure 3.2 shows two different packages with classes, interfaces, and structs. You'll notice that these names are all singular and not plural.

We'll move on to the responsibility of classes next.

A class should have only one responsibility

Responsibility is the work that has been assigned to the class. In the SOLID set of principles, the S stands for the SRP. When applied to a class, the SRP states that the class must only work on a single aspect of the feature being implemented. The responsibility of that single aspect should be fully encapsulated within the class. Therefore, you should never apply more than one responsibility to a class.

Let's look at an example to understand why:

```
public class MultipleResponsibilities
{
    public string DecryptString(
        string text,
        SecurityAlgorithm algorithm)
    {
        // ...implementation...
    }

    public string EncryptString(
        string text,
        SecurityAlgorithm algorithm)
    {
        // ...implementation...
    }

    public string ReadTextFromFile(string filename)
    {
        // ...implementation...
    }

    public string SaveTextToFile(
        string text, string filename)
    {
        // ...implementation...
    }
}
```

As you can see in the preceding code, for the `MultipleResponsibilities` class, we have our cryptography functionalities implemented with the `DecryptString` and `EncryptString` methods.

We also have file access implemented with the `ReadTextFromFile` and `SaveTextToFile` methods. This class breaks the SRP.

So, we need to break this class up into two classes, one for cryptography and the other for file access:

```
namespace CH3.Core.Security;
public class Cryptography
{
    public string DecryptString(
        string text,
        SecurityAlgorithm algorithm)
    {
        // ...implementation...
    }

    public string EncryptString(
        string text,
        SecurityAlgorithm algorithm)
    {
        // ...implementation...
    }
}
```

As we can now see from the preceding code, by moving the `EncryptString` and `DecryptString` methods to their own `Cryptography` class in the core security namespace, we have made it easy to reuse the code to encrypt and decrypt strings across different products and technology groups. The `Cryptography` class also complies with the SRP.

In the preceding code, we can see that the `SecurityAlgorithm` parameter of the `Cryptography` class is an enum and has been placed in its own source file. This helps to keep code clean, minimal, and well organized.

Now, in the following `TextFile` class, we again abide by the SRP and have a nice reusable class that is in the appropriate core filesystem namespace. The `TextFile` class is reusable across different products and technology groups:

```
namespace CH3.Core.FileSystem;
public class TextFile
{
    public string ReadTextFromFile(string filename)
    {
        // ...implementation...
    }

    public string SaveTextToFile(string text, string filename)
```

```
    {
        // ...implementation...
    }
}
```

We've looked at the responsibility of classes. Now let's take a look at organizing the contents of a class.

Class organization

The way to organize an actual class will differ between organizations, but the key is consistency. The way you will be shown to organize a class in this section is just one possible way. It is the way that I have most commonly encountered in the workplace.

The way to organize a class file is as follows:

- Class file comments
- Using statements
- The namespace
- The class
- Fields
- The constructor
- Properties
- Private methods
- Public methods

As you can see, this ordering makes it easy to know where in the code to look for class components. To make organization even easier, you can use regions. Regions are collapsible code used to group items together. When you have a long class file, regions can help to make your code much easier to work on – even more so when constructors, properties, and methods are collapsed with them.

The following code shows how you could organize your class files as we've spoken about:

```
/************************************************************
 * THE SOFTWARE IS PROVIDED "AS IS", WITHOUT WARRANTY OF ANY KIND,
EXPRESS OR
 * IMPLIED, INCLUDING BUT NOT LIMITED TO THE WARRANTIES OF
MERCHANTABILITY,
 * FITNESS FOR A PARTICULAR PURPOSE AND NONINFRINGEMENT. IN NO EVENT
SHALL THE
 * AUTHORS OR COPYRIGHT HOLDERS BE LIABLE FOR ANY CLAIM, DAMAGES OR
OTHER
```

```
 * LIABILITY, WHETHER IN AN ACTION OF CONTRACT, TORT OR OTHERWISE,
ARISING FROM,
 * OUT OF OR IN CONNECTION WITH THE SOFTWARE OR THE USE OR OTHER
DEALINGS IN THE
 * SOFTWARE.
 **********************************************************/
using System;
using System.Collections.Generic;
using System.Linq;
using System.Text;
using System.Threading.Tasks;
namespace CH3;
/// <summary>
/// Demonstration of class file organization
/// </summary>
internal class ClassOrganization
{
    #region Fields
    // Place fields at the top of your class.
    #endregion
    #region Constructors
    // Place constructors after your field declarartions.
    #endregion
    #region Properties
    // Place your properties after your constructors
    #endregion
    #region Private Methods
    // Place your private methods after your properties.
    #endregion
    #region Public Methods
    // Place your public methods after your private methods.
    #endregion
}
```

Looking at this class file, it is easy to see how such organization makes the class more manageable and easy to maintain and extend. Let's take a look at commenting for generating documentation.

Commenting for documentation generation

Documenting your source code is always a good idea. It helps other developers to understand the code and eases code adoption and maintenance.

It is always a good idea to include copyright notices at the top of each source code file and to comment on your namespaces, interfaces, classes, enums, structs, methods, and properties. Your copyright comments should be first in the source file, above the using statements, and take the form of a multiline comment that starts with /* and ends with */:

```
/**********************************************************
 * Copyright 2019 PacktPub
 *
 * Permission is hereby granted, free of charge, to any person
obtaining a copy of
 * this software and associated documentation files (the "Software"),
to deal in
 * the Software without restriction, including without limitation the
rights to use,
 * copy, modify, merge, publish, distribute, sublicense, and/or sell
copies of the
 * Software, and to permit persons to whom the Software is furnished to
do so,
 * subject to the following conditions:
 *
 * The above copyright notice and this permission notice shall be
included in all
 * copies or substantial portions of the Software.
 *
 * THE SOFTWARE IS PROVIDED "AS IS", WITHOUT WARRANTY OF ANY KIND,
EXPRESS OR
 * IMPLIED, INCLUDING BUT NOT LIMITED TO THE WARRANTIES OF
MERCHANTABILITY,
 * FITNESS FOR A PARTICULAR PURPOSE AND NONINFRINGEMENT. IN NO EVENT
SHALL THE
 * AUTHORS OR COPYRIGHT HOLDERS BE LIABLE FOR ANY CLAIM, DAMAGES OR
OTHER
 * LIABILITY, WHETHER IN AN ACTION OF CONTRACT, TORT OR OTHERWISE,
ARISING FROM,
 * OUT OF OR IN CONNECTION WITH THE SOFTWARE OR THE USE OR OTHER
DEALINGS IN THE
 * SOFTWARE.
 **********************************************************/

using System;

/// <summary>
/// The CH3.Core.Security namespace contains fundamental types used
/// for the purpose of implementing application security.
/// </summary>
namespace CH3.Core.Security
{
    /// <summary>
```

```
/// Encrypts and decrypts provided strings based on the selected
/// algorithm.
/// </summary>
public class Cryptography
{
    /// <summary>
    /// Decrypts a string using the selected algorithm.
    /// </summary>
    /// <param name="text">The string to be decrypted.</param>
    /// <param name="algorithm">
    /// The cryptographic algorithm used to decrypt the string.
    /// </param>
    /// <returns>Decrypted string</returns>
    public string DecryptString(string text, SecurityAlgorithm
algorithm)
    {
        // ...implementation...
        throw new NotImplementedException();
    }
    /// <summary>
    /// Encrypts a string using the selected algorithm.
    /// </summary>
    /// <param name="text">The string to encrypt.</param>
    /// <param name="algorithm">
    /// The cryptographic algorithm used to encrypt the string.
    /// </param>
    /// <returns>Encrypted string</returns>
    public string EncryptString(string text, SecurityAlgorithm
algorithm)
    {
        // ...implementation...
        throw new NotImplementedException();
    }
}
}
```

The preceding code sample provides an example of a documented namespace and class with documented methods. You will see that the documentation comments for the namespace and contained members start with the documentation comment /// and are directly above the item being commented on. When you type the three forward slashes, Visual Studio automatically generates the XML tags based on the line below.

For example, in the preceding code, the namespace only has a summary and so does the class, but both methods contain a summary, a couple of parameter comments, and a return comment.

The following table contains the different XML tags that you can use in your documentation comments.

Tag	Section	Purpose
`<c>`	`<c>`	Formats text as code
`<code>`	`<code>`	Provides source code as output
`<example>`	`<example>`	Provides an example
`<exception>`	`<exception>`	Describes the exceptions that can be thrown by the method
`<include>`	`<include>`	Includes XML from an external file
`<list>`	`<list>`	Adds a list or table
`<para>`	`<para>`	Adds structure to text
`<param>`	`<param>`	Describes the parameter of a constructor or method
`<paramref>`	`<paramref>`	Tags a word to identify it as a parameter
`<permission>`	`<permission>`	Describes the security accessibility of the member
`<remarks>`	`<remarks>`	Provides additional information
`<returns>`	`<returns>`	Describes the return type
`<see>`	`<see>`	Adds a hyperlink
`<seealso>`	`<seealso>`	Adds a see also entry
`<summary>`	`<summary>`	Summarizes the type or member
`<value>`	`<value>`	Describes the value
`<typeparam>`		Describes the type parameter
`<typeparamref>`		Tags a word to identify it as a type parameter

Table 3.1: Documentation XML tags

From the preceding table, it is clear that you have plenty of scope for documenting your source code. So, it is a good idea to make the best use of the available tags to document your code. The better the documentation, the quicker and easier it will be for other developers to get up to speed with using the code.

> **Note**
> Visual Studio and other IDEs fully understand XML commenting syntax, so you will have available tags listed for you. You can read more about recommended XML tags for C# code documentation at `https://learn.microsoft.com/en-us/dotnet/csharp/language-reference/xmldoc/recommended-tags`.

It is now time to look at cohesion and coupling.

Cohesion and coupling

Low cohesion and high cohesion, along with tight coupling and loose coupling, are important concepts in software engineering that have a direct impact on the quality and maintainability of code. Let's explore these concepts in the context of C# and how they can affect the quality of your code:

- **Low cohesion**:

  - Low cohesion refers to a situation where a class or module has too many responsibilities, or its functions and methods are not closely related to each other

  - In C#, low cohesion can result in classes that are difficult to understand and maintain, as they perform various unrelated tasks

  - This can lead to code that is more error-prone, harder to test, and challenging to extend or modify

- **High cohesion**:

  - High cohesion means that a class or module has a well-defined and focused set of responsibilities, and its methods and functions are closely related to those responsibilities

  - In C#, high cohesion results in code that is easier to understand, maintain, and test, as each class or module has a clear and specific purpose

  - High cohesion helps in building clean and modular code

- **Tight coupling**:

  - Tight coupling refers to a situation where two or more classes or modules are highly dependent on each other. They have strong dependencies and are interconnected.

  - In C#, tight coupling can lead to code that is difficult to maintain and modify because changes in one class can have a cascading impact on other classes.

  - Tight coupling can make code less reusable and hinder testing.

- **Loose coupling**:

  - Loose coupling means that classes or modules are designed to have minimal dependencies on each other. They interact through well-defined interfaces or abstractions, reducing their interdependence.

  - In C#, loose coupling promotes clean code by making it more modular, reusable, and easier to change without affecting other parts of the system.

  - Loose coupling is particularly important in C# for promoting testability and flexibility.

So, low cohesion and tight coupling tend to produce bad and hard-to-maintain code in C# and other programming languages. On the other hand, high cohesion and loose coupling promote clean, modular, and maintainable code. When designing software in C#, it's essential to strive for high cohesion and loose coupling to enhance code quality and ease of development and maintenance.

We'll now look at examples of coupling and cohesion.

Tight coupling

Tight coupling in C# occurs when two or more classes or components are highly dependent on each other, making it difficult to change one class without affecting the others. This can lead to several issues, such as reduced maintainability, reusability, and testability. Here's an example of tight coupling in C# and an explanation of why it's considered bad coding:

```
public class Order
{
    public decimal CalculateTotalPrice(decimal unitPrice, int
quantity)
    {
        decimal discount = DiscountCalculator.
CalculateDiscount(unitPrice, quantity);
        return unitPrice * quantity - discount;
    }
}
public class DiscountCalculator
{
    public static decimal CalculateDiscount(decimal unitPrice, int
quantity)
    {
        if (quantity >= 10)
        {
            return unitPrice * quantity * 0.1m; // 10% discount for
bulk orders
        }
        else
        {
            return 0m; // No discount
        }
    }
}
```

In this example, the `Order` class is tightly coupled to the `DiscountCalculator` class because it directly calls the `CalculateDiscount` method of `DiscountCalculator` to calculate the discount. This tight coupling leads to several issues:

- **Low maintainability**: If you need to change the discount calculation logic or introduce a new discount strategy, you would have to modify the `DiscountCalculator` class. However, this change can have unintended consequences in the `Order` class or any other class that uses `DiscountCalculator`.

- **Low reusability**: The `DiscountCalculator` class cannot be easily reused in other parts of the code base because it is closely tied to the `Order` class. In a well-designed system, discount calculation logic should be reusable across different components.

- **Low testability**: When testing the `Order` class, it's challenging to isolate and test its logic independently from `DiscountCalculator`. You are forced to test both classes together, which can make unit testing more complex.

We will now look at how we can fix this using low coupling.

Low coupling

To improve the code in the previous section and reduce tight coupling, you can introduce loose coupling through the use of interfaces or abstractions. For instance, you can define an `IDiscountCalculator` interface and inject the discount calculator as a dependency into the `Order` class, promoting better separation of concerns, maintainability, and testability:

```
public interface IDiscountCalculator
{
    decimal CalculateDiscount(decimal unitPrice, int quantity);
}
```

Now that we have an interface for calculating discounts, we can use this interface to create different types of discount calculators, such as a bulk order discount calculator:

```
public class BulkOrderDiscountCalculator : IDiscountCalculator
{
    public decimal CalculateDiscount(decimal unitPrice, int quantity)
    {
        if (quantity >= 10)
        {
            return unitPrice * quantity * 0.1m; // 10% discount for
bulk orders
        }
        else
        {
```

```
            return 0m; // No discount
        }
    }
}
```

As can be seen, `BulkOrderDiscountCalculator` implements the `IDiscountCalculator`. We can now pass in any class to the `Order` class constructor that implements `IDiscountCalculator`:

```
public class Order
{
    private readonly IDiscountCalculator discountCalculator;

    public Order(IDiscountCalculator discountCalculator)
    {
        this.discountCalculator = discountCalculator;
    }
    public decimal CalculateTotalPrice(decimal unitPrice, int
quantity)
    {
        decimal discount = discountCalculator.
CalculateDiscount(unitPrice, quantity);
        return unitPrice * quantity - discount;
    }
}
```

By using interfaces and dependency injection, you achieve loose coupling, making it easier to modify, reuse, and test individual components without affecting the others. This results in cleaner, more maintainable code.

Next, we will look at low cohesion.

Low cohesion

Low cohesion in C# refers to a situation where a class or module has multiple responsibilities that are not closely related. This results in code that is hard to understand, maintain, and test. Here's an example of low cohesion in C# and an explanation of why it's considered bad coding:

```
public class Employee
{
    public string Name { get; set; }
    public int EmployeeId { get; set; }
    public decimal Salary { get; set; }
    public Employee(string name, int employeeId, decimal salary)
    {
        Name = name;
```

```
        EmployeeId = employeeId;
        Salary = salary;
    }
    public void CalculateTax()
    {
        // Tax calculation logic
    }
    public void GeneratePayStub()
    {
        // Pay stub generation logic
    }
    public void SaveToDatabase()
    {
        // Database save logic
    }
    public void SendEmail()
    {
        // Email sending logic
    }
}
```

In this example, the `Employee` class exhibits low cohesion because it combines several unrelated responsibilities:

- **Data storage**: It stores employee information such as name, ID, and salary
- **Tax calculation**: It calculates taxes for the employee
- **Pay stub generation**: It generates pay stubs for the employee
- **Database interaction**: It has logic for saving employee data to a database
- **Email sending**: It can send emails

The following explains why low cohesion is considered bad coding:

- **Maintenance difficulty**: Code with low cohesion is difficult to maintain because different responsibilities are mixed within the same class. When one aspect of the class needs to be changed, it can impact other unrelated aspects, making it error-prone and hard to manage.
- **Reduced reusability**: Low-cohesion classes are less reusable because they often contain tightly coupled logic, making it challenging to extract and use individual components in other parts of the code base.
- **Testing complexity**: Unit testing becomes more complex when a class is responsible for multiple, unrelated tasks. Testing one functionality might require setting up or invoking unrelated functions.

In the next section, we will improve this code to make it more cohesive.

High cohesion

To improve this code and address the issue of low cohesion, you can refactor it into separate classes with single responsibilities. For example, you can have separate classes for employee information, tax calculator, pay stub generator, database interaction, and email sending. This not only makes the code more maintainable but also enhances reusability and testability:

```csharp
public class Employee
{
    public string Name { get; set; }
    public int EmployeeId { get; set; }
    public decimal Salary { get; set; }

    public Employee(string name, int employeeId, decimal salary)
    {
        Name = name;
        EmployeeId = employeeId;
        Salary = salary;
    }
}
public class TaxCalculator
{
    public decimal CalculateTax(decimal salary)
    {
        // Tax calculation logic
        // ...
    }
}
public class PayStubGenerator
{
    public void GeneratePayStub(Employee employee)
    {
        // Pay stub generation logic
        // ...
    }
}
public class DatabaseService
{
    public void SaveEmployeeToDatabase(Employee employee)
    {
        // Database save logic
        // ...
    }
}
```

```
public class EmailService
{
    public void SendEmail(string recipient, string message)
    {
        // Email sending logic
        // ...
    }
}
```

By breaking down the responsibilities into separate classes, you achieve higher cohesion and better separation of concerns, resulting in cleaner, more maintainable code. Each class now has a single, well-defined purpose, making it easier to work with and test.

We will now move on to discuss designing for change.

Designing for change

When designing for change, you should change the *what* to *how*.

The *what* is the requirement of the business. As any seasoned person involved in a role within software development will tell you, requirements frequently change. As such, the software has to be adaptable to meet those changes. The business is not interested in *how* the requirements are implemented by the software and infrastructure teams, only that the requirements are met precisely on time and on budget.

On the other hand, the software and infrastructure teams are more focused on *how* those business requirements are to be met. Regardless of the technology and processes that are adopted for the project to implement the requirements, the software and target environment must be adaptable to changing requirements.

But that is not all. You see, software versions often change with bug fixes and new features. As new features are implemented and refactoring takes place, the software code becomes deprecated and eventually obsolete. On top of that, software vendors have a road map of their software that forms part of their application life cycle management. Eventually, software versions get to the point where they are retired and no longer supported by the vendor. This can force a major migration from the current version, which will no longer be supported, to the newly supported version, and this can bring with it breaking changes that must be addressed.

Interface-oriented programming

Interface-oriented programming (IOP) helps us to program polymorphic code. Polymorphism in OOP is defined as different classes having their own implementations of the same interface. And so, by using interfaces, we can morph our software to meet the needs of the business.

Let's consider a database connection example. An application may be required to connect to different data sources. But how can the database code remain the same no matter what database is employed? Well, the answer lies in the use of interfaces.

You have different database connection classes that implement the same database connection interface, but they each have their own versions of the implemented methods. This is known as **polymorphism**. The database then accepts a database connection parameter that is of the database connection interface type. You can then pass into the database any database connection type that implements the database connection interface. Let's code this example so that it makes things a little clearer.

Start by creating a simple .NET Framework console application. Then, update the `Program` class as follows:

```
static void Main(string[] args)
{
    var program = new Program();
    program.InterfaceOrientedProgrammingExample();
}

private void InterfaceOrientedProgrammingExample()
{
    var mongoDb = new MongoDbConnection();
    var sqlServer = new SqlServerConnection();

    var db = new Database(mongoDb);
    db.OpenConnection();
    db.CloseConnection();

    db = new Database(sqlServer);
    db.OpenConnection();
    db.CloseConnection();
}
```

In this code, the `Main()` method creates a new instance of the `Program` class and then calls the `InterfaceOrientedProgrammingExample()` method. In that method, we instantiate two different database connections, one for MongoDB and one for SQL Server. We then instantiate the database with a MongoDB connection, open the database connection, and then close it. Then, we instantiate a new database using the same variable and pass in a SQL Server connection, then open the connection and close the connection.

As you can see, we only have one `Database` class with a single constructor, yet the `Database` class will work with any database connection that implements the required interface. So, let's add the `IConnection` interface:

```
public interface IConnection
{
    void Open();
    void Close();
}
```

The interface has only two methods, called Open() and Close(). Add the MongoDB class that will implement this interface:

```
public class MongoDbConnection : IConnection
{
    public void Close()
    {
        Console.WriteLine("Closed MongoDB connection.");
    }

    public void Open()
    {
        Console.WriteLine("Opened MongoDB connection.");
    }
}
```

We can see that the class implements the IConnection interface. Each method prints out a message to the console. Now, add that SQLServerConnection class:

```
public class SqlServerConnection : IConnection
{
    public void Close()
    {
        Console.WriteLine("Closed SQL Server Connection.");
    }

    public void Open()
    {
        Console.WriteLine("Opened SQL Server Connection.");
    }
}
```

The same goes for the Database class. It implements the IConnection interface, and for each method invocation, a message is printed to the console. And now for the Database class, as follows:

```
public class Database
{
    private readonly IConnection _connection;

    public Database(IConnection connection)
    {
        _connection = connection;
    }

    public void OpenConnection()
```

```
    {
        _connection.Open();
    }

    public void CloseConnection()
    {
        _connection.Close();
    }
}
```

The `Database` class accepts an `IConnection` parameter. This sets the `_connection` member variable. The `OpenConnection()` method opens the database connection, and the `CloseConnection()` method closes the database connection. It's time to run the program. You should see the following output in the console window:

```
Opened MongoDB connection.
Closed MongoDB connection.
Opened SQL Server Connection.
Closed SQL Server Connection.
```

So, now, you can see the advantage of programming to interfaces. You can see how they enable us to extend the program without having to modify the existing code. That means that if we need to support more databases, then all we have to do is write more connection objects that implement the `IConnection` interface.

Now that you know how interfaces work, we can look at how to apply them to dependency injection and inversion of control. Dependency injection helps us to write clean code that is loosely coupled and easy to test, and inversion of control enables the interchanging of software implementations as required, as long as those implementations implement the same interface.

Dependency injection and inversion of control

In C#, we have the ability to address changing software needs using **dependency injection** (**DI**) and **inversion of control** (**IoC**). These two terms do have different meanings but are often used interchangeably to mean the same thing.

With IoC, you program a framework that accomplishes tasks by calling modules. An IoC container is used to keep a register of modules. These modules are loaded when requested by the user or configuration requests them.

DI removes internal dependencies from classes. Dependent objects are then injected by an external caller. An IoC container uses DI to inject dependent objects into an object or method.

In this chapter, you will find some useful resources that will help you to understand IoC and DI. You will then be able to use these techniques in your programs.

Let's see how we can implement our own simple DI and IoC without any third-party frameworks.

An example of DI

In this example, we are going to roll our own simple DI. We will have an `ILogger` interface that will have a single method with a string parameter. We will then produce a class called `TextFileLogger` that implements the `ILogger` interface and outputs a string to a text file. Finally, we will have a `Worker` class that will demonstrate constructor injection and method injection. Let's look at the code.

The following interface has a single method that will be used for implementing classes to output a message according to the implementation of the method:

```
namespace CH3.DependencyInjection
{
    public interface ILogger
    {
        void OutputMessage(string message);
    }
}
```

The `TexFileLogger` class implements the `ILogger` interface and outputs the message to a text file:

```
using System;
namespace CH3.DependencyInjection
{
    public class TextFileLogger : ILogger
    {
        public void OutputMessage(string message)
        {
            System.IO.File.WriteAllText(FileName(), message);
        }

        private string FileName()
        {
            var timestamp = DateTime.Now.ToFileTimeUtc().ToString();
            var path = Environment.GetFolderPath(Environment.
SpecialFolder.MyDocuments);
            return $"{path}_{timestamp}";
        }
    }
}
```

The `Worker` class provides an example of constructor DI and method DI. Notice that the parameter is an interface. So, any class that implements that interface can be injected at runtime:

```
namespace CH3.DependencyInjection
{
```

```
public class Worker
{
    private ILogger _logger;

    public Worker(ILogger logger)
    {
        _logger = logger;
        _logger.OutputMessage("This constructor has been injected
with a logger!");
    }

    public void DoSomeWork(ILogger logger)
    {
        logger.OutputMessage("This method has been injected with a
logger!");
    }
}
```

The `DependencyInject` method in the `Program` class runs the example to show DI in action:

```
private void DependencyInject()
{
    var logger = new TextFileLogger();
    var di = new Worker(logger);
    di.DoSomeWork(logger);
}
```

As you can see from the code we've just looked at, we start by producing a new instance of the `TextFileLogger` class. This object is then injected into the constructor of the worker. We then call the `DoSomeWork` method and pass in the `TextFileLogger` instance. In this simple example, we have seen how to inject code into a class via its constructor and methods.

What is good about this code is it removes the dependency between the worker and the `TextFileLogger` instance. This makes it easy for us to replace the `TextFileLogger` instance with any other type of logger that implements the `ILogger` interface. So, we could have used, for example, an event viewer logger or even a database logger. Using DI is a good way to reduce coupling in your code.

How Microsoft enables DI using core .NET service classes

In .NET Core, DI is an integral part of the framework, and Microsoft provides a built-in DI container. The following code is a simple example demonstrating how to use DI with the standard .NET Core services classes for both Singleton and Transient lifetimes.

Let's create a simple interface, Ilogger, and two classes, ConsoleLogger and FileLogger, implementing this interface. We'll register these services with different lifetimes in the DI container.

First, we'll start with the ILogger interface:

```csharp
public interface ILogger
{
    void Log(string message);
}
```

This interface contains a single method called Log that accepts a string parameter, and the method does not return a value. The different implementations of this interface will provide their own way of logging messages using the Log method. Next, we'll add the ConsoleLogger class:

```csharp
public class ConsoleLogger : ILogger
{
    public void Log(string message)
    {
        Console.WriteLine($"Console Logger: {message}");
    }
}
```

This class implements the ILogger interface and implements the Log method by logging text input from the parameter to the console window. Now, we'll add the FileLogger class:

```csharp
public class FileLogger : ILogger
{
    public void Log(string message)
    {
        // Implementation to log to a file (for simplicity, not
implemented in this example)
        Console.WriteLine($"File Logger: {message}");
    }
}
```

We'll now set up DI in the console application's Program class:

```csharp
using Microsoft.Extensions.DependencyInjection;
using System;
class Program
{
    static void Main()
    {
        // Create a service collection
        var serviceProvider = new ServiceCollection()
            .AddSingleton<ILogger, ConsoleLogger>() // Singleton
```

```
lifetime
            .AddTransient<ILogger, FileLogger>()      // Transient
lifetime
            .BuildServiceProvider();
        // Resolve and use the Singleton logger
        var singletonLogger = serviceProvider.
GetRequiredService<ILogger>();
        singletonLogger.Log("This message is logged by the Singleton
Logger");
        // Resolve and use the Transient logger
        var transientLogger = serviceProvider.
GetRequiredService<ILogger>();
        transientLogger.Log("This message is logged by the Transient
Logger");

        // Check if both loggers are the same instance for Singleton
        Console.WriteLine($"Is Singleton Logger the same
instance as Transient Logger? {ReferenceEquals(singletonLogger,
transientLogger)}");
    }
}
```

In this example, `ConsoleLogger` is registered as a Singleton, meaning only one instance will be created and shared throughout the application. `FileLogger` is registered as Transient, meaning a new instance will be created every time it is requested.

When you run the program, you'll see that the Singleton logger is the same instance for each resolution, while the Transient logger is a new instance every time it's resolved.

Now that we've seen DI at work, we should also look at IoC. And we'll do that now.

An example of IoC

In this example, we are going to register dependencies with an IoC container. We will then use DI to inject the necessary dependencies.

In the following code, we have an IoC container. The container registers the dependencies to be injected in a dictionary, and reads values from the configuration metadata:

```
using System;
using System.Collections.Generic;

namespace CH3.InversionOfControl
{
    public class Container
    {
        public delegate object Creator(Container container);
```

```
        private readonly Dictionary<string, object> configuration =
new Dictionary<string, object>();
        private readonly Dictionary<Type, Creator> typeToCreator = new
Dictionary<Type, Creator>();

        public Dictionary<string, object> Configuration
        {
            get { return configuration; }
        }

        public void Register<T>(Creator creator)
        {
            typeToCreator.Add(typeof(T), creator);
        }

        public T Create<T>()
        {
            return (T)typeToCreator[typeof(T)](this);
        }

        public T GetConfiguration<T>(string name)
        {
            return (T)configuration[name];
        }
    }
}
```

Then, we create a container, and we use the container to configure metadata, register types, and create instances of dependencies:

```
private void InversionOfControl()
{
    Container container = new Container();
    container.Configuration["message"] = "Hello World!";

    container.Register<ILogger>(delegate
    {
        return new TextFileLogger();
    });

    container.Register<Worker>(delegate
    {
        return new Worker(container.Create<ILogger>());
```

```
    });
}
```

How Microsoft enables IoC using core .NET service classes

Microsoft uses its built-in DI system to enable IoC. Here's a simple example using .NET Core's built-in DI system. In this example, we'll create a simple service and inject it into a class that depends on it.

Our example will be a notification service that sends a message. Let's start with `IMessageInterface`:

```
public interface IMessageService
{
    void SendMessage(string message);
}
```

This interface we be implemented by `EmailService` to send email messages:

```
public class EmailService : IMessageService
{
    public void SendMessage(string message)
    {
        Console.WriteLine($"Sending email: {message}");
    }
}
```

With our `EmailService` class that implements `ImessageService` written, we can now add our `NotificationService` class:

```
public class NotificationService
{
    private readonly IMessageService _messageService;

    // Constructor injection - the IMessageService is injected
    public NotificationService(IMessageService messageService)
    {
        _messageService = messageService;
    }

    public void Notify(string message)
    {
```

```
        _messageService.SendMessage(message);
    }
}
```

This class uses constructor injection to obtain the implementation class of the `IMessageService` interface. The `Notify` method then passes a string into the message service to send the message.

Now, we need to configure IoC in the application's `Program` class:

```
class Program
{
    static void Main()
    {
        var serviceProvider = new ServiceCollection()
            .AddScoped<IMessageService, EmailService>() // Use
AddScoped, AddTransient, or AddSingleton based on your needs
            .AddScoped<NotificationService>()
            .BuildServiceProvider();
        var notificationService = serviceProvider.
GetRequiredService<NotificationService>();
        notificationService.Notify("Hello, World!");
    }
}
```

In this example, we define an `IMessageService` interface and an `EmailService` class that implements it. The `NotificationService` class depends on `IMessageService`, and its dependency is injected through the constructor. In the `Main` method, we set up the DI container using the `ServiceCollection` class. We register `EmailService` as the implementation of `IMessageService` and `NotificationService` with the container. We then resolve an instance of `NotificationService` from the container using `GetRequiredService`. Finally, we use `NotificationService` to send a message, and it internally uses the injected `IMessageService` to perform the action.

This example demonstrates the basics of how IoC and DI work in a .NET Core application. The actual implementation details might vary based on the specific requirements and architecture of your application.

Next up, we will look at how to limit an object's knowledge to knowing only about its close relatives using the Law of Demeter. This will help us to write a clean C# code that avoids the use of navigation trains.

The Law of Demeter

The Law of Demeter aims to remove navigation trains (dot counting), and it also aims to provide good encapsulation with loosely coupled code.

A method that understands a navigation train breaks the Law of Demeter. For example, have a look at the following code:

```
report.Database.Connection.Open(); // Breaks the Law of Demeter.
```

The line of code `report.Database.Connection.Open();` is used to open a database connection to run a report.

The Law of Demeter is a software design principle that states that an object should not have direct knowledge of the internal structure or implementation of other objects. This means that a method should only call methods of its own class or of objects that it owns, not of objects that are obtained through other objects.

In this case, the `report` object is calling the `Open()` method of the `Connection` object, which is obtained through the `Database` object. This violates the Law of Demeter because the `report` object is directly accessing the internal structure of the `Database` object, which is not its own property or method.

To adhere to the Law of Demeter, the code could be refactored to something like this:

```
var connection = report.GetDatabaseConnection();

connection.Open();
```

In this refactored code, the `report` object does not directly access the `Connection` object, but instead calls a `GetDatabaseConnection()` method to obtain the `Connection` object. The `Open()` method is then called on the connection object directly, rather than through the `report` object.

This makes the code more maintainable and easier to change in the future since any changes to the internal structure of the `Database` object will not affect the `report` object. Additionally, it improves the encapsulation of the `Database` object and promotes better separation of concerns in the code.

This line of code chains navigation as separated by the dots. You can see there are four dots. These dots should be kept to a minimum.

Each unit of code should have a limited amount of knowledge. That knowledge should only be of relevant code that is closely related. With the Law of Demeter, you must tell and not ask. Using this law, you may only call methods of objects that are one or more of the following:

- Passed as arguments
- Created locally
- Instance variables
- Globals

Implementing the Law of Demeter can be difficult, but there are advantages to telling rather than asking. One such benefit is the decoupling of your code.

It is good to see a bad example that breaks the Law of Demeter, along with one that obeys the Law of Demeter, so we will see these in the following sections.

A good and a bad example (chaining) of the Law of Demeter

In the good example, we have the report instance variable. On the report variable object instance, the method to open the connection is called. This does not break the law.

The following code is a `Connection` class with a method that opens a connection:

```
namespace CH3.LawOfDemeter
{
    public class Connection
    {
        public void Open()
        {
            // ... implementation ...
        }
    }
}
```

The `Database` class creates a new `Connection` object and opens a connection:

```
namespace CH3.LawOfDemeter
{
    public class Database
    {
        public Database()
        {
            Connection = new Connection();
        }

        public Connection Connection { get; set; }

        public void OpenConnection()
        {
            Connection.Open();
        }
    }
}
```

In the `Report` class, a `Database` object is instantiated and then a connection to the database is opened:

```
namespace CH3.LawOfDemeter
{
```

```
public class Report
{
    public Report()
    {
        Database = new Database();
    }

    public Database Database { get; set; }

    public void OpenConnection()
    {
        Database.OpenConnection();
    }
}
}
```

So far, we have seen an example of good code that obeys the Law of Demeter. But the following is code that breaks this law.

In the `Example` class, the Law of Demeter is broken because we introduce method chaining, as in `report.Database.Connection.Open()`:

```
namespace CH3.LawOfDemeter
{
    public class Example
    {
        public void BadExample_Chaining()
        {
            var report = new Report();
            report.Database.Connection.Open();
        }

        public void GoodExample()
        {
            var report = new Report();
            report.OpenConnection();
        }
    }
}
```

In this bad example, the `Database` getter is called on the report instance variable. This is acceptable. But then a call is made to the `Connection` getter that returns a different object. This breaks the Law of Demeter, as does the final call to open the connection.

Let's look at immutable objects and data structures next.

Immutable objects and data structures

In C#, setting an object to static does not make it immutable. A static object is one that belongs to the class itself, rather than to any instance of the class. It can be accessed using the class name rather than an instance name, and there is only one instance of it shared among all instances of the class.

The immutability of an object depends on its properties and methods. An immutable object is one whose state cannot be changed after it is created. This means that its properties cannot be modified, and any operations that are performed on it return a new instance of the object rather than modifying the existing instance.

To make an object immutable in C#, you can follow these guidelines:

1. Make all fields private and read-only.
2. Only allow initialization of the object through a constructor.
3. Do not provide any public setters for the object's properties.
4. Ensure that any operations performed on the object return a new instance of the object rather than modifying the existing instance.

Here is an example of an immutable class in C#:

```
public class ImmutableClass
{
    private readonly int _value;

    public ImmutableClass(int value)
    {
        _value = value;
    }

    public int Value => _value;

    public ImmutableClass Add(int value)
    {
        return new ImmutableClass(_value + value);
    }
}
```

In this example, the class has a private `readonly` field, `_value`, which can only be set through the constructor. The class also has a public property, `Value`, that exposes the value of the field but does not provide a public setter. Finally, the class has an `Add` method that returns a new instance of the class with a modified value, rather than modifying the existing instance.

By following these guidelines, we can create immutable objects in C# that cannot be modified after they are created, regardless of whether they are static or not.

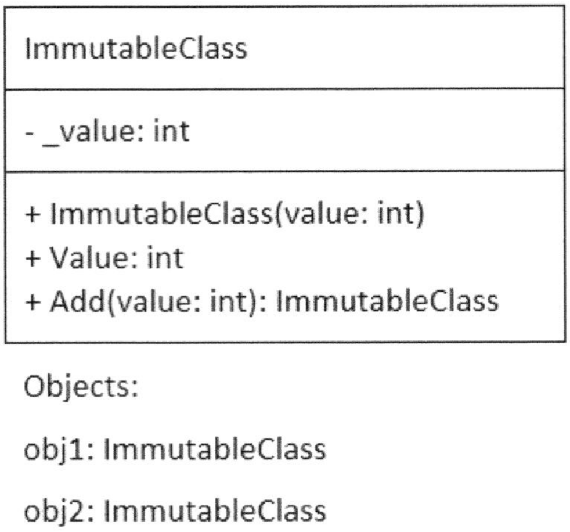

ImmutableClass
- _value: int
+ ImmutableClass(value: int) + Value: int + Add(value: int): ImmutableClass

Objects:

obj1: ImmutableClass

obj2: ImmutableClass

Figure 3.3: Immutable Objects

Let's look at this diagram in more detail:

- The ImmutableClass class is represented by a rectangle
- The class has a private _value field of the int type
- The class has an ImmutableClass(int value) constructor for initializing _value
- The class has a Value property of the int type
- The class has a method called Add(int value) that returns a new ImmutableClass object

Under the Objects section, you can create multiple instances of ImmutableClass:

- obj1: ImmutableClass
- obj2: ImmutableClass

These objects represent instances of the ImmutableClass class. You can use them to demonstrate how the Add method works, as in this example:

```
obj1 = new ImmutableClass(5);
obj2 = obj1.Add(3);
```

This creates two objects: obj1 with a value of 5 and obj2 with a value of 8 (the result of adding 5 and 3). The objects remain immutable, so obj1 and obj2 have distinct values and do not change the state of each other when the Add method is called.

Using records to create immutable objects

Records were introduced in C# 9.0, which is part of the .NET 5 release. C# 9.0 is closely associated with .NET 5, as both were released together in November 2020.

Records are a new reference type in C# that is designed to make it easier to work with immutable data. They provide a concise syntax for creating immutable objects, reducing the amount of boilerplate code that developers need to write. In addition to immutability, records come with other features that make them suitable for use in scenarios where value semantics are desired.

Here are some key features of records in C#:

- **Immutable by default**: Records are immutable by default, meaning that their properties cannot be modified after the object is created. This helps in creating objects with a predictable state and reduces the chances of introducing bugs related to mutable state.

- **Value equality**: Records automatically implement value equality. The compiler generates the `Equals` and `GetHashCode` methods based on the properties of the record. This makes it easy to compare records for equality without having to explicitly override these methods.

- **Deconstruction**: Records support deconstruction, allowing you to easily break down a record into its individual components. This can be useful in scenarios such as pattern matching or when you need to extract values from a record.

- `with` **expressions**: Records come with a `with` expression that allows you to create a new instance of the record with modified values. This is helpful for creating modified copies of immutable objects without changing the original instance.

Here's an example of a simple record in C#:

```
public record Person
{
    public string FirstName { get; init; }
    public string LastName { get; init; }
}
```

In this example, the `init` accessor is used to set the properties during object initialization, but they cannot be modified afterward.

Records are ideal for creating immutable objects due to their concise syntax, built-in support for immutability, value equality, and other features that promote good practices in managing and working with data. They contribute to more readable and maintainable code, especially in scenarios where data is expected to remain constant once it's set.

Now we have seen how easy it is to write immutable objects and data structures, we will look at data and methods in objects.

Objects should hide data and expose methods

The state of your object is stored in member variables. These member variables are pieces of data. Data should not be directly accessible. You should only provide access to data via exposed methods and properties.

Why should you hide your data and expose your methods?

Hiding data and exposing methods is known in the OOP world as **encapsulation**. Encapsulation hides the inner workings of a class from the outside world. This makes it easy to be able to change value types without breaking existing implementations that rely on the class. Data can be made read/writable, writable, or read-only providing more flexibility to you regarding data access and usage. You can also validate input and prevent data from receiving invalid values. Encapsulating also makes testing your classes much easier, and you can make your classes more reusable and extendable.

Let's look at an example.

An example of encapsulation

The following code example shows an encapsulated class. The Car object is mutable. It has properties that get and set the data values once they have been initialized by the constructor. The constructor and the set properties perform the validation of the parameter arguments. If the value is invalid, an invalid argument exception is thrown, otherwise, the value is passed back and the data value is set:

```
using System;
namespace CH3.Encapsulation
{
    public class Car
    {
        private string _make;
        private string _model;
        private int _year;

        public Car(string make, string model, int year)
        {
            Make = ValidateMake(make);
            Model = ValidateModel(model);
            Year = ValidateYear(year);
        }

        private string ValidateMake(string make)
        {
            if (make.Length >= 3)
                return make;
            throw new ArgumentException("Make must be three characters
```

```
or more.");
        }

        public string Make
        {
            get { return _make; }
            set { _make = ValidateMake(value); }
        }

        // Other methods and properties omitted for brevity.
    }
}
```

> **Note**
>
> Constructors can use different validation to setter properties. Therefore, it is a good idea to set the property in the constructor and not the field. That way, you can ensure correct validation takes place.

The benefit of the preceding code is that if you need to change the validation for the code that gets or sets the data values, you can do so without breaking the implementation.

Data structures should expose data and have no methods

The idea that data structures should expose data and have no methods is related to the concept of separation of concerns in software design. The primary concern of a data structure is to hold and organize data, while the primary concern of methods is to perform operations on that data.

Here are a few examples of data structures that expose data and have no methods:

- **Array**: An array is a simple data structure that holds a collection of elements of the same type. Arrays do not have any methods and are primarily used to store and retrieve data. Here is an example of an array of integers:

    ```
    int[] myArray = { 1, 2, 3, 4, 5 };
    ```

- **Tuple**: A tuple is a data structure that holds a collection of values of different types. Tuples do not have any methods and are primarily used to group related data together. Here is an example of a tuple that holds a name and an age:

    ```
    var person = ("John", 30);
    ```

- **Struct**: A struct is a value type that holds a collection of related data fields. Structs can have methods, but it is generally recommended to avoid adding methods to them. Here is an example of a struct that holds information about a point in a 2D coordinate system:

```
struct Point
{
    public int X;
    public int Y;
}
```

In all of these examples, the primary purpose of the data structure is to hold and organize data, and it is not necessary or appropriate to add methods to them. By keeping the concerns of data and methods separate, we can create simpler, more focused, and maintainable code.

The SOLID software methodology

SOLID is an acronym that represents a set of five design principles for writing maintainable and scalable software. These principles were introduced by Robert C. Martin and are widely used in OOP. Let's take a brief look at each of these SOLID principles.

SRP

A class should have only one reason to change, meaning that it should have only one responsibility.

The following code is an example of a wrong implementation that violates the SRP:

```
class Report
{
    public void GenerateReport() { /* ... */ }
    public void SaveToFile() { /* ... */ }
}
```

This class performs the two responsibilities of generating a report and saving it to a file. Here is the correct implementation:

```
class Report
{
    public void GenerateReport() { /* ... */ }
}
class ReportSaver
{
    public void SaveToFile(Report report) { /* ... */ }
}
```

As you can see, our correct implementation of the SRP farms out the generating of the report and saving it to a file to two separate files with single responsibilities.

Open/closed principle (OCP)

Software entities (classes, modules, and functions) should be open for extension but closed for modification.

Here is a wrong implementation that violates the OCP:

```
class Rectangle
{
    public double Width { get; set; }
    public double Height { get; set; }
}
class AreaCalculator
{
    public double CalculateArea(Rectangle rectangle)
    {
        return rectangle.Width * rectangle.Height;
    }
}
```

It is clear to see how the AreaCalculator class breaks the OCP with its CalculateArea method that takes the Rectangle object as a parameter and calculates its area. Let's see the correct implementation that does not violate the OCP:

```
abstract class Shape
{
    public abstract double CalculateArea();
}
class Rectangle : Shape
{
    public double Width { get; set; }
    public double Height { get; set; }

    public override double CalculateArea()
    {
        return Width * Height;
    }
}
```

Here, we have an abstract Shape class that has an abstract method called CalculateArea. The Rectangle class inherits the abstract Shape class and implements the CalculateArea method respecting the OCP.

Liskov substitution principle (LSP)

Subtypes must be substitutable for their base types without altering the correctness of the program.

The following code violates the LSP:

```
class Bird
{
    public virtual void Fly() { /* ... */ }
}
class Penguin : Bird
{
    public override void Fly()
    {
        throw new InvalidOperationException("Penguins cannot fly.");
    }
}
```

The LSP states that objects of a superclass should be replaceable with objects of a subclass without affecting the correctness of the program. In the given code, the Penguin class, which is a subclass of Bird, violates the LSP.

The violation occurs because the Penguin class overrides the Fly method of the base class (Bird) and throws an exception, indicating that penguins cannot fly. This behavior contradicts the expected behavior of the base class, where the Fly method is declared as a virtual method but does not define any specific behavior.

The LSP violation becomes apparent when you use an object of the Bird class (assuming it could be an instance of Penguin as well) in a context where flying is expected without checking its actual type. The code relying on the LSP may expect any bird to be able to fly based on the base class's contract, but if a Penguin is substituted, it will throw an exception, breaking the expected behavior.

In other words, the LSP violation occurs because the subclass (Penguin) introduces a behavior (Fly, throwing an exception) that is not compatible with the behavior defined by the base class (Bird). Subtypes should not alter the behavior of their base types in a way that breaks the contract established by the base class.

Here is the correct implementation:

```
interface IFlyable
{
    void Fly();
}
class Bird : IFlyable
{
    public void Fly() { /* ... */ }
}
class Penguin : IFlyable
{
```

```
    public void Fly()
    {
        throw new InvalidOperationException("Penguins cannot fly.");
    }
}
```

We start with the `IFlyable` interface that defines a `Fly` method. Different birds will implement the `IFlyable` interface and provide their own `Fly` implementation as some birds can fly and others, such as penguins, cannot.

Interface segregation principle (ISP)

A class should not be forced to implement interfaces it does not use. Here is the wrong implementation that breaks the ISP:

```
interface IWorker
{
    void Work();
    void TakeBreak();
}
class Manager : IWorker
{
    public void Work() { /* ... */ }
    public void TakeBreak() { /* ... */ }  // Manager may not need
this
}
```

The `IWorker` interface provides two methods, called `Work` and `TakeBreak`. However, some worker types may not need to take a break, yet they are forced to implement the `TakeBreak` method. We can clean this up so that the ISP is respected. Here is the correct implementation of the ISP:

```
interface IWorker
{
    void Work();
}
interface IBreakable
{
    void TakeBreak();
}
class Manager : IWorker, IBreakable
{
    public void Work() { /* ... */ }
    public void TakeBreak() { /* ... */ }
}
```

The IWorker interface has been split into two interfaces, called IWorker and IBreakable. Now, different worker types can implement only the interfaces they require.

Dependency inversion principle (DIP)

High-level modules should not depend on low-level modules. Both should depend on abstractions. Abstractions should not depend on details; details should depend on abstractions. The following code violates the DIP:

```
class LightBulb
{
    public void TurnOn() { /* ... */ }
    public void TurnOff() { /* ... */ }
}
class Switch
{
    private LightBulb bulb;
    public Switch(LightBulb bulb)
    {
        this.bulb = bulb;
    }
    public void Toggle()
    {
        // This high-level module depends on a low-level module
directly
        if (bulb.IsOn)
            bulb.TurnOff();
        else
            bulb.TurnOn();
    }
}
```

As you can see, the Switch class is dependent upon the LightBulb class. We can fix this with the code that follows:

```
interface ISwitchable
{
    void TurnOn();
    void TurnOff();
}
class LightBulb : ISwitchable
{
    public void TurnOn() { /* ... */ }
    public void TurnOff() { /* ... */ }
```

```
}
class Switch
{
    private ISwitchable device;
    public Switch(ISwitchable device)
    {
        this.device = device;
    }
    public void Toggle()
    {

if (device.IsOn)
            device.TurnOff();
        else
            device.TurnOn();
    }
}
```

We have an ISwitchable interface that provides methods for turning a device on and off. The LightBulb class implements ISwitchable so that the bulb can be turned on and off. The Switch class takes an ISwitchable device and is able to turn it on and off. In this implementation, we are using abstractions and so respect the DIP.

By following these SOLID principles, you can create more maintainable, flexible, and scalable software systems.

With this, we come to the end of the chapter, and we will now review what we've learned.

Summary

In this chapter, we learned about organizing our namespaces in folders and packages, and how good organization can help to prevent namespace classes. We then moved on to classes and responsibilities and looked at why classes should only have one responsibility. We also looked at cohesion and coupling and why it is important to have high cohesion and low coupling.

Good documentation requires public members to be correctly commented on in documentation tools, and we saw how to do this using XML comments. The importance of why you should design for change was also discussed with basic examples of DI and IoC.

The Law of Demeter showed you how to not talk to strangers but only immediate friends, and how to avoid chaining. Finally, we looked at objects and data structures, what they should hide, and what they should make public.

In the next chapter, we will briefly cover functional programming in C# and how to write clean methods that are small. We will also learn how to avoid having more than two parameters in our methods, as methods with many parameters can become unwieldy. Plus, we will learn how to avoid duplication, which can be a troublesome source of bugs when fixed in one location but still exist elsewhere in your code.

Questions

1. How can we organize our classes in C#?

2. How many responsibilities should a class have?

3. How do you comment on your code for document generators?

4. What does cohesion mean?

5. What does coupling mean?

6. Should cohesion be high or low?

7. Should coupling be tight or loose?

8. What mechanisms are available that help you design for change?

9. What is DI?

10. What is IoC?

11. Name one benefit of using immutable objects.

12. What should objects hide and show?

13. What should structures hide and show?

Further reading

- The Single Responsibility Principle by Robert C. Martin

- For more details regarding understanding the different kinds of cohesion and coupling, check out `https://www.geeksforgeeks.org/software-engineering-coupling-and-cohesion/`

- Many tutorials on IoC can be found at `https://www.tutorialsteacher.com/ioc/`

- Test Driven Development: By Example by Kent Beck

- Interface Oriented Design: With Patterns by Ken Pugh

4

Writing Clean Functions

Clean functions are methods that are small (they have two or fewer arguments) and avoid duplication. The ideal method has no parameters and does not modify the program's state. Small methods are less prone to exceptions, so you will be writing much more robust code that benefits you in the long run as you will have fewer bugs to fix.

Functional programming (FP) is a software coding methodology that treats computations as the mathematical evaluation of computations. This chapter will teach you the benefits of treating computations as the evaluation of mathematical functions in order to void changing an object's state.

Large methods (also known as functions) can be unwieldy to read and prone to errors, so writing small methods has its advantages. Hence, we will look at how large methods can be broken up into smaller methods. In this chapter, we will cover FP in C# and how to write small, clean methods.

Constructors and methods with multiple parameters can become a real pain to work with, so we will have to look for ways to work around and pass multiple parameters, as well as how to avoid using more than two parameters. The main reason for reducing the number of parameters we have is that they can become hard to read, be a source of irritation to fellow programmers, and cause visual stress if there are enough of them. They can also be a sign that the method is trying to do too much or that you need to consider refactoring your code.

In this chapter, we will cover the following topics:

- Understanding the difference between **object-oriented programming (OOP)** and FP
- Keeping methods small
- Avoiding duplication
- Avoiding multiple parameters
- Handling exceptions in FP

By the time you have worked through this chapter, you will have the skills to do the following:

- Describe FP and apply it to your C# programming
- Write small and clean functions that are readable and don't affect state
- Implement code that adheres to the **Single Responsibility Principle** (**SRP**)
- Implement correct exception handling in functional programs

Let's get started!

Technical requirements

To follow along with this chapter, you will require the following:

- The latest version of Visual Studio Community Edition
- The source code, available at `https://github.com/PacktPublishing/Clean-Code-with-CSharp-Second-Edition/tree/main/CH04`

Understanding the difference between OOP and FP

In this chapter, we will be discussing FP. Because most readers will be used to OOP, FP can feel rather alien to them to begin with.

So, in this section, we will cover an example written first as an OOP program, and secondly as a FP program.

Let's consider a simple example where we model a basic shape, such as a rectangle, using both OOP and FP approaches. We will start with the OOP code first:

```
class Rectangle
{
    public double Length { get; set; }
    public double Width { get; set; }

    // Constructor
    public Rectangle(double length, double width)
    {
        Length = length;
        Width = width;
    }
    public double CalculateArea()
    {
        return Length * Width;
    }
}
```

```
}
class Program
{
    static void Main()
    {
        // Create a rectangle object
        Rectangle myRectangle = new Rectangle(5, 3);
        // Calculate and print the area
        Console.WriteLine("Area of the rectangle: " + myRectangle.
CalculateArea());
    }
}
```

Now, we'll look at the FP version before we describe what's going on:

```
static double CalculateArea(double length, double width)
{
    return length * width;
}
class Program
{
    static void Main()
    {
        // Use the function to calculate and print the area
        double length = 5;
        double width = 3;
        Console.WriteLine("Area of the rectangle: " +
CalculateArea(length, width));
    }
}
```

Explanation of the differences

To explain the differences between FP and OOP, let's first look at OOP more closely:

1. **Class definition:**

   - OOP involves defining a class (in this case, Rectangle) to encapsulate properties (length and width) and methods (for example, CalculateArea) that operate on the data.

2. **Object instantiation:**

   - Objects (instances of the class) are created to represent specific instances of the concept (a specific rectangle with a particular length and width).

3. **State and behavior:**

   - The class encapsulates both state (properties) and behavior (methods) in a single unit.

Now, let's have a closer look at FP:

1. **Function definition:**

   - FP involves defining functions that take inputs and produce outputs without maintaining any internal state.

2. **Pure functions:**

   - Functions in FP are "pure," meaning they produce the same output for the same input and have no side effects.

3. **Data immutability:**

   - FP typically relies on immutable data. In the example, the `CalculateArea` function doesn't modify any state; it just takes inputs and produces an output.

Now, let's look at their key differences:

1. **State handling:**

   - OOP involves managing state through objects, while FP relies on immutable data and pure functions.

2. **Paradigm philosophy:**

   - OOP emphasizes encapsulation, where data and behavior are bundled together, while FP emphasizes the **separation of concerns** (**SoC**) and treating computation as the evaluation of mathematical functions.

3. **Mutability:**

   - OOP allows for mutable state within objects, whereas FP prefers immutability to avoid side effects.

Understanding and shifting between these paradigms requires a different mindset. OOP is more about organizing code around objects and their interactions, while FP focuses on composing functions and avoiding mutable state. The choice between them often depends on the problem at hand and the preferences of the developer or team.

Understanding why FP can lead to cleaner functions

FP and OOP are two different programming paradigms, each with its own strengths and weaknesses. While both paradigms can be used to write clean and robust code, FP has certain features that can contribute to cleaner and less error-prone functions compared to conventional OOP. Here are some reasons why:

1. **Immutability**:

   - In FP, immutability is often emphasized. Once a variable is assigned a value, it cannot be changed. This helps prevent unintended side effects and makes the code more predictable. In OOP, especially languages that allow mutable objects, unintended changes to object state can lead to bugs that are harder to trace.

2. **Pure functions**:

   - FP encourages the use of pure functions—functions that have no side effects and always produce the same output for the same input. Pure functions make it easier to reason about code since they don't depend on external state. In OOP, methods of objects often modify the object's state, introducing potential side effects and making it more challenging to predict the behavior of a function.

3. **Avoidance of shared state**:

   - In FP, functions operate on their inputs without modifying external state. This reduces the likelihood of shared mutable state between different parts of a program, minimizing the chance of unexpected interactions. OOP often involves shared state between objects, which can lead to complex interactions and bugs that are harder to track down.

4. **Functional composition**:

   - FP encourages composing functions by combining them to create more complex behavior. This leads to smaller, more focused functions that are easier to understand and test. In OOP, combining behavior often involves inheritance and method overriding, which can lead to complex class hierarchies that are harder to maintain.

5. **Concurrency and parallelism**:

   - FP is often considered more suitable for concurrent and parallel programming because of its emphasis on immutability and avoiding shared state. In OOP, managing shared mutable state in a concurrent environment can be challenging and error-prone.

6. **Type systems**:

   - Many FP languages have strong type systems that can catch certain types of errors at compile time. This helps prevent runtime errors that may occur due to type mismatches. While OOP languages also have type systems, the emphasis on immutability and pure functions in FP can reduce the likelihood of certain types of bugs.

7. **Easier testing**:

   - Functions in FP are often easier to test since they are designed to be pure and stateless. In OOP, testing can be more complex due to dependencies on shared state and the need to set up object hierarchies for testing.

While FP has these advantages, it's important to note that the effectiveness of a paradigm depends on the problem at hand and the context in which it is applied. Both OOP and FP have their places in modern software development, and a hybrid approach that leverages the strengths of both paradigms is also common.

We will now move on to see how unclean methods negatively impact software.

Unclean methods and how they affect software

In C#, as in any programming language, there are certain types of methods that can be considered "not clean" or problematic. These methods often exhibit characteristics that can lead to various issues in code readability, maintainability, and robustness. Here are some common types of methods that are not considered clean and the problems they can produce:

- **Methods with high cyclomatic complexity:**

  - **Problem**: Methods with high cyclomatic complexity contain a large number of branches, conditions, and decision points. These methods tend to be hard to understand, debug, and maintain.

  - **Solution**: Refactor complex methods into smaller, more focused functions and use techniques such as `switch` statements or polymorphism to simplify control flow.

- **Methods with too many parameters:**

  - **Problem**: Methods that take a large number of parameters can be challenging to call correctly and may lead to confusion and bugs.

  - **Solution**: Consider creating **data transfer objects** (**DTOs**) or using method overloads to reduce the number of parameters. Use objects or structs to bundle related data.

- **Methods with side effects:**

  - **Problem**: Methods that modify global state or have side effects can make it difficult to reason about the code's behavior and lead to unexpected results.

  - **Solution**: Aim for pure functions that don't modify state and clearly document when side effects are necessary. Minimize global state modifications.

- **Methods with poor naming**:

  - **Problem**: Methods with unclear or misleading names can lead to confusion and make the code less readable.

  - **Solution**: Use meaningful and descriptive names that convey the purpose and functionality of the method. Follow naming conventions to improve code consistency.

- **Methods with excessive length**:

  - **Problem**: Long methods can be challenging to read and understand, and they often indicate that a method is doing too much.

  - **Solution**: Break down long methods into smaller, focused functions that each perform a single task. This improves code modularity and readability.

- **Methods with nested control structures**:

  - **Problem**: Deeply nested `if` statements, loops, and switch cases can make code hard to follow and lead to logic errors.

  - **Solution**: Refactor complex control structures into smaller, more understandable methods or use early returns and guards to simplify conditional logic.

- **Methods with duplicated code**:

  - **Problem**: Repeated code in multiple methods can lead to maintenance nightmares because changes must be made in multiple places.

  - **Solution**: Extract common functionality into separate methods or classes to eliminate duplication and follow the **Don't Repeat Yourself (DRY)** principle.

- **Methods with poor error handling**:

  - **Problem**: Methods that do not handle errors or exceptions gracefully can lead to application crashes or unreliable behavior.

  - **Solution**: Implement robust error handling using `try-catch` blocks and provide meaningful error messages or log information for debugging.

- **Methods with magic numbers or hardcoded values**:

  - **Problem**: Hardcoded values can make code less maintainable and harder to understand.

  - **Solution**: Replace magic numbers with named constants or configuration values to improve code clarity and allow for easy changes.

- **Methods with poor documentation**:

  - **Problem**: Methods lacking documentation can be challenging for other developers to understand and use.

  - **Solution**: Document your methods with clear and concise comments or use tools such as XML documentation comments to provide comprehensive documentation.

In summary, clean methods in C# are characterized by simplicity, modularity, good naming, and adherence to best practices. Methods that violate these principles can lead to code that is difficult to maintain, understand, and extend. By addressing these issues, you can make your C# code base more maintainable and robust.

FP and clean methods

C# is indeed considered an OOP language, but it also supports FP concepts. FP is a programming paradigm that treats computation as the evaluation of mathematical functions and avoids changing state and mutable data. In C#, you can leverage FP techniques to write clean and efficient functions, even within an OO context. Here's how and why it's important:

- **Immutability**:

  - In FP, immutability is a fundamental concept. Immutability means that once an object is created, its state cannot be changed. You can use this concept in C# by creating immutable data structures or objects. Immutability can make your code cleaner and more predictable because you don't need to worry about unexpected changes to your data.

- **Pure functions**:

  - Pure functions are functions that have no side effects and always return the same output for the same input. Writing pure functions can make your code cleaner and more maintainable. You can write pure functions in C# by avoiding global state and minimizing side effects. This can lead to easier testing and debugging.

- **Higher-order functions**:

  - C# supports higher-order functions, which are functions that take other functions as arguments or return functions as results. You can use higher-order functions to encapsulate behavior, make your code more modular, and reduce repetition.

- **Lambda expressions**:

  - C# has lambda expressions, which are concise ways to define anonymous functions. These can be used for various FP techniques, such as filtering, mapping, and reducing data. Lambda expressions can make your code more readable and expressive.

- **Language-Integrated Query (LINQ)**:

  - LINQ is a powerful feature in C# that combines both FP and **declarative programming (DP)**. It allows you to query and manipulate data using a syntax similar to SQL. LINQ can simplify complex data operations, making your code cleaner and more efficient.

- **Functional composition**:

  - In FP, you can compose functions together to build complex behavior from simpler functions. C# allows you to create pipelines of functions using operators such as `=>` (lambda) and `|>` (pipe). This can improve code readability and maintainability.

- **Avoiding mutable state**:

  - In FP, you aim to minimize or eliminate mutable state. C# provides constructs such as `readonly` and `const` to help you create more predictable and clean code by reducing the use of mutable variables.

The importance of employing FP in C# is to make your code cleaner, more predictable, and easier to maintain. It can lead to the following benefits:

- **Improved code readability**: Functional code tends to be more concise and expressive

- **Easier debugging and testing**: Pure functions and immutability make it easier to isolate and test parts of your code

- **Reduced side effects**: Minimizing side effects leads to more predictable behavior and easier reasoning about your code

- **Enhanced modularity**: FP encourages breaking down complex problems into smaller, composable units

- **Better parallelism and concurrency**: Functional code can be more suitable for parallel processing, which is important in modern computing

While C# is primarily an OO language, its support for FP allows you to harness the benefits of both paradigms, leading to cleaner and more maintainable code.

FP examples

The only thing that sets FP aside from other methods of programming is that functions do not modify data or state. You will use FP in scenarios such as **deep learning (DL)**, **machine learning (ML)**, and **artificial intelligence (AI)** when it is necessary to perform different sets of operations on the same set of data.

The *LINQ syntax* within .NET Framework is an example of FP. So, if you are wondering what FP looks like, and if you have used LINQ before, then you have been subjected to FP and should know what it looks like.

Since FP is a deep subject and many books, courses, and videos exist on this topic, we will only touch on the topic briefly in this chapter by looking at pure functions and immutable data.

A pure function is restricted to only operating on the data that is passed into it. As a result, the method is predictable and avoids producing side effects. This benefits programmers because such methods are easier to reason about and test.

Once an immutable data object or data structure has been initialized, the contained data values will not be modified. Because the data is only set and not modified, you can easily reason about what the data is, how it is set, and what the outcome of any operation will be, given the inputs. Immutable data is also easier to test as you know what your inputs are and what outputs are expected. This makes writing test cases much easier as you don't have so many things to consider, such as object state. The benefit of immutable objects and structures is that they are thread-safe. Thread-safe objects and structures make for good DTOs that can be passed between threads.

But structs can still be mutable if they contain reference types. One way around this would be to make the reference type immutable. C# 7.2 added support for `readonly struct` and `ImmutableStruct`. So, even if our structures contain reference types, we can now use these new C# 7.2 constructs to make structures with reference types immutable.

Now, let's have a look at a pure function example. The only way to set the properties of an object is via the constructor at construction time. The class is a `Player` class whose only job is to hold the name of the player and their high score. A method is provided that updates the player's high score:

```
public class Player
{
    public string PlayerName { get; }
    public long HighScore { get; }
    public Player(string playerName, long highScore)
    {
        PlayerName = playerName;
        HighScore = highScore;
    }
    Public Player UpdateHighScore(long highScore)
    {
        return new Player(PlayerName, highScore);
    }
}
```

Notice that the `UpdateHighScore` method does not update the `HighScore` property. Instead, it instantiates and returns a new `Player` class by passing in the `PlayerName` variable, which is already set in the class, and `highScore`, which is the method parameter. You have now seen a very simple example of how to program your software without changing its state.

> **Note**
>
> FP is a very large subject and requires a mind shift that can be very difficult for both procedural and OO programmers. Since it is outside the scope of this book (to delve deep into the topic of FP), you are actively encouraged to peruse the FP resources on offer from Packt Publishing for yourself.
>
> Packt has some very good books and videos that specialize in teaching the top tiers of FP. You will find links to some Packt FP resources at the end of this chapter, in the *Further reading* section.

Before we move on, we will look at some LINQ examples since LINQ is an example of FP in C#. It will be good to have an example dataset. The following code builds a list of vendors and products. We'll start by writing the `Product` structure:

```
public struct Product
{
    public string Vendor { get; }
    public string ProductName { get; }
    public Product(string vendor, string productName)
    {
        Vendor = vendor;
        ProductName = productName;
    }
}
```

Now that we have our struct, we will add some sample data inside the `GetProducts()` method:

```
public static List<Product> GetProducts()
{
    return new List<Product>
    {
        new Product("Microsoft", "Microsoft Office"),
        new Product("Oracle", "Oracle Database"),
        new Product("IBM", "IBM DB2 Express"),
        new Product("IBM", "IBM DB2 Express"),
        new Product("Microsoft", "SQL Server 2017 Express"),
        new Product("Microsoft", "Visual Studio 2019 Community
Edition"),
        new Product("Oracle", "Oracle JDeveloper"),
        new Product("Microsoft", "Azure"),
        new Product("Microsoft", "Azure"),
        new Product("Microsoft", "Azure Stack"),
        new Product("Google", "Google Cloud Platform"),
        new Product("Amazon", "Amazon Web Services")
    };
}
```

Finally, we can start to use LINQ on our list. In the preceding example, we got a distinct list of products and ordered by the vendors' names. Now we will print out the results:

```
class Program
{
    static void Main(string[] args)
    {
        var vendors = (from p in GetProducts()
        select p.Vendor)
        .Distinct()
        .OrderBy(x => x);
        foreach(var vendor in vendors)
        Console.WriteLine(vendor);
        Console.ReadKey();
    }
}
```

In the provided C# code, the LINQ statements are used to retrieve a distinct list of vendor names from a collection of products and then order them alphabetically. The LINQ statements can be considered pure functions in the context of this code because they do not have any side effects, and their output is solely determined by their input. Here's an explanation of how these LINQ statements act as pure functions:

- `from p in GetProducts() select p.Vendor`: This LINQ statement queries the `GetProducts()` method to retrieve the `Vendor` property from each product. It transforms the input collection of products into a new sequence of vendor names. This transformation is a pure function because it does not modify the input collection or have any side effects.

- `.Distinct()`: The `Distinct()` method filters the sequence of vendor names to ensure that each vendor name appears only once in the output. This operation is also a pure function as it does not alter the original sequence and produces a new sequence based on the distinct values.

- `.OrderBy(x => x)`: The `OrderBy` method sorts the vendor names alphabetically. This sorting operation is deterministic and does not modify the input sequence but produces a new ordered sequence. It, too, is a pure function.

Overall, the LINQ statements in this code are pure functions because they take an input collection, apply various transformations to it, and produce a new collection without causing any side effects or altering the original data. This functional style of programming is one of the benefits of using LINQ in C#, as it promotes immutability and helps ensure code clarity and maintainability.

In C#, you can create an immutable type by using the `record` keyword. Here's an example of a simple immutable record a person:

```
public record Person
{
    public string FirstName { get; set; }
    public string LastName { get; set;}
    public int Age { get; set;}
    public Person(string firstName, string lastName, int age)
    {
        FirstName = firstName;
        LastName = lastName;
        Age = age;
    }
}
```

In this example, the `Person` record has three properties: `FirstName`, `LastName`, and `Age`, and it has a constructor to initialize these properties. The properties are read-only, meaning you can't change their values after the record is created.

Here's how you can use the `Person` record:

```
Person person1 = new Person("John", "Doe", 30);
Person person2 = new Person("Jane", "Smith", 25);
Console.WriteLine(person1.FirstName); // Output: John
Console.WriteLine(person2.Age);       // Output: 25
```

Because the `Person` record is immutable, you can't modify its properties directly. If you want to create a new `Person` instance with different values, you would create a new object:

```
Person updatedPerson = person1 with { Age = 35 };
```

This creates a new `Person` record with the same `FirstName` and `LastName` properties as `person1` but with an updated `Age` property.

One of the benefits of FP is that your methods are much smaller than the methods in other types of programming. Next, we will take a look at why it is good to keep methods small, as well as the techniques we can use, including FP.

Keeping methods small

As we've read before, while programming clean and readable code, it is important to keep the methods small. Preferably, in the C# world, it is best to keep methods *under 10 lines* long. The perfect length is no more than *10 lines*.

A good way to keep methods small is to consider if you should be trapping for errors or bubbling them further up the call stack. With defensive programming, you can become a little too defensive, and this can add to the amount of code you find yourself writing. Besides, methods that trap errors will be longer than methods that don't.

Let's consider the following code, which can throw an `ArgumentNullException` exception:

```
public UpdateView(MyEntities context, DataItem dataItem)
{
    InitializeComponent();
    try
    {
        DataContext = this;
        _dataItem = dataItem;
        _context = context;
        nameTextBox.Text = _dataItem.Name;
        DescriptionTextBox.Text = _dataItem.Description;
    }
    catch (Exception ex)
    {
        Debug.WriteLine(ex);
        throw;
    }
}
```

In the preceding code, we can clearly see that there are two locations where an `ArgumentNull-Exception` exception may be raised:

- The first line of code to potentially raise an `ArgumentNullException` exception is `nameTextBox.Text = _dataItem.Name;`

- The second line of code that may potentially raise the same exception is `DescriptionTextBox.Text = _dataItem.Description;`

We can see that the exception handler catches the exception when it occurs, writes it to the console, and then simply throws it back up the stack.

Notice that, from a human reading perspective, there are *eight lines* of code that form the `try-catch` block.

You can completely replace the `try-catch` exception handling with a single line of text by writing your own argument validator. To explain this, we will provide an example.

Let's start by looking at the `ArgumentValidator` class. The purpose of this class is to throw an `ArgumentNullException` exception with the name of the method that contains the `null` argument:

```
using System;
namespace CH04.Validators
```

```
{
    internal static class ArgumentValidator
    {
        public static void NotNull(
            string name,
            [ValidatedNotNull] object value
        )
        {
            if (value == null)
            throw new ArgumentNullException(name);
        }
    }
    [AttributeUsage(
        AttributeTargets.All,
        Inherited = false,
        AllowMultiple = true)
    ]
    internal sealed class ValidatedNotNullAttribute : Attribute
    {
    }
}
```

Now that we have our null validation class, we can perform a new way of validating parameters for null values in our methods. So, let's look at a simple example:

```
public ItemsUpdateView(
    Entities context,
    ItemsView itemView
)
{
    InitializeComponent();
    ArgumentValidator.NotNull("ItemsUpdateView", itemView);
    // ### implementation omitted ###
}
```

As you can clearly see, we have replaced the whole of the try-catch block with a one-liner at the top of the method. When this validation detects a null argument, an ArgumentNullException exception is thrown, preventing the code from continuing. This makes the code much easier to read and also helps with debugging.

> **Note**
>
> The `NotNull` method is called on the `ArgumentValidator` class to check the object is not null and throw an exception if it is. But you can also provide other methods in this class as well for testing string values, valid emails, and so on.

Now, we'll look at formatting functions with indentation so that they are easy to read.

Indenting code

A very long method is hard to read and follow at the best of times, especially when you have to scroll through the method many times to get to the bottom of it. However, having to do that with methods that are not properly formatted with the correct levels of indentation can be a real nightmare.

Fortunately, Visual Studio is good at taking care of this. However, arguments among teammates on the matter of indentation and whether it should be tabs or spaces, and if spaces, how many spaces, can erupt from time to time. That's why the team needs to agree on a coding style and stick to it. The code standard agreed upon can be implemented in a linting tool such as StyleCop, SonarLint, dotnet-format, or ReSharper. Again, the team will need to agree on the standard tool used for linting.

If you ever encounter any method code that is poorly formatted, then make it your own responsibility, as a professional coder, to tidy the code up before you do anything else. Any code between braces is known as a **code block**. Code within a code block should be indented by one level. Code blocks within code blocks should also be indented by one level, as shown in the following example:

```
public Student Find(List<Student> list, int id)
{
    Student r = null;
    foreach (var i in list)
    {
        if (i.Id == id)
            r = i;
    }
    return r;
}
```

The preceding example demonstrates bad indentation and also bad loop programming. Here, you can see that a list of students is being searched in order to find and return a student with the specified ID that was passed in as a parameter.

Breaking out of loops

What annoys some programmers and reduces the performance of the application is that the loop in the preceding code continues, even when the student has been found. We can improve the indentation and performance of the preceding code as follows:

```
public Student Find(List<Student> list, int id)
{
    Student r = null;
    foreach (var i in list)
    {
        if (i.Id == id)
        {
            r = i;
            break;
        }
    }
    return r;
}
```

In the preceding code, we have improved the formatting and made sure that the code is properly indented. We've added a `break` statement to the `for` loop so that the `foreach` loop is terminated when a match is found.

Not only is the code now more readable, but it also performs much better. Imagine that the code is being run against a university with 73,000 students on campus and via distance learning. Consider that if the student matches the ID that is first in the list, then without the `break` statement, the code will have to run 72,999 unnecessary computations. You can see how much of a difference the `break` statement makes to the performance of the preceding code.

We have left the return value in its original location as the compiler could complain that not all code paths return a value. This is also why we added the `break` statement. It is clear that proper indentation improves the readability of the code, thus aiding the programmer's understanding of it. This enables the programmer to make any changes that they deem necessary.

Avoiding duplication

Code can be either **DRY** or **WET**. WET code stands for **Write Every Time** and is the opposite of DRY, which stands for **Don't Repeat Yourself**, as previously mentioned. The problem with WET code is that it is the perfect candidate for *bugs*. Let's say your test team or a customer finds a bug and reports it to you. You fix the bug and pass it on, only for it to come back and bite you as many times as that code is encountered within your computer program.

Duplicate C# code can lead to increased maintenance costs. When the same code is replicated in multiple places within a project, it becomes harder to make consistent updates and bug fixes. This redundancy not only consumes more time but also introduces the risk of inconsistencies and errors.

For instance, consider the following code snippet:

```csharp
public void CalculateTotalPrice()
{
    // Code to calculate the total price
}
public void CalculateDiscountedPrice()
{
    // Same code to calculate the discounted price
}
```

In this example, both `CalculateTotalPrice` and `CalculateDiscountedPrice` functions contain identical logic for calculating prices. Any change required in this logic must be made in multiple places, which increases the likelihood of introducing errors and makes the code base more difficult to maintain. Both methods could be replaced with a single method called `CalculatePrice()`.

Now, we DRY our WET code by removing duplication. One way we can do this is by extracting the code and putting it into a method and then centralizing the method in such a way that it is accessible to all areas of the computer program that need it.

Time for an example. Imagine that you have a collection of expense items that consist of `Name` and `Amount` properties. Now, consider having to get the decimal amount for an expense item by name.

Say you had to do this 100 times. For this, you could write the following code:

```csharp
var amount = ViewModel
.ExpenseLines
.Where(e => e.Name.Equals("Life Insurance"))
.FirstOrDefault()
.Amount;
```

There is no reason why you can't write that same code 100 times. But there is a way to write it only once, thus reducing the size of your code base and making you more productive. Let's have a look at how we can do this:

```csharp
public decimal GetValueByName(string name)
{
    return ViewModel
    .ExpenseLines
    .Where(e => e.Name.Equals(name))
    .FirstOrDefault()
    .Amount;
```

To extract the required value from the `ExpenseLines` collection within your `ViewModel` class, all you have to do is pass the name of the value you require into the `GetValueName(string name)` method, as shown in the following code:

```
var amount = GetValueByName("Life Insurance");
```

That one line of code is very readable, and the lines of code to get the value are contained in a single method. So, if the method needs to be changed for whatever reason (such as a bug fix), you only have to modify the code in one place.

You can create an extension method for the `ViewModel` class to simplify the code. Here's how you can do it:

```
public static class ViewModelExtensions
{
    public static decimal GetAmountByName(this ViewModel, string name)
    {
        return viewModel.ExpenseLines
            .FirstOrDefault(e => e.Name.Equals(name))
            ?.Amount ?? 0m;
    }
}
```

In this code, we define an extension method called `GetAmountByName` for the `ViewModel` class. It takes a `name` parameter and searches for the first `ExpenseLine` instance with a matching name. If it finds a match, it returns the `Amount` value of that `ExpenseLine` instance. If no matching `ExpenseLine` is found, it returns 0 as a default value.

Now, you can use this extension method like this:

```
var viewModel = new ViewModel(); // Initialize your ViewModel instance
var amount = viewModel.GetAmountByName("Life Insurance");
```

This approach makes the code cleaner and more concise by encapsulating the logic within the `ViewModelExtensions` class and using a fluent syntax to access the amount based on the name.

The next logical step to writing good functions is to have as few parameters as possible. In the next section, we'll look at why we should have no more than two parameters, as well as how to work with just parameters, even if we need plenty more.

Avoiding multiple parameters

In this section, we'll be looking at niladic, monadic, dyadic, triadic, and polyadic methods and how we can avoid using multiple parameters.

Niladic methods are the ideal type of methods in C#. Such methods have no parameters (also known as *arguments*). Monadic methods only have one parameter. Dyadic methods have two parameters. Triadic methods have three parameters. Methods that have more than three parameters are known as polyadic methods. You should aim to keep the number of parameters to a minimum (preferably less than three).

In the ideal world of C# programming, you should do your best to avoid triadic and polyadic methods. The reason for this is not because it is bad programming but because it makes your code easier to read and understand. Methods with lots of parameters can cause visual stress to programmers and can also be a source of irritation. IntelliSense can also be difficult to read and understand as you add more parameters.

Let's look at a bad example of a polyadic method that updates a user's account information:

```csharp
public void UpdateUserInfo(int id, string username, string firstName,
string lastName, string addressLine1, string addressLine2, string
addressLine3, string addressLine3, string addressLine4, string city,
string postcode, string region, string country, string homePhone,
string workPhone, string mobilePhone, string personalEmail, string
workEmail, string notes)
{
    // ### implementation omitted ###
}
```

As shown by the UpdateUserInfo method, the code is horrible to read. How can we modify the method so that it transforms from a polyadic method into a monadic method? The answer is simple – we pass in a UserInfo object. First of all, before we modify the method, let's take a look at our UserInfo class:

```csharp
public class UserInfo
{
    public int Id { get;set; }
    public string Username { get; set; }
    public string FirstName { get; set; }
    public string LastName { get; set; }
    public string AddressLine1 { get; set; }
    public string AddressLine2 { get; set; }
    public string AddressLine3 { get; set; }
    public string AddressLine4 { get; set; }
    public string City { get; set; }
    public string Region { get; set; }
    public string Country { get; set; }
    public string HomePhone { get; set; }
    public string WorkPhone { get; set; }
    public string MobilePhone { get; set; }
    public string PersonalEmail { get; set; }
```

```
    public string WorkEmail { get; set; }
    public string Notes { get; set; }
}
```

We now have a class that contains all the information we need to pass into the `UpdateUserInfo` method. The `UpdateUserInfo` method can now be transformed from a polyadic method into a monadic method, as follows:

```
public void UpdateUserInfo(UserInfo userInfo)
{
    // ### implementation omitted ###
}
```

How much better does the preceding code look? It is smaller and much more readable. The rule of thumb should be to have less than three parameters, and ideally none. If your class is obeying the SRP, then consider implementing the *parameter object pattern*, as we have done here by replacing multiple parameters with the single `UserInfo` parameter.

> **Note**
> Refactoring tools such as ReSharper help programmers with the automatic implementation of the parameter object pattern as described here.

Implementing the SRP

All objects and methods that you write should, at most, have one responsibility and no more. Objects can have multiple methods, but those methods, when combined, should all work toward the single purpose of the object they belong to. Methods can call multiple methods, where each does different things. But the method itself should only do one thing.

A method that knows and does far too much is known as a **God method**. Likewise, an object that knows and does too much is known as a **God object**. God objects and methods are hard to read, maintain, and debug. Such objects and methods can often have the same bug repeated many times. People who are good at the programming craft will avoid God objects and God methods. Let's look at a method that is doing more than one thing:

```
public void SrpBrokenMethod(string folder, string filename, string
text, emailFrom, password, emailTo, subject, message, mediaType)
{
    var file = $"{folder}{filename}";
    File.WriteAllText(file, text);
    MailMessage message = new MailMessage();
    SmtpClient smtp = new SmtpClient();
    message.From = new MailAddress(emailFrom);
```

```
    message.To.Add(new MailAddress(emailTo));
    message.Subject = subject;
    message.IsBodyHtml = true;
    message.Body = message;
    Attachment emailAttachment = new Attachment(file);
    emailAttachment.ContentDisposition.Inline = false;
    emailAttachment.ContentDisposition.DispositionType =
DispositionTypeNames.Attachment;
    emailAttachment.ContentType.MediaType = mediaType;
    emailAttachment.ContentType.Name = Path.GetFileName(filename);
    message.Attachments.Add(emailAttachment);
    smtp.Port = 587;
    smtp.Host = "smtp.gmail.com";
    smtp.EnableSsl = true;
    smtp.UseDefaultCredentials = false;
    smtp.Credentials = new NetworkCredential(emailFrom, password);
    smtp.DeliveryMethod = SmtpDeliveryMethod.Network;
    smtp.Send(message);
}
```

SrpBrokenMethod is clearly doing more than one thing, so it breaks the SRP. We will now break this method down into a number of smaller methods that only do one thing. We will also address the issue of the polyadic nature of the method in that it has more than two parameters.

Before we begin to break down the method into smaller methods that do only one thing, we need to look at all the actions that the method is performing. The method starts by writing text to a file. It then creates an email message, assigns an attachment, and finally sends the email. So, for this, we need methods for the following:

- Write text to file
- Create an email message
- Add an email attachment
- Send email

Looking at the current method, we have four parameters that are passed into it for writing text to a file:

- One for the folder
- One for the filename
- One for the text
- One for the media type

The folder and filename can be combined into a single parameter called `filename`. If `filename` and `folder` are two separate variables that are used inside the calling code, then they can be passed into the method as a single interpolated string, such as $"{folder}{filename}".

As for the media type, this could be privately set inside a struct during construction time. We could use that struct to set the properties we need so that we can pass the struct in with the three properties as a single parameter. Let's look at the code that accomplishes this:

```
public struct TextFileData
{
    public string FileName { get; private set; }
    public string Text { get; private set; }
    public MimeType { get; }
    public TextFileData(string filename, string text)
    {
        Text = text;
        MimeType = MimeType.TextPlain;
        FileName = $"{filename}-{GetFileTimestamp()}";
    }
    public void SaveTextFile()
    {
        File.WriteAllText(FileName, Text);
    }
    private static string GetFileTimestamp()
    {
        var year = DateTime.Now.Year;
        var month = DateTime.Now.Month;
        var day = DateTime.Now.Day;
        var hour = DateTime.Now.Hour;
        var minutes = DateTime.Now.Minute;
        var seconds = DateTime.Now.Second;
        var milliseconds = DateTime.Now.Millisecond;
        return $"{year}{month}{day}@{hour}{minutes}{seconds}{milliseconds}";
    }
}
```

You can reduce the number of variables by directly using `ToString` on `DateTime.Now` and formatting it as needed. Here's the revised code:

```
private static string GetFileTimestamp()
{
    return DateTime.Now.ToString("yyyyMMdd@HHmmssfff");
}
```

This code uses a single call to `DateTime.Now` and formats the date and time components according to your desired pattern.

The `TextFileData` constructor ensures that the `FileName` value is unique by calling the `GetFileTimestamp()` method and appending it to the end of `FileName`. To save the text file, we call the `SaveTextFile()` method. Notice that `MimeType` is set internally and is set to `MimeType.TextPlain`.

We could have simply hardcoded `MimeType` as `MimeType = "text/plain";`, but the advantage of using an `enum` value is that the code is reusable, with the added benefit of you not having to remember the text for a specific `MimeType` instance or look it up on the internet. Now, we'll code enum and add a description to the `enum` value:

```
[Flags]
public enum MimeType
{
    [Description("text/plain")]
    TextPlain
}
```

Well, we've got our `enum` value, but now we need a way to extract the description so that it can be easily assigned to a variable. Therefore, we will create an extension class that will enable us to get the description of an enum value. This enables us to set `MimeType`, as follows:

```
MimeType = MimeType.TextPlain;
```

Without the extension method, the value of `MimeType` would be 0. But with the extension method, the value of `MimeType` is `"text/plain"`. You can now reuse this extension in other projects and build it up as you require.

The next class we will write is the `Smtp` class, whose responsibility it is to send an email via the SMTP protocol:

```
public class Smtp
{
    private readonly SmtpClient _smtp;
    public Smtp(Credential credential)
    {
        _smtp = new SmtpClient
        {
            Port = 587,
            Host = "smtp.gmail.com",
            EnableSsl = true,
            UseDefaultCredentials = false,
            Credentials = new NetworkCredential(credential.
EmailAddress, credential.Password),
```

```
                DeliveryMethod = SmtpDeliveryMethod.Network
        };
    }
    public void SendMessage(MailMessage mailMessage)
    {
        _smtp.Send(mailMessage);
    }
}
```

The `Smtp` class has a constructor that takes a single parameter of the `Credential` type. This credential is used to log in to the email server. The server is configured in the constructor. When the `SendMessage(MailMessage mailMessage)` method is called, the message is sent.

Let's write a `DemoWorker` class that splits the work into different methods:

```
public class DemoWorker
{
    TextFileData _textFileData;
    public void DoWork()
    {
    SaveTextFile();
    SendEmail();
    }
    public void SendEmail()
    {
        Smtp smtp = new Smtp(new Credential("fakegmail@gmail.com",
"fakeP@55w0rd"));
        smtp.SendMessage(GetMailMessage());
    }
    private MailMessage GetMailMessage()
    {
        var msg = new MailMessage();
        msg.From = new MailAddress("fakegmail@gmail.com");
        msg.To.Add(new MailAddress("fakehotmail@hotmail.com"));
        msg.Subject = "Some subject";
        msg.IsBodyHtml = true;
        msg.Body = "Hello World!";
        msg.Attachments.Add(GetAttachment());
        return msg;
    }
    private Attachment GetAttachment()
    {
        var attachment = new Attachment(_textFileData.FileName);
```

```
        attachment.ContentDisposition.Inline = false;
        attachment.ContentDisposition.DispositionType =
DispositionTypeNames.Attachment;
        attachment.ContentType.MediaType = MimeType.TextPlain.
Description();
        attachment.ContentType.Name = Path.GetFileName(_textFileData.
FileName);
        return attachment;
    }
    private void SaveTextFile()
    {
        _textFileData = new TextFileData($"{Environment.SpecialFolder.
MyDocuments}attachment", "Here is some demo text!" );
        _textFileData.SaveTextFile();
    }
}
```

The DemoWorker class shows a much cleaner version of sending an email message. The main method responsible for saving an attachment and sending it as an attachment via email is called DoWork(). This method only contains two lines of code. The first line calls the SaveTextFile() method, while the second line calls the SendEmail() method.

The SaveTextFile() method creates a new TextFileData struct and passes in the filename and some text. It then calls the SaveTextFile() method in the TextFileData struct, which is responsible for saving the text to the file specified.

The SendEmail() method creates a new Smtp class. The Smtp class has a Credential parameter, while the Credential class has two string parameters for email address and password. The email and password are used to log in to the SMTP server. Once the SMTP server has been created, the SendMessage(MailMessage mailMessage) method is called.

This method requires a MailMessage object to be passed in. So, we have a method called GetMailMethod() that builds a MailMessage object that is then passed into the SendMessage(MailMessage mailMessage) method. GetMailMethod() adds an attachment to MailMessage by calling the GetAttachment() method.

As you can see from these modifications, our code is now more compact and readable. That is the key to good quality code that is easy to modify and maintain: it must be easy to read and understand. That is why it is important for your methods to be small and clean with as few parameters as possible.

Does your method break the SRP? If it does, you should consider breaking the method up into as many methods as there are responsibilities.

Next, we will look at handling exceptions in FP.

Handling exceptions in FP

In FP, it is common to handle errors and exceptions using monads, such as the `Option` or `Either` monad. These monads allow for more declarative and composable error handling, as opposed to imperative `try-catch` blocks.

You will need to add the `LanguageExt.Core` NuGet package and add the following `using` statements:

```
using LanguageExt;
using static LanguageExt.Prelude;
```

Here is an example of using the `Option` monad in C# to handle exceptions:

```
internal class Program
{
    static void Main(string[] args)
    {
        Console.WriteLine("Hello, and welcome to the functional
programming world!");
        ExceptionHandlingUsingMonadSome();
    }
    public static bool IsValidInteger(string input)
    {
        return input is { } && int.TryParse(input, out _);
    }
    public static int GetValidIntegerFromUser(string message)
    {
        int result = 0;
        bool validInput = false;
        while (!validInput)
        {
            Console.Write(message);
            string input = Console.ReadLine();
            if (int.TryParse(input, out result))
            {
                validInput = true;
            }
            else
            {
                Console.WriteLine("Invalid input. Please enter a valid
integer.");
            }
        }
        return result;
    }
```

```
    public static Option<int> Divide(int x, int y)
    {
        return y == 0 ? None : Some(x / y);
    }
    public static void ExceptionHandlingUsingMonadSome()
    {
        int x = GetValidIntegerFromUser("Enter an integer: ");
        int y = GetValidIntegerFromUser("Enter another integer: ");
        var result = Divide(x, y);
        result.Match(Some: value => Console.WriteLine($"Result:
{value}"), None: () =>Console.WriteLine("Error: Division by zero"));
    }
}
```

In this example, the `Divide` method returns an `Option<int>` instance instead of throwing an exception when attempting to divide by zero. The `Option` type has two possible values: `Some(value)` and `None`. If the division is successful, the method returns `Some(value)` with the result. If the division fails (that is, `y` is zero), the method returns `None`.

In the `ExceptionHandlingUsingMonadSome` method, the `Divide` method is called with user input for `x` and `y`. The `Match` method is used to handle both possible cases of the `Option` type. If `result` is `Some(value)`, the result is printed to the console. If `result` is `None`, an error message is printed instead.

Using monads for error handling in FP can lead to more concise and readable code, as well as improved composability and reusability of error-handling logic.

Here's an example of using the `Either` monad for error handling in C#:

```
public static Either<string, int> Divide(int x, int y)
{
    return y == 0 ? "Division by zero" : x / y;
}
public static void ExceptionHandlingUsingMonadEither()
{
    int x = GetValidIntegerFromUser("Enter an integer: ");
    int y = GetValidIntegerFromUser("Enter another integer: ");
    var result = Divide(x, y);
    result.Match(
        Some: value => Console.WriteLine($"Result: {value}"),
        None: () => Console.WriteLine("Error: Division by zero")
    );
}
```

In this example, the `Divide` method returns an `Either<string, int>` instance instead of throwing an exception when attempting to divide by zero. The `Either` type has two possible values: `Right (value)` and `Left (error)`. If the division is successful, the method returns `Right (value)` with the result. If the division fails (that is, `y` is zero), the method returns `Left (error)` with an error message.

> **Note**
>
> `Some` and `None` are used as if `Divide` returns an `Option` type, but in this case, they are used with the `Either` type, which is conceptually similar to `Option` but represents either a success (`Some`) or an error (`None`).

In the `ExceptionHandlingUsingMonadEither` method, the `Divide` method is called with user input for `x` and `y`. The `Match` method is used to handle both possible cases of the `Either` type. If `result` is `Right (value)`, the result is printed to the console. If `result` is `Left (error)`, an error message is printed instead.

Using the `Either` monad can be useful when you need to return more detailed error messages or values that can't be represented by a simple `Option` type. It can also be useful when you need to chain together multiple operations that may fail in different ways, as the `Either` type can be used to propagate errors through a computation.

Adding comments for readability

Comments play a crucial role in enhancing the readability and maintainability of your code. They provide information about the purpose, functionality, and usage of your methods. Here's how to add comments effectively.

XML documentation comments

In C#, XML documentation comments are used to provide structured and meaningful descriptions of methods. These comments can be automatically generated as documentation for your code. Use triple slashes (`///`) to create XML comments above the method declaration:

```
/// <summary>
/// Calculates the sum of two integers.
/// </summary>
/// <param name="a">The first integer.</param>
/// <param name="b">The second integer.</param>
/// <returns>The sum of the two integers.</returns>
public int Add(int a, int b)
{
    return a + b;
}
```

By adding XML documentation comments, you help other developers understand how to use your methods and provide useful information for code analysis tools.

Inline comments

In addition to XML documentation comments, you can also use inline comments within your method code to clarify specific parts of the implementation or important details. Here's an example:

```
public void ProcessData()
{
    // Step 1: Load data from the database
    // ...

    // Step 2: Perform data processing
    // ...

    // Step 3: Save the processed data
    // ...
}
```

Variable declaration and memory management

Managing memory efficiently is crucial, especially in scenarios where your application deals with memory-intensive operations. To write clean methods in such cases, follow the practices described next.

Declaring variables close to their usage

Declare variables as close as possible to their usage. This makes it easier for developers to understand the purpose of a variable and its scope. Additionally, it can help with efficient memory management by reducing the lifetime of variables. Here's an example:

```
public void ProcessData()
{
    int total = 0;
    // Process a large data set
    for (int i = 0; i < data.Length; i++)
    {
        total += data[i];
    }
    // Use 'total' for further processing
    // ...
}
```

Disposing of resources

When your method uses resources such as database connections, file handles, or any object that implements `IDisposable`, it's essential to dispose of these resources properly. Use a `using` statement to ensure that resources are released when they are no longer needed:

```
public void ReadDataFromFile(string filePath)
{
    using (StreamReader reader = new StreamReader(filePath))
    {
        string data = reader.ReadToEnd();
        // Process data
    }
    // 'reader' is automatically disposed of at this point
}
```

Applying security in methods, especially in APIs

Security is a paramount concern when designing methods, particularly in the context of APIs that may be exposed to external users. To enhance security, consider the following aspects.

Input validation

Always validate and sanitize input parameters to prevent security vulnerabilities such as injection attacks. Ensure that user input is validated and sanitized before it is processed by your method. Here's an example:

```
public bool AuthenticateUser(string username, string password)
{
    if (string.IsNullOrEmpty(username) || string.
IsNullOrEmpty(password))
    {
        // Handle invalid input
        return false;
    }
    // Authenticate the user
    // ...
    return true;
}
```

Authentication and authorization

Implement robust authentication and authorization mechanisms to ensure that only authorized users can access sensitive methods or resources. Use authentication frameworks such as *IdentityServer* and authorization attributes to control access. Here's an example:

```
[Authorize(Roles = "Admin")]
public ActionResult DeleteUser(int userId)
{
    // Delete the user
    // ...
}
```

Protecting sensitive data

Encrypt sensitive data at rest and in transit to protect it from unauthorized access. Use encryption libraries and secure communication protocols to ensure data security. Here's an example of how to do this:

```
public string EncryptData(string data)
{
    // Use encryption libraries to encrypt 'data'
    // ...
    return encryptedData;
}
```

By addressing these considerations in your methods, you can write clean, secure, and maintainable code in C#.

And that concludes this chapter on writing clean functions. It is now time to summarize what you have learned and test your knowledge.

Summary

In this chapter, you have seen how FP can improve the safety of your code by not modifying the state, which can give rise to bugs, especially in multithreaded applications. By keeping methods small with meaningful names and no more than two parameters, you have seen how much cleaner your code is and easier to read. You have also seen how we can remove duplication in our code and the benefits of doing so. Code that is easy to read is easier to maintain and extend than code that is hard to read and decipher. And you have seen how to handle exceptions in a functional way.

In the next chapter, you will learn how to use exception handling appropriately, write your own custom C# exceptions that provide meaningful information, and write code that avoids raising `NullPointerException` exceptions.

Questions

Answer the following questions to test your knowledge of this chapter:

1. What do you call a method that has no parameters?
2. What do you call a method that has one parameter?
3. What do you call a method that has two parameters?
4. What do you call a method that has three parameters?
5. What do you call a method that has more than three parameters?
6. Which two method types should be avoided and why?
7. In layman's terms, what is FP?
8. What are some advantages of FP?
9. Name one disadvantage of FP.
10. What is WET code, and why should it be avoided?
11. What is DRY code, and why should you use it?
12. How do you dry out WET code?
13. Why should methods be as small as possible?
14. How do you implement validation without having to implement `try-catch` blocks?

Further reading

Here are some additional resources so that you can delve deeper into the realms of C# FP:

- *Functional C#* by *Wisnu Anggoro*: `https://www.packtpub.com/application-development/functional-c`. This book is devoted to C# FP and is a good place to start if you want to know more.

- *Functional Programming in C#* by *Jovan Popovic (MSFT)*: `https://www.codeproject.com/Articles/375166/Functional-programming-in-Csharp`. This is an in-depth article on functional C# programming. It contains diagrams and has a 5-star rating.

5
Exception Handling

Exception handling is an important aspect of writing reliable, robust software. When a program encounters an error, such as a division by zero, an invalid input, or something such as `Account ID not found`, it can generate an exception that can be caught and handled by the program. However, if exception handling is done poorly, it can lead to bugs, crashes, and other issues such as security issues whereby exceptions reveal valuable information to attackers and fraudsters. In this chapter, we'll cover some best practices for clean exception handling in C#, including how to write code that is readable, maintainable, and testable.

The topics covered are the following:

- Overview of exception handling in C#
- Principles of clean code and how they relate to exception handling
- Best practices for handling exceptions, including logging, using `try-catch` blocks, and handling specific exceptions
- Creating custom exceptions and when to use them
- Avoiding common mistakes in exception handling
- Debugging techniques for handling exceptions
- Testing exception handling with unit tests, integration tests, and end-to-end tests

By the end of this chapter, you should be able to do the following:

- Understand the importance of clean exception handling and its impact on software reliability and maintainability
- Apply principles of clean code to exception handling in C#
- Use best practices for handling exceptions, including logging and handling specific exceptions
- Create custom exceptions and know when to use them
- Avoid common mistakes in exception handling

- Debug exceptions effectively using Visual Studio tools
- Test exception handling with a variety of testing techniques, including unit tests, integration tests, and end-to-end tests

Let's look at the technical requirements to follow along with this chapter.

Technical requirements

To get the most from this chapter, you will need Visual Studio Community Edition. You can also use **Visual Studio Code** (**VS Code**) if you prefer. The book's source code for this chapter is located at https://github.com/PacktPublishing/Clean-Code-with-CSharp-Second-Edition/tree/main/CH05.

Overview of exception handling in C#

Exception handling is a fundamental aspect of writing robust software in C# (and in most programming languages). It is the mechanism that allows you to handle errors and unexpected situations that occur during program execution. When a C# program encounters an error, it throws an exception, which is an object that represents the error.

In C#, there are two types of exceptions: System.Exception and System.ApplicationException. Let's look at what these are:

- System.Exception is the base class for all exceptions in the .NET Framework
- System.ApplicationException is the base class for all application-specific exceptions

try-catch

A try-catch block is used to catch and handle exceptions in C#. The try block contains the code that might throw an exception, and the catch block contains the code that handles the exception. The catch block takes an exception object as a parameter, which provides information about the exception that was thrown. Here is an example of a simple try-catch block:

```
try
{
    // code that might throw an exception
}
catch (Exception ex)
{
    // code that handles the exception
}
```

You can also use multiple catch blocks to handle different types of exceptions. Here's an example:

```
try
{
    // code that might throw an exception
}
catch (DivideByZeroException ex)
{
    // code that handles a DivideByZeroException
}
catch (IOException ex)
{
    // code that handles an IOException
}
catch (Exception ex)
{
    // code that handles all other exceptions
}
```

In this example, the catch blocks handle different types of exceptions. The first catch block handles a DivideByZeroException exception, the second catch block handles an IOException exception, and the third catch block handles all other types of exceptions.

Finally, it is important to handle exceptions properly in order to prevent bugs and crashes. This involves logging exceptions, handling exceptions in a timely manner, and avoiding overly broad catch blocks. Clean exception handling can lead to more reliable and maintainable code.

try-catch-finally

In addition to try and catch blocks, a C# try-catch block can also contain a finally block. The finally block is executed after the try and catch blocks have completed, regardless of whether an exception was thrown or not. You can also have a try-finally block without a catch block.

Here's an example of a try-catch-finally block that includes a finally block:

```
try
{
    // code that might throw an exception
}
catch (Exception ex)
{
    // code that handles the exception
}
finally
{
```

```
        // code that always executes, regardless of whether an exception
was thrown or not
    }
```

In this example, if an exception is thrown within the `try` block, the `catch` block will execute and handle the exception. After the `catch` block is completed, the `finally` block will execute. If no exception is thrown within the `try` block, the `catch` block will be skipped and the `finally` block will still execute.

A `finally` block is useful for cleaning up resources that were allocated within a `try` block, such as file handles or database connections. By placing the cleanup code in the `finally` block, you ensure that it is always executed, even if an exception occurs.

Here's an example of using a `finally` block to clean up a file handle:

```
FileStream fileStream = null;
try
{
    fileStream = new FileStream("file.txt", FileMode.Open);
    // code that uses the file stream
}
catch (Exception ex)
{
    // code that handles the exception
}
finally
{
    if (fileStream != null)
    {
        fileStream.Dispose();
    }
}
```

In this example, the `finally` block disposes of the `FileStream` object, which releases the file handle and any other resources that were associated with it. By doing this in the `finally` block, you ensure that the file handle is always released, even if an exception occurs.

You can rewrite the code using a `using` statement to ensure that the `FileStream` object is disposed of properly. Here's the updated code:

```
try
{
    using (FileStream fileStream = new FileStream("file.txt",
FileMode.Open))
    {
        // code that uses the file stream
```

```
    }
}
catch (Exception ex)
{
    // code that handles the exception
}
```

With the `using` statement, the `FileStream` object will be automatically disposed of when it goes out of scope, which ensures proper resource management and eliminates the need for a separate `finally` block to call `Dispose`.

In summary, the `finally` block in a `try-catch-finally` block is used to execute code that should always run, regardless of whether an exception was thrown or not. It is useful for cleaning up resources and ensuring that your program leaves no resources behind.

We'll now look at clean code principles in exception handling.

Clean code exception-handling principles

> **Note**
>
> We have already learned about clean code principles. So, consider the following a quick refresher on the topic.

Clean code principles are a set of guidelines that aim to help developers write code that is easy to read, understand, and maintain. The principles are intended to make code more modular, reusable, and testable. Here are a few examples of clean code principles:

- **Single Responsibility Principle (SRP)**: A class should have only one reason to change.

- **Open/Closed Principle (OCP)**: Software entities (classes, modules, functions, and so on) should be open for extension but closed for modification.

- **Dependency Inversion Principle (DIP)**: High-level modules should not depend on low-level modules. Both should depend on abstractions.

When it comes to exception handling, clean code principles can help you write code that is more robust and easier to maintain. Here are a few examples of how clean code principles can apply to exception handling:

- **SRP**: In the context of custom exception classes and exception handling classes, these types of classes should handle only one type of exception. This makes the code more modular and easier to test. Additionally, methods and classes that handle exceptions should not also be responsible for business logic or other tasks unrelated to exception handling.

- **OCP**: Code that handles exceptions should be open for extension but closed for modification. This means that if you need to add new types of exceptions to your code, you should be able to do so without modifying existing exception-handling code. One way to achieve this is to use a strategy pattern to encapsulate the handling of each exception type in a separate class. The usual strategy is to create a base exception for your own software/library so that you can catch your base exception in the code, and if someone adds a new exception that derives from that base class, you do not need to modify the existing code.

- **DIP**: Code that handles exceptions should not depend on concrete implementations of external services (such as logging or notification systems). Instead, it should depend on abstractions (such as interfaces) so that different implementations can be substituted without affecting the exception-handling code.

In summary, clean code principles can help you write exception-handling code that is more modular, extensible, and testable. By following these principles, you can make your code more maintainable and less error-prone.

SRP

The SRP states that a class should have only one reason to change. When it comes to exception handling, this means that each class or method should handle only one type of exception.

By following this principle, you can make your code more modular and easier to test. Additionally, methods and classes that handle exceptions should not also be responsible for business logic or other tasks unrelated to exception handling.

Here's an example of how to use the SRP with exception handling in C#:

```
public class FileProcessor
{
    private ILogger _logger;
    public FileProcessor(ILogger logger)
    {
        _logger = logger;
    }
    public void ProcessFile(string filePath)
    {
        try
        {
            // code that reads and processes the file
        }
        catch (FileNotFoundException ex)
        {
            _logger.Error($"File not found: {ex.FileName}");
            throw;
```

```
        }
        catch (IOException ex)
        {
            _logger.Error($"Error reading file: {ex.Message}");
            throw;
        }
        catch (Exception ex)
        {
            _logger.Error($"Unexpected error: {ex.Message}");
            throw;
        }
    }
}
```

In this example, the `FileProcessor` class has a single responsibility: processing files. The class takes an `ILogger` dependency in its constructor for logging errors. The `ProcessFile` method handles three different types of exceptions:

- `FileNotFoundException`: If the file specified by the `filePath` parameter is not found, the method logs an error message and rethrows the exception

- `IOException`: If an I/O error occurs while reading the file, the method logs an error message and rethrows the exception

- `Exception`: If any other unexpected exception occurs, the method logs an error message and rethrows the exception

Here's a revised version of the `FileReader` class that uses `File.Exists` to check if the file exists before trying to read it. This allows the class to handle the `FileNotFoundException` exception more gracefully:

```
using System;
using System.IO;
public class FileProcessor
{
private ILogger _logger;
private string _filePath;
public FileProcessor(ILogger logger, string filePath){
        _logger = logger;
    _filePath = filePath;
        }
    public string ReadFile() {
        if (!File.Exists(_filePath)) {
            _logger.Error($"File {_filePath} does not exist.");
            return null;
```

```
        }
        try {
            using (StreamReader sr = new StreamReader(_filePath)) {
                string content = sr.ReadToEnd();
                return content;
            }
        }
        catch (IOException ex) {
            _logger.Error($"An IO error occurred: {ex}");
            throw;
        }
        catch (Exception ex) {
            _logger.Error($"An error occurred: {ex}");
            throw;
        }
    }
}
```

In this revised class, before attempting to read the file, we first check if the file exists using `File.Exists`. If the file does not exist, we pass an error message to the logger and return `null`, avoiding a `FileNotFoundException` exception. If the file does exist, we proceed to read the file as before, catching and handling any `IOException` exception or general `Exception` exception that might occur.

This way, we're still adhering to the SRP – the class is still only responsible for reading the file, but now it also checks if the file exists before trying to read it. This is still a single responsibility because the existence check is a necessary part of reading the file. Other parts of the program that use this class can now handle the `null` return value in the case where the file does not exist, and they can still handle any exceptions that the `ReadFile` method throws in the same way as before. This makes the code more robust and easier to understand.

We will now look at the OCP.

OCP

The OCP states that software entities (classes, modules, functions, and so on) should be open for extension but closed for modification. When it comes to exception handling, this means that your code should be able to handle new types of exceptions without modifying existing code.

By following this principle, you can make your code more flexible and easier to maintain. One way to achieve this is to use a strategy pattern to encapsulate the handling of each exception type in a separate class.

Here's an example of how to use the OCP with exception handling in C#:

```
public interface IExceptionHandler
{
```

```
    bool HandleException(Exception ex);
}
```

We have an interface called `IExceptionHandler` that has a single method called `HandleException` that takes an `exception` object as a parameter and returns a `bool` instance. We can now create exception-handling classes that implement this interface to handle specific exception types:

```
public class FileNotFoundExceptionHandler : IexceptionHandler {
    private ILogger _logger;
    public FileNotFoundExceptionHandler(ILogger logger) {
        _logger = logger;
    }
    public bool HandleException(Exception ex) {
        if (ex is FileNotFoundException) {
            _logger.LogError($"File not found:
 {((FileNotFoundException)ex).FileName}");
            return true;
        }
        return false;
    }
}
```

The `FileNotFoundExceptionHandler` class implements the `IOExceptionHandler` class to handle exceptions that are raised when a file cannot be found:

```
public class IOExceptionHandler : IExceptionHandler {
    private ILogger _logger;
    public IOExceptionHandler(ILogger logger) {
        _logger = logger;
    }
    public bool HandleException(Exception ex) {
        if (ex is IOException) {
            _logger.LogError($"Error reading file: {ex.Message}");
            return true;
        }
        return false;
    }
}
```

The `IOExceptionHandler` class handles I/O exceptions when accessing resources on disk and over a network with its own implementation of `IExceptionHandler`:

```
public class UnexpectedExceptionHandler : IExceptionHandler {
    private ILogger _logger;
    public UnexpectedExceptionHandler(ILogger logger) {
```

```
        _logger = logger;
    }
    public bool HandleException(Exception ex) {
        _logger.LogError($"Unexpected error: {ex.Message}");
        return true;
    }
}
```

The `UnexpectedExceptionHandler` class implements the `IExceptionHandler` interface to handle raised exceptions that are unexpected:

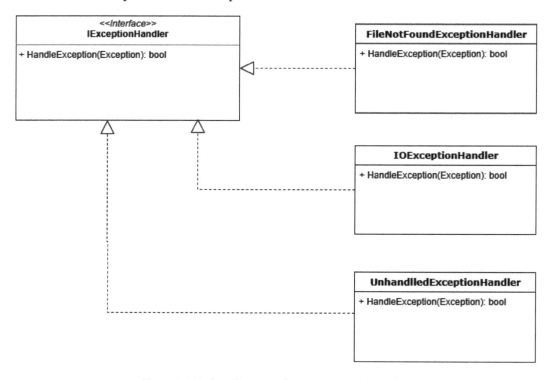

Figure 5.1: A class diagram of our exception hierarchy

As you can see from the diagram, we have an exception interface. Every time we create a new type of exception-handling class, we inherit from that interface to keep our exception classes consistent, and each exception class is responsible for handling a specific exception type, as illustrated in the following code snippet:

```
public class FileProcessor {
    private readonly IEnumerable<IExceptionHandler> _
exceptionHandlers;
```

```
    public FileProcessor(IEnumerable<IExceptionHandler>
exceptionHandlers)
    {
        _exceptionHandlers = exceptionHandlers;
    }
    public void ProcessFile(string filePath)
    {
        try
        {
            // code that reads and processes the file
        }
        catch (Exception ex)
        {
            var handled = false;
            foreach (var handler in _exceptionHandlers){
                if (handler.HandleException(ex)){
                    handled = true;
                    break;
                }
            }
            if (!handled){
                throw;
            }
        }
    }
}
```

In this example, the `FileProcessor` class takes an `IEnumerable<IExceptionHandler>` dependency in its constructor for handling exceptions. Each exception handler is implemented as a separate class that implements the `IExceptionHandler` interface. The `FileProcessor` class uses a loop to iterate through the list of exception handlers and calls the `HandleException` method on each one until an exception is handled.

Each exception handler class encapsulates the handling of a specific exception type. For example, the `FileNotFoundExceptionHandler` class handles `FileNotFoundException` exceptions by logging an error message. If a new type of exception needs to be handled, you can simply create a new exception handler class that implements the `IExceptionHandler` interface.

By using the strategy pattern to encapsulate exception handling, the code is more modular and easier to modify. You can add new types of exceptions to be handled without modifying the `FileProcessor` class or any of the existing exception handlers. If an exception is unhandled, then it will be thrown. Then, it will be up to the calling class to handle the outcome.

In summary, using the OCP with exception handling means that your code should be able to handle new types of exceptions without modifying existing code. The strategy pattern can be used to encapsulate the handling of each exception type in a separate class, making the code more flexible and easier to maintain.

DIP

The DIP states that high-level modules should not depend on low-level modules, but both should depend on abstractions. Abstractions should not depend on details, but details should depend on abstractions. When it comes to exception handling, this means that your code should depend on abstractions for logging and other operations related to exception handling, rather than depending on specific implementations.

By following this principle, you can make your code more modular and easier to test. One way to achieve this is to use **dependency injection** (**DI**) to inject abstractions for logging and other operations related to exception handling into your code.

Here's an example of how to use the DIP with exception handling in C#:

```
public interface IExceptionHandler
{
    bool HandleException(Exception ex);
}
```

We provide an interface with a single method that's implemented by our different exception-handling classes:

```
public class LoggingExceptionHandler : IExceptionHandler
{
    private readonly ILogger _logger;
    public LoggingExceptionHandler(ILogger logger)
    {
        _logger = logger;
    }
    public bool HandleException(Exception ex)
    {
        _logger.LogError(ex.ToString());
        return true;
    }
}
```

In this example, the FileProcessor class takes an IEnumerable<IExceptionHandler> dependency in its constructor for handling exceptions. The IExceptionHandler interface defines a HandleException method that takes an Exception parameter and returns a Boolean indicating whether the exception was handled.

The `LoggingExceptionHandler` class is a specific implementation of the `IExceptionHandler` interface that logs the exception using an `ILogger` abstraction.

The `FileProcessor` class uses DI to inject an `IEnumerable<IExceptionHandler>` dependency into its constructor. This allows the `FileProcessor` class to be more flexible since it can be configured with different implementations of the `IExceptionHandler` interface at runtime.

By using the `ILogger` abstraction, the `LoggingExceptionHandler` class can be used with any implementation of a logger that implements the `ILogger` interface. This allows the logging implementation to be changed without modifying the `LoggingExceptionHandler` class.

The use of the `ILogger` abstraction and the `LoggingExceptionHandler` class demonstrates the DIP, which is one of the SOLID principles of **object-oriented (OO)** design. The DIP suggests that high-level modules should not depend on low-level modules, but both should depend on abstractions. This principle helps to decouple components in a system, making it more flexible, maintainable, and easy to extend.

Let's look at this in the context of the prior code that we've written:

1. **ILogger abstraction**:

   - This is the abstraction or interface that defines the contract for logging operations.
   - It's a high-level module in the sense that it defines the behavior or API that any logger implementation must adhere to.
   - The high-level module should not be concerned with the specific details of how logging is done but should rely on this abstraction to delegate the responsibility.

2. **LoggingExceptionHandler class**:

   - This is the low-level module responsible for handling exceptions and logging error messages.
   - It's a low-level module because it deals with specific implementation details, such as catching exceptions and sending log messages to a logger.
   - However, instead of directly depending on a specific logger implementation, it depends on the `ILogger` interface, which is an abstraction.

3. The DIP is upheld as follows:

   - The high-level module, `LoggingExceptionHandler`, depends on the `ILogger` interface (abstraction), not on concrete logger implementations. This means that `LoggingExceptionHandler` is not tightly coupled to any specific logging implementation. It can work with any class that implements the `ILogger` interface.
   - Concrete logger implementations (for example, file logger, database logger, console logger) would implement the `ILogger` interface. This way, the high-level module (`LoggingExceptionHandler`) is decoupled from the low-level modules (specific logger implementations), and the dependencies are inverted.

In summary, the DIP helps to ensure that high-level modules define the behavior and depend on abstractions, while low-level modules implement the behavior and depend on those abstractions. This decoupling makes the code more flexible and allows you to change the logging implementation without modifying the `LoggingExceptionHandler` class, as long as the new implementation adheres to the `ILogger` interface.

Best practices for handling exceptions

Here are some best practices for handling exceptions in C#:

- **Only catch exceptions that you can handle**: Catching exceptions that you cannot handle can result in hiding the root cause of the exception and can lead to difficult-to-debug issues. Only catch exceptions that you can handle, and let the ones that you cannot handle propagate up the call stack.

- **Use try-catch blocks sparingly**: While `try-catch` blocks can be useful for handling exceptions, they can also negatively impact the performance of your application. Use them sparingly and only when necessary.

- **Use specific exception types**: Catching general exceptions such as `System.Exception` can make it difficult to determine the root cause of the exception. Instead, catch specific exception types that are relevant to your application.

- **Log exceptions**: Logging exceptions can help you diagnose issues and fix bugs in your application. Use a logging framework such as log4net or Serilog to log exceptions, and include relevant information such as the exception type, message, and stack trace.

- **Use a using statement for disposable objects**: Disposable objects such as database connections and file streams should be properly disposed of when they are no longer needed. Use a `using` statement to ensure that they are disposed of properly, even in the case of an exception.

- **Throw exceptions with meaningful messages**: When throwing an exception, provide a meaningful message that describes the root cause of the exception. This can make it easier to diagnose issues and fix bugs in your application. Also, we should show only user-friendly messages on the UI and hide the code details within the logs.

- **Use exception filters**: Exception filters allow you to catch exceptions based on specific criteria, such as the exception message or the exception type. This can help you handle exceptions more precisely and provide better error messages to the user.

- **Avoid catching and rethrowing exceptions**: Catching an exception and immediately rethrowing it can make it more difficult to diagnose issues and fix bugs in your application. If you need to catch an exception, handle it properly and only rethrow it if necessary.

- **Handle exceptions as close to the source as possible**: When an exception occurs, try to handle it as close to the source of the problem as possible. This can help you minimize the impact of the exception and prevent it from propagating further up the call stack.

- **Use structured exception handling**: Structured exception handling allows you to write cleaner, more readable code that is easier to maintain. Use `try-catch-finally` blocks to handle exceptions in a structured way and ensure that resources are properly cleaned up. A `finally` block is a good place to put code that needs to run regardless of whether an exception was thrown or not. This can include cleanup code for resources such as database connections, file streams, or network sockets. If the class is disposable, you can use the `using` keyword and not rely on the `finally` block.

- **Use custom exceptions**: Custom exceptions can provide more specific information about the error that occurred and make it easier to diagnose issues and fix bugs in your application. When creating custom exceptions, make sure to follow the same guidelines as standard exceptions and provide meaningful messages and proper documentation.

- **Use asynchronous exception handling**: Asynchronous exception handling can be more complex than synchronous exception handling, but it is necessary when dealing with asynchronous operations such as network requests or database queries. Use `try-catch` blocks with `await` operators to handle asynchronous exceptions in a structured way.

By following these best practices, you can write more robust and reliable code that handles exceptions effectively and helps you diagnose and fix issues more quickly.

Handling the TPL AggregateException exception

In C#, the **Task Parallel Library** (**TPL**) provides a convenient way to work with parallelism and asynchronous operations. When you are working with asynchronous tasks, it's common to use `Task.WhenAll` or `Task.WhenAny` to wait for the completion of multiple tasks. However, if any of those tasks throw an exception, the TPL will wrap those exceptions in the `AggregateException` exception. Let us look at some best practices for handling `AggregateException` in the context of the TPL.

Use await with try-catch inside async methods

When working with asynchronous code, it's common to use the `await` keyword to wait for the completion of tasks. Inside asynchronous methods, you can use a `try-catch` block to catch exceptions:

```
try
{
    await Task.WhenAll(task1, task2, task3);
}
catch (AggregateException ex)
{
    // Handle or log the exceptions
    foreach (var innerException in ex.InnerExceptions)
    {
        // Handle or log each inner exception
```

```
    }
}
```

Flatten the exception hierarchy

Instead of directly catching `AggregateException`, you can use the `Flatten` method to get a flat list of inner exceptions. This can simplify exception handling:

```
try
{
    await Task.WhenAll(task1, task2, task3);
}
catch (AggregateException ex)
{
    // Flatten the exception hierarchy
    var flattenedExceptions = ex.Flatten().InnerExceptions;
    // Handle or log the exceptions
    foreach (var innerException in flattenedExceptions)
    {
        // Handle or log each inner exception
    }
}
```

Handle individual exceptions

It's essential to loop through inner exceptions and handle them individually. This allows you to take specific actions based on the type of exception:

```
try
{
    await Task.WhenAll(task1, task2, task3);
}
catch (AggregateException ex)
{
    foreach (var innerException in ex.InnerExceptions)
    {
        if (innerException is SomeSpecificException)
        {
            // Handle specific exception type
        }
        else
        {
            // Handle or log other exceptions
        }
```

```
        }
    }
```

Handle exceptions as they occur

Instead of waiting for all tasks to complete before handling exceptions, you can handle exceptions as soon as they occur by using the ContinueWith method:

```
var task1 = SomeAsyncMethod();
var task2 = AnotherAsyncMethod();
await Task.WhenAll(
    task1.ContinueWith(t => HandleTaskException(t)),
    task2.ContinueWith(t => HandleTaskException(t))
);
// ...
void HandleTaskException(Task task)
{
    if (task.Exception != null)
    {
        foreach (var innerException in task.Exception.InnerExceptions)
        {
            // Handle or log each inner exception
        }
    }
}
```

By following these best practices, you can effectively handle AggregateException and its inner exceptions in a way that suits your application's specific requirements.

Creating custom exceptions and when to use them

Custom exceptions are a powerful tool in C# that allows you to create your own exception types with specific error messages and properties. They can be used to provide more specific information about errors that occurred and make it easier to diagnose issues and fix bugs in your application.

Here is an example of how to create a custom exception in C#:

```
public class CustomException : Exception
{
    public CustomException() : base() { }

    public CustomException(string message) : base(message) { }

    public CustomException(string message, Exception innerException) :
```

```
base(message, innerException) { }

    public int ErrorCode { get; set; }
}
```

In this example, we are creating a custom exception called `CustomException` that is inherited from the built-in `Exception` class. We are providing three constructors that allow us to create exceptions with different error messages and inner exceptions. We are also adding an `ErrorCode` property to the exception that can be used to provide additional information about the error.

Once you have created a custom exception, you can use it in your code as with any other exception. Here is an example of how to throw a custom exception:

```
public void DoSomething()
{
    try
    {
        // do something that might throw an exception
    }
    catch (Exception ex)
    {
        CustomException customEx = new CustomException("An error
occurred while doing something", ex);
        customEx.ErrorCode = 1234;
        throw customEx;
    }
}
```

In this example, we are catching an exception that might be thrown by some code and creating a new `CustomException` exception with a specific error message and inner exception. We are also setting the `ErrorCode` property on the exception to a specific value. Finally, we are rethrowing the custom exception so that it can be caught and handled by higher-level code.

Custom exceptions can be used in any situation where you need to provide more specific information about an error that occurred. This could include situations where you need to distinguish between different types of errors, provide additional information about the error, or create your own error-handling logic. By using custom exceptions, you can make your code more robust, reliable, and easier to maintain.

We'll now look at common mistakes in exception handling and how to avoid them.

Avoiding common mistakes in exception handling

Here are some common mistakes that developers make when handling exceptions in C#:

- **Catching too many exceptions**: Catching all exceptions using a `catch` block without specifying a specific exception type can lead to catching exceptions that should not be caught, such as `ThreadAbortException` or `StackOverflowException` exceptions. Catching only specific exceptions that are expected can prevent unnecessary exceptions from being caught. Here's an example:

```
try
{
    // Some code that may throw exceptions
}
catch (Exception ex)
{
    // Handle all exceptions here
}
```

  In this example, the `catch` block catches all exceptions, including exceptions that should not be caught, such as `ThreadAbortException` or `StackOverflowException` exceptions. Instead, catch only the specific exceptions that you expect to be thrown.

> **Note**
> There are situations where you simply want to log some extended information, so it is fine to catch all exceptions, log a lot of details, and then immediately rethrow them.

- **Not logging (swallowing) exceptions**: Not logging (swallowing) exceptions can cause unexpected behavior or data loss and make it difficult to diagnose issues and fix bugs in your application. Logging exceptions with detailed information such as the exception type, message, stack trace, and any relevant context information can provide valuable information to developers and system administrators. Here's an example:

```
try
{
    // Some code that may throw exceptions
}
catch (Exception ex)
{
    // Do nothing with the exception
}
```

In this example, the `catch` block catches an exception but does not log it or take any action with it. This can make it difficult to diagnose issues and fix bugs in your application. Instead, log the exception with detailed information such as the exception type, message, stack trace, and any relevant context information.

- **Not using a finally block**: Not using a `finally` block can lead to resources not being properly released or cleaned up, even if an exception is thrown. A `finally` block is designed to contain cleanup code that needs to run regardless of whether an exception is thrown or not. Here's an example:

```
try
{
    // Some code that may throw exceptions
}
catch (Exception ex)
{
    // Handle the exception
}
finally
{
    // Cleanup code that needs to run regardless of whether an
    exception is thrown or not
}
```

In this example, the `finally` block is not used to contain cleanup code that needs to run regardless of whether an exception is thrown or not.

- **Not handling exceptions at the appropriate level**: Handling exceptions too high up in the call stack can lead to a lack of context about the error that occurred and can make it difficult to diagnose the root cause of the problem. Handling exceptions closer to the source of the problem can provide more detailed information about the error and make it easier to diagnose and fix.

For example, you could have a layered architecture where an exception occurs in the data access layer but is being handled in the UI layer. In this example, the `catch` block handles the exception at a high level, which can lead to a lack of context about the error that occurred. Instead, handle exceptions closer to the source of the problem to provide more detailed information about the error and make it easier to diagnose and fix. So, for this example, you would handle the exception in the data access layer at the point where the exception occurs and not higher up in the UI layer.

Note

When we talk about handling exceptions at too high a level, it means catching exceptions higher up in the call stack than where they were thrown. For example, suppose a method in a lower level of the call stack throws an exception, but the exception is caught and handled in a method higher up in the call stack. This is an example of handling an exception at too high a level.

- **Not providing enough information in exception messages**: Exception messages that do not provide enough information about the error that occurred can make it difficult to diagnose and fix problems. Providing detailed information about the error, including any relevant context information, can make it easier to diagnose and fix issues. Here's an example:

```
try
{
    // Some code that may throw exceptions
}
catch (Exception ex)
{
    throw new Exception("An error occurred");
}
```

In this example, we are throwing a new exception without any information from the parent exception, and the exception message does not provide enough information about the error that occurred, which can make it difficult to diagnose and fix problems. It also does not reuse the original exception in the new exception.

Instead, provide detailed information about the error, including any relevant context information, to make it easier to diagnose and fix issues, and you can do this by reusing the original exception.

By avoiding these common mistakes, you can write cleaner, more reliable code that is easier to maintain and debug.

Let us now consider testing exception handling.

Testing exception handling

Testing exception handling with different types of tests involves testing the handling of exceptions in different contexts of an application. Here's how to test exception handling with unit tests, integration tests, and end-to-end tests:

- **Unit tests**: Unit tests are used to test the behavior of individual components of an application. When testing exception handling with unit tests, we can create tests that verify that expected exceptions are thrown in response to certain inputs.

  For example, we can test a method that performs division by zero and ensure that it throws a `DivideByZeroException` exception when zero is passed in as a denominator.

- **Integration tests**: Integration tests are used to test the interactions between different components of an application. When testing exception handling with integration tests, we can verify that components are handling exceptions properly when they interact with one another.

  For example, we can test a system that sends data to an external API and verify that it handles errors returned by the API properly.

- **End-to-end tests**: End-to-end tests are used to test the functionality of an application from start to finish of its operation. When testing exception handling with end-to-end tests, we can test that the application behaves correctly when it encounters unexpected errors.

  For example, we can test a web application that displays an error message to the user when a database connection fails.

In all cases, we can use assertions to verify that exceptions are thrown or handled properly. By testing exception handling with different types of tests, we can ensure that our application behaves correctly in different scenarios and that it is able to handle errors gracefully.

Unit testing exception handling

Here's an example of how to write a unit test to test exception handling in C# using the NUnit testing framework:

```
using NUnit.Framework;

[TestFixture]
public class CalculatorTests
{
    [Test]
    public void Divide_ThrowsDivideByZeroException()
    {
        // Arrange
        int numerator = 10;
        int denominator = 0;
        Calculator calculator = new();
        // Act and Assert
        Assert.Throws<DivideByZeroException>(() => calculator.
Divide(numerator, denominator));
    }
}
```

In this example, we're testing a method called `calculator.Divide` that takes two integers and returns their quotient. We're intentionally passing in a denominator value of 0, which will cause a `DivideByZeroException` exception to be thrown.

The `Assert.Throws` method is used to verify that the expected exception is thrown when we call the `calculator.Divide` method. The lambda expression passed to `Assert.Throws` is the code that we expect to throw the exception.

If the exception is not thrown, the test will fail. If the exception is thrown, the test will pass.

This is just one example of how to write a unit test to test exception handling in C#. By testing exception handling with unit tests, we can ensure that our code is able to handle unexpected errors and prevent our program from crashing.

Integration testing exception handling

Integration testing in C# involves testing the interactions between different components of an application to verify that they work together correctly. When it comes to testing exception handling, integration testing can help ensure that exceptions are propagated correctly across different components of an application.

Here's an example of how to perform integration testing of exception handling in C#.

Suppose we have a web application that retrieves data from a database and displays it to the user. When the application encounters an error retrieving data from the database, it should display an error message to the user. We can write an integration test to verify that this behavior works correctly:

1. First, we can create a test database with some sample data that our application will retrieve.

2. Next, we can write a test that simulates an error occurring when the application tries to retrieve data from the database. We can do this by configuring the test database to return an error when the application tries to execute a particular query.

3. We can then run the web application and navigate to the page that displays the data. If everything is working correctly, we should see an error message displayed to the user indicating that an error occurred when trying to retrieve data from the database.

4. Finally, we can verify that the error message is correct and contains the expected information.

Alternatively, we can use testing and mocking frameworks such as Moq, xUnit, Nunit, and MSTest to automate our tests and raise exceptions to ensure program behavior is what we expect.

Testing database integration scenarios in C# using DI is a common practice, and it allows you to isolate and test your code more effectively. In the case where you want to test a scenario where a `MongoDbException` exception is caught, you can use a mocking framework to create a mock of `IMongoCollection` that throws specific `MongoDBDriver` exceptions.

Let's go through a step-by-step example using a popular mocking framework such as Moq and a testing framework such as MSTest:

1. Install the necessary packages:

   Make sure you have the required packages installed. You can use NuGet Package Manager Console for this:

   ```
   Install-Package Moq
   Install-Package MSTest.TestFramework
   ```

2. Create the interface and class:

    Assume you have a service or class that interacts with MongoDB and uses IMongoCollection.
    Here's a simplified example:

    ```
    using MongoDB.Driver;
    public interface IDataService
    {
        void PerformDatabaseOperation();
    }
    public class DataService : IDataService
    {
        private readonly IMongoCollection<Document> _
    mongoCollection;
        public DataService(IMongoCollection<Document>
    mongoCollection)
        {
            _mongoCollection = mongoCollection;
        }
        public void PerformDatabaseOperation()
        {
            try
            {
                // Your MongoDB-related code here
                // For example, _mongoCollection.
    InsertOne(document);
            }
            catch (MongoException ex)
            {
                // Handle MongoDB exceptions
                // Log, rethrow, or perform custom actions
            }
        }
    }
    public class Document
    {
        // Your document properties
    }
    ```

3. Write the test:

    Now, let's write a test to verify the exception handling. We'll use Moq to create a mock of
    IMongoCollection that throws a MongoException exception when InsertOne is called:

    ```
    using Moq;
    using MongoDB.Driver;
    [TestClass]
    ```

```
public class DataServiceTests
{
    [TestMethod]
    public void PerformDatabaseOperation_HandlesMongoException()
    {
        // Arrange
        var mockCollection = new
Mock<IMongoCollection<Document>>();
        mockCollection .Setup(x => x.InsertOne(It.
IsAny<Document>(), null, default(CancellationToken)))
.Throws(new MongoException("Simulated MongoDB exception"));
        var dataService = new DataService(mockCollection.
Object);
        // Act
        dataService.PerformDatabaseOperation();
        // Assert
        // Add assertions as needed, depending on your specific
requirements
        // For example, you might check logs or perform other
verifications
    }
}
```

In this test, we're arranging for the mock `IMongoCollection` interface to throw a `MongoException` exception when `InsertOne` is called. The test then calls the `PerformDatabaseOperation` method, and you can assert that the exception is handled correctly or perform other necessary checks.

4.   Run the test:

Run your test using your preferred test runner (such as Visual Studio Test Explorer) and ensure that it passes.

By using DI and mocking frameworks such as Moq, you can create controlled environments for testing database integration scenarios and ensure that your code handles exceptions appropriately.

By performing integration testing of exception handling, we can ensure that our application behaves correctly when it encounters unexpected errors and that errors are propagated correctly across different components of the application. This can help us identify and fix issues before they make it into production.

End-to-end testing exception handling

End-to-end testing in C# involves testing the entire application to verify that it works correctly from the user's perspective. When it comes to testing exception handling, end-to-end testing can help ensure that the application behaves correctly when it encounters unexpected errors.

Here's an example of how to perform end-to-end testing of exception handling in C#.

Suppose we have a web application that allows users to submit a form with some data, which is then saved to a database. When the application encounters an error saving data to the database, it should display an error message to the user. We can write an end-to-end test to verify that this behavior works correctly:

1. First, we can write a test script that interacts with the web application by filling out the form and submitting it.

2. Next, we can configure the test script to simulate an error occurring when the application tries to save data to the database. We can do this by configuring the database to reject the `insert` statement.

3. We can then run the test script and verify that the error message is displayed to the user, indicating that an error occurred when trying to save data to the database.

4. Finally, we can verify that the error message is correct and contains the expected information.

By performing end-to-end testing of exception handling, we can ensure that our application behaves correctly when it encounters unexpected errors from the user's perspective. This can help us identify and fix issues before they make it into production and ensure that our users have a smooth experience using the application.

An employee management example of mocking and unit testing with correct exception handling

Handling exceptions is an essential part of writing robust and reliable code. In an employee management example, you might encounter various scenarios where exceptions need to be handled, such as database errors, file I/O issues, or validation problems.

In this section, we will write some sample code for an employee management system that employs correct exception handling and write unit tests with *Moq* objects to ensure our code works as we expect.

First, we need an `Employee` class:

```
public class Employee
{
    public int EmployeeId { get; set; }
    public string FirstName { get; set; }
    public string LastName { get; set; }
    public DateTime BirthDate { get; set; }
}
```

We can now add our `EmployeeManager` class:

```
public class EmployeeManager
{
    // Simulating a database operation
```

```
    public Employee GetEmployeeById(int employeeId)
    {
        // Assume this method might throw a database exception
        // if the employee with the given ID is not found.

        // Simulating a scenario where the employee is not found.
        throw new EmployeeNotFoundException($"Employee with ID
{employeeId} not found");
    }

    // Simulating a file I/O operation
    public void SaveEmployeeToFile(Employee employee)
    {
        // Assume this method might throw a file I/O exception
        // if there is an issue writing to the file.

        // Simulating a scenario where the file cannot be written.
        throw new FileIOException("Error writing to the employee
file");
    }
}
```

We need to handle the eventuality that an employee may not be found. So, we will add our EmployeeNotFoundException class:

```
public class EmployeeNotFoundException : Exception
{
    public EmployeeNotFoundException(string message) : base(message)
    {
    }
}
```

We also need to consider file I/O exceptions, so we will add our FileIOException class:

```
public class FileIOException : Exception
{
    public FileIOException(string message) : base(message)
    {
    }
}
```

Now, we can update our Program class that acts as the entry point for our application:

```
public class Program
{
    public static void Main()
```

```csharp
    {
        EmployeeManager employeeManager = new EmployeeManager();
        try
        {
            int employeeId = 1;
            Employee employee = employeeManager.
GetEmployeeById(employeeId);
            Console.WriteLine($"Employee {employee.FirstName}
{employee.LastName} found!");
        }
        catch (EmployeeNotFoundException ex)
        {
            Console.WriteLine($"Error: {ex.Message}");
        }
        catch (Exception ex)
        {
            // Catch any unexpected exceptions
            Console.WriteLine($"Unexpected error: {ex.Message}");
        }
        try
        {
            Employee newEmployee = new Employee
            {
                EmployeeId = 2,
                FirstName = "John",
                LastName = "Doe",
                BirthDate = new DateTime(1990, 1, 1)
            };
            employeeManager.SaveEmployeeToFile(newEmployee);
            Console.WriteLine("Employee saved to file successfully!");
        }
        catch (FileIOException ex)
        {
            Console.WriteLine($"Error saving employee to file: {ex.
Message}");
        }
        catch (Exception ex)
        {
            // Catch any unexpected exceptions
            Console.WriteLine($"Unexpected error: {ex.Message}");
        }
    }
}
```

That is our simple employee management application written.

In this example, the EmployeeManager class has methods that simulate database and file I/O operations, and these methods intentionally throw custom exceptions (EmployeeNotFoundException and FileIOException). In the Main method, exception handling is demonstrated using try, catch, and finally blocks. Custom exceptions are caught specifically, and a general Exception catch block is included to handle unexpected errors. This helps to gracefully handle exceptions and provide meaningful error messages to the user or log errors for further investigation.

Let us now add our mocking and testing classes. In this example, we'll use the *Moq* framework for creating mock objects and *NUnit* for unit testing. First, you'll need to install the necessary *NuGet* packages:

```
Install-Package Moq
Install-Package NUnit
Install-Package NUnit3TestAdapter
```

Now, let's create unit tests for the EmployeeManager class using *Moq*. First, create an EmployeeManagerTests class:

```
using Moq;
using NUnit.Framework;
using System;
[TestFixture]
public class EmployeeManagerTests
{
}
```

We'll now add our first test to the EmployeeManagerTests class that returns an employee:

```
[Test]
public void GetEmployeeById_EmployeeFound_ReturnsEmployee()
{
    // Arrange
    int employeeId = 1;
    Employee expectedEmployee = new Employee
    {
        EmployeeId = employeeId,
        FirstName = "John",
        LastName = "Doe",
        BirthDate = new DateTime(1990, 1, 1)
    };
    var mockEmployeeManager = new Mock<EmployeeManager>();
    mockEmployeeManager.Setup(manager => manager.
GetEmployeeById(employeeId)).Returns(expectedEmployee);
    // Act
```

```
        Employee actualEmployee =
            mockEmployeeManager.Object.GetEmployeeById(employeeId);
        // Assert
        Assert.AreEqual(expectedEmployee, actualEmployee);
    }
```

Next, we need to test when an employee is not found:

```
[Test]
public void GetEmployeeById_EmployeeNotFound_
ThrowsEmployeeNotFoundException()
{
    // Arrange
    int employeeId = 1;
    var mockEmployeeManager = new Mock<EmployeeManager>();
mockEmployeeManager.Setup(manager => manager.
GetEmployeeById(employeeId))
.Throws(new EmployeeNotFoundException("Employee not found"));
    // Act and Assert
    Assert.Throws<EmployeeNotFoundException>(() =>
        mockEmployeeManager.Object.GetEmployeeById(employeeId));
}
```

We now need to test for a successful file save operation:

```
[Test]
public void SaveEmployeeToFile_SuccessfulSave_NoExceptionThrown()
{
    // Arrange
    var employee = new Employee
    {
        EmployeeId = 2,
        FirstName = "John",
        LastName = "Doe",
        BirthDate = new DateTime(1990, 1, 1)
    };
    var mockEmployeeManager = new Mock<EmployeeManager>();
    mockEmployeeManager.Setup(manager => manager.
SaveEmployeeToFile(employee));
    // Act and Assert (no exception should be thrown)
    Assert.DoesNotThrow(() =>
        mockEmployeeManager.Object.SaveEmployeeToFile(employee));
}
```

Finally, we need to test for a file I/O exception being raised:

```
[Test]
public void SaveEmployeeToFile_FileIOExceptionThrown_
CatchesException()
{
    // Arrange
    var employee = new Employee
    {
        EmployeeId = 2,
        FirstName = "John",
        LastName = "Doe",
        BirthDate = new DateTime(1990, 1, 1)
    };
    var mockEmployeeManager = new Mock<EmployeeManager>();
    mockEmployeeManager.Setup(manager => manager.
SaveEmployeeToFile(employee))
                    .Throws(new FileIOException("Error saving to
file"));
    // Act and Assert
    Assert.Throws<FileIOException>(() =>
        mockEmployeeManager.Object.SaveEmployeeToFile(employee));
}
```

In these tests, we use *Moq* to create mock objects for the `EmployeeManager` class. We set up the behavior of the mock object using the `Setup` method, specifying the expected method calls and their return values or exceptions. The `Assert` statements then verify that the expected behavior occurs during the tests.

That's the end of the chapter, so let's summarize what we've learned.

Summary

We started with an overview of exception handling in C#. We saw there are two types of exceptions: `System.Exception` and `System.ApplicationException`. `System.Exception` is the base class for all exceptions in the .NET Framework, while `System.ApplicationException` is the base class for all application-specific exceptions.

Then, we moved on to review clean code exception handling using the SRP, OCP, and DIP. We saw how these principles help to keep our code clean, readable, extendable, and maintainable.

Next, we looked at best practices for exception handling. By following these best practices, we saw how we can write more robust and reliable code that handles exceptions effectively and helps us to diagnose and fix issues more quickly.

We then moved on to look at some common exception-handling mistakes and how we can avoid them. By avoiding these common mistakes, we can write cleaner, more reliable code that is easier to maintain and debug.

Next, we looked at various debugging techniques and tools for handling exceptions. These tools assist us in hunting down bugs more easily and fixing them more easily.

And finally, we looked at testing our exception handling using unit tests, integration tests, and end-to-end testing. When we know how code should act in exceptional circumstances, we can test for this. If problems are encountered, then they can be addressed and fixed.

In the next chapter, we will be looking at unit testing.

Questions

Answer the following questions to test your knowledge of this chapter:

1. What is the principle of handling exceptions as close to the source of the error as possible, and why is it important for writing clean code?

2. How can you make your exception handling more specific and targeted by catching more specific exception types rather than generic ones?

3. What is a `finally` block in a `try-catch-finally` statement, and why is it important for writing robust and maintainable code?

4. How can you use custom exception types to provide more meaningful feedback to the user and make your code more maintainable and extensible?

5. What are some best practices for logging and handling exceptions in multithreaded code?

6. How can you use the global exception handler to provide a centralized location for handling exceptions in your application?

7. Why is it important to test exception handling in your code, and what are some common approaches to testing exception handling?

8. What are some common pitfalls to avoid when writing exception-handling code, and how can you ensure that your exception handling is both effective and maintainable?

9. How does the use of exception handling impact the overall readability and maintainability of your code, and how can you strike the right balance between handling exceptions effectively and keeping your code clean and easy to understand?

Further reading

If you are interested in learning more about clean code techniques for C# exception handling, here are some resources you might find useful:

- *Clean Code: A Handbook of Agile Software Craftsmanship* by *Robert C. Martin*: This classic book provides a comprehensive overview of clean code techniques, including best practices for exception handling.

- *Exceptional C# Exception Handling* by *Avi Avni*: This article on *CodeProject* provides an in-depth guide to best practices for exception handling in C#, including tips on when to catch exceptions, how to use custom exception types, and how to handle exceptions in asynchronous code.

- *Best Practices for Handling Exceptions* by *Microsoft*: This article on the *Microsoft Docs* website provides an overview of best practices for handling exceptions in C#, including advice on how to use `try-catch` blocks, when to throw exceptions, and how to create custom exception types.

- *10 Best Practices for Handling Exceptions in C#* by *Dino Esposito*: This article on the *Redgate* website provides 10 best practices for handling exceptions in C#, including tips on how to use `finally` blocks, how to use `using` statements, and how to handle exceptions in multithreaded code.

- *Exception Handling in C# with Best Practices* by *Saineshwar Bageri*: This article on the *C# Corner* website provides a detailed guide to exception handling in C#, including best practices for logging exceptions, how to use the global exception handler, and how to use the Exception Handling Application Block in the Enterprise Library.

6

Unit Testing

Unit testing is an important aspect of software development that helps ensure the quality and correctness of code. By writing unit tests, developers can verify that their code behaves as expected and catch bugs early in the development process. In C#, there are several tools and frameworks available for writing unit tests, such as MSTest, NUnit, and xUnit. However, simply writing unit tests is not enough to ensure clean code.

To truly benefit from unit testing, developers must understand how to write effective tests that cover all critical scenarios and adhere to best practices. In this chapter, we will cover essential topics for using unit tests to write clean code in C#. We will discuss the fundamentals of unit testing, the benefits of **test-driven development** (TDD), best practices for writing effective unit tests, and how to integrate unit tests into your **software development life cycle** (SDLC).

We will be covering the following topics:

- **Understanding unit testing**: Understanding the fundamentals of unit testing, the benefits of unit testing, and how unit tests fit into the SDLC

- **Writing testable code**: Designing code that is easy to test, adhering to the SOLID principles, and using patterns such as **dependency injection** (DI) to decouple code

- **TDD**: Understanding the principles of TDD, which involves writing tests first and then writing code to make those tests pass

- **Choosing a testing framework**: Selecting a testing framework that fits your needs, such as MSTest, NUnit, or xUnit

- **Writing effective unit tests**: Writing unit tests that are concise, maintainable, and robust, covering all relevant scenarios and edge cases

- **CI/CD description:** Providing integration testing as part of your CI/CD pipeline.

- **Problem tests description:** Identify and fix "test smells".

The key learning outcomes of this chapter on using unit tests to write clean code in C# will be:

- Understanding the benefits of writing testable code and why it is important to unit test your code

- Choosing and using unit testing and mocking frameworks

- Integrating testing into the DevOps pipeline

Technical requirements

To follow along with this chapter, you will need access to Visual Studio 2022 Community Edition or later. You will find the source code for this chapter at `https://github.com/PacktPublishing/Clean-Code-with-CSharp-Second-Edition/tree/main/CH06`.

Understanding unit testing

In C#, unit tests are automated tests written to verify the behavior of a small, isolated piece of code known as a **unit**. The goal of unit testing is to ensure that the unit behaves as expected and meets the requirements and specifications defined for it.

A unit test should test the functionality of the unit in isolation, without relying on any external dependencies, such as a database or web service. The isolation of the unit test ensures that any failures are caused by issues within the unit being tested, rather than external factors. This means that unit tests are fast, efficient, and provide rapid feedback to the developer.

Unit tests should cover all relevant scenarios and edge cases for the unit being tested, including both valid and invalid input values. This helps to ensure that the unit behaves correctly in all possible situations. Unit tests should also be maintainable, meaning that they can be easily updated as changes are made to the code or requirements.

However, there are some things that unit tests should not test. Unit tests should not test external dependencies, such as a database or web service, as this goes beyond the scope of the unit being tested. Instead, these dependencies should be mocked or stubbed out to isolate the unit being tested. Additionally, unit tests should not test **non-functional requirements (NFRs)**, such as performance or security. These types of requirements should be tested through other means, such as performance testing or security testing.

Writing testable code

Writing testable code in C# is essential for ensuring that code behaves as expected and can be efficiently tested with automated tests. Here are some C#-specific tips and examples for writing testable code:

1. **Use interfaces to define dependencies**: Interfaces are a powerful tool for defining dependencies between classes. By defining dependencies through interfaces, it is easy to swap out dependencies

with test doubles, such as mocks or stubs, for testing purposes. For example, consider the following code:

```
public class OrderService
{
    private readonly IorderRepository _orderRepository;
    public OrderService(IorderRepository orderRepository)
    {
        _orderRepository = orderRepository;
    }
    public Order GetOrderById(int id)
    {
        return _orderRepository.GetById(id);
    }
}
```

In this code, the `OrderService` class depends on the `IorderRepository` interface. By defining the dependency through an interface, it is easy to create a test double, such as a mock or stub, to test the `OrderService` class in isolation.

2. **Use constructor injection to manage dependencies**: Constructor injection is a common technique used in C# to manage dependencies between classes. By passing dependencies through the constructor, it is easy to instantiate objects with the required dependencies, making it easy to write unit tests. For example, in the previous code, the `OrderService` class takes a dependency on the `IorderRepository` interface through its constructor. This makes it easy to create an instance of the `OrderService` class with a test double for the `IorderRepository` interface.

3. **Avoid static dependencies**: Static dependencies can make code difficult to test, as they are difficult to mock or stub out. Instead, use instance-based dependencies and DI to manage dependencies. For example, using our `OrderService` code, the `OrderService` class uses an instance-based dependency on the `IorderRepository` interface, making it easy to create test doubles for the interface.

4. **Use SOLID principles to write testable code**: The SOLID principles are a set of guidelines for writing clean and maintainable code. By following these principles, it is easier to write testable code. For example, the **Single Responsibility Principle (SRP)** recommends that classes should have only one responsibility, making them easier to test in isolation. The **Dependency Inversion Principle (DIP)** recommends that high-level modules should not depend on low-level modules, but both should depend on abstractions, making it easier to replace dependencies with test doubles.

Writing testable code in C# involves using interfaces to define dependencies, constructor injection to manage dependencies, avoiding static dependencies, and using SOLID principles to write clean and maintainable code. By following these best practices, it is easier to write automated tests that ensure code behaves as expected and is maintainable over time.

TDD

TDD is a software development approach in which tests are written before the actual code. The process involves iterative cycles: write a small unit test, run it (expecting it to fail initially), then write the code to make the test pass, and finally refactor the code while ensuring that all tests continue to pass. This cycle is often summarized as **Red-Green-Refactor**.

The reason why TDD is needed is that it enables early detection of defects, helps produce clearer requirements, facilitates incremental development, and enables developers to refactor with confidence.

By writing tests before writing the actual code, developers are forced to consider the desired functionality and potential edge cases. This helps catch defects at an early stage, reducing the cost and effort required for debugging later in the development cycle.

Writing tests before code encourages developers to think through the requirements and expected behavior of the system. This results in clearer and more explicit specifications for each unit of code, improving overall understanding and reducing ambiguity.

TDD encourages developers to break down the development process into small, manageable units. This incremental approach allows for more frequent integration of new features, making it easier to adapt to changing requirements and ensuring that each piece of functionality works as intended.

TDD provides a safety net for refactoring. Since the tests are written first, any changes made during refactoring can be validated by running the existing test suite. If the tests pass, developers can be more confident that the changes did not introduce new bugs.

The tests themselves serve as a form of living documentation. They provide a clear and executable specification of how the code is expected to behave. Additionally, as the code evolves, the tests are updated accordingly, creating a form of *living documentation* that stays synchronized with the code base.

We benefit from TDD with improved code quality and faster development cycles; we increase developer confidence, it is easier to collaborate on projects, and we can more easily adapt to change.

TDD leads to higher code quality by ensuring that each piece of code has a corresponding set of tests. This not only helps in identifying bugs early but also results in more modular, maintainable, and loosely coupled code.

Despite the perception that writing tests first may slow down the development process, TDD often speeds up development in the long run. It reduces the time spent on debugging and makes it easier to add new features or refactor existing code without fear of breaking existing functionality.

Developers gain confidence in their code because passing tests validate that the code behaves as expected. This confidence is crucial when making changes to the code base or when collaborating with other team members.

TDD promotes collaboration within development teams. The explicit and executable nature of tests makes it easier for team members to understand each other's code and contribute effectively.

TDD makes code more adaptable to changes in requirements. Since the code base is continuously validated by tests, developers can confidently make changes, knowing that existing functionality won't be compromised.

TDD is a powerful development methodology that contributes to the creation of robust, maintainable, and high-quality software. It aligns well with agile development practices and is widely adopted in the software industry for its numerous benefits in terms of code quality, development speed, and adaptability to changing requirements. The **Arrange, Act, Assert (AAA)** pattern is a structure used in writing automated tests to enhance clarity and maintainability. Let's take a closer look at this:

- **Arrange**: In this phase, you set up the initial conditions or context for the test. This involves preparing the test environment, initializing any necessary objects or variables, and configuring the system to be in a specific state before the actual test action occurs.

- **Act**: This is the step where the actual test action or operation takes place. It involves executing the specific functionality or behavior that you want to test. This is the point where you trigger the code or operation that you are assessing for correctness.

- **Assert**: The final phase is dedicated to verification. Here, you check whether the results of the *Act* phase align with your expectations. Assertions are used to verify that the system is in the expected state or that the expected outcome has been achieved. If the assertion passes, the test is considered successful; if it fails, it indicates a discrepancy between expected and actual outcomes.

Following the AAA pattern helps in maintaining a clear and organized structure for tests, making it easier to understand, troubleshoot, and update them. Each phase serves a distinct purpose, contributing to the overall effectiveness of the automated test.

An example of using the AAA TDD pattern

Here's a simple example in C# of using the AAA pattern. Assume you have a simple class with a method to add two numbers:

```
public class Calculator
{
    public int Add(int a, int b)
    {
        return a + b;
    }
}
```

Now, let's write a test for the Add method using the AAA pattern:

```
[TestClass]
public class CalculatorTests
{
    [TestMethod]
```

```
public void Add_ShouldReturnSumOfTwoNumbers()
{
    // Arrange
    Calculator calculator = new Calculator();
    int num1 = 5;
    int num2 = 7;

    // Act
    int result = calculator.Add(num1, num2);
    // Assert
    Assert.AreEqual(12, result);
}
}
```

In this example, the following happens:

- `Arrange`: We set up the test by creating an instance of the `Calculator` class and defining two numbers, num1 and num2

- `Act`: We call the Add method on the `calculator` object with the arranged values (num1 and num2) and store the result in the `result` variable

- `Assert`: We verify that the `result` of the Add method matches our expectations using the `Assert.AreEqual` method

This simple test checks if the Add method of the `Calculator` class correctly adds two numbers.

With TDD you can start with a failing test, then write the minimum code for it to pass. Afterward, you can refactor the code as necessary. This helps to incrementally develop your code and make changes with confidence. But which testing framework should you use? Well, the choice is yours. But to help you know which framework to choose, we will look at choosing a testing framework in the next section.

Choosing a testing framework

When it comes to choosing a testing framework for C#, there are several popular options available, including MSTest, NUnit, and xUnit. Each of these frameworks has its strengths and weaknesses, so it's important to evaluate them based on your specific needs.

Here is an extensive comparison table that highlights various aspects of MSTest, NUnit, and xUnit, three popular testing frameworks for C#:

Feature/Aspect	MSTest	NUnit	xUnit
Setup and Teardown	`[TestInitialize]`, `[TestCleanup]`	`[SetUp]`, `[TearDown]`	**Constructor, Dispose**
Test Attribute	`[TestMethod]`	`[Test]`	`[Fact]`
Test Explorer Integration	**Visual Studio**	**Visual Studio, ReSharper**	**Visual Studio, ReSharper**
Assertion Syntax	**BDD-style**	**Fluent**	**Fluent, Assert**
Parallel Execution	**Yes**	**Yes**	**Yes**
Data-Driven Tests	`[DataSource]`	`[TestCase]`	`[InlineData]`, `[ClassData]`
Test Parameterization	**Limited**	Yes (via `[TestCase]`)	Yes (`[InlineData]`, `[ClassData]`)
Theory Tests	**No**	**No**	Yes (`[Theory]`)
Test Categories/Labels	`[TestCategory]`	`[Category]`	`[Trait]`
Test Priority	`[Priority]`	`[Order]`	`[Trait]`
Ignored/Skipped Tests	`[Ignore]`	`[Ignore]`	`[Fact(Skip = Reason)]`
Test Case Source	**TestCase Class**	**External Source, Attributes**	`Inline, MemberData, ClassData`
Fixture Setup and Teardown	`[ClassInitialize]`, `[ClassCleanup]`	`[TestFixtureSetUp]`, `[TestFixtureTearDown]`	`[Collection]`, `IClassFixture`, `ICollectionFixture`
Fixture Lifespan	**Class**	**Per Test Fixture**	**Per Test Class**
Test Runner Independence	**Limited**	**Yes**	**Yes**
.NET Core Support	**Yes**	**Yes**	**Yes**
Community and Ecosystem	**Mature, Broad**	**Mature**	**Mature**
Extensibility	**Limited**	**Extensible (Add-ins)**	**Extensible (Traits Customization)**

Documentation	Good	Good	Good
License	MS-PL (Microsoft Public License)	NUnit License	Apache 2.0 License

Table 6.1: Test framework comparison table

This table provides an overview of various aspects to consider when choosing a testing framework in C#. It's important to note that the choice between MSTest, NUnit, and xUnit often depends on specific project requirements, team preferences, and existing infrastructure. Each framework has its strengths and weaknesses, so it's recommended to evaluate them based on your specific needs.

Testing framework attribute differences

Between the different testing frameworks, they all perform the same task of testing your code, but they can do things differently. One of the main differences is the use of attributes and their names. The following table provides a comparison of the differences in attribute names between the different frameworks:

Attribute	MSTest	NUnit	xUnit
[TestMethod]	Yes	[Test]	[Fact]
[TestClass]	Yes	[TestFixture]	N/A
[TestInitialize]	[ClassInitialize]	[TestFixtureSetUp]	[CollectionSetUp]
[TestCleanup]	[ClassCleanup]	[TestFixtureTearDown]	[CollectionTearDown]
[TestMethodSetUp]	N/A	[SetUp]	N/A
[TestMethodTearDown]	N/A	[TearDown]	N/A
[Ignore]	[Ignore]	[Ignore]	[Fact(Skip = "Reason")]
[DataRow]	[DataRow]	[TestCase]	[InlineData]
[DataSource]	[DataSource]	[TestCaseSource]	[MemberData]
[TestCategory]	[TestCategory]	[Category]	N/A
[Owner]	[Owner]	N/A	N/A
[Timeout]	[Timeout]	[Timeout]	[Fact(Timeout = n)]
[Description]	[Description]	[Description]	N/A

[ExpectedException]	[ExpectedException]	[ExpectedException]	[Fact]
[Assert]	**MSTest assertions**	**NUnit assertions**	**xUnit assertions**

Table 6.2: Testing framework attribute comparisons

TDD using MSTest

MSTest is a popular testing framework for C# that comes with a set of attributes and terminology to help you write and run tests. Here's an explanation of some of the most used attributes and terminology in MSTest:

- **TestMethod attribute:** The [TestMethod] attribute is used to mark a method as a test method. The method must have the signature of a void method with no parameters. The framework will execute all methods marked with this attribute as individual tests.

- **TestClass attribute:** The [TestClass] attribute is used to mark a class as a test class. All test methods within the class will be executed when the test runner executes the tests.

- **TestInitialize attribute:** The [TestInitialize] attribute is used to mark a method that should be executed before each test method is run. This is useful when you need to set up common test data or objects before running each test method.

- **TestCleanup attribute:** The [TestCleanup] attribute is used to mark a method that should be executed after each test method is run. This is useful for cleaning up test data or objects after each test.

- **TestContext property:** The TestContext property is a property of the test class that provides information about the current test run. It can be used to get information about the current test method, the test environment, and the build configuration.

- **Assert class:** The Assert class provides a set of methods for testing conditions within your tests. The most used methods include Assert.AreEqual, Assert.IsTrue, and Assert.IsFalse. These methods allow you to test whether a value is equal to an expected value or whether a condition is true or false.

- **DataTestMethod attribute:** The [DataTestMethod] attribute is used to mark a method that is a data-driven test. This attribute is used in combination with the [DataRow] attribute to provide input data to the test method.

- **DataRow attribute:** The [DataRow] attribute is used to provide input data to a data-driven test method. The attribute can be applied multiple times to a test method to provide multiple sets of input data.

By understanding and using these attributes and terminology, you can write effective and efficient tests using MSTest in C#.

TDD using NUnit

NUnit is a popular open source testing framework for C# that provides a variety of attributes and terminology to help you write and run tests. Here's an explanation of some of the most used attributes and terminology in NUnit:

- **Test attribute**: The [Test] attribute is used to mark a method as a test method. The method must have the signature of a void method with no parameters. The framework will execute all methods marked with this attribute as individual tests.

- **TestFixture attribute**: The [TestFixture] attribute is used to mark a class as a test fixture. All test methods within the class will be executed when the test runner executes the tests.

- **SetUp attribute**: The [SetUp] attribute is used to mark a method that should be executed before each test method is run. This is useful when you need to set up common test data or objects before running each test method.

- **TearDown attribute**: The [TearDown] attribute is used to mark a method that should be executed after each test method is run. This is useful for cleaning up test data or objects after each test.

- **TestContext object**: The TestContext object is a property of the test class that provides information about the current test run. It can be used to get information about the current test method, the test environment, and the build configuration.

- **Assert class**: The Assert class provides a set of methods for testing conditions within your tests. The most used methods include Assert.AreEqual, Assert.IsTrue, and Assert.IsFalse. These methods allow you to test whether a value is equal to an expected value or whether a condition is true or false.

- **ValueSource attribute**: The [ValueSource] attribute is used to mark a method that returns a set of input data to a test method. This attribute is used in combination with the [TestCase] attribute to provide input data to the test method.

- **TestCase attribute**: The [TestCase] attribute is used to provide input data to a test method. The attribute can be applied multiple times to a test method to provide multiple sets of input data.

- **Category attribute**: The [Category] attribute is used to mark a test method or test fixture with one or more categories. This allows you to organize your tests into categories for better reporting and filtering.

By understanding and using these attributes and terminology, you can write effective and efficient tests using NUnit in C#.

TDD using xUnit

xUnit is a popular open source testing framework for C# that provides a variety of attributes and terminology to help you write and run tests. Here's an explanation of some of the most used attributes and terminology in xUnit:

- **Fact attribute**: The [Fact] attribute is used to mark a method as a test method. The method must have the signature of a void method with no parameters. The framework will execute all methods marked with this attribute as individual tests.

- **Theory attribute**: The [Theory] attribute is used to mark a method as a parameterized test. This allows you to run the same test with different sets of input data. The attribute can be used in combination with the [InlineData] attribute to provide input data to the test method.

- **Test class**: xUnit does not have a separate test fixture class like NUnit or MSTest. Instead, you can define a test class with public methods that are marked with the [Fact] or [Theory] attribute.

- **Constructor**: xUnit supports a constructor for the test class. You can use the constructor to set up common test data or objects that will be used across all test methods within the class.

- **Dispose**: xUnit supports a dispose method for the test class. This can be used to clean up test data or objects after all tests within the class have been executed.

- **Assert class**: The Assert class provides a set of methods for testing conditions within your tests. The most used methods include Assert.Equal, Assert.True, and Assert.False. These methods allow you to test whether a value is equal to an expected value or whether a condition is true or false.

- **Skip attribute**: The [Skip] attribute is used to mark a test method or test class as skipped. This can be useful when you need to temporarily skip a test or group of tests.

- **Trait attribute**: The [Trait] attribute is used to mark a test method or test class with one or more traits. Traits can be used to categorize tests for better reporting and filtering.

By understanding and using these attributes and terminology, you can write effective and efficient tests using MSTest, NUnit, and xUnit in C#.

> **Note**
>
> You can understand the four-phase pattern of unit testing on the xUnit website: http://xunitpatterns.com/Four%20Phase%20Test.html. As for test doubles, there is a good article that you can read by Erik Dietrich: https://daedtech.com/introduction-to-unit-testing-part-6-test-doubles/.

The following table maps the different test framework attributes to the relevant phase of the four-phase test pattern:

Phase	Description	MSTest Attribute	NUnit Attribute	xUnit Attribute
Test Class Initialization	Set up common resources for all tests in a test class	`[ClassIni-tialize]`	`[SetUpFix-ture]`	`[Collec-tionDefini-tion]`
Test Initialization	Set up resources needed for a specific test	`[TestIni-tialize]`	`[SetUp]`	`[IUseFix-ture]`
Test Execution	Run the actual test logic	`[TestMethod]`	`[Test]`	`[Fact]`
Test Cleanup	Tear down resources after a test has executed	`[Test-Cleanup]`	`[TearDown]`	`[IClassFix-ture]`

Table 6.3: Test framework attribute mapping to the four-phase testing pattern

Running tests in Visual Studio

In Visual Studio, you can use the built-in test runner to execute your tests and view the results. The process involves a few steps:

1. **Build your solution**:

   Before running tests, ensure that your solution is built successfully. You can build your solution by pressing *Ctrl + Shift + B* or by selecting **Build** from the **Build** menu.

2. **Open Test Explorer**:

   In Visual Studio, open the **Test Explorer** window. You can do this by going to **Test | Test Explorer** or by using the *Ctrl + E, T* keyboard shortcut.

3. **Discover tests**:

   Test Explorer will automatically discover and list all the test methods in your solution. If you have just written new tests or made changes to existing ones, you may need to click the **Refresh** icon in Test Explorer to ensure it's up to date.

4. **Run tests**:

   Select the tests you want to run, right-click, and choose **Run Selected Tests**. Alternatively, you can run all tests in the solution by choosing **Run All** from the Test Explorer toolbar.

Here are the steps for viewing test results:

1. **Test Explorer window**:

    As the tests run, you'll see real-time updates in the **Test Explorer** window. Tests will be marked with a status (**Passed**, **Failed**, **Skipped**, and so on) once they complete.

2. **Output window**:

    Additional details about the test execution process and any test failures are often displayed in the **Output** window. You can open the **Output** window by going to **View** > **Output** or using the *Ctrl + W, O* shortcut.

3. **Test results summary**:

    After the tests finish running, Test Explorer provides a summary of the results, including the number of passed, failed, and skipped tests. You can also see the time it took to run the tests.

4. **Detailed test results**:

    Double-clicking on a specific test in Test Explorer will open a detailed test results window. Here, you can see the output, any error messages, and the stack trace for failed tests.

5. **Live Unit Testing** (*optional*):

    Visual Studio Enterprise Edition includes a feature called **Live Unit Testing**, which provides real-time feedback as you write or modify code. This feature automatically runs impacted tests in the background, and you can see the results directly in the code editor.

By using Test Explorer and related features in Visual Studio, you can efficiently run your tests, monitor their progress, and investigate any issues that arise during the testing process.

We have now been introduced to the different testing frameworks and seen how to run tests and view the results in Visual Studio. So, let's move on to understanding how to write effective unit tests.

Writing effective unit tests

Writing effective unit tests in C# involves several best practices and techniques that can help ensure that your tests are reliable, maintainable, and useful. Here are some tips for writing effective unit tests in C#:

- **Use a testing framework**: Use a testing framework such as NUnit, MSTest, or xUnit to help structure your tests and make them easier to write and maintain.

- **Test only one thing at a time**: Write tests that test only one aspect of your code at a time. This will make your tests more focused and easier to debug.

- **Use meaningful test names**: Use names that describe what the test is testing. This will make it easier to understand what each test is doing and to find tests that are failing.

- **Use assertions**: Use assertions to verify that the code being tested is behaving as expected. Assertions can be used to check that a value is equal to an expected value or that a condition is `true` or `false`. There are different assertion libraries available for writing readable assertions such as NUnit, xUnit, Fluent Assertions, Shoudly, NSubstitute, and Moq.

- **Test edge cases**: Test edge cases such as null inputs, empty strings, and negative values to ensure that your code handles these scenarios correctly.

- **Use test data that covers all scenarios**: Use test data that covers all possible scenarios, including the most common and uncommon scenarios.

- **Use DI**: Use DI to make your code more testable. By injecting dependencies into your code, you can easily swap out real dependencies with test doubles, such as mocks or stubs.

- **Test in isolation**: Test your code in isolation from other components to ensure that your tests are repeatable and reliable.

- **Use code coverage analysis**: Use code coverage analysis to ensure that your tests are covering all the code paths in your application.

- **Keep your tests fast**: Keep your tests fast by avoiding long-running tests and using test doubles to isolate your code.

By following these best practices and techniques, you can write effective unit tests in C# that help ensure that your code is reliable, maintainable, and bug-free.

Using code coverage analysis in Visual Studio 2022

Code coverage analysis is a technique used to measure how much of your code is executed by automated tests. It can help you identify areas of your code that are not covered by tests, allowing you to write more comprehensive test suites.

Visual Studio 2022 includes a built-in code coverage analysis tool that can be used to measure code coverage for C# projects. Here's how to use it:

1. Open your C# project in Visual Studio 2022.

2. Open the **Test Explorer** window by selecting **Test** | **Test Explorer** from the menu bar.

3. Select the tests that you want to run by selecting the checkbox next to each test. You can also select all tests in a test class or project by right-clicking on the test class or project and selecting **Run Selected Tests**.

4. Once you have selected the tests to run, right-click on the selected tests and select **Analyze Code Coverage** | **Selected Tests**.

5. Visual Studio will now run the selected tests and generate a code coverage report. The code coverage report will show you which lines of code were executed during the tests and which lines were not executed.

6.   You can view the code coverage report by selecting **Test | Analyze Code Coverage | Current Session** from the menu bar. This will open the **Code Coverage Results** window, which displays the code coverage results for the selected tests.

7.   In the **Code Coverage Results** window, you can view a code coverage report for each class and method in your project. You can also view the percentage of code coverage for each class and method.

By using the code coverage analysis tool in Visual Studio 2022, you can ensure that your tests are covering all the code paths in your application, helping you write more reliable and maintainable code.

Ensuring your unit tests themselves are correct

It is important to ensure that your unit tests themselves do not contain exceptions, as this can lead to false positives or false negatives in your test results.

One way to ensure that your unit tests do not contain exceptions is to use a testing framework such as NUnit, MSTest, or xUnit, which have built-in exception handling mechanisms. These frameworks provide methods or attributes that you can use to handle exceptions in your tests and ensure that they do not cause the test to fail.

Additionally, you can use code analysis tools such as ReSharper or CodeRush that can help identify potential exceptions in your tests. These tools can analyze your code and highlight any lines of code that may throw exceptions during execution.

Another way to ensure that your unit tests do not contain exceptions is to practice good code hygiene and follow best practices for writing tests. For example, you should ensure that your test data is valid and that your test methods are focused and only test one thing at a time. You should also use assertions to verify that the code being tested is behaving as expected.

Finally, you can run your unit tests regularly and monitor their results to ensure that they are not failing due to exceptions in the tests themselves. By following these best practices and techniques, you can ensure that your unit tests are reliable and accurate, helping you write more robust and maintainable code.

Using stubs in place of mocks

TDD is a software development methodology whereby you write your tests before writing the code that will be tested. In this process, stubs and mocks are used as test doubles to mimic the behavior of real objects.

Stubs are fake objects that return dummy test data. They do not affect the outcome of the test, and their main purpose is to set up the test scenario. For example, if you have a method that needs to fetch data from a database, you can use a stub to return a fixed set of data, allowing you to focus on testing the logic that processes this data.

Mocks, on the other hand, are also fake objects, but they are used to verify that the unit under test behaves as expected. A mock can make your test fail. It not only returns dummy data but also allows you to check whether certain methods were called during the test.

Here's a simple step-by-step example of using a stub in TDD with C#:

1. **Write a failing test**: Suppose you have a `CalculateAverage()` method in a `MathOperations` class that calculates the average of a list of numbers fetched from a database. You can write a test that checks whether this method returns the correct average for a given list of numbers. Since you haven't implemented the method yet, this test will fail.

2. **Create a stub**: To isolate the `CalculateAverage()` method from the database, you can create a stub for the database service that returns a fixed list of numbers.

3. **Make the test pass**: Implement the `CalculateAverage()` method so that it correctly calculates the average of the numbers returned by the stub. The test should now pass.

4. **Refactor**: Improve the code while keeping the functionality the same. The test should still pass after refactoring.

When using a mock object, the steps are similar, but in *step 1*, the test would also specify the expected behavior, such as which methods should be called on the mock object. In *step 3*, you would not only implement the method to make the test pass but also check that the expected interactions with the mock object occurred.

While both stubs and mocks are used in TDD, stubs are used to provide known inputs for the method under test, while mocks are used to verify interactions between the method under test and its dependencies.

Mocking data

Mocking data is the process of creating test data that simulates the behavior of real data but is specifically designed for use in unit tests. Mock data is typically created using a mocking framework, which allows you to define the behavior of the mock data and control how it is generated.

Moq is a popular mocking library in C# for creating mock objects. Let's create a simple example with step-by-step instructions:

1. **Create an interface**:

    Start by defining an interface that represents the behavior you want to mock:

    ```
    public interface ICalculator
    {
        int Add(int a, int b);
    }
    ```

2. **Create a class that uses the interface:**

Create a class that depends on the ICalculator interface:

```
public class MathService
{
    private readonly ICalculator _calculator;
    public MathService(ICalculator calculator)
    {
        _calculator = calculator;
    }
    public int AddNumbers(int a, int b)
    {
        return _calculator.Add(a, b);
    }
}
```

3. **Install Moq:**

If you haven't already, install the Moq NuGet package:

```
Install-Package Moq
```

4. **Write the test:**

Write a test where you mock the ICalculator interface using Moq:

```
using Moq;
using Xunit;
public class MathServiceTests
{
    [Fact]
    public void AddNumbers_ShouldReturnSum_
WhenUsingMockedCalculator()
    {
        // Arrange
        var calculatorMock = new Mock<ICalculator>();
        calculatorMock.Setup(calculator => calculator.Add(It.
IsAny<int>(), It.IsAny<int>()))
                      .Returns((int a, int b) => a + b);
        var mathService = new MathService(calculatorMock.
Object);
        // Act
        int result = mathService.AddNumbers(2, 3);
        // Assert
        Assert.Equal(5, result);
    }
}
```

The functions for the following elements are as follows:

- `Mock<ICalculator>`: Creates a mock object for the `ICalculator` interface.
- `Setup`: Configures the behavior of the mock. In this case, it's set up to return the sum of the two input parameters.
- `mathService.AddNumbers(2, 3)`: Calls the method being tested with the mocked dependency.
- `Assert.Equal(5, result)`: Verifies that the result is as expected.

5. **Run the test**:

Execute the test to ensure that it passes.

This example demonstrates how to use Moq to mock an `ICalculator` interface and set up behavior for testing a `MathService` class that depends on that interface. The key is to use `Mock<T>` to create a mock object and then use `Setup` to define the behavior of the mock.

By using a mocking framework to create mock data, we can isolate our unit tests from external dependencies and ensure that they are consistent and reliable. This allows us to test our code in a controlled environment, making it easier to identify and fix bugs.

When mocking is challenging or not straightforward

There are certain situations where mocking can be challenging or not straightforward. One common example is when working with `HttpClient` in C#.

The primary challenge with mocking `HttpClient` arises from the fact that it is a concrete class, and its methods are not virtual, making it difficult to create a mock or substitute. Additionally, `HttpClient` is designed to be long-lived and reused for multiple requests, which can lead to issues with managing the state of the mock.

Here are a few common challenges and ways to overcome them when dealing with `HttpClient`:

- **Non-virtual methods**:

    The methods in `HttpClient` are not virtual, so it's not straightforward to create a mock using traditional mocking frameworks such as Moq.

    Solution:

    Instead of directly mocking `HttpClient`, you can introduce an abstraction, such as an interface or a delegate, that wraps the functionality you need. Then, use DI to provide an implementation in your code and a mock implementation in your tests.

    Create a client wrapper interface called `HttpClientWrapper`:

    ```
    public interface IHttpClientWrapper
    {
    ```

```
        Task<string> GetStringAsync(string requestUri);
    }
    public class MyHttpClientWrapper : IHttpClientWrapper
    {
        private readonly HttpClient _httpClient;

        public MyHttpClientWrapper(HttpClient httpClient)
        {
            _httpClient = httpClient;
        }

        public async Task<string> GetStringAsync(string requestUri)
        {
            return await _httpClient.GetStringAsync(requestUri);
        }
    }
```

Now, in your application code, use IHttpClientWrapper instead of directly using HttpClient. In your tests, you can create a mock or a fake implementation of IHttpClientWrapper.

- **Managing the state of the HttpClient instance**:

HttpClient is designed to be reused for multiple requests to take advantage of connection pooling. Creating a new HttpClient instance for every request can lead to resource leakage. However, reusing the same HttpClient instance in tests may cause unexpected behavior due to shared state.

Solution:

Consider using a factory pattern to create instances of HttpClient in your application. This way, you can control the creation of HttpClient instances, providing a new instance for each request in your tests. Here's how it's done:

```
    public interface IHttpClientFactory
    {
        HttpClient CreateClient();
    }
    public class MyHttpClientFactory : IHttpClientFactory
    {
        public HttpClient CreateClient()
        {
            return new HttpClient();
        }
    }
```

In your application code, use `IHttpClientFactory` to create instances of `HttpClient`. In your tests, you can provide a mock implementation of `IHttpClientFactory` to control the behavior of `HttpClient` instances.

By introducing abstractions and using DI, you can make your code more testable and overcome the limitations associated with mocking concrete classes such as `HttpClient`.

Integrating tests into the continuous integration and deployment (CI/CD) pipeline

Integrating unit tests into your CI/CD pipeline can help ensure that your code is always tested and that any changes made to the code base do not introduce new bugs. Here are some steps you can take to integrate unit tests into your CI/CD pipeline:

1. Write your unit tests using a testing framework that can be automated, such as NUnit, MSTest, or xUnit.

2. Set up a build server that can automatically run your unit tests whenever code changes are made to your repository. Most build servers, such as Jenkins, Travis CI, GitHub Actions, and Azure DevOps, support running unit tests as part of the build process.

3. Configure your build server to automatically build and test your code whenever new commits are pushed to your repository. This will ensure that your unit tests are always up to date and that your code is tested as soon as changes are made.

4. Set up a code coverage analysis tool to measure the effectiveness of your tests. Many testing frameworks, such as NUnit and xUnit, come with built-in support for code coverage analysis. You can also use third-party tools such as Coverlet or OpenCover.

5. Configure your build server to report the results of your unit tests and code coverage analysis. Most build servers can generate reports or notifications that summarize the results of your tests and code coverage analysis.

By following these steps, you can ensure that your code is always tested and that any issues are caught early in the development process before they can cause problems in production. This can help improve the quality of your code and reduce the risk of bugs and errors.

Integrating tests into an Azure DevOps CI/CD pipeline

Azure DevOps provides a complete suite of tools for managing your code and building, testing, and deploying applications. Here's how you can integrate unit tests into your CI/CD pipeline using Azure DevOps:

1. Create a build pipeline in Azure DevOps that compiles your code, runs your unit tests, and generates code coverage reports. You can create a build pipeline from the **Builds** menu in the Azure DevOps dashboard.

2. Add a `Test` task to your build pipeline that runs your unit tests. Azure DevOps supports a wide variety of testing frameworks, including NUnit, xUnit, and MSTest. You can configure the `Test` task to run your tests as part of the build process.

3. Add a code coverage analysis task to your build pipeline that measures the effectiveness of your tests. Azure DevOps supports code coverage analysis for a wide variety of programming languages, including C#. You can configure the code coverage analysis task to generate reports that show the percentage of code that is covered by your tests.

Configure your build pipeline to report the results of your tests and code coverage analysis. Azure DevOps provides a variety of ways to report on the results of your tests, including charts and graphs that show the percentage of tests that pass and fail, as well as reports that show the code coverage of your tests. By following these steps, you can integrate unit tests into your CI/CD pipeline using Azure DevOps. This will help ensure that your code is always tested and that any issues are caught early in the development process before they can cause problems in production.

To finish, here is a simple example of a YAML pipeline that performs build, test, and code coverage for a C# project:

```
trigger:
- main

pool:
  vmImage: 'windows-latest'

variables:
  buildConfiguration: 'Release'

steps:
- task: NuGetToolInstaller@1

- task: NuGetCommand@2
  inputs:
    restoreSolution: '**/*.sln'

- task: VSBuild@1
  inputs:
    solution: '**/*.sln'
    msbuildArgs: '/p:Configuration=$(buildConfiguration)
/p:CollectCoverage=true /p:CoverletOutputFormat=cobertura'
    platform: '$(BuildPlatform)'
    configuration: '$(BuildConfiguration)'

- task: VSTest@2
  inputs:
    platform: '$(BuildPlatform)'
```

```
        configuration: '$(BuildConfiguration)'

- task: PublishTestResults@2
  inputs:
    testRunner: VSTest
    testRunTitle: 'Test Results'
    testResultsFiles: '**/*.trx'
    failTaskOnFailedTests: true

- task: PublishCodeCoverageResults@1
  inputs:
    codeCoverageTool: 'Cobertura'
    summaryFileLocation: '$(System.DefaultWorkingDirectory)/**/
coverage.cobertura.xml'
    failIfCoverageEmpty: true
```

This pipeline does the following:

1. It triggers any push to the main branch.

2. It runs on the latest Windows VM.

3. It installs the latest version of NuGet.

4. It restores NuGet packages for the solution.

5. It builds the solution in the Release configuration. It also enables code coverage collection in the Cobertura format.

6. It runs tests using the `VSTest` task.

7. It publishes the test results to Azure DevOps. The `PublishTestResults@2` task is used for this purpose. It expects test results in the `.trx` format.

8. It publishes the code coverage results to Azure DevOps. The `PublishCodeCoverageResults@1` task is used for this purpose. It expects Cobertura formatted coverage data.

Problem tests

In the context of software testing, "test smells" refer to indicators that a test may have issues or could be improved. These issues can affect the reliability and maintainability of the test suite. Here are some common test smells and related concepts in the context of C#:

1. **Fragility**:

   • *Description*: Fragile tests are prone to break when the application undergoes changes, even if the changes are unrelated to the functionality being tested.

   • *Example*: A test that breaks when non-essential UI changes are made.

2. **Flakiness**:

    *   *Description*: Flaky tests produce different results under the same conditions. They may pass or fail inconsistently, making it difficult to rely on their results.

    *   *Example*: A test that passes sometimes and fails other times without any code changes.

3. **Erratic tests**:

    *   *Description*: Erratic tests exhibit unpredictable behavior. They might produce different results on different test runs or environments.

    *   *Example*: A test that fails on a developer's machine but passes on the build server.

4. **Test interdependencies**:

    *   *Description*: Test interdependencies occur when the success or failure of one test is influenced by the execution of another test.

    *   *Example*: *Test B* fails because *Test A* did not clean up its test data properly.

5. **Overuse of mocks or stubs**:

    *   *Description*: Overusing mocks or stubs can lead to tests that don't accurately reflect how the real components interact.

    *   *Example*: Mocking every method call in a class, making the test too isolated from the actual system behavior.

6. **Brittleness**:

    *   *Description*: Brittle tests are overly sensitive to changes in the code or environment, leading to frequent test failures.

    *   *Example*: A test that fails when the **order of execution (OOE)** of other tests changes.

7. **Test data issues**:

    *   *Description*: Tests that rely on specific data may become problematic if the data changes or is not well maintained.

    *   *Example*: A test that assumes a specific database state, which may change over time.

8. **Hardcoding values**:

    *   *Description*: Hardcoding values in tests can make them less maintainable, especially if those values change in the application.

    *   *Example*: Asserting that a calculated value is exactly equal to a hardcoded constant.

To address these issues, consider the following best practices in C# testing:

- **Isolation of tests**: Ensure tests are independent of each other and the OOE
- **Use of test data builders**: Create flexible and maintainable test data using builders to avoid relying on hardcoded data
- **Avoiding overuse of mocks**: Mock only what is necessary for the specific test case, and favor integration tests when appropriate
- **Regular maintenance**: Update tests along with code changes and refactor them as needed to keep them robust
- **Consistent environment setup**: Ensure a consistent and reproducible test environment to reduce flakiness
- **Clear and descriptive assertions**: Use clear and descriptive assertions that focus on the behavior being tested

By addressing these test smells and following best practices, you can create a more reliable and maintainable test suite in C#.

That's the end of the chapter, so let us summarize what we've learned.

Summary

In this conversation, we discussed several topics related to unit testing in C#, including the different testing frameworks available (MSTest, NUnit, and xUnit), best practices for writing effective unit tests, and techniques for mocking data in unit tests. We also covered the importance of code coverage analysis and how to use it in Visual Studio 2022.

Overall, we emphasized the importance of writing clean and maintainable unit tests that are focused on testing one specific piece of functionality and that use descriptive naming, assertions, and the AAA pattern. We also stressed the importance of testing edge cases and exception handling, and of keeping tests isolated from external dependencies using techniques such as DI and mocking.

By following these best practices and techniques, developers can ensure that their unit tests are effective at identifying and fixing bugs in their production code and that their code is well tested, maintainable, and robust.

In *Chapter 7*, we will be discussing the design and development of APIs. But before then, you can further your reading on application testing and test your knowledge by answering the questions provided.

Questions

Answer the following questions to test your knowledge of this chapter:

1. What are the different testing frameworks available for C# and what are their strengths and weaknesses?

2. What are some best practices for writing effective unit tests in C#?

3. How can you mock data in unit tests to isolate external dependencies?

4. What is code coverage analysis and how can you use it in Visual Studio 2022 to improve the quality of your tests?

5. How can you ensure that your unit tests themselves don't contain exceptions?

Further reading

Here are some resources for further reading on application testing in C#:

*   Microsoft's official documentation on unit testing in Visual Studio: `https://docs.microsoft.com/en-us/visualstudio/test/unit-test-basics?view=vs-2022`

*   NUnit's official documentation on testing in C#: `https://docs.nunit.org/articles/nunit/intro.html`

*   xUnit's official documentation on testing in C#: `https://xunit.net/#documentation`

*   An overview of code coverage analysis in Visual Studio: `https://docs.microsoft.com/en-us/visualstudio/test/using-code-coverage-to-determine-how-much-code-is-being-tested?view=vs-2022`

*   A book on unit testing in C#: *The Art of Unit Testing: with Examples in C#* by Roy Osherove

7

Designing and Developing APIs

In this chapter, we will be looking at designing and developing APIs in C#. Today, APIs are used everywhere, from your smartphone and watch to satellites in space. It pays to fully appreciate what an API is, how APIs help consumers build apps, and what the difference between on-premises APIs and cloud APIs is. Plus, you need a good handle on API security.

In this chapter, we will be covering the following topics:

- *What is an API?*: We will cover the definition, terminologies, and other aspects of understanding what APIs are and their roles in clean code
- *API development in C#*: We will cover all the things we must consider when designing APIs
- *Web API security with OWASP*: We will cover the security implementation of OWASP in C# with example source code

By the end of the chapter, you will be able to do the following:

- Describe an API
- Describe the differences between on-premises and cloud APIs
- Describe the API design process
- Implement OWASP security best practices to secure your APIs

Technical requirements

You will need the latest community edition of Visual Studio/Visual Code if you want to write the code provided in this chapter. The code can be found at `https://github.com/PacktPublishing/Clean-Code-with-CSharp-Second-Edition/tree/main/CH07/CH07`.

What is an API?

API stands for **application programming interface**. It is a set of rules and protocols that allows one software application to interact with another. APIs define the methods and data formats that applications can use to request and exchange information. They enable different software systems to communicate with each other, making it possible for developers to use the functionality of one application in another.

APIs can be used for various purposes, including the following:

- **Data retrieval**: An API allows one application to request data from another. For example, a weather application might use an API to fetch current weather data from a weather service.

- **Functionality integration**: APIs enable the integration of different software services. For instance, a payment processing API allows an eCommerce website to securely process payments using a third-party payment gateway.

- **Automation**: APIs facilitate automation by allowing different software components to communicate and perform tasks without manual intervention. This is commonly seen in the integration of various tools and services in a development or operations workflow.

- **Accessing third-party services**: Many companies provide APIs to allow developers to access their services or data. For example, social media platforms often have APIs that allow developers to integrate social features into their applications.

APIs can use various protocols for communication, including HTTP, **Representational State Transfer** (**REST**), SOAP, and others. The choice of protocol often depends on the specific requirements of the application and the services it interacts with. RESTful APIs, which use HTTP and are based on REST principles, are quite common in web development due to their simplicity and scalability.

APIs help different consumers build loosely coupled applications

An API plays a crucial role in enabling smooth interaction and collaboration between different software components or systems. When designed with loose coupling in mind, an API allows various consumers to build applications smoothly. Here's how:

- **Decoupling of implementation details**: An API abstracts away the underlying implementation details of a system or service, exposing only the necessary functionalities. This separation allows consumers to interact with the service without needing to understand or be dependent on the internal workings of the provider.

- **Interoperability**: APIs facilitate interoperability by providing a standardized way for different systems to communicate. This standardization ensures that so long as consumers adhere to the API specifications, they can seamlessly integrate with the service, regardless of the technologies used on either side.

- **Flexibility and versioning**: Loosely coupled APIs provide flexibility in the sense that changes to the internal implementation of a service don't necessarily impact the consumers. Consumers interact with the API contract, and so long as the contract remains stable, they can upgrade or change the underlying service without disrupting their applications.

- **Scalability**: APIs allow for scalable architectures by enabling the distribution of workloads. As different components can interact through APIs, they can be deployed independently and scaled horizontally, supporting the growth of the overall system without tightly coupling the components.

- **Specialized functionality**: APIs often expose specific functionalities or services, allowing consumers to leverage specialized features without having to implement them from scratch. This promotes code reuse and efficiency in application development.

- **Technology diversity**: Loosely coupled APIs enable diverse technologies to work together. Consumers can choose the programming languages, frameworks, or platforms that best suit their needs, so long as they adhere to the agreed-upon API specifications.

- **Reduced dependencies**: Since APIs abstract away the internal details of a service, consumers are less dependent on the specific technologies or implementations used by the provider. This reduces the risk of tight dependencies that can hinder the evolution of both the provider and consumer applications.

- **Ease of maintenance**: When an API is loosely coupled, updates or changes to the provider's service can be made without affecting the consumers, so long as the API contract remains intact. This ease of maintenance is crucial for long-term sustainability and adaptability.

A well-designed API with loose coupling fosters a more agile and collaborative development environment. It allows different consumers to build applications smoothly by providing a standardized interface, abstracting away implementation details, and supporting flexibility, scalability, and interoperability. This approach promotes modular, maintainable, and extensible software architectures.

Idempotent and non-idempotent operations

The term **idempotent** in the context of HTTP methods refers to the property that a certain operation can be repeated multiple times with the same effect as if it were only performed once. In other words, making the same request multiple times should produce the same result as making the request once.

Here's a breakdown of the concept:

- **Idempotent operation**:

  - If an operation is idempotent, performing it multiple times has the same outcome as performing it once

  - It doesn't matter if the operation is repeated – the system's state or the result remains the same

  - This property is particularly important in distributed systems and network communication to ensure predictable and consistent behavior

- **Examples**:

  - **GET**: Retrieving data is an idempotent operation. Fetching the same resource multiple times doesn't change the resource on the server.

  - **PUT**: Updating a resource using PUT is idempotent. Repeatedly sending the same update request won't change the state beyond the first update.

  - **DELETE**: Deleting a resource is idempotent. If you delete a resource, it's gone, and deleting it again won't change the fact that it's gone.

- **Not idempotent**:

  - **POST**: Submitting a form or creating a new resource using POST is generally not idempotent. Submitting the same POST request multiple times might result in the creation of multiple resources or different outcomes.

- **Why it matters**:

  - In network communication, especially in scenarios where requests can be retried due to network issues, having idempotent operations helps ensure that even if a request is duplicated, the system remains in a consistent state.

Understanding whether an operation is idempotent is crucial for designing robust and predictable systems, especially in the context of web APIs and distributed architectures. It allows developers to make informed decisions about the appropriate HTTP methods to use based on the desired behavior of their applications.

HTTP verbs

Hypertext Transfer Protocol (**HTTP**) defines a set of request methods, often referred to as HTTP verbs or HTTP methods. These methods indicate the desired action to be performed on a resource identified by a given **Uniform Resource Identifier** (**URI**). Here are the primary HTTP verbs:

- **GET**:

  - **Description**: Retrieve data from the server

  - **Example**: Fetch the content of a web page, retrieve information from a database, and so on

  - **Idempotent**: Yes (repeating the same GET request multiple times has the same effect)

- **POST**:

  - **Description**: Submit data to be processed to a specified resource

  - **Example**: Submit a form, upload a file, or create a new resource on the server

  - **Idempotent**: No (repeating the same POST request may have different effects)

- **PUT:**

  - **Description**: Update a resource or create a new resource if it does not exist
  - **Example**: Update the details of a user, create a new record in a database, and so on
  - **Idempotent**: Yes (repeating the same PUT request has the same effect)

- **PATCH:**

  - **Description**: Apply partial modifications to a resource
  - **Example**: Update only specific fields of a resource without affecting the entire resource
  - **Idempotent**: No (repeating the same PATCH request may have different effects)

- **DELETE:**

  - **Description**: Request the removal of a resource
  - **Example**: Delete a user account, remove a record from a database, and so on
  - **Idempotent**: Yes (repeating the same DELETE request has the same effect)

- **HEAD:**

  - **Description**: Retrieve the headers of a resource, without the body content
  - **Example**: Check if a resource has been modified without downloading the entire content
  - **Idempotent**: Yes (repeating the same HEAD request has the same effect)

- **OPTIONS:**

  - **Description**: Get information about the communication options available for a resource
  - **Example**: Retrieve the allowed methods for a resource, discover **cross-origin resource sharing (CORS)** policies, and so on
  - **Idempotent**: Yes (repeating the same OPTIONS request has the same effect)

- **TRACE:**

  - **Description**: Perform a message loop-back test along the path to the target resource
  - **Example**: Debugging and diagnostic purposes
  - **Idempotent**: Yes (repeating the same TRACE request has the same effect)

- **CONNECT**:

  - **Description**: Establish a network connection to a resource, typically for use with a proxy

  - **Example**: Establish a tunnel to the server identified by the target resource

  - **Idempotent**: No (repeating the same CONNECT request may have different effects)

Not all methods are used in typical web applications, and their usage depends on the desired actions and the semantics of the application. Each HTTP method has its specific use cases, and adherence to their intended purposes helps ensure a well-designed and RESTful API.

Important API design topics you must consider

API design is a crucial aspect of building successful and maintainable software systems. The following design topics are essential considerations for creating effective APIs:

- **Clarity**:

  - **Importance**: Clarity ensures that the API is easy to understand, both in terms of its purpose and how to use it. Well-documented and straightforward APIs reduce the learning curve for developers and make integration more efficient.

  - **Problems**: Lack of clarity can lead to misunderstandings, increased development time, and errors in implementation. It can hinder adoption and collaboration among developers.

- **Consistency**:

  - **Importance**: Consistency in API design promotes a unified and predictable experience for developers. Uniformity in naming conventions, response formats, and endpoint structures simplifies usage.

  - **Problems**: Inconsistent APIs can confuse developers, leading to errors and frustration. It also complicates maintenance and may result in a steeper learning curve.

- **Reusability**:

  - **Importance**: Reusable components and patterns in API design enhance efficiency and reduce redundancy. A well-designed API allows developers to leverage existing functionality across different parts of an application or even in different projects.

  - **Problems**: Without a focus on reusability, developers may duplicate efforts, leading to code bloat, increased maintenance, and a higher likelihood of introducing bugs.

- **Testability**:

  - **Importance**: APIs should be designed with testability in mind to ensure the reliability of the services they provide. Testable APIs simplify the development of automated tests, aiding in the identification of issues early in the development process.

  - **Problems**: Inadequate testability can result in undetected bugs, decreased software quality, and increased difficulty in troubleshooting and debugging.

- **Security**:

  - **Importance**: Security is paramount in API design to protect sensitive data and prevent unauthorized access. Proper authentication, authorization, and data encryption are critical components.

  - **Problems**: Insecure APIs are vulnerable to data breaches, unauthorized access, and other security threats, potentially leading to significant legal and financial consequences.

- **Reliability**:

  - **Importance**: Reliable APIs ensure consistent performance and availability. Redundancy, error handling, and graceful degradation are essential considerations.

  - **Problems**: Unreliable APIs can disrupt services, lead to data loss, and damage the reputation of the system. Downtime and service interruptions may have serious consequences for users and stakeholders.

- **Maintainability**:

  - **Importance**: APIs should be designed for ease of maintenance to accommodate future changes and updates. Clean code, modularization, and versioning strategies contribute to maintainability.

  - **Problems**: Poorly maintainable APIs can become obsolete, challenging to update, and prone to breaking changes. This can result in resistance to adopting new features or improvements.

- **Observability**:

  - **Importance**: Observability provides insights into the performance and behavior of an API. Logging, monitoring, and metrics collection are crucial for understanding how the API is used and identifying issues.

  - **Problems**: Lack of observability hinders the ability to diagnose problems, optimize performance, and proactively address potential issues. It can lead to slower response times in identifying and resolving issues.

In summary, neglecting these API design topics can lead to various problems, including the following:

- **Increased development time**: Developers may struggle to understand and use poorly designed APIs, leading to increased development time

- **Reduced adoption**: Inconsistencies, lack of clarity, and poor documentation can discourage developers from adopting and integrating with an API

- **Security risks**: Inadequate security measures can expose sensitive data, leading to security breaches and legal consequences

- **Unreliable services**: Without a focus on reliability, APIs may experience downtime, affecting the availability and performance of services

- **Higher maintenance costs**: Poorly maintainable APIs are more challenging and costly to update, leading to resistance to making necessary improvements

Addressing these design topics from the outset is critical to building APIs that are robust, user-friendly, and capable of supporting the evolving needs of both developers and the systems they interact with.

How can clean code help API design and development?

Clean code principles, as advocated by Robert C. Martin and other software engineering experts, emphasize writing code that is easy to read, understand, and maintain. The application of clean code practices is beneficial not only in general software development but also specifically in the context of API design and development. Here's how clean code can help in API development:

- **Readability**:
  - **Benefit**: Clean code is highly readable, making it easier for developers to understand the logic and functionality of the API
  - **Impact**: Improved readability aids in faster onboarding for new developers, reduces the chances of introducing bugs, and facilitates collaboration among team members

- **Maintainability**:
  - **Benefit**: Clean code is designed to be maintainable, making it easier to update, extend, and modify as requirements evolve
  - **Impact**: An API built with maintainability in mind allows for seamless updates, reduces technical debt, and makes it easier for developers to work on the code base over time

- **Simplicity**:
  - **Benefit**: Clean code promotes simplicity by avoiding unnecessary complexity and keeping code concise

- **Impact**: A simple API is easier to use and understand, reducing the likelihood of errors and making it more accessible to a broader audience of developers

- **Consistency**:

  - **Benefit**: Clean code adheres to consistent coding styles and conventions, providing a uniform experience for developers working on the API

  - **Impact**: Consistency in code style and structure makes it easier for multiple developers to collaborate, reduces confusion, and improves the overall code base quality

- **Reduced cognitive load**:

  - **Benefit**: Clean code minimizes cognitive load by using meaningful names, proper organization, and straightforward logic

  - **Impact**: Developers can focus more on the problem-solving aspect of API development rather than grappling with complex or unclear code, leading to increased productivity

- **Effective documentation**:

  - **Benefit**: Clean code often requires less documentation because the code itself is self-explanatory

  - **Impact**: While documentation is crucial, having clean and self-explanatory code reduces the reliance on extensive documentation, making the API more user-friendly

- **Testability**:

  - **Benefit**: Clean code is inherently more testable, allowing for the creation of robust test suites

  - **Impact**: Well-tested APIs are more reliable, as issues can be identified and addressed early in the development process, reducing the likelihood of bugs in production

- **Refactoring**:

  - **Benefit**: Clean code facilitates easy refactoring, allowing developers to make changes without fear of introducing errors

  - **Impact**: APIs that can be refactored easily are more adaptable to evolving requirements and can be improved over time without disrupting existing functionality

- **Collaboration**:

  - **Benefit**: Clean code encourages collaboration among team members by providing a common and easily understandable code base

  - **Impact**: Collaboration is more effective when developers can quickly grasp the purpose and design of the API, leading to smoother development workflows

- **Error handling**:

  - **Benefit**: Clean code includes clear and effective error-handling mechanisms

  - **Impact**: Well-defined error handling in APIs improves robustness and helps developers diagnose and address issues more efficiently

Applying clean code principles in API design and development contributes to better readability, maintainability, and collaboration. It results in APIs that are more user-friendly, adaptable to change, and less prone to errors, ultimately enhancing the overall quality of the software.

The API design process

The process of designing a successful API involves several key steps, from understanding requirements to testing and documentation. Here's a comprehensive guide to a successful API design process:

- **Define the purpose and goals**:

  - **Objective**: Clearly define the purpose of the API and its goals. Understand the problem it aims to solve and the value it provides to users.

- **Understand the users**:

  - **Objective**: Identify the target audience and understand their needs. Know who will be consuming the API and what kind of functionality they expect.

- **Gather requirements**:

  - **Objective**: Collect and document functional and non-functional requirements. Consider factors such as performance, scalability, security, and integration with other systems.

- **Design the data model**:

  - **Objective**: Define the data structures and entities that the API will handle. Design a clear and intuitive data model that aligns with the requirements.

- **Choose the right protocols and standards**:

  - **Objective**: Select appropriate communication protocols (for example, HTTP/HTTPS), data formats (for example, JSON, XML, and so on), and any relevant industry standards.

- **Design endpoints**:

  - **Objective**: Define the API's endpoints that represent the various functionalities. Clearly articulate the request and response structures for each endpoint.

- **Handle authentication and authorization**:

  - **Objective**: Implement secure authentication and authorization mechanisms. Decide whether the API will use API keys, OAuth, or other authentication methods.

- **Implement error handling**:

  - **Objective**: Design a robust error-handling strategy. Provide meaningful error messages, status codes, and guidance for developers in case of issues.

- **Prioritize simplicity and consistency**:

  - **Objective**: Keep the API design simple, intuitive, and consistent. Follow established conventions and naming patterns to enhance developer experience.

- **Consider versioning**:

  - **Objective**: Plan for versioning to accommodate future changes without breaking existing implementations. Decide whether to include the version in the URL or headers.

- **Think about pagination and filtering**:

  - **Objective**: If the API deals with large datasets, design mechanisms for pagination and filtering to improve performance and user experience

- **Address security concerns**:

  - **Objective**: Implement security best practices, including data encryption, secure connections (HTTPS), and protection against common vulnerabilities such as SQL injection and **cross-site scripting (XSS)**

- **Test thoroughly**:

  - **Objective**: Conduct comprehensive testing, including unit testing, integration testing, and performance testing. Ensure that the API functions as expected and can handle various scenarios.

- **Document extensively**:

  - **Objective**: Create clear and comprehensive documentation for the API. Include details about endpoints, request and response formats, authentication, error handling, and usage examples.

- **Provide code samples and SDKs**:

  - **Objective**: If possible, offer code samples and **software development kits (SDKs)** in popular programming languages to simplify integration for developers

- **Implement rate limiting**:

  - **Objective**: If applicable, implement rate limiting to prevent abuse and ensure fair usage of the API resources

- **Plan for monitoring and analytics**:

  - **Objective**: Set up monitoring tools and analytics to track API usage, identify performance bottlenecks, and gather insights for future improvements

- **Prepare to scale**:

  - **Objective**: Design the API to scale horizontally and vertically. Consider potential bottlenecks and plan for additional resources as usage grows.

- **Launch and iterate**:

  - **Objective**: Launch the API and gather feedback from users. Iterate on the design based on real-world usage and evolving requirements.

- **Maintain and support**:

  - **Objective**: Provide ongoing support, address issues promptly, and consider future enhancements. Regularly update documentation and communicate changes to users.

By following a systematic and thoughtful API design process, you increase the likelihood of creating a successful, user-friendly, and maintainable API that meets the needs of both developers and the business.

API security risks and their mitigations

API security is crucial to protect the integrity, confidentiality, and availability of data and services that are exchanged between different software applications. Here are some common API security risks and their mitigations:

1. **Unauthorized access and authentication issues**:

   I.   **Risk**: If an API is not properly secured, unauthorized users might gain access to sensitive data or perform actions they shouldn't be allowed to

   II. **Mitigations**:

   - Use strong authentication mechanisms such as API keys, OAuth, or JSON Web Tokens (JWT)

   - Implement proper access controls and authorization mechanisms to restrict access based on roles and permissions

2. **Data exposure and lack of encryption:**

   I.   **Risk:** Transmitting data in an unencrypted format can lead to data exposure and potential breaches

   II. **Mitigations:**

   - Use HTTPS (TLS/SSL) to encrypt data in transit
   - Employ encryption for sensitive data at rest
   - Implement secure coding practices to avoid unintentional data exposure

3. **Injection attacks:**

   I.   **Risk:** Malicious users might inject harmful code (for example, via SQL injection) through API requests, compromising the underlying system

   II. **Mitigations:**

   - Use parameterized queries to prevent SQL injection
   - Validate and sanitize input data to mitigate injection attacks
   - Employ **web application firewalls (WAFs)** to filter and monitor HTTP traffic

4. **Denial of service (DoS) attacks:**

   I.   **Risk:** Attackers may overwhelm the API with a high volume of requests, causing it to become slow or unresponsive

   II. **Mitigations:**

   - Implement rate limiting to control the number of requests from a single client
   - Use load balancers to distribute traffic and mitigate the impact of DoS attacks
   - Monitor and analyze traffic patterns to detect and mitigate abnormal behavior

5. **Insecure direct object references (IDOR):**

   I.   **Risk:** Improperly implemented access controls may allow attackers to access unauthorized resources.

   II. **Mitigations:**

   - Implement proper authorization checks to ensure users can only access their own data
   - Use unique identifiers instead of predictable sequential IDs

6. **Lack of logging and monitoring**:

   I.   **Risk**: Without proper logging and monitoring, it becomes challenging to detect and respond to security incidents

   II.   **Mitigations**:

   - Implement comprehensive logging of API activities
   - Set up real-time monitoring to detect unusual patterns or behavior
   - Regularly review logs and generate alerts for suspicious activities

7. **Insufficient rate limiting**:

   I.   **Risk**: Without proper rate limiting, APIs are vulnerable to abuse, leading to performance issues or data breaches

   II.   **Mitigations**:

   - Implement rate limiting to control the number of requests per minute or hour
   - Use token buckets or sliding window algorithms to manage rate limits

8. **Broken function-level authorization**:

   I.   **Risk**: Inadequate enforcement of function-level access controls may lead to unauthorized access to specific API functionalities

   II.   **Mitigations**:

   - Implement proper role-based access controls
   - Regularly audit and review access permissions to ensure they align with the principle of least privilege

9. **Insecure third-party integrations**:

   I.   **Risk**: Security vulnerabilities in third-party APIs or libraries can expose the entire system to risks

   II.   **Mitigations**:

   - Keep third-party components up to date with the latest security patches
   - Vet and monitor the security posture of third-party APIs before integrating them

10. **Inadequate error handling**:

    I.   **Risk**: Improper error handling may reveal sensitive information to attackers

II.   **Mitigations**:

* Implement generic error messages to avoid exposing sensitive details

* Log errors internally while presenting user-friendly error messages to clients

It's important to note that API security is an ongoing process, and organizations should regularly assess and update their security measures to adapt to evolving threats. Security best practices should be integrated into the development life cycle, and continuous monitoring is essential to identify and address new vulnerabilities promptly.

On-premises APIs versus cloud APIs

On-premises APIs and cloud APIs refer to where the API infrastructure is hosted and managed. Let's break down the differences between the two, along with their respective pros and cons, including security considerations.

On-premises APIs

* **Definition**: On-premises APIs are hosted on servers and infrastructure within an organization's physical location or data center. The organization has complete control over the servers, network, and overall infrastructure.

* **Pros**:

  * **Control**: Organizations have full control over hardware, software, and network configurations

  * **Customization**: Tailor-made solutions can be implemented to meet specific security and compliance requirements

  * **Performance**: On-premises solutions may offer lower latency and faster response times since the infrastructure is within the organization's premises

* **Cons**:

  * **Cost**: Higher upfront costs for hardware, software, and ongoing maintenance

  * **Scalability**: Scaling up requires additional hardware purchases and may take longer

  * **Maintenance**: Organizations are responsible for all maintenance tasks, including security updates and patches

* **Security pros and cons**:

  * **Pros**:

    * **Control**: Direct control over security measures and configurations

    * **Isolation**: Greater ability to implement physical security measures

- **Cons**:

  - **Responsibility**: Organizations are solely responsible for all security aspects, which may be challenging for smaller entities

  - **Updates**: Timely application of security updates depends on the organization's diligence

Cloud APIs

- **Definition**: Cloud APIs are hosted on servers provided by a third-party cloud service provider. The infrastructure is off-site and accessed via the internet.

- **Pros**:

  - **Cost**: Lower upfront costs as organizations don't need to invest in physical hardware

  - **Scalability**: Easily scale resources up or down based on demand

  - **Maintenance**: The cloud provider handles infrastructure maintenance and updates

- **Cons**:

  - **Dependency**: Organizations rely on the cloud service provider's infrastructure and service availability

  - **Limited customization**: Some organizations may find it challenging to implement highly customized solutions due to cloud provider limitations

  - **Data transfer costs**: Costs may be incurred for data transfer between the organization and the cloud provider

- **Security pros and cons**:

  - **Pros**:

    - **Expertise**: Cloud providers often have dedicated security teams and expertise

    - **Compliance**: Many cloud providers comply with industry-specific security standards

  - **Cons**:

    - **Dependence**: Security relies on the cloud provider's practices, and organizations need to trust the provider's security measures

    - **Data location**: Concerns about data residing in different geographical locations, potentially subject to different legal jurisdictions

Security considerations

1. **Data encryption**: Both on-premises and cloud solutions should implement strong encryption protocols for data in transit and at rest

2. **Access control**: Implement robust access controls to ensure that only authorized individuals or systems can interact with the API

3. **Audit logging**: Both environments should maintain detailed logs for monitoring and auditing purposes

4. **Compliance**: Ensure that the chosen solution aligns with relevant industry compliance standards (for example, GDPR, HIPAA, and so on)

5. **Incident response**: Have a well-defined incident response plan to address security breaches promptly

Ultimately, the choice between on-premises and cloud APIs depends on an organization's specific requirements, resources, and strategic goals.

API development in C#

API development in C# typically involves creating web services using a framework such as ASP.NET Web API or ASP.NET Core. These frameworks provide the tools and infrastructure needed to build robust and scalable APIs. Here's a general overview of the steps involved in API development in C#:

- **Choose a framework**:

  - **Options**: ASP.NET Web API (for traditional .NET Framework) or ASP.NET Core (for cross-platform development)

  - **Selection criteria**: Consider factors such as platform compatibility, performance, and feature sets

- **Set up your development environment**:

  - **Install tools**: Install Visual Studio, the primary IDE for C# development

  - **Create a project**: Use Visual Studio to create a new ASP.NET Web API or ASP.NET Core project

- **Define the API structure**:

  - **Create controllers**: In ASP.NET, controllers handle incoming requests and produce responses. In ASP.NET Core, these are typically derived from `Controller` or `ControllerBase` classes.

  - **Define endpoints**: Use attributes such as `[HttpGet]`, `[HttpPost]`, and so on to define HTTP methods and their corresponding endpoints.

- **Model your data**:

  - **Create models**: Define data models or classes that represent the structure of the data you will handle in your API

- **Implement CRUD operations**:

  - **Controller methods**: Write methods in your controller to handle **Create, Read, Update, and Delete (CRUD)** operations

  - **Use HTTP verbs**: Decorate methods with attributes such as `[HttpGet]`, `[HttpPost]`, and so on to specify the HTTP verb they respond to

- **Handle routing**:

  - **Attribute routing**: Use attribute routing to define custom route templates for your endpoints

- **Implement validation**:

  - **Input validation**: Validate input data using attributes such as `[Required]`, `[StringLength]`, and so on or custom validation logic

- **Implement authentication and authorization**:

  - **Identity framework**: Utilize ASP.NET Identity for user management

  - **Authorization attributes**: Use attributes such as `[Authorize]` to control access to API endpoints

- **Handle errors**:

  - **Global exception handling**: Implement global exception handling to provide consistent error responses

  - **Use HTTP status codes**: Return appropriate HTTP status codes for different scenarios

- **Add middleware**:

  - **Configure middleware**: Use middleware components to add cross-cutting concerns such as logging, CORS, and so on

- **Implement versioning**:

  - **Choose a versioning strategy**: Decide on API versioning (URL-based, header-based, and so on) and implement it

- **Testing**:

  - **Unit testing**: Write unit tests for your controller methods using testing frameworks such as MSTest, NUnit, or xUnit

  - **Integration testing**: Conduct integration tests to ensure the entire API works as expected

- **Documentation**:

  - **Use Swagger/OpenAPI**: Integrate Swagger or OpenAPI to automatically generate API documentation

  - **XML comments**: Add XML comments to your code for better documentation generation

- **Implement security**:

  - **HTTPS**: Enforce the use of HTTPS to secure data in transit

  - **Secure APIs**: Implement security best practices, such as input validation, to protect against common vulnerabilities

- **Configure dependency injection**:

  - **Use a dependency injection container**: Configure and use the built-in dependency injection container to manage dependencies

- **Optimize performance**:

  - **Caching**: Implement caching mechanisms where applicable to improve performance

  - **Asynchronous programming**: Utilize async/await patterns for I/O-bound operations to improve responsiveness

- **Logging and monitoring**:

  - **Integrate logging**: Use logging frameworks such as Serilog or NLog for logging

  - **Set up monitoring**: Implement monitoring tools to track API usage and identify performance issues

- **Deploy the API**:

  - **Choose a hosting environment**: Deploy to IIS, Azure, Docker, or another hosting environment based on your requirements

  - **Configure deployment settings**: Set up environment-specific configurations

- **Continuous integration/continuous deployment (CI/CD)**:

  - **Set up a CI/CD pipeline**: Implement a CI/CD pipeline for automated testing and deployment

- **Scale and maintain**:

  - **Scaling strategies**: Plan for scalability using strategies such as load balancing, caching, and efficient database access

  - **Ongoing maintenance**: Regularly update dependencies, address security vulnerabilities, and implement enhancements based on user feedback

By following these steps, you can develop a robust and well-structured API in C# that meets the needs of your users and the requirements of your application.

Web API security with OWASP

OWASP stands for **Open Web Application Security Project** and is a nonprofit organization that focuses on improving the security of software. It provides freely accessible resources and tools to help organizations and developers build secure applications. OWASP collaborates with the security community and provides guidance on best practices for securing web applications and APIs.

The OWASP Top 10 is a regularly updated document that highlights the most critical security risks to web applications. It is widely recognized as a valuable resource for understanding and mitigating common security vulnerabilities. The list is compiled based on input from security experts globally and is intended to raise awareness about the most significant threats.

The OWASP Top 10 typically includes vulnerabilities such as injection attacks, broken authentication, security misconfigurations, and more. Developers and security professionals use the OWASP Top 10 as a guide to prioritize their efforts in securing web applications.

The OWASP API Security Project focuses specifically on addressing security concerns related to APIs. As modern applications increasingly rely on APIs to communicate and share data, securing these interfaces is of paramount importance. The project provides resources, tools, and best practices to help organizations and developers secure their APIs effectively.

The OWASP API Security Project covers various aspects of API security, including authentication mechanisms, authorization, data protection, and addressing common API vulnerabilities. The project aims to create awareness about API security risks and provide practical guidance on mitigating those risks.

Importance of OWASP adherence in C# API development

For C# API development, adherence to OWASP guidelines and best practices is crucial for several reasons:

- **Risk mitigation**: Following OWASP guidelines helps mitigate common security risks and vulnerabilities associated with web applications and APIs, reducing the likelihood of exploitation.

- **Compliance**: Many industries and organizations have compliance requirements that mandate adherence to security standards. Following OWASP guidelines contributes to compliance with security standards and regulations.

- **User trust**: Secure APIs enhance user trust by protecting sensitive data and ensuring the confidentiality, integrity, and availability of services.

- **Application longevity**: Adhering to OWASP best practices helps ensure the longevity of your C# API by making it more resilient to emerging security threats and reducing the need for frequent security patches.

- **Developer awareness**: The OWASP API Security Project serves as a valuable resource for developers, raising awareness about the importance of API security and providing practical guidance for implementation.

- **Community support**: Being part of the larger OWASP community provides access to resources, tools, and a network of security professionals. This collaborative environment can be beneficial for addressing security challenges in C# API development.

- **Continuous improvement**: OWASP regularly updates its resources and guidance based on the evolving threat landscape. By staying informed about the latest recommendations, C# API developers can continuously improve the security posture of their applications.

> **Note**
>
> You can find out more about OWASP at `https://owasp.org/www-project-api-security/`.

Leveraging OWASP resources and following the guidelines from the OWASP API Security Project is essential for securing C# APIs. It helps developers identify and address security risks, build more robust applications, and contribute to a global effort to enhance the overall security of software systems.

Creating an OWASP-compliant API

Creating a step-by-step OWASP-compliant API involves several considerations. We will step through the process with explanations for each step. For brevity, we'll focus on key aspects, such as authentication, input validation, and secure communication:

1. **Step 1 – set up a new ASP.NET Core Web API project**: Create a new ASP.NET Core Web API project in Visual Studio or your preferred IDE. Ensure you have the necessary dependencies and configure your project.

2. **Step 2 – add Swagger for API documentation**: Use the *Swashbuckle.AspNetCore* NuGet package to integrate the Swagger for API documentation in the `Startup` class:

```
public void ConfigureServices(IServiceCollection services)
{
    // Other configurations...
    // Add Swagger
    services.AddSwaggerGen(c =>
```

```
    {
        c.SwaggerDoc("v1", new OpenApiInfo { Title = "My API",
Version = "v1" });
    });
}
public void Configure(IApplicationBuilder app,
IHostingEnvironment env)
{
    // Other configurations...
    // Enable Swagger middleware
    app.UseSwagger();
    app.UseSwaggerUI(c =>
    {
        c.SwaggerEndpoint("/swagger/v1/swagger.json", "My API
V1");
    });
}
```

This code configures Swagger in your ASP.NET Core project, making it accessible at `/swagger`.

1. **Step 3 – implement JWT authentication**: For OWASP compliance, consider using JWT for authentication, configuring the tokens in the `Startup` class:

```
// Install necessary NuGet packages: Microsoft.AspNetCore.
Authentication.JwtBearer
// In Startup.cs
public void ConfigureServices(IServiceCollection services)
{
    // Other configurations...

    // Add authentication
    services.AddAuthentication(JwtBearerDefaults.
AuthenticationScheme)
        .AddJwtBearer(options =>
        {
            options.TokenValidationParameters = new
TokenValidationParameters
            {
                ValidateIssuer = true,
                ValidateAudience = true,
                ValidateLifetime = true,
                ValidateIssuerSigningKey = true,
                ValidIssuer = "your-issuer",
                ValidAudience = "your-audience",
                IssuerSigningKey = new
SymmetricSecurityKey(Encoding.UTF8.GetBytes("your-secret-key"))
```

```
            };
        });
    }
```

Replace placeholders such as "your-issuer", "your-audience", and "your-secret-key" with your specific values.

2. **Step 4 – secure API endpoints**: Apply the [Authorize] attribute to secure specific endpoints or controllers:

```
[ApiController]
[Route("api/[controller]")]
[Authorize] // Requires authentication for all actions in this
controller
public class MyController : ControllerBase
{
    [HttpGet]
    public IActionResult Get()
    {
        // Your implementation
    }
    [HttpPost]
    public IActionResult Post([FromBody] MyModel model)
    {
        // Your implementation
    }
}
```

3. **Step 5 – implement input validation**: Use data annotations for input validation:

```
public class MyModel
{
    [Required]
    public string Name { get; set; }
    [EmailAddress]
    public string Email { get; set; }
}
```

This ensures that the Name property is required and that the Email property must be a valid email address.

4. **Step 6 – write unit tests**: Write unit tests using a testing framework such as xUnit:

```
public class MyControllerTests
{
    [Fact]
    public void Get_ReturnsOkResult()
```

```
    {
        // Arrange
        var controller = new MyController();
        // Act
        var result = controller.Get();
        // Assert
        Assert.IsType<OkResult>(result);
    }
    [Fact]
    public void Post_WithValidModel_
ReturnsCreatedAtActionResult()
    {
        // Arrange
        var controller = new MyController();
        var validModel = new MyModel { Name = "John Doe", Email
= "john.doe@example.com" };
        // Act
        var result = controller.Post(validModel);
        // Assert
        var createdAtActionResult = Assert.
IsType<CreatedAtActionResult>(result);
        Assert.Equal("ActionName", createdAtActionResult.
ActionName);
    }
}
```

5. **Step 7 – testing with Postman**:

- **Obtain a JWT token**:

  - Use an authentication endpoint to obtain a JWT token. This typically involves sending a POST request with valid credentials.

  - Extract the token from the response.

- **Set up authorization in Postman**:

  - In Postman, set up authorization for your requests using the obtained JWT token. You can usually add it to the request headers using the **Bearer Token** option.

- **Test endpoints**:

  - Send requests to your secured API endpoints using Postman.

  - Verify that the responses match your expectations and that the security mechanisms are working as intended.

Remember to adapt these steps and code snippets to your specific requirements and security policies. OWASP compliance is an ongoing process, so stay updated on security best practices and adapt your API accordingly.

Implementing OWASP-compliant two-factor authentication (2FA)

Implementing 2FA involves adding an additional layer of security to the authentication process, typically requiring users to provide a second form of verification in addition to their password. Here is a step-by-step walkthrough of creating a 2FA method for securing a C# API while aiming for OWASP compliance:

1. **Set up your ASP.NET Core Web API project**: Create a new ASP.NET Core Web API project in Visual Studio or your preferred IDE.

2. **Install the required NuGet packages**: Install the necessary packages for implementing 2FA. For this example, we'll use ASP.NET Core Identity and Google Authenticator:

    ```
    dotnet add package Microsoft.AspNetCore.Identity
    dotnet add package OtpNet
    ```

3. **Set up ASP.NET Core Identity**: Configure ASP.NET Core Identity in your `Startup` class so that you can manage user authentication and identity-related operations:

    ```csharp
    public void ConfigureServices(IServiceCollection services)
    {
        // Other configurations...
        Services.AddDbContext<ApplicationDbContext>(
            options => options.UseSqlServer(
                Configuration.GetConnectionString(
                    "DefaultConnection")
                )
        );
        services.AddDefaultIdentity<IdentityUser>(
            options => options.SignIn
                .RequireConfirmedAccount = true
        ).AddEntityFrameworkStores<ApplicationDbContext>();
    }
    ```

4. **Enable 2FA**: Enable 2FA for users in the `IdentityUser` class:

    ```csharp
    public class ApplicationUser : IdentityUser
    {
        [PersonalData]
        public string TwoFactorSecretKey { get; set; }
    }
    ```

5. **Generate and store a secret key:** When a user registers, generate a secret key for 2FA and store it securely:

```
// In your registration logic
var user = new ApplicationUser { UserName = email, Email = email
};
var result = await _userManager.CreateAsync(user, password);
if (result.Succeeded)
{
    // Generate and store secret key
    var secretKey = KeyGeneration.GenerateRandomKey(20);
    user.TwoFactorSecretKey = Base32Encoding.
ToString(secretKey);
    await _userManager.UpdateAsync(user);
}
```

6. **Implement 2FA setup:** Allow users to set up 2FA in your user profile or settings controller:

```
public IActionResult EnableTwoFactorAuthentication()
{
    var user = await _userManager.GetUserAsync(User);
    var model = new EnableTwoFactorAuthViewModel {
        HasAuthenticator = await _userManager
            .GetAuthenticatorKeyAsync(user) != null
    };
    return View(model);
}
[HttpPost]
public async Task<IActionResult> EnableTwoFactorAuthentication(
    EnableTwoFactorAuthViewModel model)
{
    if (!ModelState.IsValid)
        return View(model);
    var user = await _userManager.GetUserAsync(User);
    var verificationCode = model.Code.Replace(" ", string.
Empty).Replace("-", string.Empty);
    var isCodeValid = await _userManager.
VerifyTwoFactorTokenAsync(user, _userManager.Options.Tokens.
AuthenticatorTokenProvider, verificationCode);
    if (!isCodeValid) {
        ModelState.AddModelError(string.Empty, "Verification
code is invalid.");
        return View(model);
    }
    await _userManager.SetTwoFactorEnabledAsync(user, true);
    return RedirectToAction(
```

```
            "EnableTwoFactorAuthentication");
    }
```

7. **Implement 2FA login**: Modify the login process so that it includes 2FA within your login logic:

```
var result = await _signInManager.PasswordSignInAsync(model.
Email, model.Password, model.RememberMe, lockoutOnFailure:
true);
if (result.Succeeded)
{
    var user = await _userManager.FindByEmailAsync(model.Email);
    if (await _userManager.GetTwoFactorEnabledAsync(user))
    {
        if (!await _userManager.GetTwoFactorClientAsync(user,
"Authenticator"))
        {
            return
RedirectToAction("EnableTwoFactorAuthentication");
        }
        return RedirectToAction("TwoFactorAuthentication");
    }
    // Handle regular login success
}
// Handle other login results
```

8. **Implement 2FA verification**: Create a method for users to verify their 2FA in your controller:

```
public IActionResult TwoFactorAuthentication()
{
    return View();
}
[HttpPost]
public async Task<IActionResult>
TwoFactorAuthentication(TwoFactorAuthViewModel model)
{
    if (!ModelState.IsValid)
    {
        return View(model);
    }
    var user = await _signInManager.
GetTwoFactorAuthenticationUserAsync();
    var verificationCode = model.Code.Replace(" ", string.
Empty).Replace("-", string.Empty);
    var isCodeValid = await _userManager.
VerifyTwoFactorTokenAsync(user, _userManager.Options.Tokens.
AuthenticatorTokenProvider, verificationCode);
    if (!isCodeValid)
```

```
        {
              ModelState.AddModelError(string.Empty, "Verification
code is invalid.");
              return View(model);
        }
        await _signInManager.SignInAsync(user, model.RememberMe);
        return RedirectToAction("Index");
}
```

9. **Implement 2FA recovery**: Implement a recovery mechanism for 2FA in your user profile settings controller (optional):

```
public IActionResult ResetTwoFactorAuthentication()
{
    return View();
}
[HttpPost]
public async Task<IActionResult> ResetTwoFactorAuthentication()
{
    var user = await _userManager.GetUserAsync(User);
    await _userManager.ResetAuthenticatorKeyAsync(user);
    return RedirectToAction("EnableTwoFactorAuthentication");
}
```

10. **Test with Postman**:

   I.   **Register a user**: Use a POST request to your registration endpoint to create a user.

   II. **Enable 2FA**: Use a POST request to enable a 2FA endpoint that will enable 2FA for the registered user.

   III. **Login**: Use a POST request to your login endpoint, providing the username, password, and 2FA code.

   IV. **2FA setup**: Send a GET request to your 2FA setup endpoint to check if the user has set up 2FA.

   V.   **Reset 2FA (optional)**: Use a POST request to reset the 2FA endpoint to reset the user's 2FA.

Ensure that your Postman requests include appropriate headers and follow the API's authentication and authorization requirements.

This example provides a basic implementation of 2FA in an ASP.NET Core API. Depending on your application's requirements and the desired level of security, you may need to adjust and enhance this implementation. Additionally, ensure that your code complies with OWASP security guidelines and regularly update dependencies to address any security vulnerabilities.

OpenID Connect (OIDC) and OAuth 2.0 (OAuth2)

OIDC and OAuth2 are protocols that play essential roles in modern authentication and authorization systems. They are often used together, and both contribute to the security of web applications. Here's an overview of each.

OAuth 2.0 (OAuth2)

- **Definition**: OAuth 2.0 is an open standard protocol that allows secure authorization between applications. It enables third-party applications to obtain limited access to a user's resources without exposing their credentials.

- **Key components**:

  - **Resource owner**: The entity that owns the resources (usually a user)

  - **Client**: The application that requests access to resources on behalf of the resource owner

- **Authorization server**: The server that authenticates the resource owner and issues access tokens after getting authorization.

- **Resource server**: The server hosting the protected resources. It is capable of accepting and responding to protected resource requests using access tokens.

- **Flows**: OAuth2 defines various grant types or flows, including Authorization Code, Implicit, Resource Owner Password Credentials, and Client Credentials.

OpenID Connect (OIDC)

- **Definition**: OpenID Connect is an identity layer built on top of OAuth 2.0. It allows clients to verify the identity of the end user based on the authentication performed by an authorization server.

- **Key components**:

  - **ID token**: A JWT containing identity information about the authenticated user

  - **UserInfo endpoint**: An endpoint where additional user claims can be retrieved after authentication

- **Roles**:

  - **Relying party (RP)**: The client application that relies on the identity provider for authentication

  - **OpenID provider (OP)**: The identity provider that authenticates the user and provides identity information

Relationship with OWASP

OWASP is a nonprofit organization that focuses on improving the security of software. It provides resources, tools, and best practices to help developers build secure applications.

Relationship with OAuth2 and OIDC

OAuth2 and OIDC are important components of secure web application development, and they align with several key OWASP security principles:

- **Authentication and authorization**: OAuth2 and OIDC address authentication and authorization concerns, providing a standardized way to secure access to resources and authenticate users.

- **Secure communication**: Both protocols emphasize secure communication. OAuth2 tokens, especially when used with HTTPS, help protect against eavesdropping and man-in-the-middle attacks.

- **Protecting user credentials**: OAuth2 enables access without exposing user credentials to third-party applications. This aligns with OWASP's recommendations to avoid exposing sensitive information.

- **Session management**: OIDC, through the ID token and UserInfo endpoint, provides a structured way to manage user sessions securely.

- **Reducing credential exposure**: OAuth2's Authorization Code flow helps in reducing the exposure of user credentials by allowing authorization without exposing the user's password directly.

- **Secure token storage**: Proper handling of tokens, such as access tokens and ID tokens, is crucial for security. This aligns with OWASP principles related to secure storage and management of sensitive information.

- **Protection against CSRF and clickjacking**: Proper implementation of OAuth2 and OIDC helps mitigate CSRF and clickjacking attacks, which are concerns highlighted by OWASP.

- **Standardized security practices**: OAuth2 and OIDC provide standardized security practices for authentication and authorization, contributing to a more consistent and robust security posture.

Developers and security professionals need to be aware of and implement these protocols securely, adhering to the guidelines provided by both OWASP and the respective specifications of OAuth2 and OIDC.

A basic OIDC and OAuth2 OWASP-compliant example

Setting up a fully OWASP-compliant OAuth 2.0 and OIDC implementation involves several considerations, and the implementation can vary based on the identity provider and client application specifics. However, I'll provide a basic example using ASP.NET Core and IdentityServer4 as the identity provider:

1. **Create a new ASP.NET Web Core project**: Create a new ASP.NET Core Web API project in Visual Studio or using the command line:

```
dotnet new webapi -n CH07_MyApi
```

2. **Install the required NuGet packages**: Install the necessary packages for OAuth 2.0 and OIDC:

```
dotnet add package IdentityServer4
dotnet add package IdentityServer4.AspNetIdentity
dotnet add package Microsoft.AspNetCore.Authentication.
OpenIdConnect
```

3. **Configure IdentityServer4**: Set up IdentityServer4 in your Startup class:

```
public void ConfigureServices(IServiceCollection services)
{
    // Other configurations...
    services.AddIdentityServer()
        .AddDeveloperSigningCredential()
        .AddInMemoryApiResources(Config.GetApiResources())
        .AddInMemoryClients(Config.GetClients())
        .AddAspNetIdentity<ApplicationUser>();
}
```

Now, configure the app so that it uses IdentityServer and authentication:

```
public void Configure(IApplicationBuilder app,
IHostingEnvironment env)
{
    // Other configurations...
    app.UseIdentityServer();
    app.UseAuthentication();
    // Other middleware...
}
```

Create a Config class to provide some in-memory configurations:

```
public static class Config
{
    public static IEnumerable<ApiResource> GetApiResources()
    {
        return new List<ApiResource>
        {
            new ApiResource("CH07_MyApi", "CH07: My API")
        };
    }
    public static IEnumerable<Client> GetClients()
    {
        return new List<Client>
        {
            new Client
            {
```

```
                    ClientId = "CH07_MyApiClient",
                    ClientSecrets = { new Secret("CH07_MyApiSecret".
    Sha256()) },
                    AllowedGrantTypes = GrantTypes.
    ClientCredentials,
                    AllowedScopes = { "CH07_MyApi" }
                }
            };
        }
    }
```

4. **Secure API endpoints**: Protect your API endpoints by using the `Authorize` attribute in your controller:

```
[Authorize]
[ApiController]
[Route("api/[controller]")]
public class MyController : ControllerBase
{
    [HttpGet]
    public IActionResult Get()
    {
        // Your secure API logic
        return Ok(new { message = "Secure data from the API" });
    }
}
```

5. **Client application setup**: Create a simple client application (for example, ASP.NET Core MVC) to demonstrate the OIDC flow:

```
dotnet new mvc -n CH07_MyApiClient
```

In the client's `Startup.cs` file, configure OIDC:

```
public void ConfigureServices(IServiceCollection services)
{
    // Other configurations...
    services.AddAuthentication(options =>
    {
        options.DefaultScheme = CookieAuthenticationDefaults.
AuthenticationScheme;
        options.DefaultChallengeScheme = "oidc";
    })
    .AddCookie()
    .AddOpenIdConnect("oidc", options =>
    {
```

```
            options.Authority = "https://localhost:5001";
            options.ClientId = "CH07_MyApiClient";
            options.ClientSecret = "CH07_MyApiSecret";
            options.ResponseType = "code";
            options.SaveTokens = true;
            options.Scope.Add("CH07_MyApi");
        });
    }
```

6. **Secure MVC views**: Protect your MVC views by requiring the user to log in:

```
[Authorize]
public class HomeController : Controller
{
    public IActionResult Index()
    {
        return View();
    }
}
```

7. **Test the setup**:

   I.   Run the IdentityServer4 project (`https://localhost:5001`).

   II. Run the API project (`https://localhost:5003`).

   III. Run the MVC client project (`https://localhost:5002`).

Visit `https://localhost:5002` in your browser; you should be redirected to log in. After logging in, you should see the secure data that was retrieved from the API.

This is a basic example, and you should further enhance it based on your specific requirements. Additionally, always ensure that your implementation adheres to OWASP guidelines and best practices for secure authentication and authorization.

Summary

An API is a set of rules and protocols that enables one software application to interact with another. APIs facilitate communication between different software systems, allowing them to exchange data and functionality. There are different types of APIs, including web APIs, library APIs, and operating system APIs.

API operations can be categorized as idempotent or non-idempotent. Idempotent operations can be repeated multiple times without them changing the result, making them safer for retries in case of failures. Non-idempotent operations, on the other hand, may yield different results with each execution.

APIs often use HTTP verbs to define the operation that should be performed. Common HTTP verbs include GET (retrieve data), POST (create data), PUT (update data), and DELETE (remove data).

API design involves considering aspects such as endpoint structure, data format (typically JSON or XML), error handling, versioning, and authentication. A well-designed API promotes ease of use, scalability, and maintainability.

The API design process involves defining requirements, designing the interface, specifying endpoints, documenting the API, and testing thoroughly. Iterative refinement is crucial to ensure the API meets user needs.

Security is a critical aspect of API development. This includes secure communication using HTTPS, authentication (API keys and OAuth), authorization, input validation, and protection against common security threats such as injection attacks and XSS.

The choice between on-premises and cloud APIs depends on factors such as infrastructure requirements, scalability, and accessibility. Cloud APIs offer the advantage of scalability and accessibility, while on-premises APIs provide more control over infrastructure.

API development involves creating endpoints, handling data formats, implementing authentication and authorization, and ensuring scalability and performance. Frameworks and tools are commonly used for API development.

OWASP provides guidelines for securing web APIs. Common security considerations include proper authentication, authorization, input validation, encryption, and protection against OWASP's Top 10 security risks.

In conclusion, understanding and implementing best practices in API design, development, and security are essential for creating robust and reliable software systems that can seamlessly communicate and share data.

Questions

Answer the following questions to test your knowledge of this chapter:

1. How can you ensure security in a C# API, and what are some best practices for handling authentication and authorization?

2. What is OWASP, and why is it significant in the field of web application security?

3. Explain the role of OIDC in the context of identity authentication. How does it differ from OAuth 2.0?

4. What are the key roles in OAuth 2.0, and how do they interact in the authorization process?

Further reading

Here are some resources for further reading on writing clean C# APIs with clean architecture:

- *API in C#: The Best Practices of Design and Implementation*: https://www.udemy.com/course/api-in-csharp/: This course provides an in-depth explanation of how to design and implement a type or an API that takes care of its users, encapsulates types, codes in a good style, refactors the code, and throws and handles exceptions properly.

- *Clean Architecture With .NET 6 - C# Corner*: https://www.c-sharpcorner.com/article/clean-architecture-with-net-62/: This article provides a brief on what a clean architecture is and how to design a solution in .NET 6 while following this architecture.

- *Clean Architecture Solution Template GitHub - ardalis/CleanArchitecture*: https://github.com/ardalis/CleanArchitecture: This GitHub repository provides a starting point for Clean Architecture with ASP.NET Core.

- *Introduction To Clean Architecture And Implementation With ASP.NET Core*: https://www.bytehide.com/blog/clean-architecture-csharp: This article provides an introduction to clean architecture and its implementation with ASP.NET Core.

- *Hands-On Design Patterns with C# and .NET Core | Packt*: https://www.packtpub.com/product/hands-on-design-patterns-with-c-and-net-core/9781789133646: This book provides an overview of **object-oriented programming** (OOP) and SOLID principles. It provides an in-depth explanation of the **Gang of Four** (GoF) design patterns, including creational, structural, and behavioral.

- *Software Architecture with C# 9 and .NET 5 - Second Edition*: https://www.packtpub.com/product/software-architecture-with-c-9-and-net-5-second-edition/9781800566040: This book enables you to acquire the key skills, knowledge, and best practices required to become an effective software architect.

- *ASP.NET Core - SOLID and Clean Architecture (.NET 5 and Up)*: https://www.oreilly.com/library/view/aspnet-core/9781803231228/: This book by Trevoir Williams is set to release in February 2023.

- *PacktPublishing/Clean-Architecture-with-.NET – GitHub*: https://github.com/PacktPublishing/Clean-Architecture-with-.NET: This GitHub repository by Packt Publishing provides a starting point for Clean Architecture with .NET.

Addressing Cross-Cutting Concerns

In modern software development, addressing cross-cutting concerns is essential for building robust and maintainable applications. Cross-cutting concerns refer to aspects of a software system that cut across multiple modules or components, often resulting in code duplication and scattered implementation. These concerns include logging, error handling, security, caching, and more.

In this chapter, we will explore various techniques and strategies in C# for effectively addressing cross-cutting concerns.

By the end of this chapter, you will have a solid understanding of the concepts, techniques, and best practices required to address cross-cutting concerns in your C# projects effectively.

> **Note**
>
> This chapter has no source code and aims to be a general introduction to the many aspects of cross-cutting concerns that you need to be aware of as a software developer and programmer. In *Chapter 9*, we will be building a reusable cross-cutting concerns project with plenty of source code, and we will be using the PostSharp **aspect-oriented programming** (AOP) framework to build the project.

In this chapter, we will cover the following topics:

- A definition of cross-cutting concerns
- Importance and impact on software development
- Common examples of cross-cutting concerns

The learning outcomes of the chapter are:

- You will be able to define what cross-cutting concerns are, their importance, and their impact on software development
- You will have seen examples of cross-cutting concerns and know how to address them

The next section will define what cross-cutting concerns are.

A definition of cross-cutting concerns

Cross-cutting concerns refer to aspects of a software system that cut across multiple modules or components, affecting the behavior and functionality of the application as a whole. Unlike core **functional requirements (FRs)**, which are typically confined to specific modules or components, cross-cutting concerns permeate multiple parts of the code base and have an impact on the overall system.

Here are some common cross-cutting concerns encountered in software development, along with their descriptions:

- **Logging**: Logging applies to all layers. Logging involves capturing and recording relevant information about the application's runtime behavior, errors, and events. It helps in diagnosing issues, tracking application flow, and providing insights into system behavior for troubleshooting and analysis.

- **Error handling and exception management**: Error handling and exception management apply to all layers. Error handling encompasses the process of gracefully managing and responding to errors and exceptions that occur during application execution. It involves handling and recovering from exceptions, logging error details, and presenting meaningful error messages to users.

- **Security and authorization**: Security and authorization primarily apply to the Presentation Layer (input validation, authentication) and Data Access Layer (data integrity, authorization). However, aspects of security can apply to all layers. Security concerns involve protecting the application from unauthorized access, ensuring data confidentiality, and enforcing proper user authentication and authorization mechanisms. This includes user authentication, access control, data encryption, and secure communication protocols.

- **Caching**: Caching primarily applies to the Data Access Layer to cache data and improve performance and to the Presentation Layer for caching user interface states. Caching is the process of storing frequently accessed data in a temporary storage area to improve performance and reduce the need for expensive operations. It involves caching results of computationally intensive operations, database queries, or external API responses.

- **Performance optimization**: Performance optimization applies to all layers. Performance optimization focuses on improving the speed, efficiency, and resource utilization of an application. It includes techniques such as optimizing algorithms, reducing database queries, minimizing network roundtrips, and using efficient data structures.

- **Transaction management**: Transaction management primarily applies to the Data Access Layer where transactions are managed and in the Business Logic Layer's transaction management. Transaction management deals with maintaining data integrity and consistency when multiple operations need to be executed as an atomic unit. It ensures that either all operations within a transaction are completed successfully or none of them take effect, thereby preventing data inconsistencies.

- **Cross-cutting validation**: Cross-cutting validation applies to all layers. Cross-cutting validation involves applying validation rules or constraints that are applicable across different parts of the application. It includes input validation, data integrity checks, and enforcing business rules consistently throughout the system.

- **Auditing and compliance**: Auditing and compliance apply to all layers. Auditing refers to the tracking and recording of actions performed within the application, ensuring compliance with regulations, policies, and industry standards. It involves capturing and storing information about user actions, system changes, and access to sensitive data.

- **Localization and internationalization**: Localization and internationalization primarily apply to the Presentation Layer where user-facing text is displayed, and potentially the Business Logic Layer and Data Access Layer if they deal with locale-specific logic or data. Localization and internationalization concerns involve adapting the application to support multiple languages, cultural preferences, and regional formats. This includes providing translations, date and time formatting, currency conversion, and support for different character encodings.

- **Monitoring**: Monitoring applies to all layers. The monitoring concern involves monitoring the application's performance, health, and usage patterns. It includes capturing metrics, tracking resource utilization, identifying bottlenecks, and generating reports for analysis and optimization.

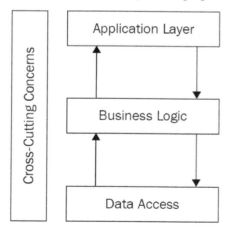

Figure 8.1: Cross-cutting concerns

These cross-cutting concerns require special attention as they transcend specific modules or components, and their proper handling is essential for building reliable, maintainable, and high-performing software applications.

Importance and impact on software development

Addressing cross-cutting concerns is of paramount importance in software development due to their significant impact on the overall quality, maintainability, and performance of the application. Here are some key reasons why addressing cross-cutting concerns is crucial:

- **Modularity and code organization**: By addressing cross-cutting concerns, developers can modularize and encapsulate these concerns separately from the core business logic. This separation promotes better code organization, reduces code duplication, and improves the maintainability and understandability of the code base.

- **Maintainability and reusability**: Properly addressing cross-cutting concerns leads to cleaner and more maintainable code. It allows developers to make changes or enhancements to the cross-cutting concern in one place, which automatically propagates those changes throughout the application. This reduces the risk of introducing bugs and makes it easier to modify or extend the application in the future.

- **Separation of concerns (SoC)**: Addressing cross-cutting concerns enables a clear SoC between the core functionality and the pervasive aspects of the system. This separation enhances code readability, improves the overall design of the application, and makes it easier to reason about and test individual components.

- **Consistency and standardization**: Cross-cutting concerns, when addressed uniformly, ensure consistent implementation and behavior across the entire application. This consistency improves the user experience, reduces the likelihood of errors, and establishes coding standards that enhance collaboration among developers.

- **Performance and efficiency**: By addressing performance-related cross-cutting concerns, such as caching or optimizing database queries, developers can significantly improve the speed and efficiency of the application. This leads to better user experiences, reduced response times, and optimized resource utilization.

- **Debugging and troubleshooting**: Properly handling cross-cutting concerns facilitates effective debugging and troubleshooting. Separating these concerns from the core logic makes it easier to isolate and identify issues, track application flow, and capture relevant information for error diagnosis.

- **Scalability and extensibility**: Addressing cross-cutting concerns promotes scalability and extensibility. When these concerns are modularized and encapsulated, it becomes easier to introduce new features, adapt to changing requirements, and scale the application without disrupting the core functionality.

- **Compliance and security**: Cross-cutting concerns such as security and compliance can have legal, regulatory, and reputational implications for applications. Addressing these concerns ensures that the application meets industry standards, protects sensitive data, and mitigates security risks.

Addressing cross-cutting concerns positively impacts software development by improving modularity, maintainability, performance, and code organization. It enables developers to separate concerns, achieve consistency, enhance debugging and troubleshooting, and build scalable and extensible applications. By giving due attention to these pervasive aspects, developers can deliver high-quality, robust, and reliable software systems.

Common examples of cross-cutting concerns

In this section, we will be looking at examples of cross-cutting concerns and how they can be handled.

Logging

Logging is a common example of a cross-cutting concern that cuts across multiple modules or components in an application. It involves capturing and recording relevant information about the application's runtime behavior, errors, and events. Here are some common examples of logging that would be addressed as cross-cutting concerns:

- **Error logging**: When an error occurs during application execution, it is crucial to log detailed information about the error, including the stack trace, error message, and any relevant contextual data. Error logging provides a valuable resource for troubleshooting and diagnosing issues. It can be addressed as a cross-cutting concern by implementing a centralized error-handling mechanism that captures and logs errors from different parts of the application.

- **Informational logging**: Informational logging involves capturing important events or milestones during the execution of the application. This can include logging application startup, shutdown, significant configuration changes, or specific user actions. By addressing informational logging as a cross-cutting concern, developers can capture these events consistently across various modules and components.

- **Metrics**: Metrics focuses on measuring and logging performance-related metrics, such as response times, execution times of critical operations, or resource utilization. By implementing metrics as a cross-cutting concern, developers can capture performance data from different components and use it to identify bottlenecks, optimize code, and improve overall application performance. Metric gathering is not usually done with standard logging libraries, but with dedicated libraries such as `app.metrics`.

- **Debug logging**: Debug logging involves capturing additional information during the development and testing phases to aid in debugging and troubleshooting. This can include logging variable values, intermediate results, or specific code execution paths. By addressing debug logging as a cross-cutting concern, developers can enable/disable debug logging globally or for specific components, allowing for efficient debugging and reducing noise in production logs.

To handle logging as a cross-cutting concern, developers can leverage logging frameworks or libraries available in C#, such as log4net, NLog, Serilog, or the built-in logging capabilities in .NET Core and .NET Framework. These frameworks provide standardized logging APIs and features, including configurable log levels, log formatting, log filtering, and support for various log destinations (for example, console, file, database, or external services).

By implementing a centralized logging approach, developers can ensure consistent logging practices throughout the application. This involves modularizing logging code, encapsulating it within dedicated logging components, and utilizing appropriate logging levels and log message formats. Additionally, developers can configure the logging framework to capture and store logs in a centralized location, making it easier to analyze and monitor the application's behavior.

Addressing logging as a cross-cutting concern improves the maintainability, troubleshooting, and monitoring capabilities of the application. It enables developers to capture and analyze important runtime information, aiding in diagnosing issues, identifying performance bottlenecks, and ensuring reliable application behavior.

Error handling and exception management

Error handling and exception management are critical cross-cutting concerns that span multiple modules or components in an application. They involve managing and responding to errors and exceptions that occur during application execution. Here are some common examples of error handling and exception management as cross-cutting concerns:

- **Centralized exception handling**: Implementing centralized exception handling allows for consistent and uniform handling of exceptions throughout the application. This involves capturing exceptions at a high level, logging relevant information about the exception, and presenting meaningful error messages to users. By addressing exception handling as a cross-cutting concern, developers can ensure that exceptions are handled consistently across different modules, promoting maintainability and reducing code duplication.

- **Error logging and reporting**: When an error occurs, it is crucial to log detailed information about the error for troubleshooting and analysis. This includes logging the exception stack trace, error message, relevant contextual data, and any additional information that can assist in diagnosing the issue. By addressing error logging and reporting as a cross-cutting concern, developers can implement a standardized mechanism to capture and log errors from different parts of the application, facilitating efficient debugging and problem resolution.

- **Error recovery and graceful degradation**: Cross-cutting error handling also involves implementing strategies for error recovery and graceful degradation. This includes handling recoverable errors, retrying failed operations, providing fallback mechanisms, and ensuring the application can gracefully handle errors without crashing or negatively impacting the user experience. By addressing error recovery and graceful degradation as cross-cutting concerns, developers can implement consistent error-handling strategies that promote application resilience and user satisfaction.

- **Exception propagation and wrapping**: Exception propagation and wrapping are cross-cutting concerns that involve properly handling and propagating exceptions across different layers of the application. This includes catching exceptions at appropriate levels, wrapping them in custom exceptions if necessary, and propagating them to higher-level components or system boundaries. By addressing exception propagation and wrapping as cross-cutting concerns, developers can ensure that exceptions are appropriately handled, allowing for better SoC and improved code readability.

- **User-friendly error messages**: Providing meaningful and user-friendly error messages is an important aspect of error handling. It involves crafting error messages that are informative, clear, and actionable for users, helping them understand the cause of the error and guiding them toward potential solutions. By addressing user-friendly error messages as a cross-cutting concern, developers can standardize the process of generating and presenting error messages, ensuring consistency and a positive user experience across the application.

To handle error handling and exception management as cross-cutting concerns, developers can follow best practices such as:

- Implementing a centralized exception-handling mechanism, such as a global exception handler or middleware, to capture and handle exceptions uniformly

- Logging exceptions and relevant contextual information using a logging framework or library

- Using structured exception types and custom exception classes to provide specific error information and differentiate between different types of exceptions

- Implementing appropriate error recovery strategies, such as retry mechanisms or fallback options, to handle recoverable errors gracefully

- Providing user-friendly error messages that communicate the problem clearly and suggest possible actions for resolution

- Establishing error-handling policies and guidelines that are followed consistently throughout the application development process

By addressing error handling and exception management as cross-cutting concerns, developers can improve application robustness, maintainability, and user satisfaction by ensuring consistent and effective handling of errors and exceptions across the entire application.

Security and authorization

Security and authorization are vital cross-cutting concerns in application development. They encompass measures to protect the application from unauthorized access, ensure data confidentiality, and enforce proper user authentication and authorization mechanisms. Here are some common examples of security and authorization as cross-cutting concerns:

- **User authentication**: User authentication is a crucial aspect of security and authorization. It involves verifying the identity of users accessing the application. Addressing user authentication as a cross-cutting concern involves implementing a standardized authentication mechanism, such as username/ password authentication, token-based authentication (for example, **JSON Web Token (JWT)**), or integration with external authentication providers (for example, **Open Authorization (OAuth)**). This ensures consistent authentication across different modules or components of the application.

- **Access control**: Access control is another important aspect of security and authorization. It involves determining which actions and resources a user is permitted to access based on their roles, permissions, or privileges. Addressing access control as a cross-cutting concern involves implementing a centralized authorization mechanism that enforces access control rules consistently across the application. This can be achieved through **role-based access control (RBAC)**, **attribute-based access control (ABAC)**, or other access control models.

- **Data encryption**: Data encryption is a critical security measure to protect sensitive data from unauthorized access or interception. It involves encrypting data at rest (stored in databases or files) and data in transit (communication over networks). Addressing data encryption as a cross-cutting concern involves implementing encryption algorithms or utilizing encryption libraries/frameworks to ensure that sensitive data is encrypted and decrypted consistently across different parts of the application.

- **Input validation**: Input validation is a security concern that involves validating and sanitizing user input to prevent security vulnerabilities such as SQL injection, **cross-site scripting (XSS)**, or command injection attacks. Addressing input validation as a cross-cutting concern involves implementing a standardized input validation mechanism that validates user input consistently across the application. This helps mitigate common security risks associated with malicious or malformed input.

- **Security auditing and logging**: Security auditing and logging involve capturing and monitoring security-related events, user actions, and system changes for compliance and troubleshooting purposes. Addressing security auditing and logging as cross-cutting concerns involves implementing a centralized logging mechanism that captures security-related events consistently across different components. This allows for effective monitoring, analysis, and forensic investigations in case of security incidents, and therefore security logs should be kept separate from standard logs for security reasons.

- **Secure communication**: Secure communication ensures the confidentiality and integrity of data exchanged between the application and external systems or clients. Addressing secure communication as a cross-cutting concern involves utilizing secure communication protocols, such as HTTPS/TLS, and implementing certificate management practices to encrypt and authenticate communication channels. This ensures that sensitive information remains protected during transit.

- **Security configuration management (SCM)**: SCM involves managing and securing configuration settings, such as database connection strings, API keys, or access control policies. Addressing SCM as a cross-cutting concern involves implementing secure storage mechanisms for sensitive configuration settings, enforcing access control to configuration files, and following secure coding practices to prevent configuration-related vulnerabilities.

To handle security and authorization as cross-cutting concerns, developers can follow best practices such as:

- Adopting established security frameworks and libraries that provide robust authentication and authorization mechanisms

- Implementing secure coding practices, including input validation, output encoding, and protection against common security vulnerabilities

- Regularly updating and patching software components and libraries to address security vulnerabilities

- Conducting security testing, including penetration testing and code reviews, to identify and address security weaknesses

- Establishing secure development guidelines and providing training to developers to ensure security considerations are integrated into the development process

By addressing security and authorization as cross-cutting concerns, developers can ensure that security measures are consistently applied throughout the application. This helps protect sensitive data, prevent unauthorized access, and maintain the integrity and confidentiality of the application and its users. It also helps in compliance with regulatory requirements and builds trust with users by demonstrating a commitment to safeguarding their information.

By implementing security and authorization as cross-cutting concerns, developers can achieve the following benefits:

- **Consistency**: Addressing security and authorization consistently across the application ensures that security measures are applied uniformly, reducing the risk of overlooking vulnerabilities or creating inconsistencies that could be exploited by attackers.

- **Modularity**: Treating security and authorization as cross-cutting concerns allows for modularization and encapsulation of security-related logic. This promotes code reusability, maintainability, and SoC, making it easier to enforce security policies and make changes or updates when needed.

- **Reduced duplication**: Handling security and authorization as cross-cutting concerns avoids duplicating security-related code across different modules or components. Instead, developers can centralize security logic, reducing redundancy and simplifying maintenance efforts.

- **Scalability**: When security and authorization are addressed as cross-cutting concerns, they can be scaled and applied consistently as the application grows. This ensures that security measures can adapt to evolving requirements and accommodate increased user access and data volumes.

- **Auditability**: Centralizing security-related logging and auditing enables comprehensive monitoring and analysis of security events. It facilitates compliance audits, forensic investigations, and the detection of potential security breaches or suspicious activities.

- **Interoperability**: By addressing security and authorization as cross-cutting concerns, developers can integrate with external authentication providers, identity management systems, or security frameworks more easily. This enables seamless interoperability with other systems or services, ensuring a cohesive and secure application ecosystem.

Addressing security and authorization as cross-cutting concerns is crucial for developing robust and secure applications. It helps protect sensitive data, mitigate security risks, and maintain user trust. By implementing standardized security practices and consistently applying them across the application, developers can create a secure foundation that underpins the entire **software development life cycle** (SDLC).

Caching

Caching is a common cross-cutting concern in software development that involves storing frequently accessed or computationally expensive data in a temporary storage location for faster retrieval. It helps improve application performance, reduce latency, and minimize resource consumption. Here are some common examples of caching that would be addressed as cross-cutting concerns:

- **Data caching**: Data caching involves caching frequently accessed data from data sources such as databases, external APIs, or filesystems. This can include caching the results of database queries, the responses from API calls, or the contents of files. By addressing data caching as a cross-cutting concern, developers can implement a caching layer that sits between the application and the data source, allowing for efficient retrieval of data without the need to access the original source repeatedly.

- **Query result caching**: Query result caching focuses on caching the results of computationally expensive or frequently executed queries. This can be particularly beneficial in scenarios where the same query is executed multiple times with the same parameters. By addressing query result caching as a cross-cutting concern, developers can cache the results of queries in memory or a distributed cache, reducing the time and resources required for query execution.

- **HTTP response caching**: HTTP response caching involves caching the responses of HTTP requests to avoid redundant network traffic and improve response times. This is especially useful for static or semi-static content that does not frequently change. By addressing HTTP response caching as a cross-cutting concern, developers can configure caching headers and mechanisms to cache responses at various levels, such as the client-side cache, proxy servers, or the application server itself.

- **View or fragment caching**: View or fragment caching focuses on caching parts or sections of a user interface that are expensive to generate or compute. This can include caching the rendered output of a view, a component, or a portion of a web page. By addressing view or fragment caching as a cross-cutting concern, developers can cache the pre-rendered output and serve it directly without the need for costly computations, enhancing the application's responsiveness.

- **Object caching**: Object caching involves caching instances of objects or complex data structures to improve performance. This can be helpful when the creation or retrieval of objects is time-consuming or resource-intensive. By addressing object caching as a cross-cutting concern, developers can cache objects in memory or a distributed cache, enabling faster access and reducing the need for expensive object creation or retrieval operations.

To handle caching as a cross-cutting concern, developers can adopt various strategies:

- **Utilizing caching frameworks or libraries**: Use existing caching frameworks or libraries, such as Redis, Memcached, or the built-in caching mechanisms provided by web frameworks such as ASP.NET Core or ASP.NET MVC. These frameworks provide APIs and configurations for implementing caching strategies easily.

- **Setting caching policies**: Define caching policies that determine when and for how long data should be cached. This includes considering factors such as data volatility, expiration times, cache invalidation mechanisms, and cache eviction strategies.

- **Applying cache dependencies**: Establish dependencies between cached items and the underlying data sources to ensure the cache remains synchronized with the data. Invalidate or update the cache when the underlying data changes to maintain data consistency.

- **Employing cache management techniques**: Implement techniques such as cache partitioning, cache compression, or cache throttling to optimize cache usage and manage cache resources efficiently.

- **Measuring and monitoring cache performance**: Use monitoring tools and techniques to track cache hit rates, cache misses, and cache effectiveness. This allows for performance optimization and identifying potential cache-related issues.

By addressing caching as a cross-cutting concern, developers can enhance the performance and scalability of applications, reduce the load on data sources, and improve overall user experience by minimizing response times and resource consumption.

Performance optimization

Performance optimization is a crucial cross-cutting concern in software development that focuses on improving the speed, efficiency, and resource utilization of an application. It involves identifying and addressing bottlenecks, reducing unnecessary computations, and optimizing algorithms and data structures. Here are some common examples of performance optimization that would be addressed as cross-cutting concerns:

- **Algorithmic optimization**: Algorithmic optimization involves improving the efficiency of algorithms and data structures used in the application. This includes analyzing the complexity of algorithms, identifying opportunities for algorithmic improvements (such as replacing a linear search with a binary search), and selecting the most appropriate data structures for efficient data manipulation (for example, using a hash table instead of a linear list). Addressing algorithmic optimization as a cross-cutting concern helps ensure that efficient algorithms and data structures are used consistently throughout the application.

- **Caching**: Caching, as discussed earlier, is a performance optimization technique that involves storing frequently accessed or computationally expensive data in temporary storage. By caching data or computation results, developers can reduce the need to recalculate or retrieve the same data repeatedly, improving application response times and reducing resource usage. Addressing caching as a cross-cutting concern involves implementing a caching layer that can be utilized across different modules or components of the application.

- **Lazy loading**: Lazy loading is a technique that defers the loading of resources or data until they are needed. This helps reduce the initial load time and resource consumption, especially for large or complex applications. By addressing lazy loading as a cross-cutting concern, developers can implement mechanisms to load resources or data on demand, ensuring that only the necessary components are loaded when required.

- **Database optimization**: Database optimization focuses on improving the performance of database operations. This includes optimizing database queries by using appropriate indexes, reducing unnecessary database roundtrips, and optimizing database schema design. Addressing database optimization as a cross-cutting concern involves utilizing best practices and techniques to optimize database access and reduce the overhead of database operations across the application.

- **Multithreading and asynchronous processing**: Multithreading and asynchronous processing techniques are used to leverage parallelism and maximize the utilization of system resources. By performing computationally intensive or long-running tasks in separate threads or asynchronously, the application can maintain responsiveness and improve overall throughput. Addressing multithreading and asynchronous processing as cross-cutting concerns involves implementing concurrency patterns, utilizing thread pools, or employing asynchronous programming techniques consistently throughout the application.

- **Resource management**: Efficient resource management is essential for optimal application performance. This involves properly managing resources such as memory, file handles, network connections, and database connections. Addressing resource management as a cross-cutting concern includes employing techniques such as object pooling, connection pooling, and proper disposal of resources to minimize resource leaks and maximize resource reuse.

- **Code profiling and performance monitoring**: Code profiling and performance monitoring are important practices for identifying performance bottlenecks and areas of improvement. This includes using profiling tools to analyze the performance characteristics of the application, identifying hotspots in the code, and measuring the impact of optimization efforts. Addressing code profiling and performance monitoring as cross-cutting concerns involves incorporating performance analysis and monitoring techniques into the development and testing processes.

To handle performance optimization as a cross-cutting concern, developers can follow these approaches:

- Conducting performance testing and analysis to identify bottlenecks and areas for improvement

- Utilizing profiling tools and techniques to measure and analyze the performance characteristics of the application

- Applying optimization strategies at various levels, such as algorithmic optimizations, database optimizations, or resource management optimizations

- Utilizing performance counters, logging, and monitoring tools to gather real-time performance metrics and identify performance issues in production environments

- Regularly reviewing and optimizing critical code paths, frequently accessed modules, and performance-sensitive operations

- Applying performance optimization techniques consistently across the application, considering the impact on code readability and maintainability

- Utilizing caching mechanisms appropriately to reduce redundant computations and improve data retrieval performance

- Considering scalability and future growth when optimizing performance to ensure that the application can handle increasing workloads and user demands

- Collaborating with the operations team or infrastructure specialists to optimize server configurations, network settings, and other infrastructure-related factors that impact performance

- Keeping up to date with advancements in technology, frameworks, and libraries that offer performance improvements and incorporating them into the application where applicable

By addressing performance optimization as a cross-cutting concern, developers can significantly enhance the speed, responsiveness, and efficiency of their applications. Optimized performance not only improves user experience but also reduces infrastructure costs, increases application scalability, and allows the application to handle larger workloads effectively.

Transaction management

Transaction management is a vital cross-cutting concern in software development that ensures data integrity and consistency when executing multiple operations as part of a single logical unit of work. It involves coordinating and managing transactions across different components or modules of an application. Here are some common examples of transaction management that would be addressed as cross-cutting concerns:

- **Database transactions**: Database transactions are used to maintain data consistency and integrity when performing multiple database operations. This includes inserting, updating, or deleting records within a database. Addressing database transactions as a cross-cutting concern involves utilizing the transaction management capabilities provided by the database system or using transaction management frameworks available in the programming language or framework being used. This ensures that all database operations within a transaction are executed atomically (all-or-nothing) and that changes are persisted reliably.

- **Distributed transactions**: Distributed transactions involve coordinating and managing transactions that span across multiple independent systems or services. In a distributed environment, where data and operations are distributed across different resources or microservices, ensuring transactional consistency becomes challenging. Addressing distributed transactions as a cross-cutting concern involves employing distributed transaction management protocols or frameworks that provide mechanisms for coordinating and synchronizing the participants involved in the transaction. This ensures that all operations across the distributed systems either commit or roll back together to maintain data integrity.

- **Application-level transactions**: Application-level transactions involve managing logical units of work that span beyond the boundaries of a single database. This includes coordinating operations across multiple components or services within an application. Addressing application-level transactions as a cross-cutting concern requires implementing transaction management mechanisms within the application. This can be achieved through programming language constructs, transaction management frameworks, or custom transaction management logic. It ensures that related operations are executed atomically and consistently across different modules or components.

- **Resource management**: Resource management in transaction management involves ensuring that resources used during a transaction, such as file handles, network connections, or external services, are properly acquired, utilized, and released. This includes managing resource locks, connection pooling, and handling resource failures. Addressing resource management as a cross-cutting concern involves implementing appropriate resource management patterns, using connection pooling techniques, and handling exceptions or failures that may occur during resource usage.

- **Transaction monitoring and logging**: Transaction monitoring and logging involve capturing relevant information and events related to transactions for monitoring, auditing, and troubleshooting purposes. This includes logging transaction details, tracking transaction status, and recording any exceptions or errors that occur during the transaction. Addressing transaction monitoring and logging as a cross-cutting concern involves implementing a centralized logging mechanism that captures transaction-related events consistently across different components or services. This facilitates monitoring, analysis, and debugging of transactional behavior.

To handle transaction management as a cross-cutting concern, developers can follow these practices:

- Utilize transaction management frameworks or libraries provided by the programming language or framework being used. These frameworks abstract the complexities of transaction coordination and provide mechanisms for managing transactions easily.

- Design and structure the application in a way that promotes modularization and SoC. This helps isolate transactional logic from business logic, making it easier to manage and coordinate transactions across different components.

- Ensure that transactions are properly defined and scoped to encapsulate related operations that need to be treated as a single unit of work. This helps maintain data consistency and integrity.

- Handle transaction failures and exceptions appropriately by implementing mechanisms for rollback, retry, or compensation. This ensures that the application can recover from transactional errors and maintain data consistency.

- Implement proper transaction isolation levels to balance the requirements of data consistency, concurrency, and performance.

- Monitor and log transaction-related events to facilitate troubleshooting, auditing, and performance analysis.

By addressing transaction management as a cross-cutting concern, developers can ensure data integrity, consistency, and reliability when performing complex operations that involve multiple resources or services.

Validation

Validation is a critical cross-cutting concern in software development that involves ensuring the correctness, integrity, and compliance of data entered or processed by an application. It encompasses various forms of data validation, including input validation, business rule validation, and data format validation. Here are some common examples of validation that would be addressed as cross-cutting concerns:

- **Input validation**: Input validation focuses on validating user input to ensure it meets the required format, length, and constraints. This includes checking for the presence of mandatory fields, validating data types, and performing range or pattern checks. Addressing input validation as a cross-cutting concern involves implementing validation logic at a centralized level that can be applied consistently across different parts of the application. This can be achieved through the use of validation frameworks or libraries that provide validation rules, annotations, or attributes.

- **Business rule validation**: Business rule validation ensures that data adheres to the specific rules and constraints defined by the business logic of an application. This can involve complex validations, such as verifying that certain fields are in a valid state, performing calculations or cross-field validations, or checking for data dependencies. Addressing business rule validation as a cross-cutting concern involves implementing a centralized validation layer or service that can evaluate and enforce business rules consistently across different modules or components of the application.

- **Data format validation**: Data format validation ensures that data is in the correct format or follows specific formatting rules. This can include validating email addresses, phone numbers, postal codes, URLs, or any other data format specific to the application's domain. Addressing data format validation as a cross-cutting concern involves utilizing regular expressions, parsing libraries, or dedicated formatting/validation libraries to validate and enforce the desired data formats consistently throughout the application.

- **Domain-specific validation**: Domain-specific validation refers to validations that are specific to the application's domain or industry requirements. This can involve compliance checks, regulatory validations, or domain-specific constraints. Addressing domain-specific validation as a cross-cutting concern involves understanding and implementing the specific validation requirements applicable to the application's domain. This may involve integrating with external validation services, utilizing domain-specific validation libraries, or implementing custom validation logic.

To handle validation as a cross-cutting concern, developers can follow these practices:

- Utilize validation frameworks or libraries that provide pre-built validation rules, validators, or annotations. These frameworks simplify the implementation of validation logic and promote consistency.

- Implement validation logic at a centralized level to enforce validation rules consistently across different parts of the application. This ensures that validations are not duplicated and that changes or updates to validation rules can be applied universally.

- Leverage declarative validation approaches, such as annotations or attributes, to associate validation rules directly with the data models or objects being validated. This promotes code readability and reduces the coupling between validation logic and business logic.

- Implement custom validation logic, when necessary, especially for complex business rules or domain-specific validations. This can be achieved through custom validation classes, functions, or extensions that encapsulate specific validation requirements.

- Provide meaningful and user-friendly validation error messages that communicate validation failures clearly to users, helping them understand and correct their input.

- Regularly review and update validation rules to accommodate changes in business requirements, regulatory compliance, or data format standards.

By addressing validation as a cross-cutting concern, developers can ensure data integrity, improve application robustness, and enhance the overall user experience by providing accurate and valid data inputs. Centralizing and standardizing validation logic across the application leads to code reusability, maintainability, and a consistent approach to data validation.

Auditing and compliance

Auditing and compliance are crucial cross-cutting concerns in software development that focus on tracking and ensuring adherence to security policies, regulations, and internal guidelines. These concerns involve capturing and logging relevant events, monitoring user activities, and enforcing compliance with specific requirements. Here are some common examples of auditing and compliance that would be addressed as cross-cutting concerns:

- **Audit logging**: Audit logging involves capturing and recording relevant events and activities within an application for later review and analysis. This includes logging actions such as user logins, data modifications, access attempts, and system changes. Addressing audit logging as a cross-cutting concern involves implementing a centralized logging mechanism that captures audit events consistently across different components or modules of the application. This helps in maintaining an audit trail, facilitating compliance, and aiding in security incident investigation.

- **Access control**: Access control ensures that only authorized users have appropriate access to resources or functionalities within the application. This includes enforcing user authentication, RBAC, and permissions management. Addressing access control as a cross-cutting concern involves implementing a centralized access control mechanism that can be applied consistently across different parts of the application. This can be achieved through the use of access control frameworks or libraries that provide the necessary features and capabilities.

- **Compliance with security standards**: Compliance with security standards involves adhering to specific security requirements, regulations, or industry best practices. This can include compliance with standards such as the **Payment Card Industry Data Security Standard (PCI DSS)**, the **Health Insurance Portability and Accountability Act (HIPAA)**, or the **General Data Protection Regulation (GDPR)**. Addressing compliance with security standards as a cross-cutting concern involves implementing security controls, encryption mechanisms, data protection measures, and privacy safeguards. It may also involve conducting security assessments, vulnerability scans, or penetration testing to ensure compliance.

- **Data privacy and protection**: Data privacy and protection involve safeguarding sensitive or **personally identifiable information (PII)** collected or processed by the application. This includes encrypting data at rest and in transit, implementing secure communication protocols, and enforcing data anonymization or pseudonymization where required. Addressing data privacy and protection as a cross-cutting concern involves implementing data protection measures consistently throughout the application, incorporating security frameworks or libraries, and following privacy guidelines and regulations.

- **Compliance auditing and reporting**: Compliance auditing and reporting involve generating reports or providing evidence of compliance with specific regulations or internal policies. This includes generating compliance reports, tracking user activities, and ensuring proper documentation of security controls and procedures. Addressing compliance auditing and reporting as a cross-cutting concern involves implementing mechanisms to capture relevant data and events, generating compliance reports, and providing audit trails and documentation when required.

- **Incident response (IR) and forensics**: IR and forensics involve handling security incidents, investigating breaches, and performing forensic analysis. This includes capturing and preserving relevant data, identifying the root cause of security incidents, and implementing remediation measures. Addressing IR and forensics as a cross-cutting concern involves implementing mechanisms to detect and respond to security incidents, incorporating **security IR (SIR)** frameworks, and ensuring proper logging and retention of relevant data.

To handle auditing and compliance as cross-cutting concerns, developers can follow these practices:

- Implement a centralized logging and auditing mechanism that captures relevant events consistently across the application

- Utilize security frameworks, libraries, or APIs that provide built-in functionality for access control, authentication, and encryption

- Regularly review and update security policies, ensuring they align with applicable regulations and industry best practices

- Conduct security assessments, vulnerability scans, or penetration testing to identify potential security risks and vulnerabilities

- Monitor and analyze audit logs to detect any suspicious or unauthorized activities

- Implement mechanisms for generating compliance reports and providing evidence of adherence to regulations or internal policies

- Establish IR and forensics procedures to promptly handle security incidents, investigate breaches, and take necessary remedial actions

- Regularly train and educate developers, administrators, and users on security best practices, compliance requirements, and the importance of adhering to security policies

- Conduct periodic security audits and assessments to evaluate the effectiveness of security controls, identify areas for improvement, and ensure ongoing compliance with regulations

- Maintain documentation of security measures, policies, procedures, and compliance efforts to demonstrate accountability and facilitate audits or regulatory inspections

By addressing auditing and compliance as cross-cutting concerns, developers can ensure that their applications meet security standards, adhere to regulations, and protect sensitive data. Implementing consistent security controls, monitoring user activities, and maintaining compliance with applicable regulations contribute to the overall security posture of the application and instill trust among users and stakeholders.

Localization and internationalization

Localization and internationalization are important cross-cutting concerns in software development that deal with making applications accessible and adaptable to different languages, cultures, and regions. These concerns involve enabling the localization of user interfaces, handling date and time formats, managing multilingual content, and accommodating cultural preferences. Here are some common examples of localization and internationalization that would be addressed as cross-cutting concerns:

- **User interface localization**: User interface localization involves adapting the application's user interface elements, such as labels, buttons, menus, and messages, to different languages and locales. This includes providing translations for user-facing text and ensuring proper rendering and layout for different character sets and writing systems. Addressing user interface localization as a cross-cutting concern involves designing the application with localization in mind, externalizing user interface strings, and utilizing localization frameworks or libraries that support resource files or key-value pairs for different languages.

- **Date and time formats**: Date and time formats vary across different regions and cultures. Addressing date and time formats as a cross-cutting concern involves correctly formatting and displaying dates, times, and time zones according to the user's locale and preferences. This can be achieved by utilizing localization libraries or functions that provide built-in date and time formatting capabilities or by leveraging platform-specific localization APIs.

- **Currency and number formats**: Currency and number formats also vary across different regions and locales. Addressing currency and number formats as a cross-cutting concern involves formatting and displaying currency values, decimal separators, and digit grouping based on the user's locale. This can be achieved by utilizing localization libraries or functions that support currency and number formatting rules specific to different cultures.

- **Multilingual content management**: Managing and displaying multilingual content, such as articles, product descriptions, or error messages, is an essential aspect of localization. Addressing multilingual content management as a cross-cutting concern involves designing a **content management system** (CMS) or utilizing localization tools that allow for the efficient translation and management of content in different languages. This includes supporting workflows for content translation, integrating with translation services or teams, and providing mechanisms for content versioning and synchronization across languages.

- **Cultural considerations**: Cultural considerations encompass various aspects, such as language directionality (for example, left-to-right or right-to-left), address formats, name formats, and cultural preferences. Addressing cultural considerations as a cross-cutting concern involves accommodating cultural differences in the application's design and behavior. This may include utilizing internationalization libraries or functions that handle language directionality, allowing for customizable address formats, and providing options for personal name formats based on different cultural conventions.

- **Time zone handling**: Time zone handling is crucial for applications serving users across different regions. Addressing time zone handling as a cross-cutting concern involves correctly capturing, storing, and displaying date and time values relative to the user's time zone. This includes utilizing time zone databases, converting time values between time zones, and providing mechanisms for users to set their preferred time zone.

To handle localization and internationalization as cross-cutting concerns, developers can follow these practices:

- Design the application with localization in mind from the beginning, considering factors such as text expansion, layout flexibility, and language support.

- Externalize user-facing strings and utilize resource files or key-value pairs to store localized text. This allows for easy translation and adaptation to different languages.

- Utilize localization frameworks or libraries that provide built-in functionality for user interface localization, date and time formatting, and number and currency formatting.

- Support customizable language and locale settings for users to choose their preferred language and cultural preferences.

- Collaborate with localization teams or services to ensure accurate and contextually appropriate translations of user interface text and content.

- Test the application with different language settings, regions, and locales to identify and address any localization-related issues.

- Keep language and locale-specific content separate from the application's logic and functionality, allowing for easier updates and additions of new translations.

- Provide mechanisms for users to switch languages or locales within the application, allowing them to seamlessly navigate between different language versions.

- Consider cultural considerations when designing features or interactions, such as accommodating different name formats or addressing cultural sensitivities.

- Stay up to date with language and cultural conventions, as they may evolve over time. Regularly update language packs, localization resources, and translation files to reflect changes and improvements.

- Consider the use of machine translation technologies or services to streamline the translation process and support faster localization updates.

- Document localization processes and guidelines to ensure consistency and facilitate future updates or maintenance.

By addressing localization and internationalization as cross-cutting concerns, developers can create applications that cater to a global audience, providing a localized and culturally relevant user experience. Implementing robust localization practices and utilizing appropriate tools and frameworks simplifies the process of adapting the application to different languages, regions, and cultural requirements, ultimately increasing the accessibility and usability of the application for users around the world.

Logging and monitoring

Logging and monitoring are essential cross-cutting concerns in software development that involve capturing and analyzing application events, errors, and performance metrics. These concerns encompass logging relevant information, detecting anomalies, and ensuring the stability and reliability of the application.

To handle logging and monitoring as cross-cutting concerns, developers can follow these practices:

- Utilize logging frameworks or libraries that provide flexible and configurable logging capabilities. These frameworks often offer log levels, log formatting options, and various logging targets.

- Implement centralized logging mechanisms that can capture and store log entries consistently across different components or modules of the application.

- Define and follow logging conventions and best practices to ensure consistent and meaningful log messages across the application. This includes capturing relevant contextual information, timestamps, and appropriate log levels for different types of events.

- Implement structured exception handling to capture and log detailed error information when exceptions occur. Use exception-handling frameworks or custom error handlers to centralize error logging and reporting.

- Set up performance monitoring tools or instrumentation to collect performance metrics and track application performance. Analyze the collected data to identify performance bottlenecks and optimize resource usage.

- Integrate security monitoring tools or services to detect and respond to security-related events or anomalies. Implement log analysis and correlation techniques to identify potential security breaches or suspicious activities.

- Utilize infrastructure monitoring tools or services to monitor the health, availability, and performance of the application's underlying infrastructure components. Set up alerts or notifications to proactively address issues and ensure optimal system performance.

- Implement log analysis and reporting mechanisms to extract meaningful insights from the collected log data. Utilize log analysis tools or log management platforms to search, filter, and generate reports based on specific criteria or patterns.

- Regularly review and analyze log data to identify recurring issues, spot anomalies, and improve the application's stability, performance, and security.

- Ensure proper log retention and archival practices based on compliance or regulatory requirements.

By addressing logging and monitoring as cross-cutting concerns, developers can gain valuable insights into their application's behavior, diagnose issues more effectively, and proactively respond to security incidents or performance bottlenecks. Logging and monitoring play a crucial role in maintaining the reliability, security, and performance of the application throughout its life cycle.

Summary

Throughout this chapter, we have explored the definition and importance of cross-cutting concerns in software development. These concerns are FRs that affect multiple parts of an application and can have a significant impact on its overall design and quality.

We have examined various common examples of cross-cutting concerns, including logging, error handling and exception management, security and authorization, caching, performance optimization, transaction management, validation, localization and internationalization, and monitoring. These concerns often require repetitive code or modifications throughout the application, making them challenging to manage and maintain.

By properly handling cross-cutting concerns, developers can improve code maintainability, enhance system performance, increase security, and facilitate internationalization and localization efforts. Identifying and addressing these concerns early in the development process is crucial for building high-quality and maintainable applications.

In summary, cross-cutting concerns are integral to software development, and effectively managing them is essential for developing robust and efficient applications. Using AOP techniques, developers can successfully address these concerns, resulting in modular and maintainable software systems

We will take a deeper look at AOP with code examples in *Chapter 9*, as we cover the PostSharp framework.

As we bring this chapter to a close, let's summarize what we have learned about addressing cross-cutting concerns.

Questions

Answer the following questions to test your knowledge of this chapter:

1. Define cross-cutting concerns.
2. Why are cross-cutting concerns important?
3. How do cross-cutting concerns impact software development?
4. List some examples of cross-cutting concerns.

Further reading

Here are some recommended resources for further reading on C# cross-cutting concerns and AOP:

- *Aspect-Oriented Programming in .NET* by *Matthew D. Groves*: This book provides a good introduction to AOP and how it can be applied in .NET applications.

- *AOP in .NET: Practical Aspect-Oriented Programming* by *Matthew D. Groves*: Another resource by Matthew Groves, this book focuses specifically on applying AOP in .NET, which is a common approach to managing cross-cutting concerns.

- *Dependency Injection in .NET* by *Mark Seemann*: While not specifically focused on cross-cutting concerns, this book covers the principles of **dependency injection** (**DI**), which is a technique commonly used to address cross-cutting concerns in a modular way.

- *Pro .NET Benchmarking: The Art of Performance Measurement* by *Andrey Akinshin*: Performance is a cross-cutting concern that often needs attention. This book can help you understand how to measure and improve the performance of your C# applications.

- **Pluralsight courses**: Pluralsight offers various courses on C# and .NET development. Courses such as *Applied Asynchronous Programming with Patterns in C#* or *Building Scalable APIs with GraphQL and Relay in C#* may touch upon cross-cutting concerns.

- **Official Microsoft documentation**: The official Microsoft documentation is always a valuable resource. Check the documentation for specific frameworks and libraries you are using, such as ASP.NET Core, for guidance on handling cross-cutting concerns.

- **Articles and blogs**: Explore blogs and articles from the C# and .NET community. Websites such as Medium, Dev.to, and personal blogs of experienced developers often contain insightful articles on various aspects of C# development, including dealing with cross-cutting concerns.

- **GitHub repositories**: Look for open source projects on GitHub that address cross-cutting concerns. Studying the code of well-designed projects can provide practical insights into how to handle these concerns effectively.

These resources should provide you with a solid foundation and practical insights into C# cross-cutting concerns and AOP.

9

AOP with PostSharp

Aspect-oriented programming (AOP) can be used with **object-oriented programming (OOP)**. An aspect is an attribute applied to classes, methods, parameters, and properties that, at compile time, weaves code into the class, method, parameter, or property to which it is applied. This approach allows the cross-cutting concerns of a program to be moved from the business source code to a class library. Concerns are added where needed as attributes. The compiler then weaves the required code in at runtime. This keeps your business code small and readable. In this chapter, we will be using PostSharp.

We will be covering the following topics:

- How AOP works with PostSharp
- Extending the aspect framework
- Project – Cross-cutting concerns reusable library
- PostSharp and build pipeline considerations
- Dynamic AOP with `Castle.DynamicProxy`

By the end of the chapter, you will understand the following:

- How to use PostSharp in Visual Studio
- How to create your own reusable library that utilizes the PostSharp AOP framework

Let's review the technical requirements for following along with this chapter.

Technical requirements

You will need the following tools installed to follow along with this tutorial:

- Visual Studio Community Edition
- PostSharp (essentials): `https://www.postsharp.net/`

- PostSharp documentation: `https://doc.postsharp.net/?pk_vid=919254c8a0a73ae51691117837edbc2f`

- The book's source code: `https://github.com/PacktPublishing/Clean-Code-with-CSharp-Second-Edition/tree/main/CH09/CH09_AopWithPostSharp`

AOP

AOP is a programming paradigm that aims to modularize and manage cross-cutting concerns in software systems. In traditional programming approaches, cross-cutting concerns, such as logging, security, transaction management, and error handling, tend to be scattered across different modules or components, leading to code duplication and tangled dependencies. AOP provides a way to encapsulate and centralize these concerns, making the code more modular, maintainable, and easier to understand.

At its core, AOP introduces a new construct called an "aspect." An aspect represents a modular unit of cross-cutting functionality that can be applied to multiple parts of a system. It allows developers to separate concerns related to the core functionality of the system from cross-cutting concerns. This separation enhances code modularity and improves the system's overall structure.

AOP achieves this separation by introducing the concept of "join points" and "pointcuts." A join point represents a specific point in the execution of a program, such as method invocations, object creations, or exception handling. A pointcut is a declarative expression that specifies which join points should be intercepted by an aspect. By defining pointcuts, developers can specify locations in the code where the cross-cutting concerns need to be applied.

Once pointcuts are defined, AOP frameworks provide mechanisms to intercept the execution at those join points and execute the corresponding aspect code. The aspect code, often referred to as "advice," contains the behavior associated with the cross-cutting concern. This advice can be executed before, after, or around the join points, allowing developers to inject additional functionality without modifying core business logic.

AOP also introduces the concept of "weaving." Weaving is the process of applying aspects to the target code base, either statically or dynamically. In static weaving, an aspect is woven into the code base during the compilation phase, resulting in modified bytecode or source code. Dynamic weaving, on the other hand, applies aspects during runtime, often through the use of proxies or bytecode manipulation techniques:

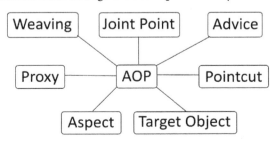

Figure 9.1: Elements of AOP

By utilizing AOP, developers can address cross-cutting concerns more effectively. Some benefits of using AOP include the following:

1. **Modularity**: AOP allows for cleaner **separation of concerns (SoC)** by encapsulating cross-cutting functionality in aspects. This leads to modular code that is easier to develop, maintain, and test.

2. **Code reusability**: Aspects can be reused across multiple components or modules, reducing code duplication and promoting code reuse. This results in more efficient and maintainable code bases.

3. **Improved readability**: AOP helps to improve code readability by removing the clutter of cross-cutting concerns from core business logic. Aspects provide a centralized and explicit way of expressing such concerns, making the code base easier to understand.

4. **Runtime configuration**: AOP frameworks often provide mechanisms for configuring aspects at runtime. This flexibility allows developers to enable or disable specific aspects or adjust their behavior without modifying the underlying code base.

5. **SoC**: AOP promotes a clear separation between the core functionality of the system and cross-cutting concerns. This separation makes the code base more modular and maintainable, facilitating collaboration among developers working on different aspects of the system.

AOP is a programming paradigm that provides a powerful mechanism to address cross-cutting concerns in software systems. By encapsulating these concerns in aspects and applying them to join points through weaving, AOP enhances code modularity, maintainability, and readability. It enables developers to focus on core business logic while handling cross-cutting concerns in a modular and reusable manner.

AOP frameworks

AOP frameworks, such as PostSharp, can be a valuable tool for C# programmers to keep business logic separate from AOP concerns. PostSharp integrates directly into the C# build process and provides a wide range of AOP features that can be applied to the code base.

Here's how PostSharp can be utilized to achieve separation between business logic and AOP concerns:

*   **Attribute-based programming**: PostSharp allows developers to define aspects using attributes. By applying these attributes to classes, methods, or properties, developers can specify the cross-cutting concerns that need to be applied. This approach keeps AOP concerns clearly separated from business logic code.

*   **Compile-time weaving**: PostSharp performs weaving during the compilation process, modifying **intermediate language** (IL) code before it gets compiled into the final executable. This means that aspects are applied at compile time, enabling early validation and minimizing runtime overhead. The modified IL code contains the woven aspects, while the original business logic remains untouched.

> **Note**
> Understanding the distinction between compile-time modification and dynamic AOP is crucial when considering unit-testing strategies. Compile-time modifications provide a clear and predictable testing environment, while dynamic AOP introduces runtime variability that requires careful consideration in the testing process.

- **Aspect composition**: PostSharp supports aspect composition, allowing multiple aspects to be combined and applied to the same code element. This feature enables developers to apply multiple cross-cutting concerns without introducing code duplication or tangled dependencies. Aspects can be applied individually or as a group, providing flexibility in managing different AOP concerns.

- **SoC**: PostSharp helps C# programmers to separate business logic from AOP concerns by keeping aspects separate from the core code base. Developers can define and maintain aspects independently, making it easier to manage and modify the AOP behavior without directly modifying business logic. This separation enhances code modularity and improves the overall structure of the system.

- **Configuration and fine-grained control**: PostSharp provides configuration options that allow developers to fine-tune the behavior of aspects. Developers can specify when and where aspects should be applied, enable or disable specific aspects based on runtime conditions, or provide custom parameters to influence aspect behavior. This configurability helps in keeping business logic clean and unaffected by the specifics of AOP concerns.

- **Integration with existing code bases**: PostSharp seamlessly integrates with existing C# code bases, requiring minimal changes to the code structure. Developers can apply aspects selectively to specific classes or methods, ensuring that only necessary parts of the code are affected by AOP concerns. This integration facilitates the adoption of AOP in both new and legacy projects without disrupting the existing code base.

By utilizing PostSharp or similar AOP frameworks, C# programmers can effectively keep business logic separate from AOP concerns. They can define and manage aspects independently, apply them selectively, and easily modify AOP behavior without directly modifying the core code base. This separation promotes code modularity, maintainability, and readability, making it easier to manage cross-cutting concerns in C# applications. Let's now look at how AOP works with PostSharp.

How AOP works with PostSharp

You add the PostSharp package to your project. Then, you annotate your code with attributes. The C# compiler builds your code into binary, and then PostSharp analyzes the binary and injects the implementation of aspects. Although binaries are modified with injected code at compile time, your project's source code remains unaltered. This means you can keep your code nice, clean, and simple, which in turn makes maintenance, reuse, and extending existing code bases much easier in the long term.

PostSharp has some really good ready-made patterns for you to utilize. These cover **Model-View-ViewModel (MVVM)**, caching, multithreading, logging and architecture validation, and more. But the good news is that if none of these meets your requirements, then you can automate your own patterns by extending the aspect framework and/or the architecture framework.

With the aspect framework, you develop your simple or composite aspect, apply it to the code, and validate its usage. As for the architectural framework, you develop your custom architectural constraints. Before we delve into cross-cutting concerns, let's briefly take a look at extending the aspect and architectural frameworks.

You need to add the `PostSharp.Redist` NuGet package when writing aspects and attributes. Once done, if you find that your attributes and aspects are not working, then right-click on the project and select **Add PostSharp to Project**. After you've done this, your aspects should work.

Extending the aspect framework

In this section, we are going to develop a simple aspect and apply it to some code. Then, we will validate the usage of our aspect.

Developing our aspect

Our aspect will be a simple one that is composed of a single transformation. We will derive our aspect from a primitive aspect class. Then, we will override some methods known as advice. If you would like to know how to create a composite aspect, you can read how to do so at `https://doc.postsharp.net/complex-aspects`.

Injecting behaviors before and after the method execution

The `OnMethodBoundaryAspect` aspect implements the decorator pattern. With this aspect, you can execute logic before and after the execution of a target method. The following table provides a list of advice methods that are available in the `OnMethodBoundaryAspect` class:

Advice method	Description
`OnEntry(MethodExe-cutionArgs)`	Used when the method's execution starts, before any user code.
`OnSuccess(MethodEx-ecutionArgs)`	Used when the method's execution succeeds (that is, returns without an exception), after any user code.
`OnException(Metho-dExecutionArgs)`	Used when the method execution fails with an exception, after any user code. It is equivalent to a `catch` block.
`OnExit(MethodExecu-tionArgs)`	Method executed after the body of methods to which this aspect is applied, even when the method exists with an exception (this method is invoked from the finally block).

Table 9. 1: List of active methods

For our simple aspect, we are going to look at all methods in use. Before we begin, add PostSharp to your project. If you have already downloaded PostSharp, you can right-click on your project and then select **Add PostSharp to Project**. After that, add a new folder to your project called `Aspects`, and then add a new class called `LoggingAspect`:

```
[PSerializable]
public class LoggingAspect : OnMethodBoundaryAspect { }
```

The `[PSerializeable]` attribute is a custom attribute that, when applied to a type, causes PostSharp to generate a serializer for use by `PortableFormatter`. Now, override the `OnEntry` method:

```
public override void OnEntry(MethodExecutionArgs args) {
    Console.WriteLine("The {0} method has been entered.", args.Method.
Name);
}
```

The `OnEntry` method is executed before any user code. Now, override the `OnSuccess` method:

```
publicoverridevoid OnSuccess(MethodExecutionArgs args) {
    Console.WriteLine("The {0} method executed successfully.", args.
Method.Name);
}
```

The `OnSuccess` method runs after the user code has completed without an exception. Override the `OnExit` method:

```
Public override void OnExit(MethodExecutionArgs args) {
    Console.WriteLine("The {0} method has exited.", args.Method.Name);
}
```

The `OnExit` method executes when the user method completes successfully or unsuccessfully and exits. It is equivalent to a `finally` block. Finally, override the `OnException` method:

```
publicoverridevoid OnException(MethodExecutionArgs args) {
    Console.WriteLine("An exception was thrown in {0}.", args.Method.
Name);
}
```

The `OnException` method executes when the method execution fails with an exception, after any user code. It is equivalent to a `catch` block.

The next step is to write two methods we can apply `LoggingAspect` to. We'll add `SuccessfulMethod`:

```
[LoggingAspect]
private static void SuccessfulMethod() {
    Console.WriteLine("Hello World, I am a success!");
}
```

`SuccessfulMethod` uses `LoggingAspect` and prints a message to the console. Now, let's add `FailedMethod`:

```
[LoggingAspect]
private static void FailedMethod() {
    Console.WriteLine("Hello World, I am a failure!");
    var x = 1;
    var y = 0;
    var z = x / y;
}
```

`FailedMethod` uses `LoggingAspect` and prints a message to the console. Then, it performs a division-by-zero operation, which results in `DivideByZeroException`. Call both of these methods from your `Main` method, and then run through your project. You should see the following output:

```
The SuccessfulMethod has been entered.
Hello World, I am a success!
The SuccessfulMethod executed successfully
The FailedMethod has been entered.
Hello World, I am a failure!
```

An exception was thrown in FailMethod. At this point, the debugger will cause the program to exit. That's it. As you can see, creating your own PostSharp aspects to meet your needs is a simple process. Now, we will look at adding our own architectural constraint.

Extending the architectural framework

An architectural constraint is the adoption of custom design patterns that must be respected across all modules. We will implement a scalar constraint that validates an element of code.

Our scalar constraint, called `BusinessRulePatternValidation`, will validate that any class deriving from the `BusinessRule` class must have a nested class named `Factory`. Start by adding a `BusinessRulePatternValidation` class:

```
[MulticastAttributeUsage(MulticastTargets.Class, Inheritance =
MulticastInheritance.Strict)]
publicclass BusinessRulePatternValidation : ScalarConstraint { }
```

`MulticastAttributeUsage` designates that this validation aspect will only work with classes and inheritance allowed. Let's override the `ValidateCode` method:

```
Public override void CodeValidation(object target)
{
    var targetType = (Type)target;
    if (targetType.GetNestedType("Factory") == null)
    {
```

```
        Message.Write(
            targetType, SeverityType.Warning,
            "10",
            "You must include a 'Factory' as a nested type for {0}.",
            targetType.DeclaringType,
            targetType.Name);
    }
}
```

Our `ValidateCode` method checks whether the target object has a nested `Factory` type. If the `Factory` type is not present, then an exception message is written to the output window. Add a `BusinessRule` class:

```
[BusinessRulePatternValidation]
public class BusinessRule  { }
```

The `BusinessRule` class is empty and devoid of `Factory`. It has our `BusinessRulePatternValidation` attribute assigned to it, which is an architectural constraint. Build your project, and you will see a message in the output window. We will now start to build a reusable class library that you can extend and use in your own projects to address cross-cutting concerns.

Project – Cross-cutting concerns reusable library

In this section, we will be working through writing a reusable library for addressing various cross-cutting concerns. It will have limited functionality, but it will give you the knowledge you need to further expand the project for your own needs. The class library you will be creating will be a .NET standard library so that it can be used for apps that target both .NET Framework and .NET Core. You will also create a .NET Framework console application to see the library in action.

The concerns we will be handling as we progress through the project are as follows:

- Caching
- Logging
- Exception handling
- Security
- Validation
- Resource pool
- Configuration settings
- Instrumentation

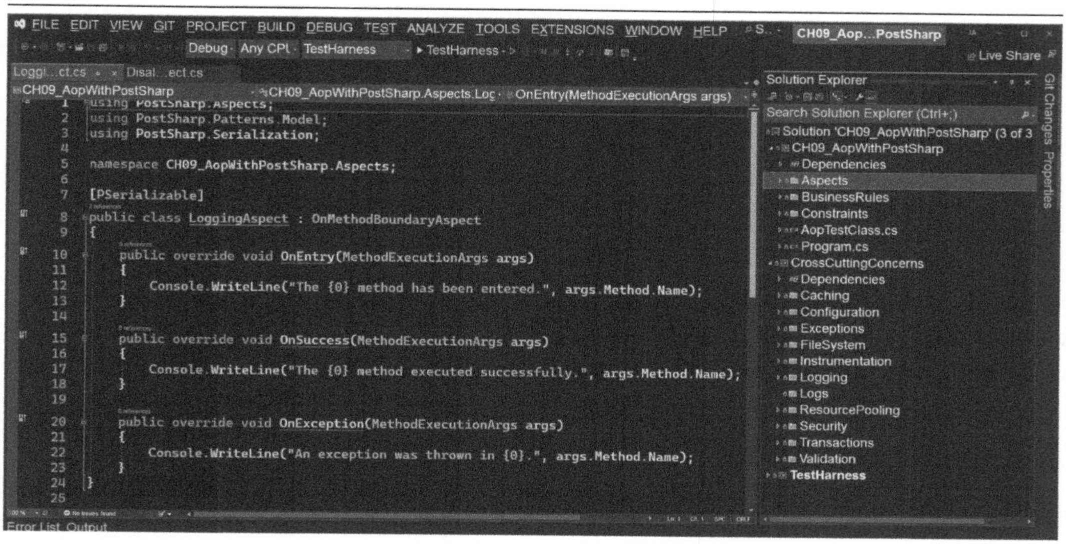

Figure 9.2: Screenshot of the project you'll be creating

Start by creating a new .NET standard class library called `CrossCuttingConcerns`. Then, add a .NET Framework console application to `TestHarness` solution and select **Do not use high-level statements**. We will be adding reusable functionality to address various concerns, starting with caching.

Adding a caching concern

Caching is a storage technique for improving performance when accessing various kinds of resources. The cache used can be memory, a filesystem, or a database. The type of cache you use will be dependent on the needs of the project. For our demonstration, we will be using memory caching to keep things simple.

Add a folder called `Caching` to the `CrossCuttingConcerns` project. Then, add a class called `MemoryCache`. Add the following NuGet packages to the project:

- `PostSharp`

- `PostSharp.Patterns.Common`

- `PostSharp.Patterns.Diagnostics`

- `System.Runtime.Caching`

Update the `MemoryCache` class with the following code:

```
public static class MemoryCache {
    public static T GetItem<T>(string itemName, TimeSpan timeInCache,
Func<T> itemCacheFunction) {
        var cache = System.Runtime.Caching.MemoryCache.Default;
        var cachedItem = (T) cache[itemName];
        if (cachedItem != null) return cachedItem;
```

```
        var policy = new CacheItemPolicy {AbsoluteExpiration =
DateTimeOffset.Now.Add(timeInCache)};
        cachedItem = itemCacheFunction();
        cache.Set(itemName, cachedItem, policy);
        return cachedItem;
    }
}
```

The GetItem method takes the name of the cached item, itemName, the length of time the item is to remain in the cache, timeInCache, and the function to call to place the item in the cache if it is not already there, itemCacheFunction. Add a new class to the TestHarness project and call it TestClass. Then, add GetCachedItem and GetMessage methods, as shown:

```
public string GetCachedItem() {
    return MemoryCache.GetItem<string>("Message", TimeSpan.
FromSeconds(30), GetMessage);
}
private string GetMessage() {
    return "Hello, world of cache!";
}
```

The GetCachedItem method gets a string called "Message" from the cache. If it is not in the cache, then it will be stored in the cache by the GetMessage method for 30 seconds.

Update your Main method in the Program class to call the GetCachedItem method, as shown:

```
var harness = new TestClass();
Console.WriteLine(harness.GetCachedItem());
Console.WriteLine(harness.GetCachedItem());
Thread.Sleep(TimeSpan.FromSeconds(1));
Console.WriteLine(harness.GetCachedItem());
```

The first call to GetCachedItem stores the item in the cache and then returns it. The second call obtains the item from the cache and returns it. The sleeping thread invalidates the cache, and so the last call stores the item in the cache before returning it.

Adding file logging capabilities

In our project, logging, auditing, and instrumentation processes will send their output to a text file. So, we will need a class to manage adding files if they don't exist, and then adding the output to those files and saving them. Add a FileSystem folder to the class library. Then, add a class called LogFile. Set the class as public static and add the following member variables:

```
private static string _location = string.Empty;
private static string _filename = string.Empty;
private static string _file = string.Empty;
```

The _location variable is assigned to the folder for the entry assembly. The _filename variable is assigned the name of the file with the file extension. We need to add a Logs folder at runtime (if it does not exist). So, we will add an AddDirectory method to the FileSystem class:

```
private static void AddDirectory() {
    if (!Directory.Exists(_location))
        Directory.CreateDirectory("Logs");
}
```

The AddDirectory method checks whether the location exists. If it does not exist, then the directory is created. Next, we need to deal with adding a file if it does not exist. So, add an AddFile method:

```
private static void AddFile() {
    _file = Path.Combine(_location, _filename);
    if (File.Exists(_file)) return;
    using (File.Create($"Logs\\{_filename}")) {
    }
}
```

In the AddFile method, we combine the location and filename. If the filename already exists, then we exit the method; otherwise, we create a file. If we don't use the using statement, we will encounter IOException when we create our first record, but subsequent saves will be fine. So, by using the using statement, we avoid the exception and log the data. We can now write a method that actually saves the data to a file. Add an AppendTextToFile method:

```
public static void AppendTextToFile(string filename, string text) {
    _location = $"{Path.GetDirectoryName(Assembly.GetEntryAssembly()?.
Location)}\\Logs";
    _filename = filename;
    AddDirectory();
    AddFile();
    File.AppendAllText(_file, text);
}
```

The AppendTextToFile method takes a filename and text and sets the location to that of the entry assembly. It then ensures that the file and directory exist. Then, it saves the text to the specified file. Our file logging capabilities are now taken care of, so now, we can move on to look at our logging concern.

Adding a logging concern

Most applications need some form of logging. The usual methods of logging are to the console, filesystem, event logs, and database. In our project, we will only focus on console and text file logging. Add a folder called `Logging` to the class library. Then, add a file called `ConsoleLoggingAspect` and update it as follows:

```
[PSerializable]
public class ConsoleLoggingAspect : OnMethodBoundaryAspect { }
```

The `[PSerializable]` attribute informs PostSharp to generate a serializer for use by `PortableFormatter`. `ConsoleLoggingAspect` inherits from `OnMethodBoundaryAspect`. The `OnMethodBoundaryAspect` class has methods that we can override to add code before a method body executes, after a method body executes, when a method body executes successfully, and when an exception is encountered. We will override these methods to output a message to the console. This can be a very useful tool when it comes to debugging to see whether code actually gets called and whether it successfully completes or encounters an exception. We will start by overriding the `OnEntry` method:

```
public override void OnEntry(MethodExecutionArgs args) {
    Console.WriteLine($"Method: {args.Method.Name}, OnEntry().");
}
```

The `OnEntry` method executes before the body of our method does, and our override prints out the name of the method being executed and its own name. Next, we'll override the `OnExit` method:

```
public override void OnExit(MethodExecutionArgs args) {
    Console.WriteLine($"Method: {args.Method.Name}, OnExit().");
}
```

The `OnExit` method executes after the body of our method has finished executing, and our override prints out the name of the method that has been executed and its own name. Now, we'll add an `OnSuccess` method:

```
public override void OnSuccess(MethodExecutionArgs args) {
    Console.WriteLine($"Method: {args.Method.Name}, OnSuccess().");
}
```

The `OnSuccess` method executes after the body of the method it is applied to has finished and returns without exception. When our override executes, it prints out the name of the executed method and its own name. The last method we will override is the `OnException` method:

```
public override void OnException(MethodExecutionArgs args) {
    Console.WriteLine($"An exception was thrown in {args.Method.Name}.
{args}");
}
```

The OnException method executes when an exception is encountered, and in our override, we print out the name of the method and the argument's object. To apply the attribute, use ConsoleLoggingAspect. To add a text file logging aspect, add a class called TextFileLoggingAspect. TextFileLoggingAspect is identical to ConsoleLoggingAspect, apart from the contents of the overridden methods. The OnEntry, OnExit, and OnSuccess methods call the LogFile.AppendTextToFile method and append the contents to the Log.txt file. The OnException method does the same, except it appends the contents to the Exception.log file. Here is the OnEntry example:

```
public override void OnEntry(MethodExecutionArgs args) {
    LogFile.AppendTextToFile("Log.txt", $"\nMethod: {args.Method.
Name}, OnEntry().");
}
```

That is our logging taken care of. Now, we'll move on to adding our exceptions concern.

Adding an exception-handling concern

It is inevitable with software that exceptions will be experienced by users of the software. So, there needs to be some way to log them. The normal way of logging exceptions is to store the error in a file on the user's system, such as with Exception.log. That's what we'll do in this section. We will inherit from the OnExceptionAspect class and write our exception data to the Exception.log file, which will be located in the Logs folder of our application.

OnExceptionAspect wraps the tagged method in a try-catch block. Add a new Exceptions folder to the class library, and then add a file called ExceptionAspect with the following code:

```
[PSerializable]
public class ExceptionAspect : OnExceptionAspect {
    public string Message { get; set; }
    public Type ExceptionType { get; set; }
    public FlowBehavior Behavior { get; set; }

    public override void OnException(MethodExecutionArgs args) {
        var message = args.Exception != null ? args.Exception.Message
: "Unknown error occurred.";
        LogFile.AppendTextToFile(
            "Exceptions.log", $"\n{DateTime.Now}: Method: {args.
Method}, Exception: {message}"
        );
        args.FlowBehavior = FlowBehavior.Continue;
    }

    public override Type GetExceptionType(System.Reflection.MethodBase
targetMethod) {
```

```
            return ExceptionType;
    }
}
```

The `ExceptionAspect` class is assigned the `[PSerializable]` aspect and inherits from `OnExceptionAspect`. We have three properties: `Message`, `ExceptionType`, and `FlowBehavior`. `Message` contains the exception message, `ExceptionType` contains the type of exception encountered, and `FlowBehavior` determines whether execution continues once the exception is handled or whether the process terminates. The `GetExceptionType` method returns the type of exception that was thrown. The `OnException` method starts by constructing an error message. It then logs the exception to the file by calling `LogFile.AppendTextToFile`. Finally, the flow of the exception's behavior is set to continue.

All you have to do to use the `ExceptionAspect` aspect is add it as an attribute to your method. We have now covered exception handling. So, we'll move on to adding our security concern.

Adding a security concern

The security needs will be specific to the project being worked on. The most common concerns are that users are authenticated and authorized to access and use various parts of the system. In this section, we will use the decorator pattern to implement a secure component with role-based methods.

Security is a very large subject in itself and beyond the scope of this book. There are many good APIs out there, such as the various Microsoft APIs. Refer to `https://docs.microsoft.com/en-us/dotnet/standard/security/` for more information, and for OAuth 2.0, refer to `https://oauth.net/code/dotnet/`. We will leave you to select and implement your own method of security. In this chapter, we simply add our own custom-defined security using the decorator pattern. You can use this as a base for implementing any of the aforementioned security methods.

Add a new folder called `Security`, and add an interface to it called `ISecureComponent`:

```
public interface ISecureComponent {
    void AddData(dynamic data);
    int EditData(dynamic data);
    int DeleteData(dynamic data);
    dynamic GetData(dynamic data);
}
```

Our secure component interface contains the preceding four methods, which are self-explanatory. The `dynamic` keyword means that any type of data can be passed in as a parameter and that any type of data can be returned from the `GetData` method. Next, we need an abstract class that implements the interface. Add a class called `DecoratorBase`, as shown:

```
public abstract class DecoratorBase : ISecureComponent {
    private readonly ISecureComponent _secureComponent;
```

```
    public DecoratorBase(ISecureComponent secureComponent)
    {
        _secureComponent = secureComponent;
    }
}
```

The `DecoratorBase` class implements `ISecureComponent`. We declare a member variable of the `ISecureComponent` type and set it in the default constructor. We need to add missing methods of `ISecureComponent`. Add an `AddData` method:

```
public virtual void AddData(dynamic data) {
    _secureComponent.AddData(data);
}
```

This method will take any type of data and then pass it into the call to the `AddData` method of `_secureComponent`. Add missing methods for `EditData`, `DeleteData`, and `GetData`. Now, add a class called `ConcreteSecureComponent`, which implements `ISecureComponent`. For each method, write a message to the console. For the `DeleteData` and `EditData` methods, also return a value of 1. Return "Hi!" for `GetData`. The `ConcreteSecureComponent` class is the class that executes the secure work that we are interested in.

> **Note**
>
> In the context of ASP.NET, you can use the `HTTPContext` class to obtain the currently logged-in user. For non-web applications such as console applications, you can use either `Thread.CurrentPrinciple` or `WindowsIdentity.GetCurrent()`, depending on the authentication mechanism being used.

We need a way to validate the user and obtain their role. The role will be checked before executing any methods. So, add the following struct:

```
public readonly struct Credentials {
    public static string Role { get; private set; }
    public Credentials(string username, string password) {
        switch (username)
        {
            case "System" when password == "Administrator":
                Role = "Administrator";
                break;
            case "End" when password == "User":
                Role = "Restricted";
                break;
            default:
```

```
            Role = "Imposter";
            break;
        }
    }
}
```

To keep things simple, the struct takes a username and password and sets the appropriate role. Restricted users have fewer privileges than administrators. The final class for our security concern is the `ConcreteDecorator` class. Add the class, as follows:

```
public class ConcreteDecorator : DecoratorBase {
    public ConcreteDecorator(ISecureComponent secureComponent) :
base(secureComponent) { }
}
```

The `ConcreteDecorator` class inherits the `DecoratorBase` class. Our constructor takes a type of `ISecureComponent` and passes it to the base class. Add an `AddData` method:

```
public override void AddData(dynamic data) {
    if (Credentials.Role.Contains("Administrator") || Credentials.
Role.Contains("Restricted")) {
        base.AddData((object)data);
    } else {
        throw new UnauthorizedAccessException("Unauthorized");
    }
}
```

`AddMethod` checks the user's role against the allowed `Administrator` and `Restricted` roles. If the user is in one of these roles, then the `AddData` method is executed in the base class; otherwise, `UnauthorizedAccessException` is thrown. The rest of the methods follow this same pattern. Override the rest of the methods, but make sure the `DeleteData` method can only be executed by administrators.

We will now put our security concerns to work. Create a new class called `ConcreteSecureComponent` that inherits from `ISecureComponent` and implement its methods. Add the following line to the top of the `Program` class:

```
private static readonly ConcreteDecorator ConcreteDecorator = new
ConcreteDecorator(new ConcreteSecureComponent());
```

We are declaring and instantiating a concrete decorator object and passing in a concrete secure object. This object will be referenced in our data methods. Update the `Main` method, as follows:

```
private static void Main(string[] _) {
    new Credentials("End", "User");
    DoSecureWork();
```

```
        Console.WriteLine("Press any key to exit.");
        Console.ReadKey();
}
```

We assign the username and password to the `Credentials` struct. This causes `Role` to be set. We then call the `DoWork` method. The `DoWork` method will be responsible for calling data methods. We then pause for the user to press any key and exit. Add a `DoSecureWork` method:

```
private static void DoSecureWork() {
    AddData();
}
```

The `DoSecureWork` method calls each of the data methods that call the data methods on the concrete decorator. Add an `AddData` method:

```
[ExceptionAspect]
private static void AddData() {
    ConcreteDecorator.AddData("Hello, world!");
}
```

The `ExceptionAspect` class is applied to the `AddData` method. This will ensure any errors are logged to the `Exceptions.log` file. The parameter is set to `true`, so an error message will also be printed in the console window. The method itself calls the `AddData` method on the `ConcreteDecorator` class. Add the rest of the methods by following the same procedure. Then, run your code. You should see the following output:

Press any key to continue.

We now have a working role-based object, complete with exception handling. Our next step is to implement our validation concern.

Adding a validation concern

All user-entered data should be validated as it could be malicious, incomplete, or in the wrong format. You need to ensure that your data is clean and cannot cause harm. For our demonstration concern, we will implement null validation. Start by adding a folder called `Validation` to the class library. Then, add a new class called `AllowNullAttribute`:

```
[AttributeUsage(AttributeTargets.Parameter | AttributeTargets.
ReturnValue | AttributeTargets.Property)]
public class AllowNullAttribute : Attribute { }
```

This attribute allows nulls on parameters, return values, and properties. Now, add a `ValidationFlags` enum to a new file of the same name:

```
[Flags]
public enum ValidationFlags {
    Properties = 1,
    Methods = 2,
    Arguments = 4,
    OutValues = 8,
    ReturnValues = 16,
    NonPublic = 32,
    AllPublicArguments = Properties | Methods | Arguments,
    AllPublic = AllPublicArguments | OutValues | ReturnValues,
    All = AllPublic | NonPublic
}
```

These flags are used to determine which items an aspect can be applied to. Next, we'll add a class called `ReflectionExtensions`:

```
public static class ReflectionExtensions {
    private static bool IsCustomAttributeDefined<T>(this
ICustomAttributeProvider value) where T
        : Attribute  {
        return value.IsDefined(typeof(T), false);
    }
    public static bool AllowsNull(this ICustomAttributeProvider value)
{
        return value.IsCustomAttributeDefined<AllowNullAttribute>();
    }
    public static bool MayNotBeNull(this ParameterInfo arg){
        return !arg.AllowsNull() && !arg.IsOptional && !arg.
ParameterType.IsValueType;
    }
}
```

The `IsCustomAttributeDefined` method returns `true` if the attribute type is defined on this member, and `false` otherwise. The `AllowsNull` method returns `true` if the `AllowNull` attribute is already applied, and `false` if not. The `MayNotBeNull` method checks to see whether nulls are allowed, whether the parameter is optional, and what type of value the parameter is. A Boolean value is then returned by performing logical AND operations on these values. It's time to add `DisallowNonNullAspect`:

```
[PSerializable]
public class DisallowNonNullAspect : OnMethodBoundaryAspect {
    private int[] _inputArgumentsToValidate;
    private int[] _outputArgumentsToValidate;
```

```
        private string[] _parameterNames;
        private bool _validateReturnValue;
        private string _memberName;
        private bool _isProperty;
        public DisallowNonNullAspect() : this(ValidationFlags.AllPublic) {
    }

        public DisallowNonNullAspect(ValidationFlags validationFlags) {
            ValidationFlags = validationFlags;
        }
        public ValidationFlags ValidationFlags { get; set; }
    }
```

This class has the `PSerializable` attribute applied to inform PostSharp to generate a serializer for `PortableFormatter`. It also inherits the `OnMethodBoundaryAspect` class. We then declare variables to hold the input and output arguments as validated parameter names, return value validation and the member name, and check whether the item being validated is a property. The default constructor is configured to allow the validator to be applied to all public members. We also have a constructor that takes a `ValidationFlags` value and a `ValidationFlags` property. Now, we'll override the `CompileTimeValidate` method:

```
public override bool CompileTimeValidate(MethodBase method) {
    var methodInformation = MethodInformation.
GetMethodInformation(method);
    var parameters = method.GetParameters();
    if (!ValidationFlags.HasFlag(ValidationFlags.NonPublic) &&
!methodInformation.IsPublic) return false;
    if (!ValidationFlags.HasFlag(ValidationFlags.Properties) &&
methodInformation.IsProperty)
        return false;
    if (!ValidationFlags.HasFlag(ValidationFlags.Methods) &&
!methodInformation.IsProperty) return false;
    _parameterNames = parameters.Select(p => p.Name).ToArray();
    _memberName = methodInformation.Name;
    _isProperty = methodInformation.IsProperty;


    var argumentsToValidate = parameters.Where(p => p.MayNotBeNull()).
ToArray();
    _inputArgumentsToValidate = ValidationFlags.
HasFlag(ValidationFlags.Arguments) ? argumentsToValidate.Where(p =>
!p.IsOut).Select(p => p.Position).ToArray() : new int[0];
    _outputArgumentsToValidate = ValidationFlags.
HasFlag(ValidationFlags.OutValues) ? argumentsToValidate.Where(p =>
p.ParameterType.IsByRef).Select(p => p.Position).ToArray() : new
int[0];
    if (!methodInformation.IsConstructor) {
        _validateReturnValue = ValidationFlags.
```

```
HasFlag(ValidationFlags.ReturnValues) && methodInformation.
ReturnParameter.MayNotBeNull();
    }
    var validationRequired = _validateReturnValue || _
inputArgumentsToValidate.Length > 0 || _outputArgumentsToValidate.
Length > 0;

    return validationRequired;
}
```

This method ensures that the aspect is correctly applied at compile time. If the aspect is applied to a wrong type of member, then `false` is returned. Otherwise, it returns `true`. We now override the `OnEntry` method:

```
public override void OnEntry(MethodExecutionArgs args) {
    foreach (var argumentPosition in _inputArgumentsToValidate) {
        if (args.Arguments[argumentPosition] != null) continue;
        var parameterName = _parameterNames[argumentPosition];

        if (_isProperty) {
            throw new ArgumentNullException(parameterName,
                $"Cannot set the value of property '{_memberName}' to
null.");
        } else {
            throw new ArgumentNullException(parameterName);
        }
    }
}
```

This method checks the input arguments to validate. If any arguments are `null`, then `ArgumentNullException` is thrown; otherwise, the method exits without throwing an exception. Let's override the `OnSuccess` method now:

```
public override void OnSuccess(MethodExecutionArgs args) {
    foreach (var argumentPosition in _outputArgumentsToValidate) {
        if (args.Arguments[argumentPosition] != null) continue;
        var parameterName = _parameterNames[argumentPosition];
        throw new InvalidOperationException($"Out parameter
'{parameterName}' is null.");
    }

    if (!_validateReturnValue || args.ReturnValue != null) return;

    if (_isProperty) {
        throw new InvalidOperationException($"Return value of property
'{_memberName}' is null.");
```

```
    }
        throw new InvalidOperationException($"Return value of method '{
    memberName}' is null.");
    }
```

The `OnSuccess` method validates the output parameters to validate. If any arguments are `null`, then `InvalidOperationException` will be thrown. The next thing we need to do is add a private class for extracting method information. Add the following class to the bottom of the `DisallowNonNullAspect` class before the closing brace:

```
private class MethodInformation { }
```

Add the following three constructors to the `MethodInformation` class:

```
    private MethodInformation(ConstructorInfo constructor) :
    this((MethodBase)constructor) {
        IsConstructor = true;
        Name = constructor.Name;
    }

    private MethodInformation(MethodInfo method) : this((MethodBase)
    method) {
        IsConstructor = false;
        Name = method.Name;
        if (method.IsSpecialName &&
        (Name.StartsWith("set_", StringComparison.Ordinal) ||
        Name.StartsWith("get_", StringComparison.Ordinal))) {
            Name = Name.Substring(4);
            IsProperty = true;
        }
        ReturnParameter = method.ReturnParameter;
    }

    private MethodInformation(MethodBase method)
    {
        IsPublic = method.IsPublic;
    }
```

These constructors differentiate between constructors and methods and perform the necessary initialization of the method. Add the following method:

```
private static MethodInformation CreateInstance(MethodInfo method) {
    return new MethodInformation(method);
}
```

The `CreateInstance` method creates a new instance of the `MethodInformation` class based on the `MethodInfo` data of the method passed in and returns that instance. Add a `GetMethodInformation` method:

```
public static MethodInformation GetMethodInformation(MethodBase
methodBase) {
    var ctor = methodBase as ConstructorInfo;
    if (ctor != null) return new MethodInformation(ctor);
    var method = methodBase as MethodInfo;
    return method == null ? null : CreateInstance(method);
}
```

This method casts `methodBase` to `ConstructorInfo` and checks for `null`. If `ctor` is not `null`, then a new `MethodInformation` class is generated based on the constructor. However, if `ctor` is `null`, then `methodBase` is cast to `MethodInfo`. If the method is not `null`, then the `CreateInstance` method is called, passing in the method. Otherwise, `null` is returned. Finally, add the following properties to the class:

```
public string Name { get; private set; }
public bool IsProperty { get; private set; }
public bool IsPublic { get; private set; }
public bool IsConstructor { get; private set; }
public ParameterInfo ReturnParameter { get; private set; }
```

These properties are properties of the method that has the aspect applied. We have now finished writing our validation aspect. You can now use the validator to allow nulls by attaching the `AllowNull` attribute. You can disallow nulls by attaching `DisallowNonNullAspect`. Now, we'll add our transaction concern.

Adding a transaction concern

Transactions are processes that must run to completion or roll back. Add a new `Transactions` folder to the class library, and then add a `RequiresTransactionAspect` class:

```
[PSerializable]
[AttributeUsage(AttributeTargets.Method)]
public sealed class RequiresTransactionAspect : OnMethodBoundaryAspect
{
    public override void OnEntry(MethodExecutionArgs args) {
        var transactionScope = new
TransactionScope(TransactionScopeOption.Required);
        args.MethodExecutionTag = transactionScope;
    }

    public override void OnSuccess(MethodExecutionArgs args) {
        var transactionScope = (TransactionScope)args.
MethodExecutionTag;
```

```
            transactionScope.Complete();
        }

    public override void OnExit(MethodExecutionArgs args) {
        var transactionScope = (TransactionScope)args.
MethodExecutionTag;
        transactionScope.Dispose();
    }
}
```

The OnEntry method starts the transaction, the OnSuccess method completes the transaction, and the OnExit method disposes of the transaction. To use the aspect, add RequiresTransactionAspect to your method. To log any exceptions that prevent the completion of the transaction, you can also assign the [ExceptionAspect(consoleOutput: false)] aspect. Next, we'll add our resource pool concern.

Adding a resource pool concern

Resource pools are a good way to improve performance when multiple instances of an object are expensive to create and destroy. We will create a very simple resource pool for our needs. Add a folder called ResourcePooling, and then add a ResourcePool class:

```
public class ResourcePool<T> {
    private readonly ConcurrentBag<T> _resources;
    private readonly Func<T> _resourceGenerator;

    public ResourcePool(Func<T> resourceGenerator) {
        _resourceGenerator = resourceGenerator ??
                            throw new
ArgumentNullException(nameof(resourceGenerator));
        _resources = new ConcurrentBag<T>();
    }

    public T Get() => _resources.TryTake(out T item) ? item : _
resourceGenerator();
    public void Return(T item) => _resources.Add(item);
}
```

This class creates a new resource generator and stores resources in ConcurrentBag. When an item is requested, it issues a resource from the pool. If one does not exist, then it is created, added to the pool, and issued to the caller:

```
var pool = new ResourcePool<Course>(() => new Course()); // Create a
new pool of Course objects.
var course = pool.Get(); // Get course from pool.
pool.Return(course); // Return the course to the pool.
```

The code you've just seen shows you how to use the `ResourcePool` class to create a pool, obtain a resource, and return it to the pool.

Adding a configuration settings concern

Configuration settings should always be centralized. Since desktop applications store their settings in the `app.config` file and web applications store their settings in `Web.config`, we can use `ConfigurationManager` to access the application settings. Add the `System.Configuration.ConfigurationNuGet` library to your class library and test the harness. Then, add a folder called `Configuration` and the following `Settings` class:

```
public static class Settings {
    public static string GetAppSetting(string key) {
        return System.Configuration.ConfigurationManager.
AppSettings[key];
    }

    public static void SetAppSettings(this string key, string value) {
        System.Configuration.ConfigurationManager.AppSettings[key] =
value;
    }
}
```

This class will get and set app settings in the `Web.config` file and the `App.config` file. To include the class in your files, add the following `using` statement:

```
using static CrossCuttingConcerns.Configuration.Settings;
```

The following code shows you how to use the methods:

```
Console.WriteLine(GetAppSetting("Greeting"));
"Greeting".SetAppSettings("Goodbye, my friends!");
Console.WriteLine(GetAppSetting("Greeting"));
```

Using the static import, you don't have to include the class prefix. You can extend the `Settings` class to get connection strings or to do whatever configuration you need in your apps.

Adding an instrumentation concern

Our final cross-cutting concern is that of instrumentation. We use instrumentation to profile our application and see how long it takes for methods to execute. Add an `Instrumentation` folder to the class library, and then add an `InstrumentationAspect` class, as shown:

```
[PSerializable]
[AttributeUsage(AttributeTargets.Method)]
```

```
public class InstrumentationAspect : OnMethodBoundaryAspect {
    public override void OnEntry(MethodExecutionArgs args) {
        LogFile.AppendTextToFile("Profile.log",
            $"\nMethod: {args.Method.Name}, Start Time: {DateTime.
Now}");
        args.MethodExecutionTag = Stopwatch.StartNew();
    }

    public override void OnException(MethodExecutionArgs args) {
        LogFile.AppendTextToFile("Exception.log",
            $"\n{DateTime.Now}: {args.Exception.Source} - {args.
Exception.Message}");
    }

    public override void OnExit(MethodExecutionArgs args) {
        var stopwatch = (Stopwatch)args.MethodExecutionTag;
        stopwatch.Stop();
        LogFile.AppendTextToFile("Profile.log",
            $"\nMethod: {args.Method.Name}, Stop Time: {DateTime.Now},
Duration: {stopwatch.Elapsed}");
    }
}
```

As you can see, the instrumentation aspect only applies to methods, times the start and stop times of the method, and logs the profile information to the `Profile.log` file. If an exception is encountered, then the exception is logged to the `Exception.log` file.

PostSharp and build pipeline considerations

When it comes to integrating PostSharp into a build pipeline, there are a few key considerations:

1. **Installation on build server**: PostSharp is typically installed on the build server as part of the build process. This ensures that the necessary PostSharp tasks and tools are available during the compilation of your code. The build server needs to have PostSharp installed globally, or at least in a location accessible during the build process. This may involve using tools such as NuGet to manage PostSharp as a package or manually installing it on the build server.

2. **Build process integration**: In your project file (for example, `.csproj` for a C# project), you would typically include references to PostSharp targets or tasks. These references inform the build system to execute PostSharp tasks during the build process. PostSharp tasks will analyze your code and apply the specified aspects. This step usually occurs after the compilation of the source code.

3. **Configuration**: You may need to configure PostSharp within your project. This configuration includes specifying which aspects to apply, configuring aspect behavior, and other settings relevant to your application's needs.

4. **License considerations**: If you're using a licensed version of PostSharp, ensure that the build server has the necessary license information. Some licensing models may require additional configuration to work seamlessly in a **continuous integration (CI)** environment.

5. **Build server compatibility**: Ensure that your build server is compatible with the version of PostSharp you're using. PostSharp evolves over time, and new versions might introduce changes that affect the build process.

6. **Integration with CI/CD tools**: PostSharp integrates well with popular CI/CD tools such as Jenkins, TeamCity, Azure DevOps, and others. You may need to configure your CI/CD pipeline to include steps for installing PostSharp and executing the necessary build tasks.

Integrating PostSharp into a build pipeline involves installing it on the build server, configuring your project files to include PostSharp tasks, and ensuring that the build server has the necessary dependencies and licenses. The specifics may vary based on the build system and tools you are using. Always refer to the latest documentation for PostSharp and your chosen CI/CD system for the most accurate and up-to-date information.

Dynamic AOP with Castle.DynamicProxy

AOP allows you to separate cross-cutting concerns from your main business logic. Using a dynamic AOP library such as `Castle.DynamicProxy` in C# allows you to add aspects at runtime. Here's a minimal example demonstrating dynamic AOP with `Castle.DynamicProxy`. You will need to add `Castle.DynamicProxy` to your project. Start by adding a `LoggingAspect` class:

```
using Castle.DynamicProxy;
using System;
public class LoggingAspect : IInterceptor
{
    public void Intercept(IInvocation invocation)
    {
        Console.WriteLine($"Before method {invocation.Method.Name}");

        // Invoke the original method
        invocation.Proceed();

        Console.WriteLine($"After method {invocation.Method.Name}");
    }
}
```

This class implements the `IInterceptor` interface. Upon receipt of an invocation, the `LoggingAspect` class writes a message to the console, invokes the original methods, and then closes by writing another message to the console. Next, add a `Calculator` class, which we'll use for our target class:

```
public class Calculator
{
```

```
public virtual int Add(int a, int b)
{
    Console.WriteLine("Adding numbers");
    return a + b;
}
}
```

All this class does is add two integers and return the result. Now, update the `Program` class's `Main` method as follows:

```
static void Main()
{
    // Create a proxy generator
    ProxyGenerator generator = new ProxyGenerator();

    // Create the target object
    Calculator calculator = new Calculator();

    // Create the proxy with the logging aspect
    Calculator proxy = generator
.CreateClassProxyWithTarget<Calculator>(calculator, new
LoggingAspect());

    // Call the method on the proxy
    int result = proxy.Add(3, 5);
    Console.WriteLine($"Result: {result}");
}
```

In this example, we have a `Calculator` class with an `Add` method. We also have a `LoggingAspect` class that implements the `IInterceptor` interface from `Castle.DynamicProxy`. This interceptor logs a message before and after the method is called.

The `Main` method demonstrates how to create a dynamic proxy using `Castle.DynamicProxy`. The `LoggingAspect` class is added to the `Calculator` class at runtime. When you call the `Add` method on the proxy, the logging aspect intercepts the method call, logs messages, and then proceeds with the original method.

This is a minimal example, but you can extend it to include more complex aspects and handle various cross-cutting concerns dynamically.

We now have a functional and reusable cross-cutting concerns library. Let's summarize what we have learned in this chapter.

Summary

We started the chapter by learning what AOP is, and we also discussed AOP frameworks that enable the separation of cross-cutting concerns from business logic when you are programming. This helps you to focus on business logic and keep your code clean and succinct.

Next, we covered how AOP works with PostSharp. We covered extending the aspect framework by developing our own aspect, injecting aspect behaviors before and after method execution, and extending the architectural framework.

Finally, we built a reusable library to address various cross-cutting concerns. These concerns included caching, logging, exception handling, security, validation, resource pool, configuration settings, and instrumentation concerns.

In the next chapter, we will look at using tools to help you improve your code quality. But before then, test your knowledge and then further your reading.

Questions

1. What is an aspect and how do you apply one?
2. What is an attribute and how do you apply one?
3. How do aspects and attributes work together?
4. How does the build process work with aspects?

Further reading

Here is a list of resources specifically about addressing AOP and PostSharp in C#:

- PostSharp documentation: `https://doc.postsharp.net/`
- Introduction to AOP and PostSharp: `https://www.codeproject.com/Articles/337564/Introduction-to-Aspect-Oriented-Programming-AOP-an`
- Questions tagged with [postsharp]: `https://stackoverflow.com/questions/tagged/postsharp`
- AOP with PostSharp: Aspect Oriented Programming with PostSharp - YouTube: `https://www.youtube.com/watch?v=dtx4Vnbe570&t=20s`
- PostSharp samples: `https://github.com/postsharp/PostSharp.Samples`

Please note that the availability of these resources may vary, and some of them may require a subscription or purchase to access the full content. Additionally, some of the resources might be specific to older versions of PostSharp, so make sure to check the documentation and version compatibility for the most up-to-date information.

10

Using Tools to Improve Code Quality

As a programmer, enhancing code quality is one of your chief concerns. Improving the quality of your code demands the utilization of various tools. Tools designed to improve your code and speed up development include **code metrics**, **quick actions**, the **JetBrains dotTrace** profiler, **JetBrains ReSharper**, and **Telerik JustDecompile**.

This is what we'll be doing in this chapter. To do so, we will cover the following topics:

- Defining good-quality code
- Performing code cleanup and calculating code metrics
- Performing code analysis
- Using quick actions
- Using the JetBrains dotTrace profiler
- Using JetBrains ReSharper
- Using Telerik JustDecompile

By the end of this chapter, you will be able to do the following:

- Use code metrics to measure software complexity and maintainability
- Use quick actions to make changes using a single command
- Profile your code and analyze bottlenecks with JetBrains dotTrace
- Refactor code using JetBrains ReSharper
- Decompile code and generate a solution using Telerik JustDecompile

Technical requirements

To follow along with this chapter, you will need the following:

- Visual Studio 2019 or higher

- JetBrains ReSharper

- JetBrains dotTrace profiler

- Telerik JustDecompile

- The source code for this chapter: `https://github.com/PacktPublishing/Clean-Code-with-CSharp-Second-Edition/tree/main/CH10`

Code analysis

Visual Studio provides a code analysis toolset that helps developers improve code quality, find issues, and maintain coding standards.

Open the **CH4** project. Then, from the **Project** menu, select the **CH4 Properties** menu item. This will bring up the **Properties** dialog box for the **CH4** project. From the left-hand tabs, select the **Code Analysis** tab. You should see the following screen:

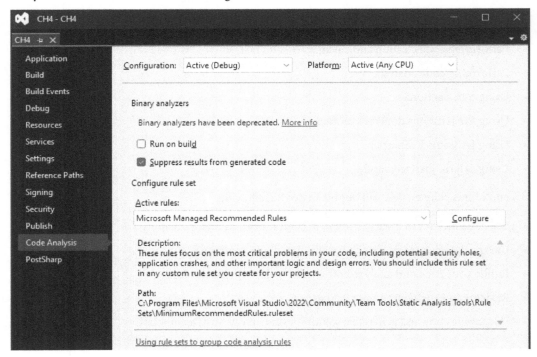

Figure 10.1: The Code Analysis page for the CH4 project

From this page, you can select the active rules that you want to use. Clicking on the **Configure** button brings up the ruleset editor dialog:

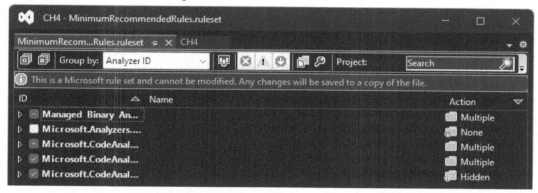

Figure 10.2: The Code Analysis page's ruleset editor dialog

By default, we are using **Microsoft Managed Recommended Rules**, which can be found in the `C:\ Program Files\Microsoft Visual Studio\2022\Community\Team Tools\ Static Analysis Tools\Rule Sets\MinimumRecommendedRules.ruleset` file. When a ruleset is opened, you can select and deselect rules that you would like to have applied during code analysis.

You can click on ruleset files and open them in Visual Studio. If you open a ruleset file in Notepad, you will see that it is an XML file. So, any text editor that can read XML can be used to open, view, and edit these files.

Once you have configured your rules, you are ready to perform code analysis on your project. To manually run code analysis, select **Analyze | Run Code Analysis | On Solution**. To view the results, you will need to open the **Error List** tab. Select **View | Error List** to open the **Error List** tab if it is closed.

For our **CH4** solution, you will see the following in the **Error List** tab:

	Code	Description	Project	File	Line	Suppression State
A	CA0507	Post-build Code Analysis (FxCopCmd.exe) has been deprecated in favor of FxCop analyzers, which run during build. Refer to https://aka.ms/fxcopanalyzers to migrate to FxCop analyzers.				Active
ℹ	IDE0250	Struct can be made 'readonly'	CH4	Credential.cs	9	Active
ℹ	IDE0250	Struct can be made 'readonly'	CH4	DataItem.cs	9	Active
ℹ	IDE0017	Object initialization can be simplified	CH4	DemoWorker.cs	30	Active
ℹ	IDE0250	Struct can be made 'readonly'	CH4	Product.cs	9	Active
ℹ	IDE0060	Remove unused parameter 'args'	CH4	Program.cs	13	Active
ℹ	IDE0060	Remove unused parameter 'userInfo' if it is not part of a shipped public API	CH4	Program.cs	58	Active

Figure 10.3: The Error List tab after running code analysis on the CH4 solution

As shown in *Figure 10.3*, our solution has one warning and six suggestions under **Information**. In this instance, we can address the warning by upgrading from Post-build Code Analysis to FxCop analyzers that run during the build process. Then, we can process each of the six suggestions provided as information on how we can improve our code.

Using quick actions

Another handy tool that I like to use is the **Quick Action** tool. Appearing as a screwdriver (✎), a lightbulb (💡), or an error light bulb (💡) on a line of code, quick actions enable you to use a single command that will generate code, refactor code, suppress warnings, perform code fixes, and add using statements.

Look at the screenshot shown in *Figure 10.4*:

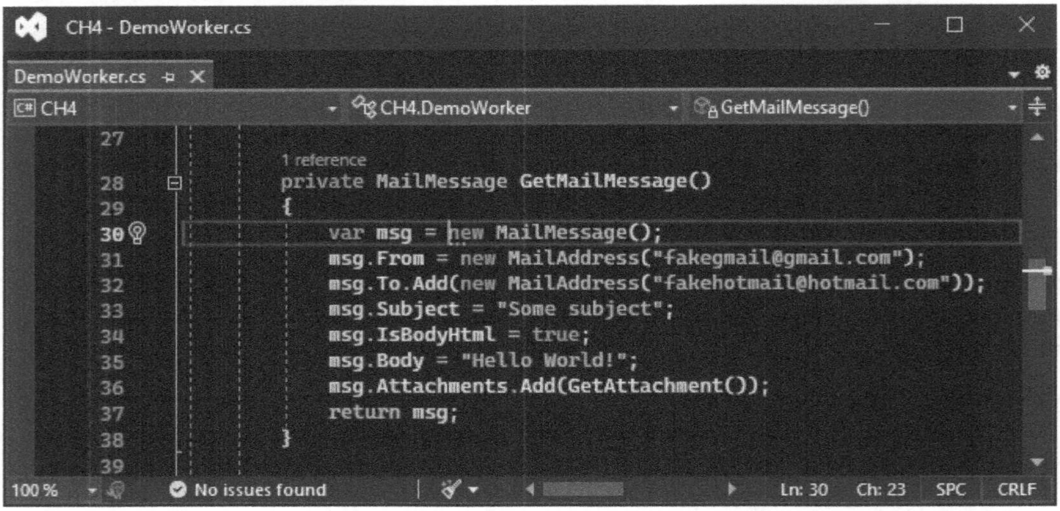

Figure 10.4: The VS editor showing the Quick Action Bulb

The GetMailMessage method in the DemoWorker class has line 30 highlighted with a lightbulb in the left-hand margin:

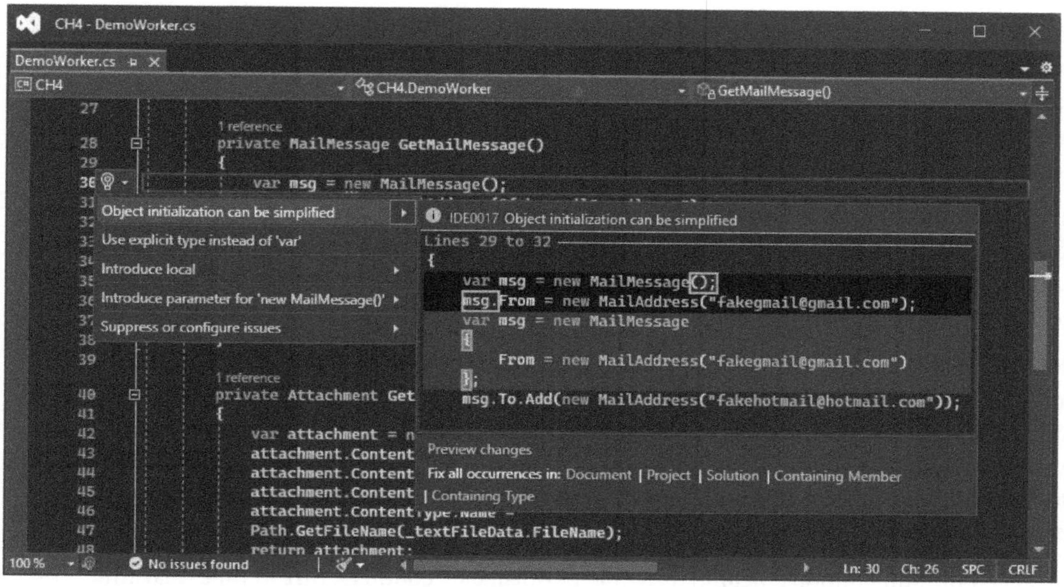

Figure 10.5: The Quick Action tool displaying quick actions that can be performed on line 30

We can see that we have several quick actions available to us that we can perform on line 30. Object initialization can be simplified, we can use an explicit type instead of `var`, introduce a local, introduce method parameters, and even suppress configuration issues. Using these suggestions, we would have a reusable method with simplified code that is more succinct and easier to read.

> **Pro tip**
>
> Warnings can be really bad in your code, such as "this variable is not used," because they can underline subtle bugs and other issues with your code. You can change the default severity levels of warnings to errors and prevent your code from compiling. This will force you to change the code that's been flagged to clean code with the issue removed. You can read more about quick actions on the Microsoft website: `https://learn.microsoft.com/en-us/visualstudio/ide/quick-actions?view=vs-2022`.

Using the JetBrains dotTrace profiler

The JetBrains dotTrace profiler is a part of the JetBrains ReSharper Ultimate license. Since we will be looking at both tools, I recommend that you download and install JetBrains ReSharper Ultimate before we continue.

> **Pro tip**
>
> JetBrains does have a trial version available if you don't already own a copy. There are versions available for Windows, macOS, and Linux.

The JetBrains dotTrace profiling tool works with Mono, .NET Framework, and .NET Core. All application types are supported by the profiler, and you can use the profiler to analyze and track down performance issues with your code base. The profiler will help you get to the bottom of such problems that cause 100% CPU usage, 100% of the disk I/O, maxing out the memory or running into overflow exceptions, and many other issues.

Many applications perform **HyperText Transfer Protocol** (**HTTP**) requests. The profiler will analyze how the application is processing these requests, and it will also do the same with **Structured Query Language** (**SQL**) queries on a database. Static methods and unit tests can be profiled, and you can view the results from within Visual Studio. There is also a standalone version that you can use.

There are four basic profiling options – **Sampling**, **Tracing**, **Line-by-Line**, and **Timeline**. The first time you start looking at the performance of an application, you may decide to use Sampling, which provides an accurate measurement of call time. Tracing and Line-by-Line offer more detailed profiling, but they do add more overhead (memory and CPU usage) to the program being profiled. Timeline is like sampling and collects application events over time. Between them, no problem can't be tracked down and resolved.

Advanced profiling options include real-time performance counters, thread time, real-time CPU instructions, and thread cycle time. The real-time performance counters measure the time between method entry and exit. Thread time measures the thread running time. Based on the CPU register, the real-time CPU instructions provide an accurate time of method entry and exit.

The profiler can attach to running .NET Framework 4.0 (or later) or .NET Core 3.0 (or later) applications and processes, profile local applications, and profile remote applications. These include standalone applications, .NET Core applications, **Internet Information Services** (**IIS**)-hosted web applications, IIS Express-hosted applications, .NET Windows Services, **Windows Communication Foundation** (**WCF**) services, Windows Store and **Universal Windows Platform** (**UWP**) applications, any .NET processes (started after you run the profiling session), desktop or console applications based on Mono, and Unity editor or standalone Unity applications.

To access the profiler in Visual Studio 2022 from the menu, select **Extensions** | **ReSharper** | **Profile** | **Show dotTrace Performance Profiler**:

Figure 10.6: The dotTrace Performance Profiler with no snapshots collected

In *Figure 10.6*, the dotTrace profiler has been configured to profile the performance of the **CH4** project using the **Timeline profiling** type. If you have multiple projects in your solution, you can change the project being profiled and add projects to be profiled, and you can change the profile type. Here, the profile types are Timeline, Sampling, Tracing, and Line-by-Line. We'll profile **CH4** using the **Sampling profiling** type, the output of which can be seen in *Figure 10.7*:

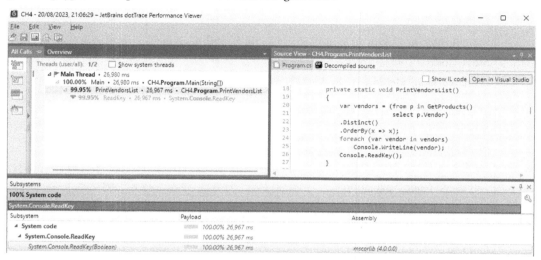

Figure 10.7: The result of the dotTrace Performance Profiler on the CH4 project

From *Figure 10.7*, we can drill down into threads and the code subsystems and view the decompiled code. There is also the option to show the **Intermediate Language** (**IL**) code. Here, we can see the payload, the assembly name, and its version, and we can also see how many milliseconds it took to run the code.

Here, you can view **Thread Tree**, **Call Tree**, **Plan List**, and **Hot Spots**. These different views of the profile can help you determine if there are any bottlenecks and long-running pieces of code. Then, from this information, you can determine what areas of the code base need to be improved upon performance-wise.

> **Pro tip**
> Visual Studio has its own profiler that you can use. To learn more about Visual Studio's profiler, visit the Microsoft website at `https://learn.microsoft.com/en-us/visualstudio/profiling/profiling-feature-tour?view=vs-2022`.

Using JetBrains ReSharper

In this section, we'll look at how JetBrains ReSharper can help you improve your code. ReSharper is quite an extensive tool, and just as with the profiler, which is a part of the Ultimate edition of ReSharper, we will only be scratching the surface. However, hopefully, you will come to appreciate what the tool is and what it can do for you to improve your Visual Studio coding experience:

Refactoring Feature	Visual Studio (Base)	ReSharper
Rename	✔	✔
Extract Method	✔	✔
Extract Interface/Class	✔	✔
Move Code	✔	✔
Inline Variable/Method	✔	✔
Change Signature	✔	✔
Encapsulate Field	✔	✔
More Refactoring Options		✔
Intelligent Code Analysis		✔
Advanced Code Navigation		✔
Live Templates		✔
Code Quality Inspections		✔
Context-Aware Code Completion		✔
Performance Improvements		✔
Unit Testing Integration		✔

Table 10.1: Visual Studio and ReSharper refactoring tools comparison

Here are a few benefits of using ReSharper:

- With ReSharper, you can analyze your code quality.
- It provides options for improving your code, removing code smells, and fixing coding problems.
- With the navigation system, you can completely traverse your solution and jump to any item of interest. You have many different helpers, which include extended IntelliSense, code reorganization, and more.
- Refactoring benefits from ReSharper's offerings, which can be localized or solution-wide.
- You can also generate source code using ReSharper, such as base classes and superclasses, and inline methods.
- Here, code can be cleaned up in keeping with your company's coding policies to get rid of unused imports and other unused code.

Pro tip

You can refactor using Visual Studio's in-built refactoring tools or ReSharper. ReSharper performs better refactoring, but it does come with a slight performance penalty within Visual Studio. There is some really good refactoring help on the Microsoft website at `https://learn.microsoft.com/en-us/visualstudio/ide/refactoring-in-visual-studio?view=vs-2022`.

You can visit the **ReSharper** menu from the Visual Studio **Extensions** menu. When in the code editor, right-clicking on a piece of code will bring up a context menu with the appropriate menu items. The **ReSharper** menu item in the context menu is **Refactor This...**, as shown in the following screenshot:

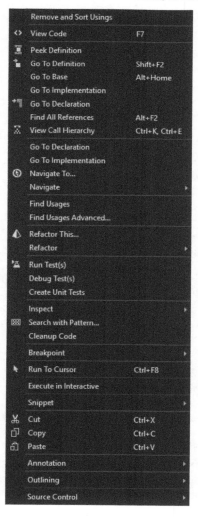

Figure 10.8: The Visual Studio context menu showing the ReSharper Refactor This… menu option

Open the **CH4** project in Visual Studio. Now, from the Visual Studio menu, run **Extensions | ReSharper | Inspect | Code Issues in Solution**. ReSharper will process the solution and then display the **Inspection Results** window, as shown in the following screenshot:

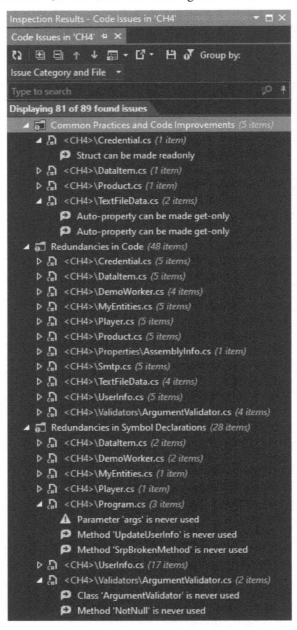

Figure 10.9: The Inspection Results window showing results for the CH4 solution inspection

We can see that ReSharper found 89 issues with the **CH4** solution:

- 5 x **Common Practices and Code Improvements**

- 48 x **Redundancies in Code**

- 28 x **Redundancies in Symbol Declarations**

You can expand each of these groups and double-click on each item in the list. Doing so will take you to the specific line of code so that you can implement the suggestions.

Open the **GoodCodeBadCode.sln** solution from the first edition of this book or GitHub repository of this chapter in Visual Studio.. ReSharper can also generate **dependency diagrams**. To generate a dependency diagram for our solution, select **Extensions | ReSharper | Architecture | Show Project Dependency Diagram**. This will display the project dependency diagram for our solution. The black container box called CH06 is the namespace, and the gray/blue boxes prefixed with CH06_ are projects, as illustrated in the following screenshot:

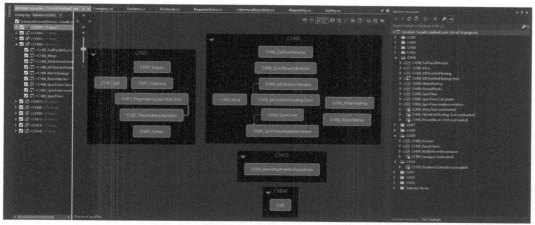

Figure 10.10: The ReSharper architecture dependency diagram

As you can see from the project dependency diagram in the CH06 namespace, there is a project dependency between CH06_SpecFlow and CH06_SpecFlow.Implementation. Similarly, you can also generate type dependency diagrams using ReSharper. Select **Extensions | ReSharper | Architecture | Type Dependencies Diagram**.

If we generate the diagram for ConcreteClass in the CH10_AddressingCrossCuttingConcerns project, then the diagram will be generated, but only the ConcreteComponent class will be displayed initially. Right-click on the ConcreteComponent box on the diagram and select **Add All Referenced Types**. You will see the addition of the ExceptionAttribute class and the IComponent interface. Right-click on the ExceptionAttribute class and select **Add All Referenced Types**; you will end up with the following output:

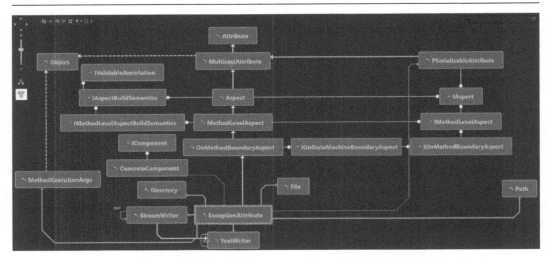

Figure 10.11: The ReSharper type dependency diagram

What's wonderful about this tool is that you can order the diagram elements by namespace. This can be useful for massive solutions with multiple large projects and deep-nested namespaces. Though it's good that we can right-click on code and go to the item declaration, you can't beat visually seeing the lay of the land in terms of the project that you are working on, and that is why this tool can be really useful. Here is an example of a typed dependencies diagram organized by namespaces:

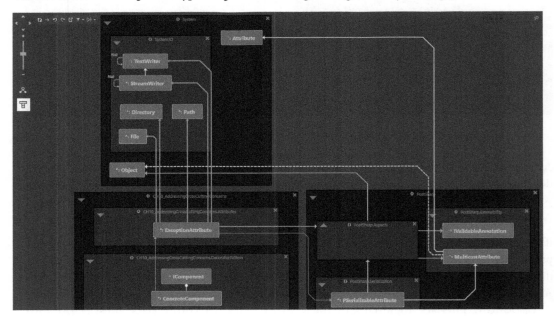

Figure 10.12: The ReSharper type dependency diagram

Often, I could have used a diagram such as this in my day-to-day work. This diagram is technical documentation that will help developers find their way around a complex solution. They will be able to see which namespaces are available and how everything is interlinked. This will empower developers with the correct knowledge as to where new classes, enums, and interfaces should be placed when performing new development, but also, they will know where to find objects if they are performing maintenance. This diagram is also good for finding duplicate namespaces, interfaces, and object names.

Now, let's look at coverage. Proceed as follows:

1. Select **Extensions | ReSharper | Cover | Cover Application**.

2. The **Coverage Configuration** dialog will be displayed.

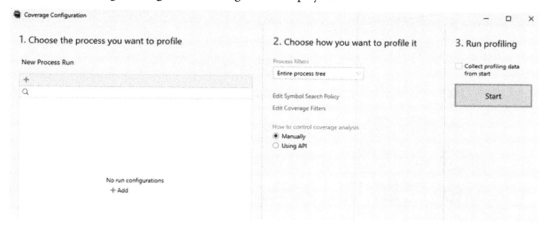

Figure 10.13: The Resharper coverage configuration screen. This image
is only to show the layout; text readability is not required.

3. Click on +**Add** to create a run configuration. This will bring up the New Run Configuration dialog as shown in Figure 10.14.

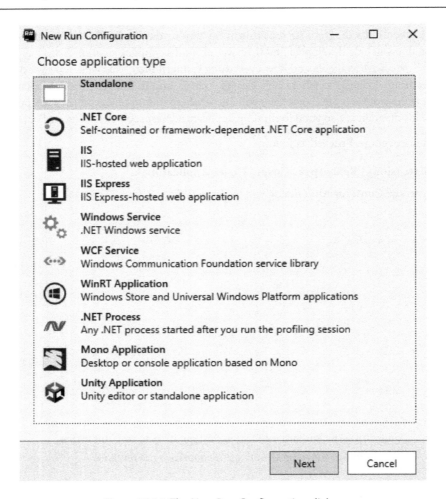

Figure 10.14: The New Run Configuration dialog

4. Select **Standalone** and then click on the **Next** button.

5. Select your executable and provide a name for your run configuration as shown in Figure 10.15.

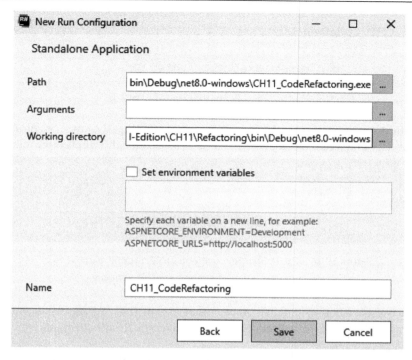

Figure 10.15: The next step of the New Run Configuration dialog

6. You can select a .NET app from the bin folder. Then once you are done click on the Save button.

7. The **Coverage Configuration** dialog should look similar to *Figure 10.16* depending upon the version of the JetBrains tools you are using. Tick the **Collect profiling data from start** checkbox.

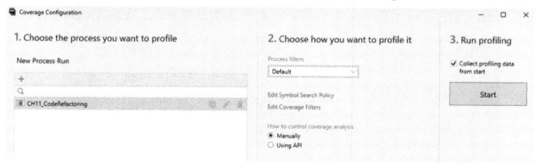

Figure 10.16: Coverage Configuration dialog. This image is only to
show the layout; text readability is not required.

8. Click the **Run** button to start the application and collect profiling data. ReSharper will display the following dialog:

Figure 10.17 – The ReSharper snapshot dialog

The application will then run. As the application is running, the coverage profiler will be collecting data. Our selected executable is a console application that displays the following data:

```
D:\git\Clean-Code-with-CSha   ×    +   ∨

AdapteeOperation() has just executed.
The sum of the integers 1, 2, 3, 4, 5, 6, 7, 8, 9 squared is 285.
Press any key to exit.
```

Figure 10.18 – The ReSharper coverage profiler running in the
console window Our application's console window

9. Click the console window, and then press any key to exit. The coverage dialog will disappear, and storage will then be initialized. Finally, the **Coverage Results Browser** window will be displayed, as shown here:

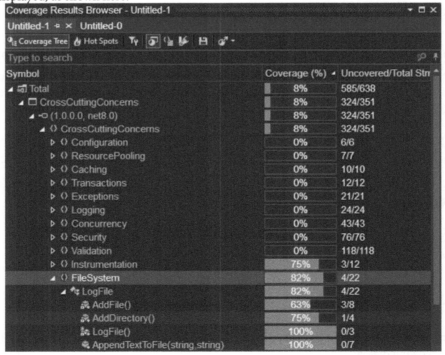

Figure 10.19 – The ReSharper Coverage Results Browser window

This window contains really useful information. It provides a visual indicator of code that was not called, marked in red. The code that was executed is marked in green. Using this information, you can see if the code is dead code that can be removed or was not executed due to the path that was taken through the system but is still required, was commented out for testing purposes, or was simply not called because the developer forgot to add the call in the correct place or a condition check was wrong.

> **Pro tip**
>
> When removing dead code, you need to be extra vigilant as sometimes what appears as dead code may get executed under certain scenarios. So, it is best to take extra care when removing code classified as dead code, just in case you do delete code by accident that is actually required.

To go to the item of interest, you just have to double-click on the item. Once you've done this, you will be taken to the specific code you are interested in.

Now that you've been introduced to ReSharper and had a look at tools that can assist you in writing good, clean C# code, it is time to look at our next tool, called *Telerik JustDecompile*.

Using Telerik JustDecompile

> **Pro tip**
>
> You can learn about Visual Studio's in-built decompilation tools and processes on the Microsoft Learn website: `https://learn.microsoft.com/en-us/visualstudio/debugger/decompilation?view=vs-2022`.

I have used Telerik JustDecompile on several occasions, for things such as tracking down bugs in third-party libraries, recovering essential project source code that has been lost, checking the strength of assembly obfuscation, and learning purposes. It is a tool that I highly recommend as it has proven its worth many times over the years.

The decompilation engine is open source and you can obtain the source code from `https://github.com/telerik/justdecompileengine`, so you are free to contribute to the project and write extensions for it. You can download Windows Installer from the Telerik website at `https://www.telerik.com/products/decompiler.aspx`. All source code is fully navigable. The decompiler is available as a standalone application or as a Visual Studio extension. You can create VB.NET or C# projects from assemblies that you decompile, and you can extract and save resources from the decompiled assemblies.

Download and install Telerik JustDecompile. Once you've done this, we'll go through the decompilation process and generate a C# project from an assembly. You may be prompted to install other tools during the installation process, but you can deselect the other offerings from Telerik.

Run the Telerik JustDecompile standalone application. Find a .NET assembly and then drag it into the left pane of Telerik JustDecompile. It will decompile the code and display the code tree on the left. If you select an item on the left, the code will be shown on the right, as shown in the following screenshot:

Figure 10.20: The Telerik JustDecompile window

As you can see, the decompilation process is fast and it does a pretty good job of decompiling our assembly. The decompilation is not perfect, but in most cases, it does the job. Proceed as follows:

1. In the dropdown to the right of the **Plugins** menu item, select **C#**.
2. Then, click on **Tools | Create Project**.
3. You will sometimes be prompted to select the .NET version to target; other times, you won't be.
4. Then, you will be asked where to save the project.
5. The project will then be written to that location.

Once you've done this, you can open the project in Visual Studio and work on it. Should you encounter any problems, Telerik will log the issues in your code and provide an email. You can always email them with any issues you encounter. They are good at responding to and fixing problems.

Continuous integration with GitHub Actions and CodeQL

In this section, we will look at continuous integration with GitHub Actions and CodeQL.

GitHub Actions can be utilized to set up a workflow for continuous integration with CodeQL analysis in a C# project. Here's a simplified YAML example:

```yaml
name: CodeQL Analysis

on:
  push:
    branches:
      - main

jobs:
  analyze:
    runs-on: ubuntu-latest

    strategy:
      matrix:
        language: [csharp]

    steps:
    - name: Checkout repository
      uses: actions/checkout@v2

    - name: Set up CodeQL
      uses: github/codeql-action/init@v1
      with:
        languages: ${{ matrix.language }}

    - name: Build and Run CodeQL analysis
      run: |
        dotnet build
        codeql database create --language=csharp --source-root .
--database ${{ runner.workspace }}/codeql-database
        codeql analyze --database ${{ runner.workspace }}/codeql-
database
```

In this example, the workflow triggers each push to the main branch, checks out the code, sets up CodeQL for C#, builds the project, and runs CodeQL analysis.

CodeQL supports multiple languages, including C#. It allows you to find and fix security vulnerabilities, making it a valuable tool for code quality and security.

With that, we have finished looking at various tools. Now, let's summarize what we have learned.

Summary

In this chapter, you saw how code metrics provide several measurements of code quality, and how easy it is to generate them. Code metrics include the number of lines – including blank lines – versus the number of executable lines of code, the cyclomatic complexity, the level of cohesion and coupling, and how maintainable your code is. The refactoring color codes are green for "good", yellow for "ideally needs refactoring", and red for "definitely needs refactoring".

You then saw how easy it is to provide a static code analysis of projects and view the results. Viewing and modifying rulesets that govern what gets analyzed and what doesn't get analyzed was also covered. Then, you experienced quick actions and learned how to perform bug fixes, add `using` statements, and refactor code with a single command.

Then, we used the JetBrains dotTrace profiler to measure our application's performance, track down bottlenecks, and identify hungry methods that take up the most processing time. The next tool we looked at was JetBrains ReSharper, which enables us to inspect code for various problems and potential improvements. We identified a couple of them and made the necessary changes and saw how easy it was to improve the code with this tool. Then, we looked at creating architectural diagrams for dependencies and type dependencies.

Finally, we looked at Telerik JustDecompile, a very useful tool that can be used to decompile assemblies and generate projects in either C# or VB.NET from them. This can be very useful when bugs are encountered or the program needs to be expanded, but you no longer have access to the existing source code.

In the chapters that follow, we will mainly be looking at code and how we can refactor it. But for now, test your knowledge with the following questions and further your reading with the links provided in the *Further reading* section.

Questions

Answer the following questions to test your knowledge of this chapter:

1. What are code metrics, and why should we use them?
2. Name six code metric measurements.
3. What is code analysis, and why is it useful?
4. What are quick actions?
5. What is JetBrains dotTrace used for?
6. What is JetBrains ReSharper used for?
7. Why use Telerik JustDecompile to decompile assemblies?

Further reading

To learn more about the topics that were covered in this chapter, take a look at the following resources:

- Official Microsoft documentation on code metrics: `https://docs.microsoft.com/en-us/visualstudio/code-quality/code-metrics-values?view=vs-2019`

- Official Microsoft documentation on quick actions: `https://learn.microsoft.com/en-us/visualstudio/ide/quick-actions?view=vs-2022&viewFallbackFrom=vs-2020`

- JetBrains dotTrace profiler: `https://www.jetbrains.com/profiler/`

- Automating your workflows with GitHub Actions: `https://docs.github.com/en/actions`.

- Performing semantic code analysis with CodeQL: `https://codeql.github.com/`

11
Refactoring C# Code

In this chapter, we will look at the problem code and how to refactor it. In the industry, problematic code is normally termed **code smell**. It is code that compiles, runs, and does what it is supposed to do. The reason it is problem code is that it becomes unreadable, complex in nature, and makes the code base hard to maintain and extend further down the line. Such code should be refactored as soon as it's feasible to do so. It is technical debt, and in the long run, if you don't deal with it, it will bring the project to its knees. When this happens, you are looking at an expensive redesign and must recode the application from scratch.

So, what is refactoring? Refactoring is the process of taking existing code that works and rewriting it such that the code becomes clean. As you have already discovered, clean code is easy to read, easy to maintain, and easy to extend.

In this chapter, we will cover the following topics:

- Identifying application-level code smells and how we can address them
- Identifying class-level code smells and how we can address them
- Identifying method-level code smells and how we can address them

After working your way through this chapter, you will be able to do the following:

- Identify different kinds of code smells
- Understand why the code is classed as a code smell
- Refactor code smells so they become clean code

We'll start our look at refactoring code smells by looking at application-level code smells.

Technical requirements

You will need the following prerequisites for this chapter:

- Visual Studio 2019 or higher
- PostSharp

The code files for this chapter can be found at https://github.com/PacktPublishing/Clean-Code-with-CSharp-Second-Edition/tree/main/CH11.

Application-level code smells

Application-level code smells are problem code scattered through the application and affect every layer. No matter what layer of the software you find yourself in, you will see the same problematic code appearing over and over again. If you don't address these issues now, then you will find that your software will start to die a slow and agonizing death.

In this section, we will look at application-level code smells and how we can remove them. Let's start with Boolean blindness.

Boolean blindness

Boolean data blindness refers to information loss as determined by functions that work on Boolean values. Using a better structure provides better interfaces and classes that keep data, making for a more pleasant experience in working with data.

Let's look at the problem of Boolean blindness via this code sample:

```
public void BookConcert(string concert, bool standing)
{
    if (standing)
    {
        // Issue standing ticket.
    }
    else
    {
        // Issue sitting ticket.
    }
}
```

This method takes a string for the concert's name and a Boolean value indicating whether the person is standing or seated. Now, we can call the code as follows:

```
private void BooleanBlindnessConcertBooking()
{
```

```
        var booking = new ProblemCode.ConcertBooking();
        booking.BookConcert("Solitary Experiments", standing: true);
}
```

If someone new to the code saw the `BooleanBlindnessConcertBooking()` method, do you think they would instinctively know what `true` stands for? I think not. They would be blind to what it means. So, they would have to either use IntelliSense or locate the method being referred to, to find the meaning. They are Boolean blind. So, how can we cure them of this blindness?

Well, a simple solution would be to replace the Boolean with an enum. Let's start by adding our enum, which is called `TicketType`:

```
[Flags]
internal enum TicketType
{
    Seated,
    Standing
}
```

Our enum identifies two types of ticket types: `Seated` and `Standing`. Now, let's add our `ConcertBooking()` method:

```
internal void BookConcert(string concert, TicketType ticketType)
{
    if (ticketType == TicketType.Seated)
    {
        // Issue seated ticket.
    }
    else
    {
        // Issue standing ticket.
    }
}
```

The following code shows how to call the newly refactored code:

```
private void ClearSightedConcertBooking()
{
    var booking = new RefactoredCode.ConcertBooking();
    booking.BookConcert("Chrom", TicketType.Seated);
}
```

Now, if that new person came along and looked at this code, they would see that we are booking a concert to see the band `Chrom` and that we want seated tickets.

Combinatorial explosion

Combinatorial explosion is a *byproduct* of the same thing being performed by different pieces of code using different combinations of parameters. Let's look at an example that adds numbers:

```csharp
public int Add(int x, int y)
{
    return x + y;
}

public double Add(double x, double y)
{
    return x + y;
}

public float Add(float x, float y)
{
    return x + y;
}
```

Here, we have three methods that all add numbers. The return types and parameters are all different. Is there a better way? Yes – through the use of generics. By using generics, you can have a single method that is capable of working with different types. And so, we will be using generics to solve our addition problem. This will allow us to have a single addition method that will accept integers, doubles, or floats. Let's have a look at our new method:

```csharp
public T Add<T>(T x, T y)
    where T : struct // Add a value type constraint, assuming you want
to support only value types
{
    // Ensure that T supports the + operator
    if (typeof(T).GetMethod("op_Addition") == null)
    {
        throw new InvalidOperationException("Type T must support the +
operator.");
    }

    return (dynamic)x + (dynamic)y;
}
```

This generic method is called with a specific type assigned to T. It performs the addition and returns the result. Only one version of the method is required for the different .NET types that can be added together.

The method will only accept value types based on the value type constraint. We check the type to ensure that it will accept the + operator. Then, we perform the addition and return the correct type.

To call the code for `int`, `double`, and `float` values, we would do the following:

```
var addition = new RefactoredCode.Maths();
addition.Add<int>(1, 2);
addition.Add<double>(1.2, 3.4);
addition.Add<float>(5.6f, 7.8f);
```

We have just eliminated three methods and replaced them with a single method that performs the same task.

Contrived complexity

When you can develop code with simple architecture, but instead implement an advanced and rather complex architecture, this is known as **contrived complexity**. Unfortunately, I have suffered having to work on such systems and it is a proper pain and cause of stress. What you find with such systems is that they tend to have a high turnover of staff. They lack documentation, and no one seems to know the system or can answer questions from onboarders – the poor souls who have to learn the system to maintain and extend it.

My advice to all super-intelligent software architects is that when it comes to software, **Keep It Simple, Stupid (KISS)**. Remember, the days of permanent employment with jobs for life appear to be a thing of the past now. Oftentimes, programmers are more for chasing the money than showing lifelong loyalty to the business. So, with the business relying on the software for revenue, you need a system that is easy to understand, to onboard new staff, maintain, and extend. Ask yourself this question: If the systems that you are responsible for suddenly experienced yourself and all staff assigned to them walking out and finding new opportunities, would the new staff who take over be able to hit the ground running? Or would they be left stressed out and scratching their heads?

Also, bear in mind that if you have only one person on the team who understands that system and they die, move on to a new location, or retire, where does that leave you and the rest of the team? And even more than that, where does it leave the business?

I cannot stress enough that you are to KISS. The only reason for creating complex systems and not documenting them and sharing the architectural knowledge is to hold the business over a barrel so that they keep you on and you can bleed them dry. I have seen this happen in different companies I have worked for. Don't do it. In my experience, the more complicated a system is, the quicker it dies a death and has to be rewritten.

> **Note**
>
> KISS code is normally self-explanatory and easy to read. Complex code is often not easy to read, so it needs to be well documented. But in my extensive experience, people start with good intentions to document complex code and make it a mandatory policy. But then, with tight deadlines, ever-growing demands, and even lazy programmers, I have found that documentation is one of the first casualties of a complex system with complex code. And in the end, nobody wants to work on it because they don't understand it. And so, this can lead to a high developer turnaround.

In *Chapter 10*, *Using Tools to Improve Code Quality*, you learned how to use Visual Studio tools to discover the *cyclomatic complexity* and *depth of inheritance*. You also learned how to produce dependency diagrams with ReSharper. Use these tools to discover problem areas in the code, then focus on those areas. Reduce cyclomatic complexity down to a value of 10 or less, then reduce the depth of inheritance on all objects down to no greater than 1.

Once you've done this, make sure all classes only perform the tasks that they are meant to. Aim to keep methods small. A good rule of thumb is to have no more than around 10 lines of code per method. As for method parameters, replace long parameter lists with parameter objects. And where you have a lot of out parameters, refactor the method so that it returns a tuple or object. Identify any multithreading, and make sure that the code being accessed is thread-safe.

Also, look for the Quick Tips icons. These will normally suggest one-click refactorings for the line of code they highlight. I recommend that you use them. These were mentioned in *Chapter 10*, *Using Tools to Improve Code Quality*.

The next code smell to consider is the data clump.

Data clump

A **data clump** occurs when you see the same fields appearing together in different classes and parameter lists. Their names usually follow the same pattern. This is normally a sign that a class is missing from the system. The reduction in system complexity will come by identifying the missing class and generalizing it. Don't be put off by the fact that the class may only be small, and never think of a class as being unimportant. If there is a need for a class to simplify the code, then add it.

Let's see a simple example:

```
Order order = new Order
{
    OrderId = 1,
    OrderDate = DateTime.Now,
    CustomerFirstName = "John",
    CustomerLastName = "Doe"
};
```

In this code, the `Order` class has two properties called `CustomerFirstName` and `CustomerLastName`. These same properties are part of a `Customer` class. So, what we should do is replace them with a `Customer` class property, as follows:

```
Order order = new Order
{
    OrderId = 1,
    OrderDate = DateTime.Now,
    Customer = new Customer { "John", "Doe" }
};
```

The code is much cleaner because instead of having the same two properties in the `Customer` class and the `Order` class, we now only have them in the `Customer` class. In the `Order` class, we have a property that defines `Customer`, in which we can set the customer's first and last name.

Deodorant comments

When a comment uses nice words to excuse bad code, this is known as a **deodorant comment**. If the code is bad, then refactor it to make it good and remove the comment. If you don't know how to refactor it to make it good, then ask for help. If there is no one to ask who can help you, then post your code on Stack Overflow or present your case to ChatGPT. Some very good programmers on StackOverflow can be a real help to you. Just make sure you follow the rules when posting! Also, ChatGPT is good at taking complex code, simplifying it, and even correcting it. The main advantage of using ChatGPT over StackOverflow is that you get real-time answers to your questions.

Duplicate code

Duplicate code is code that occurs more than once. Problems that arise from duplicate code include increased maintenance costs per duplication. When a developer is fixing a piece of code, it costs the business time and money. Fixing one bug is *technical debt (programmer's pay) x 1*. But if there are 10 duplications of that code, that's *technical debt x 10*. So, the more that code is duplicated, the more expensive it is to maintain. Then, there is the boredom factor of having to fix the same problem in multiple locations and the fact that duplication may get overlooked by the programmer doing the bug fix.

It is best to refactor the duplicate code so that only one copy of the code exists. Often, the easiest way to do this is to add it to a new reusable class in your current project and place it in a class library. The benefit of placing reusable code in a class library is that other projects can use the same file.

The .NET standard libraries can be accessed by all C# project types on Windows, Linux, macOS, iOS, and Android. When writing reusable libraries, it is best to stick with the standard libraries to avoid code issues when targeting different deployment platform targets, and only use platform-specific libraries when the standard libraries do not meet your needs.

Another alternative for removing boilerplate code is to use **aspect-oriented programming** (AOP). We looked at AOP in the previous chapter. You essentially move boilerplate code into an aspect. The aspect then decorates the method it is applied to. When the method is compiled, the boilerplate code is then weaved into place. This enables you only to write code that meets the business requirements inside the method. The aspect applied to the method hides the essential code, but not part of what the business has asked for. This coding technique is nice and clean, and it works well.

You can also write decorators using the decorator pattern, as you also saw in the previous chapter. The decorator wraps concrete class operations in such a way that you can add new code without affecting the expected operation of the code. A simple example would be to wrap the operation in a `try/catch` block, as you saw previously in *Chapter 8, Addressing Cross-Cutting Concerns*.

Lost intent

If you can't easily understand the intent of the source code, then it has lost its intent. One of the biggest pains for programmers is when you have code scattered in all manner of namespaces instead of neatly placed in the correct namespace where it should be. This makes it hard to find what you are looking for and can cause a drop in personal performance that gets picked up by your colleagues and can even result in disciplinary action where you are forced to explain your drop in productivity.

> **Note**
> If you ever find yourself in a position where you are onboarded to a massive code base where code is incorrectly placed in namespaces and classes, making it hard to understand and follow the code, then it is best to speak out and bring it to the manager's attention as technical debt.

The first thing to do is look at the namespace and the class name. These should indicate the purpose of the class. Then, check the contents of the class, and look for code that looks out of place. Once you have identified such code, refactor the code and place it in the right location.

The next thing to do is to look at each of the methods. Are they only doing one thing well or doing multiple things not so well? If yes, then refactor them. For large methods, look for code that can be extracted into a method. Aim to make the code of the class read like a book. Keep refactoring the code until the intent is clear, and only what is in the class needs to be in the class.

Don't forget to put the tools to work that you learned how to use in *Chapter 10, Using Tools to Improve Code Quality*. The mutation of variables is the code smell we will look at next.

The mutation of variables

The mutation of variables means they are hard to understand and reason about. This makes them difficult to refactor.

A mutable variable gets changed multiple times by different operations. This makes the reasoning of why the value is higher, significantly more difficult. Not only that but because the variable is mutating from different operations, this makes it difficult to extract sections of code into other small and more readable methods. Mutable variables can also require more checking, which adds complexity to the code.

> **Note**
> When you have multiple places that mutate a variable, you can be certain that your code is not thread-safe. This can lead to unpredictable behavior during testing and at runtime.

Look to refactor small sections of code by extracting them out to methods. If there is a lot of branching and looping, see if there is an easier way to do things to remove the complexity. If you are using multiple out values, consider returning an object or tuple. Aim to remove the mutability of the variable to make it easier to reason about and know why it is the value that it is, and from where it is getting set. Remember that the smaller the method that holds a variable, the easier it will be to determine where the variable is getting set, and why.

Look at the following example:

```
[InstrumentationAspect]
public class Mutant
{
    public int IntegerSquaredSum(List<int> integers)
    {
        var squaredSum = 0;
        foreach (var integer in integers)
        {
            squaredSum += integer * integer;
        }
        return squaredSum;
    }
}
```

The method takes a list of integers. Then, it loops through the integers, squares them, and adds them to the squaredSum variable, which is returned when the method exits. Notice the iterations and the fact that the local variable is getting updated in each iteration. We can improve on this using LINQ. The following code shows the improved, refactored version:

```
public class Function
{
    [InstrumentationAspect]
    public int IntegerSquaredSum(List<int> integers)
    {
        return integers.Sum(integer => integer * integer);
    }
}
```

In this version, AsParallel() allows the LINQ query to be processed in parallel, taking advantage of multiple cores and potentially improving performance. However, keep in mind that not all operations benefit from parallelization, and it's essential to consider the nature of the computation and the size of the input data.

Also, note that this change assumes that the `InstrumentationAspect` aspect and the surrounding context are thread-safe. If there are other shared resources or stateful operations within the aspect or the calling code, additional synchronization mechanisms may be necessary to ensure overall thread safety. Compile and run the program; you will see the following:

```
The sum of the integers 1, 2, 3, 4, 5, 6, 7, 8, 9 squared is 285.
The sum of the integers 1, 2, 3, 4, 5, 6, 7, 8, 9 squared is 285.
Press any key to exit.
```

Figure 11.1: Output shown by both versions of the code

Both versions of the code produce the same output.

You will have noticed that both versions of the code have [InstrumentationAspect] applied to them. We added this aspect to our reusable library in *Chapter 8, Addressing Cross-Cutting Concerns*. When you run the code, you will find a `Logs` folder in the `Debug` folder. Open the `Profile.log` file in Notepad; you will see the following output:

```
Method: IntegerSquaredSum, Start Time: 01/07/2020 11:41:43
Method: IntegerSquaredSum, Stop Time: 01/07/2020 11:41:43, Duration:
00:00:00.0005489
Method: IntegerSquaredSum, Start Time: 01/07/2020 11:41:43
Method: IntegerSquaredSum, Stop Time: 01/07/2020 11:41:43, Duration:
00:00:00.0000027
```

Figure 11.2: The contents of a profile log

The output shows that the `ProblemCode.IntegerSquaredSum()` method was the slowest version, taking **548.9** nanoseconds to run. On the other hand, the `RefactoredCode.IntegerSquaredSum()` method was much faster, taking only **2.7** nanoseconds to run.

By refactoring the loop to use LINQ, we avoided mutating a local variable. We also reduced the time it took to process the calculation by **546.2** nanoseconds. Such a small improvement is not noticeable to the human eye. But if you perform such calculations on big data, then you will experience a noticeable difference.

> **Note**
>
> When performing benchmarking, you need to run the same code multiple times. A good library to use when benchmarking your code is `BenchmarkDotNet`: `https://benchmarkdotnet.org/`.

Now, let's discuss the oddball solution.

The oddball solution

When you see a problem that's been solved differently throughout the source code, this is known as an **oddball solution**. This can happen because of different programmers having their own style of programming, and no standards being put in place. It can also happen through ignorance of the system, in that the programmer does not realize a solution already exists.

A way to refactor oddball solutions is to write a new class that encompasses the behavior that is being repeated in different ways. Add the behavior to the class in the cleanest way that is the most performant. Then, replace the oddball solutions with the newly refactored behavior.

You can also unite different system interfaces using the **adapter pattern**:

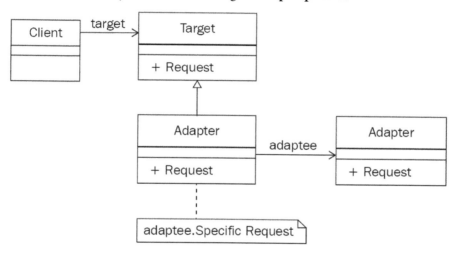

Adapter Pattern

Figure 11.3: Apapter pattern

The `Target` class is the domain-specific interface that is used by `Client`. An existing interface that needs adapting is called `Adaptee`. The `Adapter` class adapts the `Adaptee` class to the `Target` class. Finally, the `Client` class communicates objects that conform to the `Target` interface. Let's implement the adapter pattern. Add a new class called `Adaptee`:

```
public class Adaptee
{
    public void AdapteeOperation()
    {
        Console.WriteLine($"AdapteeOperation() has just executed.");
    }
}
```

The `Adaptee` class is very simple – it contains a method called `AdapteeOperation()` that prints out a message to the console. Now, add the `Target` class:

```csharp
public class Target
{
    public virtual void Operation()
    {
        Console.WriteLine("Target.Operation() has executed.");
    }
}
```

The `Target` class is also very simple and contains a virtual method called `Operation()` that prints out a message to the console. Now, we'll add the `Adapter` class, which wires `Target` and `Adaptee` together:

```csharp
public class Adapter : Target
{
    private readonly Adaptee _adaptee = new Adaptee();

    public override void Operation()
    {
        _adaptee.AdapteeOperation();
    }
}
```

The `Adapter` class inherits the `Target` class. Then, we create a member variable to hold our `Adaptee` object and initialize it. After, we have a single method, which is the overridden `Operation()` method of the `Target` class. Finally, we will add our `Client` class:

```csharp
public class Client
{
    public void Operation()
    {
        Target target = new Adapter();
        target.Operation();
    }
}
```

The `Client` class has a single method called `Operation()`. This method creates a new `Adapter` object and assigns it to a `Target` variable. Then, it calls the `Operation()` method on the `Target` variable. If you call a new `Client().Operation()` method and run the code, you will see the following output:

Fugure 11.4: Adaptee code console out

As you can see, the method that gets executed is called `Adaptee.AdapteeOperation()`. Now that you have successfully learned how to implement the adapter pattern to solve oddball solutions, we will look at shotgun surgery.

Shotgun surgery

Making a single change that requires making changes to multiple classes is known as **shotgun surgery**. This can sometimes be down to excessive refactoring of code due to divergent changes being encountered. This code smell increases the propensity for introducing bugs such as those caused by a missed chance. You also increase the possibility of merge conflicts since the code needs to change in so many areas that programmers end up stepping on each other's toes. The code is so convoluted that it induces cognitive overload in programmers. This results in new programmers having a steep learning curve because of the nature of the software.

The version control history will provide a history of the changes that have been made to the software over time. This can help you identify all the areas that are changed every time a new piece of functionality is added or when a bug is encountered. Once these areas have been identified, you can look to move the changes to a more localized area of the code base. This way, when a change is required, you only have to focus on one area of the program and not many areas. This makes maintaining the project a lot easier.

Duplicate code is a good candidate for refactoring into a single class that is appropriately named, and that is placed in the correct namespace. Also, consider all the different layers of your application. Are they really necessary? Can things be simplified? In a database-driven application, is it really necessary to have DTOs, DAOs, domain objects, and the like? Could database access be simplified in any way? Architecture must be flexible. DTOs are often necessary, but we don't always need them. So, use DTOs when they are needed, and avoid them when they're not needed. These are just some ideas for reducing the size of the code base, and thus reducing the number of areas that must be modified to effect a change.

Other things to look at are the level of coupling and cohesion. Coupling needs to be kept to an absolute minimum. One way to accomplish this is to inject dependencies via constructors, properties, and methods. The injected dependencies would be of a specific interface type. Let's code a simple example. Add an interface called `IService`:

```
public interface IService
{
    void Operation();
}
```

The interface contains a single method called `Operation()`. Now, add a class called `Dependency` that implements `IService`:

```
public class Dependency : IService
{
```

```csharp
    public void Operation()
    {
        Console.WriteLine("Dependency.Operation() has executed.");
    }
}
```

The Dependency class implements the `IService` interface. In the `Operation()` method, a message is printed to the console. Now, let's add the `LooselyCoupled` class:

```csharp
public class LooselyCoupled
{
    private readonly IService _service;

    public LooselyCoupled(IService service)
    {
        _service = service;
    }

    public void DoWork()
    {
        _service.Operation();
    }
}
```

As you can see, the constructor takes a type of `IService` and stores it in a member variable. The call to `DoWork()` calls the `Operation()` method within the `IService` type. The `LooselyCoupled` class is just that loosely coupled, and it is easy to test.

By reducing coupling, you make classes easier to test. By removing code that does not belong in a class and placing it where it does belong, you improve the readability, maintainability, and extensibility of the application. You lessen the learning curve for anyone coming on board, and there is less chance of introducing bugs when you perform maintenance or new development.

Now, let's have a look at solution sprawl.

Solution sprawl

The single responsibility that is implemented within different methods, classes, and even libraries suffers from solution sprawl. This can make code hard to read and understand. The result is that code becomes harder to maintain and extend.

To fix the problem, move the implementation of the single responsibility into the same class. This way, the code is in just one location and does what it needs to. This makes code easy to read and understand. The result is that the code can be easily maintained and extended.

Uncontrolled side effects

Uncontrolled side effects are those issues that rear their ugly heads in production because the quality assurance tests are unable to capture them. When you encounter these problems, the only option you have is to refactor the code so that it is fully testable and variables can be viewed during debugging to make sure they are set appropriately.

Suppose you have a method called `ProcessData` that is supposed to transform a given dataset. However, due to uncontrolled side effects, this method also modifies a global variable or state outside its context. This can lead to unintended and unpredictable results, especially when the method is called in different parts of the program.

To address uncontrolled side effects, it's generally recommended to design functions and methods to be pure and avoid modifying external state. Encapsulation, immutability, and carefully managing shared resources can help prevent unintended consequences of side effects in a program.

That concludes our look at application-level code smells. Now, we will move on and look at class-level code smells.

Class-level code smells

Class-level code smells are localized problems with the class in question. The kinds of problems that can plague a class are things such as cyclomatic complexity and depth of inheritance, high coupling, and low cohesion. Your aim when writing a class is to keep it small and functional. The methods in the class should be there, and they should be small. Only do what needs to be done in the class – no more, no less. Work to remove class dependency and make your classes testable. Remove code that should be placed elsewhere to where it belongs. In this section, we'll address class-level code smells and how to refactor them, starting with cyclomatic complexity.

Cyclomatic complexity

When a class has a large number of branches and loops, it has an increased cyclomatic complexity. Ideally, the code should have a cyclomatic complexity value of *between 1 and 10*. Such code is simple and without risks. Code with a cyclomatic complexity of 11-20 is complex but low risk. When the cyclomatic complexity of the code is between 21-50, then the code requires attention as it is too complex and poses a medium risk to your project. And if the code has a cyclomatic complexity of more than 50, then such code is high risk and is not testable. A piece of code that has a value above 50 must be refactored immediately.

The goal of refactoring is to get the cyclomatic value down to between 1-10. Start by replacing `switch` statements followed by `if` expressions.

Replacing switch statements with the factory pattern

In this section, you will learn how to replace a `switch` statement with the factory pattern. First, we will need a `Report` enum:

```
[Flags]
public enum Report
{
    StaffShiftPattern,
    EndofMonthSalaryRun,
    HrStarters,
    HrLeavers,
    EndofMonthSalesFigures,
    YearToDateSalesFigures
}
```

The `[Flags]` attribute enables us to extract the name of the enum. The `Report` enum provides a list of reports. Now, let's add our `switch` statement:

```
public void RunReport(Report report)
{
    switch (report)
    {
        case Report.EndofMonthSalaryRun:
            Console.WriteLine("Running End of Month Salary Run
Report.");
            break;
        case Report.EndofMonthSalesFigures:
            Console.WriteLine("Running End of Month Sales Figures
Report.");
            break;
        case Report.HrLeavers:
            Console.WriteLine("Running HR Leavers Report.");
            break;
        case Report.HrStarters:
            Console.WriteLine("Running HR Starters Report.");
            break;
        case Report.StaffShiftPattern:
            Console.WriteLine("Running Staff Shift Pattern Report.");
            break;
        case Report.YearToDateSalesFigures:
            Console.WriteLine("Running Year to Date Sales Figures
Report.");
            break;
        default:
```

```
            Console.WriteLine("Report unrecognized.");
            break;
    }
}
```

Our method accepts a report and then decides on what report to execute. When I started as a junior VB6 programmer in 1999, I was responsible for building a report generator from scratch for the likes of Thomas Cook, ANZ, BNZ, Vodafone, and a few other big companies. There were many reports, and I was responsible for writing a massive case statement that dwarfed this one. But my system worked well. However, by today's standards, there are much better ways of creating this same code and I would do things very differently.

Let's use the factory method to run our reports without using a `switch` statement. Add a file called `IreportFactory`, as shown here:

```
public interface IReportFactory
{
    void Run();
}
```

The `IReportFactory` interface only has one method, called `Run()`. This method will be used by the implementing classes to run their reports. We'll only add one report class, called `StaffShiftPatternReport`, which implements `IReportFactory`:

```
public class StaffShiftPatternReport : IReportFactory
{
    public void Run()
    {
        Console.WriteLine("Running Staff Shift Pattern Report.");
    }
}
```

The `StaffShiftPatternReport` class implements the `IReportFactory` interface. The implemented `Run()` method prints a message to the screen. Add a report called `ReportRunner`:

```
public class ReportRunner
{
    public void RunReport(Report report)
    {
        var reportName = $"CH11_CodeRefactoring.RefactoredCode.
{report}Report, CH11_CodeRefactoring";
        var factory = Activator.CreateInstance(
            Type.GetType(reportName) ?? throw new
InvalidOperationException("Invalid operation occurred in
ReportRunner")
        ) as IReportFactory;
```

```
        factory?.Run();
    }
}
```

The `ReportRunner` class has a method called `RunReport`. It accepts a parameter of the `Report` type. With `Report` being an enum with the `[Flags]` attribute, we can obtain the name of the `report` enum. We can use this to build the name of the report. Then, we can use the `Activator` class to create an instance of the report. If `reportName` returns null when we're getting the type, `InvalidOperationException` is thrown. The factory is cast to the `IReportFactory` type. Then, we call the Run method on the factory to generate the report.

This code is much better than a very long `switch` statement. However, we need to know how to improve the readability of conditional checks within an `if` statement. We'll look at that next.

Improving the readability of conditional checks within an if statement

`if` statements can break the single responsibility and the open/closed principles. Look at the following example:

```
public string GetHrReport(string reportName)
{
    if (reportName.Equals("Staff Joiners Report"))
        return "Staff Joiners Report";
    else if (reportName.Equals("Staff Leavers Report"))
        return "Staff Leavers Report";
    else if (reportName.Equals("Balance Sheet Report"))
        return "Balance Sheet Report";
}
```

The `GetReport()` class has three responsibilities: the staff joiners report, the staff leavers report, and the balance sheet report. This breaks the SRP because the method should only be concerned with HR reports and it is returning HR and finance reports. As far as the open/closed principle is concerned, every time a new report is needed, we will have to extend this method. Let's refactor the method so that we no longer need the `if` statement. Add a new class called `ReportBase`:

```
public abstract class ReportBase
{
    public abstract void Print();
}
```

The `ReportBase` class is an abstract class with an abstract `Print()` method. We will add the `NewStartersReport` class, which inherits the `ReportBase` class:

```
internal class NewStartersReport : ReportBase
{
```

```
    public override void Print()
    {
        Console.WriteLine("Printing New Starters Report.");
    }
}
```

The NewStartersReport class inherits the ReportBase class and overrides the Print() method. The Print() method prints a message to the screen. Now, we will add the LeaversReport class, which is pretty much the same:

```
public class LeaversReport : ReportBase
{
    public override void Print()
    {
        Console.WriteLine("Printing Leavers Report.");
    }
}
```

LeaversReport inherits the ReportBase class and overrides the Print() method. The Print() method prints a message to the screen. We can now call the reports as follows:

```
ReportBase newStarters = new NewStartersReport();
newStarters.Print();

ReportBase leavers = new LeaversReport();
leavers.Print();
```

Both reports inherit the ReportBase class, so they can be instantiated and assigned to a ReportBase variable. The Print() method can then be called on the variable, and the correct Print() method will be executed. The code now adheres to the single responsibility principle and the open/closed principle.

The next thing we will look at is a divergent change code smells.

Divergent change

When you need to make a change in one location and find yourself having to change many unrelated methods, then this is known as a **divergent change**. Divergent changes take place within a single class and are the result of a poor class structure. Copying and pasting code is another reason this problem arises.

To fix the problem, move the code causing the problem to its own class. If the behavior and state are shared between classes, then consider implementing inheritance using base classes and subclasses as appropriate.

The benefits of fixing divergent change-related problems include easier maintenance as changes will be located within a single location. This makes supporting the application a whole lot easier. It also removes duplicate code from the system, which just so happens to be the next thing we will discuss.

Downcasting

When a base class is cast to one of its children, this is known as **downcasting**. This is a code smell as the base class should not know about the classes that inherit it. For example, consider the Animal base class. Any type of animal can inherit the base class. But an animal can only be of one type. For example, felines are felines and canines are canines. It would be absurd to cast a feline to a canine and vice versa.

It is even more absurd to downcast an animal to one of its subtypes. That would be like saying a monkey is the same as a camel and is good at transporting humans and cargo long distances through the desert. This just does not make sense. So, you should never be downcasting. Upcasting various animals such as monkeys and camels to the Animal type is valid because felines, canines, monkeys, and camels are all types of animals.

Excessive literal use

When using literals, it is very easy to introduce coding errors. An example would be a spelling mistake in a string literal. It is best to assign literals to constant variables. String literals should be placed in resource files for localization, especially if you plan to deploy your software to different locations around the world.

Feature envy

When a method spends more time processing source code in classes other than the one that it is in, this is known as **feature envy**. We will see an example of this in our Authorization class. But before we do, let's have a look at our Authentication class:

```
public class Authentication
{
    private bool _isAuthenticated = false;

    public void Login(ICredentials credentials)
    {
// Checking of credentials omitted for brevity.
        _isAuthenticated = true;
    }

    public void Logout()
    {
        _isAuthenticated = false;
    }

    public bool IsAuthenticated()
    {
```

```
                return _isAuthenticated;
        }
    }
```

Our `Authentication` class is responsible for logging people in and out, as well as identifying whether they are authenticated or not. Let's add our `Authorization` class:

```
public class Authorization
{
    private Authentication _authentication;

    public Authorization(Authentication authentication)
    {
        _authentication = authentication;
    }

    public void Login(ICredentials credentials)
    {
        _authentication.Login(credentials);
    }

    public void Logout()
    {
        _authentication.Logout();
    }

    public bool IsAuthenticated()
    {
        return _authentication.IsAuthenticated();
    }

    public bool IsAuthorized(string role)
    {
        // Dummy example. You would check user is in role.
        return IsAuthenticated && role.Contains("Administrator");
    }
}
```

As you can see, our `Authorization` class is doing more than it is supposed to. There is one method that validates whether the user is authorized to carry a role. The role that's passed in is checked to see whether it is the administrator role. If it is, then the person is authorized. But if the role is not the administrator role, then the person is not authorized.

However, if you look at the other methods, they are doing no more than calling the same methods in the Authentication class. So, in the context of this class, the authentication methods are an example of feature envy. Let's remove the feature envy from the Authorization class:

```csharp
public class Authorization
{
    private ProblemCode.Authentication _authentication;

    public Authorization(ProblemCode.Authentication authentication)
    {
        _authentication = authentication;
    }

    public bool IsAuthorized(string role)
    {
        return _authentication.IsAuthenticated() && role.
Contains("Administrator");
    }
}
```

You will see that the Authorization class is a lot smaller now, and only does what it needs to. There is no longer any feature envy.

Next up, we will look at an inappropriate intimacy code smell.

Inappropriate intimacy

A class engages in inappropriate intimacy when it relies on the implementation details held in a separate class. Does the class that has this reliance need to exist? Can it be merged with the class that it relies on? Or is there shared functionality that is better off being extracted into its own class?

Classes should not rely on each other as this causes coupling, and it can also affect cohesion. A class should ideally be self-contained, and classes should know as little about each other as possible.

Indecent exposure

When a class reveals its internal details, this is known as **indecent exposure**. This breaks the OOP principle of *encapsulation*. Only that which should be public should be public. All other implementations that don't need to be public should be hidden by using the appropriate access modifiers.

Data values should not be public. They should be private, and they should only be modifiable via constructors, methods, and properties. They should also only be retrievable via properties.

The large class (the God object)

The large class, also known as the God object, is all things to all parts of the system. It is a large, unwieldy class that simply does far too much. When you attempt to read the object, the intent of the code may be clear when you read the class name and see what namespace it is in, but then when you come to look at the code, the intent of the code can become lost.

A well-written class should have the name of its intent and should be placed in the appropriate namespace. The contents of the class should follow the company coding standards. Methods should be kept as small as possible, and method parameters should be kept to the absolute bare minimum. Only the methods that belong in the class should be in the class. Member variables, properties, and methods that don't belong in the class should be removed and placed in the correct files in the correct namespace.

To keep classes small and focused, don't inherit classes if there is no need. If there is a class that has five methods, and you will only ever use one of them, is it possible to move that method out into its own reusable class? Remember the single responsibility principle. A class should only have a single responsibility. For example, a file class should only handle operations and behaviors associated with files. A file class should not be performing database operations. You get the idea.

When writing a class, you should aim to make it as small, clean, and readable as you can.

The lazy class (the freeloader and the lazy object)

A **freeloading** class is one that hardly does anything to be useful. When you encounter such classes, you can merge their contents with other classes that have the same kind of intentions.

You can also attempt to collapse the inheritance hierarchy. Remember that the ideal depth of inheritance is *1*. So, if your classes have a larger value for their depth of inheritance, then they are good candidates for moving back up the inheritance tree. You may also want to consider using inline classes for really small classes.

The middleman class

The middleman class does no more than delegate functionality to other objects. In situations like this, you can get rid of the middleman and deal with the objects that carry out the responsibility directly.

Also, remember that you need to keep the depth of inheritance down. So, if you cannot get rid of the class, look to merge it with existing classes. Look at the overall design of that area of code. Could it all be refactored in some way to reduce the amount of code and the number of different classes?

The orphan class of variables and constants

It is not good practice to have a lone class that holds variables and constants for multiple different parts of the application. When you encounter such a situation, it can be hard for the variables to have any real meaning and their context can be lost. It is better to move constants and variables to areas that use them. If constants and variables will be used by multiple classes, then they should be assigned to a file within the root of the namespace they will be used in.

Here are some issues associated with having orphan classes:

- **Lack of cohesion**: Orphan classes may lack a clear, focused responsibility or purpose. When a class contains variables and constants that are used in various parts of a system, it may become a dumping ground for unrelated functionalities. This lack of cohesion can make the code base harder to understand and maintain.

- **Global state**: Classes with shared variables and constants can introduce global state, making it challenging to reason about the state of the system at any given point. Changes to the state in one part of the system may have unintended consequences in other parts, leading to difficult-to-trace bugs.

- **Dependency issues**: If multiple components of a system depend on a class with shared variables and constants, changes to that class can have a cascading effect on various parts of the code base. This can increase the risk of introducing bugs and make the system more fragile to changes.

- **Scoping and encapsulation**: Orphan classes might not adhere to proper scoping and encapsulation principles. Ideally, variables and constants should be defined in the smallest scope possible, and their visibility should be limited to the parts of the system that genuinely need them. Orphan classes may violate these principles, leading to potential issues related to code maintainability and modularity.

- **Maintenance challenges**: As the code base evolves, maintaining and extending functionality in orphan classes can become challenging. Developers may need to sift through unrelated code to understand the purpose and impact of changes, leading to inefficiencies and an increased likelihood of introducing errors.

To address these issues, it's generally advisable to follow good software design principles, such as creating classes with well-defined responsibilities, adhering to encapsulation, minimizing global state, and promoting modular and maintainable code. If variables and constants are used in multiple parts of the system, consider organizing them in a way that aligns with the structure and responsibilities of the system components. This can contribute to a more coherent and maintainable code base.

Primitive obsession

Primitive obsession is a code smell that occurs when primitive data types (such as strings, integers, and others) are used to represent domain concepts, instead of creating dedicated classes or structures to encapsulate that logic. This can lead to code that is harder to understand, maintain, and extend. Let's consider an example by using `CreditCardNumber`, which demonstrates primitive obsession:

```
public class PaymentProcessor
{
    // Primitive obsession example
    public bool ProcessPayment(string creditCardNumber, decimal
amount)
    {
        // Validate credit card number format
```

```
        if (!IsValidCreditCardNumber(creditCardNumber))
        {
            Console.WriteLine("Invalid credit card number format.");
            return false;
        }
        // Perform payment processing logic
        Console.WriteLine($"Processing payment of {amount:C} using
credit card ending in {GetLastFourDigits(creditCardNumber)}.");
        // More payment processing code...
        return true;
    }
    // Primitive obsession: Credit card number validation logic
    private bool IsValidCreditCardNumber(string creditCardNumber)
    {
        // Simplified credit card number validation logic
        // Check length, format, etc.
        return !string.IsNullOrEmpty(creditCardNumber) &&
creditCardNumber.Length == 16 && creditCardNumber.All(char.IsDigit);
    }
    // Primitive obsession: Extracting last four digits from a credit
card number
    private string GetLastFourDigits(string creditCardNumber)
    {
        return creditCardNumber.Length >= 4 ? creditCardNumber.
Substring(creditCardNumber.Length - 4) : string.Empty;
    }
}
```

In this example, we have the following:

1. **Primitive obsession**: `creditCardNumber` is represented as a primitive string. While it's a valid representation, it lacks the encapsulation and validation logic that could be associated with a more specialized type.

2. **Code smell**: The `ProcessPayment` method deals with validating the credit card number and extracting the last four digits directly. This logic could be better encapsulated within a dedicated `CreditCard` class.

- **Validation logic**: The validation logic for the credit card number is scattered within the `ProcessPayment` method, making it harder to reuse or modify independently.

A better approach to address the primitive obsession code smell would be to create a dedicated `CreditCard` class that encapsulates the credit card-related logic:

```
public class CreditCard
{
```

```
    public string Number { get; }
    public CreditCard(string number)
    {
        if (!IsValidCreditCardNumber(number))
        {
            throw new ArgumentException("Invalid credit card number
format.", nameof(number));
        }
        Number = number;
    }
    public string LastFourDigits => Number.Length >= 4 ? Number.
Substring(Number.Length - 4) : string.Empty;
    private bool IsValidCreditCardNumber(string number)
    {
        // Credit card number validation logic
        return !string.IsNullOrEmpty(number) && number.Length == 16 &&
number.All(char.IsDigit);
    }
}
public class PaymentProcessor
{
    public bool ProcessPayment(CreditCard creditCard, decimal amount)
    {
        Console.WriteLine($"Processing payment of {amount:C} using
credit card ending in {creditCard.LastFourDigits}.");
        // More payment processing code...
        return true;
    }
}
```

In this improved version, the `CreditCard` class encapsulates the validation logic, and the `ProcessPayment` method of `PaymentProcessor` now accepts a `CreditCard` instance, making the code more maintainable, modular, and aligned with object-oriented design principles.

Refused bequest

When a class inherits from another class but does not use all its methods, this is known as **refused bequest**. A common reason for this happening is when the subclass is completely different from the base class. For example, a `building` base class is used by different building types, but then a `car` object inherits `building` because it has properties and methods to do with windows and doors. This is wrong.

When you encounter this, consider whether a base class is necessary. If it is, then create one and inherit from it. Otherwise, add the functionality to the class that was inherited from the wrong type.

Speculative generality

A class that is programmed with functionality that is not needed now but may be needed in the future suffers from speculative generality. Such code is dead code and adds maintenance overhead as well as code bloat. It is best to remove these classes when you see them.

Tell, Don't Ask

The *Tell, Don't Ask* software principle informs us, as programmers, that we are to bundle data with the methods that will operate on that data. Our objects must not ask for data and then operate on it! They must tell the logic of an object to perform a specific task on that object's data.

If you find objects that contain logic and that ask other objects for data to carry out their operations, then combine the logic and the data into a single class.

Temporary fields

Temporary fields are member variables that are not needed for an object's entire lifetime.

You can perform refactoring by removing the temporary fields and the methods that operate upon them to their own class. You will end up with clearer code that is well organized.

Method-level smells

Method-level code smells are problems within the method itself. Methods are the workhorses that either make the software function well or poorly. They should be well organized and do only what they are expected to do – no more and no less. It is important to know about the kinds of problems and issues that can arise because of poorly constructed methods. We will address what to look out for in terms of method-level code smells, and what we can do to address them. We'll start with the black sheep method.

The black sheep method

Out of all the methods in the class, a black sheep method will be noticeably different. When you encounter a black sheep method, you must consider the method objectively. What is its name? What is the method's intent? When you have answered these questions, you can decide to remove the method and place it where it truly belongs.

Cyclomatic complexity

When a method has too many loops and branches, this is known as **cyclomatic complexity**. This code smell is also a class-level code smell; we saw how we can reduce the problems with branching when we looked at replacing `switch` and `if` statements. As for loops, they can be replaced with LINQ statements. LINQ statements have the added benefit of being functional code since LINQ is a functional query language.

Contrived complexity

When a method is unnecessarily complex and can be simplified, this complexity is termed contrived complexity. Simplify the method to make sure that its contents are human-readable and understandable. Then, look to refactor the method and reduce its size to the smallest number of lines that is practical.

Dead code

When a method exists but is not used, this is known as **dead code**. The same goes for constructors, properties, parameters, and variables. They should be identified and removed.

> **Note**
>
> Visual Studio and other refactoring tools will often inform you of dead code that can be removed. Different tools may have different keypress combinations to rectify the code, so make sure you know the commands, such as *CTRL +*, to boost your productivity. But be careful – sometimes, they can be wrong.

Excessive data return

When a method returns more data than is needed by each client that calls it, this code smell is known as **excessive data return**. Only the data that is required should be returned. If you find that there are groups of objects with different requirements, then you should maybe consider writing different methods that appeal to both groups and only return what is necessary to those groups.

Feature envy

A method that has feature envy spends more time accessing data in other objects than it does in its own object. We saw this in action when we looked at feature envy in the *Class-level code smells* section.

A method should be kept small, and most of all, its main functionality should be localized to that method. If it is doing more in other methods than its own, then there is scope for moving some of the code out of the method and into its own method.

Identifier size

Identifiers can be either too short or too long. Identifiers should be descriptive and succinct. The main thing to consider when naming variables is their context and location. In a localized loop, a single letter may be appropriate. But if the identifier is at the class level, then it will need a human-understandable name to give it context. Avoid using names that lack context, and that are ambiguous or cause confusion.

Inappropriate intimacy

Methods that rely too heavily on implementation details in other methods or classes display inappropriate intimacy. These methods need to be refactored and possibly even removed. The main thing to bear in mind is that the methods use the internal fields and methods of another class.

To perform refactoring, you can move the methods and fields to where they need to be used. Alternatively, you can extract the fields and methods into a class of their own. Inheritance can replace delegation when the subclass is being intimate with the superclass.

Long lines (God lines)

Long lines of code can be very hard to read and decipher. This makes it difficult for programmers to debug and refactor such code. Where it is possible, the line can be formatted so that any periods and any code after a comma appear on a new line. But such code should also be refactored to make it small.

Lazy methods

A lazy method does very little work. It may delegate its work to other methods, and it may simply call a method on another class that does what it is supposed to. If any of these are the case, then it may pay to get rid of the methods and place code within the methods where it is needed. You could, for instance, use an inline function such as a Lambda.

Long methods (God methods)

A long method is a method that has outgrown itself. Such methods may lose their intent and perform more tasks than they are expected to. You can use the IDE to select parts of the method, and then select extract method or extract class to move portions of the method to their own method and even their own class. A method should only be responsible for doing a single task.

Long parameter lists (too many parameters)

Three or more parameters are classed as the long parameter list code smell. You can tackle this problem by replacing the parameters with a method call. An alternative is to replace the parameters with a parameter object.

Message chains

A message chain occurs when a method calls an object that calls another object that calls another object and so on. Previously, you saw how to deal with message chains when we looked at the Law of Demeter. Message chains break this law as a class should only communicate with its nearest neighbor. Refactor the classes to move the required state and behavior closer to where it is needed.

The middleman method

When all a method does is delegate work out to others to complete, it is a middleman method and can be refactored and removed. But if there is functionality that can't be removed, then merge it in the area that it is being used in.

Oddball solutions

When you see multiple methods doing the same thing but doing it differently, then this is an oddball solution. Choose the method that best implements the task, and then replace the method calls to the other methods with calls to the best method. Then, delete the other methods. This will leave only one method and one way of implementing the task that can be reused.

Speculative generality

A method that is not used anywhere in the code is known as a speculative generality code smell. It is essentially dead code, and all dead code should be removed from the system. Such code provides a maintenance overhead and also provides unnecessary code bloat.

Summary

In this chapter, you were introduced to a variety of code smells and how to remove them through refactoring. We stated that there are application-level code smells, which permeate throughout all the layers of the application, class-level code smells, which run throughout the class, and method-level code smells, which affect the individual methods.

First of all, we covered application-level code smells, which consisted of Boolean blindness, combinatorial explosion, contrived complexity, data clump, deodorant comments, duplicate code, lost intent, mutation of variables, oddball solutions, shotgun surgery, solution sprawl, and uncontrolled side effects.

We then went on to look at class-level code smells, including cyclomatic complexity, divergent change, downcasting, excessive literal use, feature envy, inappropriate intimacy, indecent exposure, and the large object, also known as the God object. We also covered the lazy class, also known as the freeloader and the lazy object, middleman, orphan classes of variables and constants, primitive obsession, refused bequest, speculative generality, Tell, Don't Ask, and temporary fields.

Finally, we moved on to method-level code smells. We discussed black sheep, cyclomatic complexity, contrived complexity, dead code, feature envy, identifier size, inappropriate intimacy, long lines, also known as the God lines, the lazy method, the long method, also known as the God method, the long parameter list, also known as too many parameters, message chains, middleman, oddball solutions, and speculative generality.

In the next chapter, we will continue looking at code refactoring with the use of ReSharper.

Questions

Answer the following questions to test your knowledge of this chapter:

1. What are the three main categories of code smell?
2. Name the different types of application-level code smells.
3. Name the different types of class-level code smells.
4. Name the different types of method-level code smells.
5. What kinds of refactoring can you perform to clean up various code smells?
6. What is cyclomatic complexity?
7. How can we overcome cyclomatic complexity?
8. What is contrived complexity?
9. How can we overcome contrived complexity?
10. What is a combinatorial explosion?
11. How do we overcome a combinatorial explosion?
12. What should you do when you find deodorant comments?
13. If you have bad code but don't know how to fix it, what should you do?
14. Where is a good place to ask questions and get answers when it comes to programming issues?
15. In what ways can a long parameter list be reduced?
16. How can a large method be refactored?
17. What is the maximum length for a clean method?
18. Within what range of numbers should your program's cyclomatic complexity be?
19. What is the ideal depth of inheritance value?
20. What is speculative generality and what should you do about it?
21. If you encounter an oddball solution, what course of action should you take?
22. What refactorings would you perform if you encountered a temporary field?
23. What is a data clump, and what should you do about it?
24. Explain the refused bequest code smell.
25. What law do message chains break?
26. How should message chains be refactored?
27. What is feature envy?
28. How do you remove feature envy?
29. What pattern can you use to replace `switch` statements that return objects?

30. How can we replace `if` statements that return objects?

31. What is solution sprawl, and what can be done to tackle it?

32. Explain the Tell, Don't Ask principle.

33. How does the Tell, Don't Ask principle get broken?

34. What are the symptoms of shotgun surgery, and how should they be addressed?

35. Explain lost intent and what can be done about it.

36. How can loops be refactored, and what benefits do the refactorings bring?

37. What is a divergent change, and how would you go about refactoring it?

Further reading

To learn more about the topics that were covered in this chapter, take a look at the following resources:

- *Refactoring – Improving the Design of Existing Code*, by Martin Fowler and Kent Beck
- `https://refactoring.guru/refactoring`: A good site on design patterns and code smells
- `https://www.dofactory.com/net/design-patterns`: A very good C#-based site on various design patterns

12

Functional Programming

Functional programming is a powerful paradigm that offers a different approach to writing code by treating computation as the evaluation of mathematical functions. In this chapter, we will explore various aspects of functional programming in C#, showcasing how it can lead to more expressive, modular, and maintainable code.

We are going to cover the following topics:

- Overview of functional programming in C#
- First-class functions and Lambda expressions
- High-order functions
- Immutability and pure functions
- Functional composition
- Option types and the Maybe monad
- Functional error handling
- Functional data transformation and pipeline
- Lazy evaluation
- Pattern matching
- Currying and partial application
- Concurrency and partial application

By completing this chapter, you will be able to do the following:

- Understand functional programming in C#
- Apply the functional techniques to your code

Technical requirements

To complete this chapter, you will require the following:

- Visual Studio

- The source code for this chapter: `https://github.com/PacktPublishing/Clean-Code-with-CSharp-Second-Edition/tree/main/CH12`

Imperative versus functional programming

Imperative and functional programming are two different programming paradigms that dictate how you structure your code and solve problems. Let's explore both paradigms using C# code examples.

Imperative programming

Imperative programming focuses on describing how to perform tasks step by step, just like giving a series of instructions to a computer. It's centered around mutable state and using statements to modify the state directly.

Here's an example of imperative programming in C#:

```
using System;
class ImperativeExample
{
    static void Main()
    {
        int sum = 0;

        for (int i = 1; i <= 10; i++)
        {
            sum += i;
        }

        Console.WriteLine("Sum of numbers from 1 to 10: " + sum);
    }
}
```

In this example, we're using a `for` loop to iteratively update the sum variable, which is an example of imperative programming. We're telling the computer exactly how to perform the task step by step.

Functional programming

Functional programming, on the other hand, treats computation as the evaluation of mathematical functions and avoids changing state and mutable data. It focuses on immutability and the use of higher-order functions.

Here's an example of functional programming in C#:

```csharp
using System;
using System.Linq;
class FunctionalExample
{
    static void Main()
    {
        var numbers = Enumerable.Range(1, 10);
        int sum = numbers.Sum();

        Console.WriteLine("Sum of numbers from 1 to 10: " + sum);
    }
}
```

In this example, we're using the LINQ extension Sum method on a sequence of numbers. The functional approach involves using higher-order functions (functions that take other functions as arguments or return functions) and avoiding mutable state.

In the context of **object-oriented programming (OOP)** and C#, the term "state" refers to the current values of the attributes or properties of an object. An object's state represents the data it holds at any given moment. Let's break down the concept of state and how it relates to classes and immutable structs/records in C#.

State in classes

In C#, classes are a fundamental building block of OOP. A class is a blueprint for creating objects, and objects created from the same class share the same structure and behavior. The state of an object instantiated from a class is determined by the values of its fields and properties.

Here's a simple example:

```csharp
public class Person
{
    private string name;
    private int age;
    public string Name { get; set; }
    public int Age { get; set; }
}
```

In this example, the Person class has two fields (name and age) that contribute to the state of an instance of the class. You can create objects of this class and set their state using the properties:

```csharp
Person person1 = new Person();
person1.Name = "John";
person1.Age = 30;
```

State in immutable structs/records

In contrast to classes, structs and records in C# are value types and are often used to represent immutable data structures. Immutable means that the state of an instance cannot be changed after it is created. Instead of modifying the state, you create new instances with the desired state.

Here's an example using an immutable record:

```
public record ImmutablePerson(string Name, int Age);
```

In this case, the ImmutablePerson record has two properties (Name and Age). Since records are immutable, you cannot change the values once an instance is created. Instead, you must create a new instance with the updated state:

```
ImmutablePerson person1 = new ImmutablePerson("John", 30);
ImmutablePerson person2 = person1 with { Age = 31 };
```

In the second line, a new instance, person2, is created with the same Name but a different Age. The original instance, person1, remains unchanged.

Understanding and managing the state of objects is crucial in OOP, and choosing between classes and immutable structs/records depends on the specific requirements of your application. Immutable types can offer benefits in terms of safety, concurrency, and reasoning about code but may involve more memory allocation due to the creation of new instances. Classes, on the other hand, allow for mutability but require careful management to avoid unintended side effects.

Key differences

Let's look at the key differences between these approaches:

- **State and mutability**:
  - **Imperative**: It focuses on changing state and mutable data directly
  - **Functional**: It emphasizes immutability and avoids changing state directly
- **Control flow**:
  - **Imperative**: It relies on explicit control flow statements such as loops and conditionals
  - **Functional**: It leverages higher-order functions and expressions for control flow
- **Side effects**:
  - **Imperative**: It can lead to more side effects due to mutable state changes
  - **Functional**: It minimizes side effects, making it easier to reason about code

- **Code style**:

  - **Imperative**: It often involves more explicit step-by-step instructions
  - **Functional**: It focuses on composing functions to transform data

The following table compares imperative and functional programming:

Feature	Imperative Programming	Functional Programming
Paradigm	Uses statements to change a program's state	Focuses on declaring functions and avoiding state changes
Mutability	Emphasizes mutable state and variables	Emphasizes immutability and avoids mutable state
Control flow	Relies on explicit control flow structures (loops, conditionals)	Uses higher-order functions, recursion, and expressions for control flow
Side effects	Commonly involves side effects and changes to the external state	Avoids side effects and aims for pure functions without side effects
State management	Uses objects and classes to manage state	Relies on immutable data structures and avoids shared mutable state
Functions	May have side effects and don't necessarily adhere to mathematical functions	Emphasizes pure functions with no side effects following mathematical functions
Coding style	Tends to be more procedural and imperative	Tends to be more declarative and expression-oriented
Error handling	Often uses exception handling for error management	Encourages the use of monads or other functional constructs for error handling
Parallelism	May require manual management of concurrency and parallelism	Facilitates parallelism through immutability and pure functions
Readability	Code may be more verbose with explicit state changes	Code is often more concise and readable due to the absence of mutable state and side effects

Table 12.1: Imperative versus functional programming

Both programming paradigms have their merits and are suitable for different scenarios. It's common to use a mix of both paradigms depending on the problem at hand and the preferences of the developer.

Overview of functional programming in C#

Functional programming in C# is a programming paradigm that emphasizes writing code in a declarative and immutable manner, treating computation as the evaluation of mathematical functions. In this approach, functions are first-class citizens, which means they can be assigned to variables, passed as arguments to other functions, and returned as results from functions. The central idea is to model computations as the composition of pure functions, where the output solely depends on the input, without any side effects or mutable state.

Here are some key characteristics of functional programming in C#:

- **Immutability**: In functional programming, data is treated as immutable, meaning once created, it cannot be changed. Instead of modifying existing data, functional programs create new data with updated values, which helps in maintaining a more predictable and reliable state.

- **Pure functions**: Pure functions are functions that produce the same output for a given set of inputs and have no side effects. This property makes them easy to reason about and test. They don't modify the external state or interact with the outside world, making them isolated and independent.

- **Higher-order functions**: C# supports higher-order functions, which are functions that can take other functions as arguments or return functions as results. This enables powerful abstractions and code reuse, promoting modularity and composability.

- **Lambda expressions**: Lambda expressions are concise and anonymous functions that facilitate writing functional code in C#. They allow developers to define simple functions directly at the call site without the need for explicit method declarations.

- **Option types and the Maybe monad**: Functional programming in C# often involves using option types, such as `Nullable<T>`, or custom types such as `Option<T>`, to handle the absence of a value without resorting to null references. The Maybe monad is frequently employed to handle computations with possible null results elegantly.

- **Functional data transformation and pipelines**: Functional programming encourages transforming data using pure functions and building pipelines, which are sequences of operations, to process data from one step to another. This enables the creation of expressive and concise code.

- **Pattern matching**: C# 7.0 and later versions support pattern matching, a feature that's common in functional programming languages. Pattern matching allows developers to match the structure of data and perform different operations based on patterns, leading to more readable and efficient code.

- **Concurrency and parallelism**: Functional programming facilitates writing concurrent and parallel code with less contention and complexity. By avoiding shared mutable state, functional programs can often achieve better scalability and safety in multi-threaded scenarios.

Functional programming in C# is not about eliminating imperative programming altogether but rather about utilizing the functional paradigm in appropriate situations to improve code quality, maintainability, and expressiveness. By embracing these functional techniques, C# developers can design more robust, scalable, and maintainable applications while taking advantage of the language's expressive power and extensive libraries.

First-class functions and Lambda expressions

In C#, functions are considered first-class citizens, which means they can be treated just like any other data type, such as integers or strings. This enables functions to be assigned to variables, passed as arguments to other functions, and returned as results from functions. In essence, functions can be manipulated and used as data, making them a powerful tool for abstraction and code reuse.

Lambda expressions in C#

Lambda expressions are a concise way to define anonymous functions in C#. They provide a compact syntax for creating delegates or expression trees. A Lambda expression consists of input parameters (if any), the Lambda operator (=>), and the function body. The function body can be a single expression or a block of statements enclosed in curly braces.

The general syntax of a Lambda expression in C# is as follows:

```
(parameters) => expression
```

Here's an example of a simple Lambda expression that adds two numbers:

```
Func<int, int, int> add = (a, b) => a + b;
```

In this example, we define a Lambda expression that takes two integers (a and b) as input parameters and returns their sum (a + b). Func<int, int, int> is a delegate type that represents a function that takes two integers as input and returns an integer as output. We assign our Lambda expression to a variable called add, and we can now use this variable as if it were a regular function.

Lambda expressions are commonly used when working with higher-order functions or LINQ in C#. For instance, they can be used in LINQ's Where, Select, OrderBy, and other methods to specify filtering, projection, and ordering operations succinctly.

Here's an example of using a Lambda expression with LINQ's Where method:

```
List<int> numbers = new List<int> { 1, 2, 3, 4, 5, 6, 7, 8, 9, 10 };
List<int> evenNumbers = numbers.Where(num => num % 2 == 0).ToList();
```

In this example, we use a Lambda expression within the Where method to filter out the even numbers from the numbers list, and the result is stored in the evenNumbers list.

Lambda expressions simplify the syntax of defining small, single-purpose functions, and they are particularly valuable in functional programming as they allow functions to be created directly at the call site without the need for explicit method declarations. They enhance code readability and maintainability, especially when working with collections and LINQ queries in C#.

Higher-order functions

In C#, a higher-order function is a function that takes one or more functions as arguments or returns a function as its result. This concept is an essential aspect of functional programming and enables powerful abstractions and code reusability.

There are two main types of higher-order functions in C#:

- **Functions that take other functions as arguments**: These higher-order functions accept one or more functions as parameters. They can then apply those functions to data or invoke them within their own implementation. By passing different functions as arguments, the higher-order function can be customized to perform various operations without needing separate implementations for each case.

In functional programming, one of the key principles is immutability. In C#, you can use LINQ to achieve a non-mutating state. Here's an example of a higher-order function that takes functions as arguments and uses LINQ without violating the non-mutating state concept:

```
using System;
using System.Collections.Generic;
using System.Linq;
class Program
{
    static void Main()
    {
        // Example usage
        List<int> numbers = new List<int> { 1, 2, 3, 4, 5 };

        // High-order function: TransformList
        var squaredNumbers = TransformList(numbers, x => x * x);
        // Print the original and transformed lists
        Console.WriteLine("Original numbers: " + string.Join(",
", numbers));
        Console.WriteLine("Squared numbers: " + string.Join(",
", squaredNumbers));
    }
    // High-order function that applies a transformation to each
    element of a list
    static List<TOutput> TransformList<TInput,
TOutput>(List<TInput> inputList, Func<TInput, TOutput>
```

```
transformFunc)
    {
        // Using LINQ to project each element of the input list
    using the provided transformation function
        return inputList.Select(transformFunc).ToList();
    }
}
```

In this example, the `TransformList` function is a higher-order function that takes a list and a transformation function as arguments. It uses LINQ's `Select` method to project each element of the input list using the provided transformation function and then converts the result into a list.

The key point here is that the original list (numbers) remains unchanged, and a new list (`squaredNumbers`) is created with the transformed values. This adheres to the non-mutating state concept in functional programming.

- **Functions that return functions**: These higher-order functions create and return new functions as their result. The returned functions can be customized or parameterized based on the input arguments to the higher-order function. This technique is useful for creating specialized functions on the fly without the need to explicitly define them beforehand.

Here's an example of a higher-order function in C# that returns a function:

```
public static Func<int, int, int> GetMathOperation(string
operation)
{
    switch (operation)
    {
        case "add":
            return (a, b) => a + b;
        case "subtract":
            return (a, b) => a - b;
        case "multiply":
            return (a, b) => a * b;
        case "divide":
            return (a, b) => b != 0 ? a / b : throw new
ArgumentException("Cannot divide by zero.");
        default:
            throw new ArgumentException("Invalid operation.");
    }
}
```

In this example, `GetMathOperation` is a higher-order function that takes a string representing a math operation and returns a function (`Func<int, int, int>`) accordingly. Depending on the input string, it returns different Lambda functions that perform the specified math operation.

Higher-order functions in C# facilitate code reuse, abstraction, and modularity. They enable developers to create more flexible and expressive code by parameterizing behavior and promoting separation of concerns. These functions are commonly used in functional programming paradigms and are particularly valuable when combined with Lambda expressions and LINQ, allowing for concise and elegant code that is easier to maintain and understand.

Immutability and pure functions

Immutability refers to the property of an object whose state cannot be changed after it is created. In C#, this means that once an object is instantiated, its internal state, including the values of its properties, cannot be modified. Instead of modifying the existing object, any updates or modifications result in the creation of a new object with the updated values.

Immutability is commonly associated with functional programming in C# and has several benefits:

- **Predictable behavior**: Since immutable objects cannot change state, their behavior remains consistent throughout the program's execution, making the code easier to reason about and debug.

- **Thread safety**: Immutable objects are inherently thread-safe since multiple threads cannot modify their state concurrently. This simplifies concurrent programming and reduces the risk of data corruption or race conditions.

- **Caching and optimization**: Immutability allows for caching and optimizing objects since their values remain constant. This can lead to performance improvements in certain scenarios, along with improved testability due to the lack of a mutable state, which can make tests predictable.

Here's an example of an immutable record in C#:

```
Public record Point(int x, int y);
```

In this example, the `Point` record is immutable because it has read-only properties, X and Y. Once a `Point` object is created, its X and Y values cannot be changed.

A pure function is a function that, given the same input, always produces the same output and has no side effects. In C#, this means that a pure function doesn't modify the global state, modify input parameters, perform I/O operations, or have any observable effect beyond computing the return value.

Pure functions are a fundamental concept in functional programming and have several advantages:

- **Deterministic behavior**: Since pure functions produce the same output for the same input, they offer deterministic behavior, which is crucial for predictability and testability

- **Easy testing**: Pure functions are easy to test because their behavior is entirely determined by their inputs, and they do not rely on the external state or resources

- **Referential transparency**: Pure functions exhibit referential transparency, meaning that a function call can be replaced with its return value without affecting the program's behavior

Here's an example of a pure function in C#:

```
public static int PerformOperation(Func<int, int, int> operation, int
a, int b) {
    return operation(a, b);
}
```

The C# code defines a function, `PerformOperation`, in the context of functional programming. It takes a binary operation represented by the `Func<int, int, int>` delegate, along with two integers (a and b), and applies the operation, returning the result. The code embraces the functional programming principle of first-class functions, treating operations as parameters. If the provided operation adheres to purity principles (the same output for the same input and no side effects), the `PerformOperation` function is also considered pure. This design promotes composability and clarity in functional programming by allowing different operations to be easily passed and applied. By embracing immutability and pure functions, C# developers can design more maintainable, reliable, and parallelizable code.

Functional programming techniques encourage the use of immutable data structures and pure functions whenever possible, promoting better code quality and enabling developers to write robust and scalable applications.

Functional composition

Functional composition in C# refers to the practice of combining multiple functions to create a new function. The result of one function becomes the input for another function, allowing developers to chain and compose functions to perform more complex operations in a concise and declarative manner. This technique is a core concept in functional programming and enables code reuse and modularity.

There are several ways to achieve functional composition in C#, including using Lambda expressions, LINQ, and higher-order functions. Let's explore some examples of functional composition in C#.

Using Lambda expressions

```
Func<int, int> addOne = x => x + 1;
Func<int, int> doubleValue = x => x * 2;
Func<int, int> composedFunction = x => doubleValue(addOne(x));
int result = composedFunction(5); // result = doubleValue(addOne(5)) =
doubleValue(6) = 12
```

In this example, we define two simple functions, `addOne` and `doubleValue`. Then, we create a new function called `composedFunction`, which applies `addOne` first and then passes the result to `doubleValue`. The `result` variable holds the value that was obtained by composing the two functions.

Using LINQ and extension methods

```
List<int> numbers = new List<int> { 1, 2, 3, 4, 5 };
IEnumerable<int> transformedNumbers = numbers.Select(x => x +
1).Where(x => x % 2 == 0);
```

In this example, we use the LINQ Select and Where extension methods to compose two functions together. The Select method adds 1 to each element in the numbers list and the Where method filters out the even numbers from the result.

Using higher-order functions

```
Func<int, int> addOne = x => x + 1;
Func<int, int> doubleValue = x => x * 2;
Func<int, int> ComposeFunctions(Func<int, int> func1, Func<int, int>
func2)
{
    return x => func2(func1(x));
}
Func<int, int> composedFunction = ComposeFunctions(addOne,
doubleValue);
int result = composedFunction(5); // result = doubleValue(addOne(5)) =
doubleValue(6) = 12
```

In this example, we create a higher-order function, ComposeFunctions, which takes two functions as arguments and returns a new function that applies the second function to the result of the first function. We then use this higher-order function to compose addOne and doubleValue.

Functional composition in C# allows developers to build complex behavior by combining simpler functions in a way that promotes code reuse and clarity. It enhances the readability and maintainability of code by breaking down complex operations into smaller, composable functions. By leveraging functional composition techniques, developers can design more expressive and concise code, making their applications easier to understand and maintain.

Option types and the Maybe monad

Option types and the Maybe monad are concepts that are used in functional programming to handle the absence of a value or represent a computation that might fail. While C# doesn't have built-in support for option types and the Maybe monad, we can implement them using custom classes or leverage third-party libraries such as LanguageExt and CSharpFunctionalExtensions to achieve similar functionality.

Option types represent the presence or absence of a value, providing a safe alternative to using null references. Instead of directly returning null when a value is not found or when an operation fails, option types allow us to explicitly indicate the absence of a value.

Here's an example of an option type in C#:

```
public class Option<T>
{
    private readonly T value;

    public bool HasValue { get; }
    public T Value => HasValue ? value : throw new
InvalidOperationException("Option has no value.");

    private Option() => HasValue = false;
    private Option(T value) { HasValue = true; this.value = value; }

    public static Option<T> Some(T value) => new Option<T>(value);
    public static Option<T> None() => new Option<T>();
}
```

The provided code defines a generic class, Option<T>, that represents an optional value, similar to the concept of an "option" or "maybe" type in functional programming. This class has two possible states:

- Some: This represents a case where the option has a value. It is constructed using the Some method, which takes a value of the T type.

- None: This represents a case where the option has no value. It is constructed using the None method.

The class also has properties:

- HasValue: This indicates whether the option has a value

- Value: This returns the value if HasValue is true; otherwise, it throws an InvalidOperationException error

The constructor and properties are designed to ensure that an instance of Option<T> can only be in one of the two states.

You can achieve similar functionality using C# nullable types, which were introduced in C# 8.0. Here's how you might rewrite the code using a nullable type:

```
public class Option<T>
{
    public T? Value { get; }

    public bool HasValue => Value.HasValue;

    private Option(T? value) => Value = value;
```

```
    public static Option<T> Some(T value) => new Option<T>(value);
    public static Option<T> None() => new Option<T>(null);
}
```

In this version, the `Value` property is of the `T?` type (nullable type), allowing it to represent both cases of having a value (`HasValue` is `true`) and having no value (`Value` is `null`). The `Some` method sets the value, and the `None` method creates an instance with a null value.

This approach simplifies the code by leveraging nullable types, but it's worth noting that the semantic meaning of `Option<T>` and nullable types is not the same. The `Option<T>` type explicitly communicates the intention of representing an optional value, whereas nullable types may have different use cases.

Usage of option types in C#

```
Option<int> GetPositiveNumber(int num)
{
    if (num > 0)
        return Option<int>.Some(num);
    else
        return Option<int>.None();
}

Option<int> result = GetPositiveNumber(-5);

if (result.HasValue)
{
    int value = result.Value;
    Console.WriteLine($"Positive number found: {value}");
}
else
{
    Console.WriteLine("No positive number found.");
}
```

In this usage example, the `GetPositiveNumber` function returns an `Option` type to indicate whether a positive number was found or not.

The Maybe monad in C#

The Maybe monad is a construct that's used to chain computations that may produce null results or fail gracefully. It allows us to avoid null reference exceptions and handle potential errors more elegantly and functionally.

Here's an example of a Maybe monad in C# using extension methods:

```
public static class MaybeExtensions
{
    public static Maybe<T> ToMaybe<T>(this T value) => new
Maybe<T>(value);
}
public class Maybe<T>
{
    private readonly T value;

    public bool HasValue { get; }
    public T Value => HasValue ? value : throw new
InvalidOperationException("Maybe has no value.");

    private Maybe() => HasValue = false;
    public Maybe(T value) { HasValue = true; this.value = value; }
}
```

In this example, we define a `Maybe<T>` class, and the `MaybeExtensions` class provides an extension method to convert a value into a Maybe monad.

Let's look at the use of the Maybe monad in C#:

```
Maybe<int> result = GetPositiveNumber(-5).ToMaybe();
if (result.HasValue)
{
    int value = result.Value;
    Console.WriteLine($"Positive number found: {value}");
}
else
{
    Console.WriteLine("No positive number found.");
}
```

In this example, we chain the `Maybe` monad with the `Option` type from the previous example using the `ToMaybe()` extension method.

By using the `Option` type and the `Maybe` monad in C#, we can create safer and more expressive code by explicitly handling scenarios where values may be absent, or operations may fail. These functional programming concepts promote better error handling and can lead to more robust and reliable applications.

Functional error handling

Functional error handling in C# involves using functional programming techniques to handle and propagate errors more elegantly and robustly. It focuses on avoiding exceptions and mutable state for error handling and instead relies on data structures and monads to represent and manage errors in a functional and declarative way.

There are several approaches to functional error handling in C#:

- **Option types and the Maybe monad**: As discussed earlier, **Option** types and the **Maybe** monad can be used to represent the absence of a value or the success/failure of an operation without resorting to null references or exceptions. Instead of throwing exceptions, functions can return **Option** types or **Maybe** monads, allowing callers to handle the absence of results or potential errors explicitly.

  Here's an example of using Option types for error handling in C#:

  ```
  public Option<int> TryParseInt(string input)
  {
      if (int.TryParse(input, out int result))
          return Option<int>.Some(result);
      else
          return Option<int>.None();
  }
  ```

- **Either monad**: The `Either` monad is a construct that represents a result that can be either a success value (`Right`) or an error value (`Left`). This approach allows functions to return either the successful result or an error message, making it easier to propagate and functionally handle errors.

  Here's an example of using the `Either` monad for error handling in C#:

  ```
  public Either<int, string> TryParseInt(string input)
  {
      if (int.TryParse(input, out int result))
          return Either<int, string>.Left(result);
      else
          return Either<int, string>.Right("Invalid input");
  }
  ```

- **Railway-oriented programming** (**ROP**): ROP is an error-handling approach where functions return a result object that contains both the success value and any potential error messages. It enables composing functions together in a way that automatically handles errors and propagates them without breaking the execution flow.

Here's an example of using ROP for error handling in C#:

```
public Result<int> TryParseInt(string input)
{
    if (int.TryParse(input, out int result))
        return Result.<int>.Success(result);
    else
        return Result.<int>.Failure("Invalid input");
}
```

In this approach, the `Result<T>` class represents the result of an operation, which can be either a success, `Success`, or a failure, `Failure`. The `Result` object contains both the success value (if applicable) and an error message (if there was a failure).

Functional error handling in C# encourages developers to handle errors explicitly using data structures such as `Option` types, the `Maybe` monad, the `Either` monad, and `Result` objects. By relying on functional programming concepts, developers can create more reliable and maintainable code that elegantly handles and propagates errors throughout their applications. Additionally, these approaches make it easier to reason about and test error scenarios and lead to more robust and predictable code.

Incorporating functional error-handling techniques in C# can greatly enhance the reliability and maintainability of code. Each of the mentioned approaches – `Option` types, the `Maybe` monad, the `Either` monad, and `Result` objects – has its use cases, and choosing the right one depends on the specific requirements and design preferences.

Option types

Use case: Option types are suitable when an operation might result in a value or nothing (null). They help eliminate null reference exceptions and make it explicit that a value might be absent.

Example: Returning `Option<string>` instead of a nullable string when searching for an item in a collection. This communicates that the item may or may not be found.

The Maybe monad

Use case: Similar to `Option` types, `Maybe` monads represent computations that may fail. They are beneficial for chaining operations, where any failure in the chain causes subsequent operations to short-circuit.

Example: Using a `Maybe` monad to chain a series of data transformations where any step might fail, preventing unnecessary computation in case of failure.

The Either monad

Use case: `Either` monads are useful when there are two distinct outcomes, often representing success and failure. They allow for more detailed error information and can be used to propagate context about the failure.

Example: A function returning `Either<ErrorType, ResultType>`, where `ErrorType` contains information about the failure and `ResultType` represents the successful result.

Result objects

Use case: `Result` objects are suitable for scenarios where you want to communicate both success and failure explicitly. They often include additional information about the error.

Example: A function returning `Result<string, ErrorType>` where the string represents a successful result, and `ErrorType` contains details about the failure.

Choosing the right approach depends on the level of granularity you need for error handling, the complexity of your application, and your team's familiarity with these concepts. Additionally, consider whether you want to short-circuit on the first error that's encountered or accumulate multiple errors before halting execution. In any case, adopting these functional programming concepts for error handling in C# can lead to more robust, testable, and comprehensible code.

Functional data transformation and pipelines

Functional data transformation and pipelines in C# refer to the practice of using functional programming techniques to transform data through a sequence of operations, creating a concise and declarative flow. Instead of using imperative loops and mutable state to modify data, functional data transformation relies on higher-order functions, Lambda expressions, and LINQ to apply a series of operations to the data without changing its original state.

Functional data transformation involves using pure functions to transform input data into new output data. The transformation functions take the input data and return a new data structure with the desired changes. These functions do not modify the original data; instead, they create new data based on the input.

Here's an example of functional data transformation in C# using the LINQ `Select` and `Where` methods:

```
List<int> numbers = new List<int> { 1, 2, 3, 4, 5 };
// Transform the numbers into their squares
List<int> squares = numbers.Select(x => x * x).ToList();
// Filter out the even numbers
List<int> evenNumbers = numbers.Where(x => x % 2 == 0).ToList();
```

In this example, `Select` and `Where` are LINQ methods that are used for functional data transformation. The `Select` method transforms each element of the `numbers` list into its square, and the `Where` method filters out the even numbers.

Functional pipelines combine multiple data transformation operations into a sequence, creating a pipeline that processes data from one step to another. Each operation in the pipeline takes the output of the previous operation as input, allowing for a chain of transformations that can be composed and extended easily.

Here's an example of a functional pipeline in C#:

```
List<int> numbers = new List<int> { 1, 2, 3, 4, 5 };
List<int> result = numbers
    .Where(x => x % 2 == 0)        // Filter out the even numbers
    .Select(x => x * x)            // Transform the remaining numbers
into their squares
    .OrderByDescending(x => x)     // Sort the squared numbers in
descending order
    .ToList();
```

In this example, the pipeline starts with the numbers list and applies a sequence of operations using LINQ methods. First, it filters out the even numbers, then transforms the remaining numbers into their squares, and finally sorts the squared numbers in descending order.

Functional data transformation and pipelines in C# promote a more expressive and concise way of processing data. By using functional programming techniques, developers can create clean and readable code that is easier to understand, test, and maintain. Additionally, functional pipelines allow for better separation of concerns and enable developers to build complex data transformations by composing simple functions into a chain of operations.

The **Task Parallel Library** (**TPL**) in C# provides powerful tools for parallelizing and concurrently executing tasks. When combined with functional data transformation and pipelines, it can lead to efficient parallel processing. The TPL Dataflow library is particularly helpful for building data-centric parallel applications with a focus on pipelining.

Let's consider a simple example of using the TPL Dataflow for data transformation.

TPL Dataflow is a library that provides dataflow components to help increase the robustness of concurrency-enabled applications. These dataflow components are useful when you have multiple operations that must communicate with one another asynchronously or when you want to process data as it becomes available.

One way to use TPL Dataflow for parallel data transformation is to use the TransformBlock<TInput, TOutput> class, which represents a dataflow block that invokes a provided function for every data element received. You can link multiple transform blocks together to create a pipeline of data transformations and use the ActionBlock<TInput> class to perform an action on the final output.

Here is an example of a simple console app that uses TPL Dataflow for parallel data transformation:

```
using System;
using System.Threading.Tasks;
using System.Threading.Tasks.Dataflow;

namespace CH12_Async
{
```

```
class Program
{
    static async Task Main(string[] args)
    {
        // Create some sample data
        int[] data = new int[10];
        Random random = new Random();
        for (int i = 0; i < data.Length; i++)
        {
            data[i] = random.Next(1, 100);
        }

        // Create the dataflow blocks
        var multiplyByTwo = new TransformBlock<int, int>(x => x *
2);
        var addFive = new TransformBlock<int, int>(x => x + 5);
        var printResult = new ActionBlock<int>(x => Console.
WriteLine(x));

        // Link the blocks together
        var options = new DataflowLinkOptions {
PropagateCompletion = true };
        multiplyByTwo.LinkTo(addFive, options);
        addFive.LinkTo(printResult, options);

        // Post data to the first block
        foreach (var item in data)
        {
            multiplyByTwo.Post(item);
        }

        // Mark the first block as complete
        multiplyByTwo.Complete();

        // Wait for the last block to complete
        await printResult.Completion;

        // Print a message
        Console.WriteLine("Dataflow completed.");
    }
}
```

In this example, we have the following:

- `BufferBlock<int>` is used to store the input data
- `TransformBlock<int, string>` is used for two parallel transformations
- `ActionBlock<string>` is used to process the final results

This code creates three dataflow blocks: a transform block that multiplies the input by two, a transform block that adds five to the input, and an action block that prints the input to the console. It then links the blocks together using the LinkTo method, and sets the PropagateCompletion option to true, which means that when a source block completes, it will signal the completion to its target block, and so on until the action block completes. It then posts some sample data to the first block, marks the first block as complete, and waits for the last block to complete. The output of the program should look something like this:

```
17
29
39
23
35
27
21
19
25
37
Dataflow completed.
```

Your numbers will be different, but the data output format should be the same. This example demonstrates how TPL Dataflow can be used to create a simple parallel data transformation pipeline, taking advantage of immutability and functional programming concepts in a concurrent setting.

Lazy evaluation

Lazy evaluation in C# is a functional programming technique that postpones the evaluation of an expression or computation until the result is needed. Instead of immediately computing the value of an expression when it is defined, lazy evaluation allows the value to be computed only when it is requested for the first time. This can improve performance and reduce unnecessary computations, especially for expensive or time-consuming operations.

In C#, lazy evaluation is commonly achieved using the `Lazy<T>` class, which is part of the .NET Framework. The `Lazy<T>` class allows us to defer the execution of a computation and ensures that the computation is executed only once, no matter how many times the value is accessed.

Here's an example of lazy evaluation in C# using `Lazy<T>`:

```csharp
using System;
public class Example
{
    private static Lazy<int> lazyValue = new Lazy<int>(() =>
ComputeValue());
    private static int ComputeValue()
    {
        // Some expensive computation
        Console.WriteLine("Computing the value...");
        return 42;
    }
    public static void Main()
    {
        Console.WriteLine("Before accessing the value.");

        // The computation is not executed until we access the Value
property.
        int value = lazyValue.Value;

        Console.WriteLine($"Value: {value}");

        // The computation is executed only once, subsequent accesses
use the cached result.
        int cachedValue = lazyValue.Value;

        Console.WriteLine($"Cached Value: {cachedValue}");
    }
}
```

In this example, we use the `Lazy<T>` class to create a lazy-evaluated value called `lazyValue`. The `ComputeValue()` method represents some expensive computation that we want to defer. When we run the `Main()` method, we print a message before accessing the value. Then, when we access the `Value` property of `lazyValue`, the `ComputeValue()` method is executed for the first time, and `result (42)` is cached. Subsequent accesses to the `Value` property do not recompute the value and instead use the cached result, as demonstrated by the `"Cached Value"` message.

`Lazy<T>` and asynchronous functions (`async` and `Task<T>`) in C# serve distinct purposes. `Lazy<T>` is designed for deferred and single initialization, allowing the instantiation of an object to be postponed until it is accessed for the first time. The initialization is synchronous, ensuring it occurs only once, and subsequent requests return the cached instance. It's particularly useful for scenarios where the cost of creating the object is high, and you want to avoid unnecessary instantiation. On the other hand, asynchronous functions, which are marked with the `async` keyword and utilize `Task<T>`, are employed for non-blocking and concurrent execution of operations. They enable the program to continue with other tasks while waiting for asynchronous operations, making them well-suited for scenarios involving parallelism or asynchronous I/O, where blocking operations would hinder overall performance. While `Lazy<T>` focuses on deferred instantiation and single initialization, asynchronous functions excel in scenarios requiring concurrent and non-blocking execution.

Lazy evaluation is particularly useful when you're dealing with computationally intensive operations or data that might not be required during the entire execution of a program. By deferring computations until they are needed, lazy evaluation can lead to more efficient and performant code, making it an essential technique for functional programming in C#.

Pattern matching

Functional pattern matching in C# is a technique that's used to match the structure of data against a series of patterns and execute specific code blocks based on the matched pattern. It allows developers to express complex conditional logic in a more concise and declarative way, making code more readable and maintainable.

In C#, functional pattern matching can be achieved using the `switch` statement with the `case` pattern matching feature that was introduced in C# 7.0. With this feature, you can pattern match on various types, constant values, or even custom patterns using the `when` keyword.

Here's an example of functional pattern matching in C#:

```
public class Shape
{
}
public class Circle : Shape
{
    public double Radius { get; set; }
}

public class Rectangle : Shape
{
    public double Width { get; set; }
    public double Height { get; set; }
}

public class Triangle : Shape
{
    public double SideA { get; set; }
    public double SideB { get; set; }
    public double SideC { get; set; }
}
public class Program
```

```
{
    public static void Main()
    {
        Shape shape = new Rectangle { Width = 3, Height = 4 };

        double area = CalculateArea(shape);

        Console.WriteLine($"Area: {area}");
    }
public static double CalculateArea(Shape shape)
    {
        switch (shape)
        {
            case Circle circle:
                return Math.PI * circle.Radius * circle.Radius;
            case Rectangle rectangle:
                return rectangle.Width * rectangle.Height;
            case Triangle triangle when IsRightAngled(triangle):
                double s = (triangle.SideA + triangle.SideB +
triangle.SideC) / 2;
                return Math.Sqrt(s * (s - triangle.SideA) * (s -
triangle.SideB) * (s - triangle.SideC));
            default:
                throw new ArgumentException("Unsupported shape
type.");
        }
    }

    public static bool IsRightAngled(Triangle triangle)
    {
        return Math.Pow(triangle.SideA, 2) + Math.Pow(triangle.SideB,
2) == Math.Pow(triangle.SideC, 2)
            || Math.Pow(triangle.SideB, 2) + Math.Pow(triangle.SideC,
2) == Math.Pow(triangle.SideA, 2)
            || Math.Pow(triangle.SideC, 2) + Math.Pow(triangle.SideA,
2) == Math.Pow(triangle.SideB, 2);
    }
}
```

In this example, we have a Shape class and three derived classes called Circle, Rectangle, and Triangle. The CalculateArea method uses the switch statement with pattern matching to calculate the area of the given shape based on its type and properties. We use pattern matching to extract data from the shape variable and execute the corresponding code block based on the shape's type. The when keyword is used to match right-angled triangles and calculate their area accordingly.

Functional pattern matching in C# allows for more expressive and clear code when handling complex branching scenarios, especially when working with polymorphic types. It is a powerful tool for functional programming and enhances the readability and maintainability of code, making it easier to handle multiple cases and scenarios concisely and efficiently.

Currying and partial application

Currying and partial application are techniques that are used in functional programming to transform functions, but they differ in their approach and application.

Currying

Definition: Currying is a process in which a function that takes multiple arguments is transformed into a sequence of functions, each taking a single argument.

Resulting function: The resulting curried function returns a new function with each invocation, expecting one argument at a time until all the original arguments are supplied.

Here's an example:

```
// Curried function
Func<int, Func<int, int>> addCurried = x => y => x + y;
// Usage
var addWith5 = addCurried(5);
int result = addWith5(3); // Result: 8
```

Partial application

Definition: Partial application involves fixing a certain number of arguments of a function, creating a new function with fewer parameters.

Resulting function: The resulting partially applied function can be invoked with the remaining arguments to produce a specialized version of the original function.

Here's an example:

```
// Original function
Func<int, int, int> add = (x, y) => x + y;
// Partial application
Func<int, int> addWith5 = x => add(x, 5);
// Usage
int result = addWith5(3); // Result: 8
```

Key differences

Arity: Currying involves transforming a function into a sequence of single-argument functions, while partial application fixes a subset of arguments in a multi-argument function.

Usage: Currying is primarily concerned with transforming functions for a more flexible composition, allowing for the creation of functions with varying arities. Partial application, on the other hand, focuses on creating specialized versions of functions with fixed parameters.

Syntax: Currying often relies on creating nested functions or using language features that explicitly support currying, while partial application can be achieved through various means, such as Lambda expressions or library functions.

Currying and partial application are related concepts in functional programming, but they address different aspects of function transformation. Currying decomposes a function's arity, while partial application fixes some arguments, creating specialized functions.

Concurrency with functional programming

Concurrency with functional programming in C# involves handling concurrent and parallel execution of code in a way that avoids shared mutable state and embraces functional programming principles. It focuses on creating independent, immutable data and pure functions to manage concurrent operations, promoting safety, modularity, and scalability.

Here are some key aspects of concurrency with functional programming in C#:

- **Immutable data**: Functional programming encourages the use of immutable data structures, where data cannot be modified after creation. By avoiding a shared mutable state, concurrent operations can work independently without interfering with each other's data. Immutable data reduces the risk of race conditions and other concurrency-related bugs.

- **Pure functions**: Pure functions, which produce the same output for the same input and have no side effects, are inherently suitable for concurrent programming. Since pure functions don't rely on a shared state, they can be executed concurrently without worrying about data corruption or unintended interactions.

- **Functional data transformation**: Functional programming encourages data transformation using pure functions and pipelines. When dealing with concurrent operations, functional data transformation ensures that the original data remains intact, and each operation generates new data without modifying existing structures.

- **Asynchronous programming**: Asynchronous programming is a common technique in C# for handling concurrency. Using the `async` and `await` keywords, developers can create asynchronous functions that allow concurrent execution without blocking the main thread. This enables better responsiveness in applications, especially for tasks such as I/O operations or network requests.

Let's consider a simple example of processing data asynchronously using functional programming concepts in C#. In this example, we'll use `async` and `await` along with functional-style composition to transform a collection of integers asynchronously:

```csharp
using System;
using System.Collections.Generic;
using System.Linq;
using System.Threading.Tasks;
class Program
{
    static async Task Main()
    {
        List<int> inputNumbers = Enumerable.Range(1, 10).
ToList();
        // Async data processing pipeline
        var result = await ProcessDataAsync(inputNumbers,
            async data => await DoubleAsync(data),
            async data => await AddFiveAsync(data),
            async data => await SquareAsync(data)
        );
        Console.WriteLine("Result: " + string.Join(", ",
result));
    }
    static async Task<List<int>> ProcessDataAsync(List<int>
data, params Func<List<int>, Task<List<int>>>[] transformations)
    {
        // Compose asynchronous transformations
        var composedTransformation = transformations.
Aggregate(async (currentData, transformation) => await
transformation(await currentData));

        // Apply the composed transformation to the input data
        return await composedTransformation(data);
    }
    static async Task<List<int>> DoubleAsync(List<int> data)
    {
        await Task.Delay(100); // Simulate asynchronous
operation
        return data.Select(x => x * 2).ToList();
    }
    static async Task<List<int>> AddFiveAsync(List<int> data)
    {
        await Task.Delay(100); // Simulate asynchronous
operation
        return data.Select(x => x + 5).ToList();
    }
```

```
static async Task<List<int>> SquareAsync(List<int> data)
{
    await Task.Delay(100); // Simulate asynchronous
operation
    return data.Select(x => x * x).ToList();
}
}
```

In this example, the `ProcessDataAsync` function takes a list of integers and a series of asynchronous transformation functions as parameters. Then, it composes these transformations using functional programming techniques and applies them to the input data.

`DoubleAsync`, `AddFiveAsync`, and `SquareAsync` are asynchronous transformation functions that simulate asynchronous operations by using `await Task.Delay(100)`.

This example demonstrates the use of functional-style composition to create a pipeline of asynchronous data transformations, providing a clean and expressive way to process data asynchronously in a functional programming manner.

- **Functional concurrency patterns**: Functional programming principles can be applied to concurrency in C# to improve code reliability, readability, and maintainability. Let's look at some functional concurrency patterns in C#:

  - **Immutable data**:

    - **Principle**: Make use of immutable data structures to ensure that data remains unchanged during concurrent operations. This eliminates the need for locks and helps prevent race conditions.

    - **Example**: Instead of modifying a shared data structure, create new instances with the desired changes.

  - **Pure functions**:

    - **Principle**: Design functions to be pure, meaning they produce the same output for the same input and have no side effects. Pure functions simplify reasoning about concurrency since they don't rely on or modify shared state.

    - **Example**: Avoid functions that modify global variables or have side effects on shared data.

  - **Map and reduce**:

    - **Principle**: Utilize `map` and `reduce` operations to parallelize tasks. The `map` operation applies a function to each element independently, while the `reduce` operation combines the results. This pattern is well-suited for parallel processing.

    - **Example**: Use `Parallel.ForEach` or PLINQ for parallelizing map operations, and aggregate results with a reduction function.

- **Concurrency models (actors)**:

  - **Principle**: Implement the actor model, where actors are isolated entities that communicate through messages. Each actor has its state and processes messages sequentially, avoiding a shared mutable state.

  - **Example**: Use frameworks such as Akka.NET or design custom actor systems to implement the actor model in C#.

- **Async/await**:

  - **Principle**: Leverage `async` and `await` to write asynchronous code in a more functional style. This allows for the composition of asynchronous operations without resorting to callback-based patterns.

  - **Example**: Use `async` functions to represent asynchronous operations and compose them using `await` for more readable and maintainable asynchronous code.

- **Software Transactional Memory (STM)**:

  - **Principle**: Implement STM to manage shared state in a concurrent environment. STM provides a way to encapsulate transactions, ensuring that updates to shared data are atomic and consistent.

  - **Example**: Libraries such as `System.Threading.Channels` in C# offer primitives for building transactional systems.

- **Functional Reactive Programming (FRP)**:

  - **Principle**: FRP allows you to express computations over time as functions, making it easier to handle asynchronous events. Libraries such as **Reactive Extensions (Rx)** provide functional constructs for working with asynchronous and event-driven code.

  - **Example**: Use Rx to handle and compose asynchronous events in a functional and declarative manner.

By applying these functional concurrency patterns, developers can write concurrent code that is more modular, easier to reason about, and less prone to common concurrency issues such as race conditions and deadlocks.

By combining functional programming principles with concurrency techniques such as asynchronous programming, C# developers can create robust and scalable concurrent applications. Functional programming helps manage complexity and reduces the likelihood of concurrency bugs by promoting immutable data, pure functions, and functional data transformation. As a result, functional programming in C# can lead to more reliable and maintainable concurrent code bases.

Next, we'll look at recursion.

Recursion

Recursion is a programming concept where a function calls itself to solve a problem. In the context of functional programming in C#, recursion is a powerful technique that's used to solve complex problems by breaking them down into simpler subproblems that can be solved recursively.

In functional programming, the focus is on expressing computations as the evaluation of mathematical functions rather than changing state or modifying variables. Recursion aligns well with this paradigm because it allows you to define functions that operate on smaller pieces of data, gradually reducing the problem's size until a base case is reached, at which point the solution can be computed and propagated back up the call stack.

Here's a step-by-step explanation of how recursion works in functional C# programming:

1. **Base case**: Every recursive function needs a base case. This is the simplest form of the problem that can be solved directly without further recursion. Without a base case, the recursion would continue indefinitely, leading to a stack overflow.

2. **Divide and conquer**: The problem is divided into smaller subproblems that are similar to the original problem but with reduced complexity. Each recursive call operates on a smaller dataset.

3. **Recursive call**: Inside the function, you call the same function you're defining, but with the smaller subproblem as the input. This is the heart of recursion. The function will keep calling itself with smaller and smaller subproblems until the base case is reached.

4. **Combining results**: As the recursion unwinds (that is, the base case is hit and the calls start returning), the results from the recursive calls are combined to solve the original problem. This combining process often involves mathematical operations, list concatenation, or other similar operations.

Here's a simple example of calculating the factorial of a number using recursion in functional C#:

```
using System;
class Program
{
    static int Factorial(int n)
    {
        // Base case
        if (n == 0)
            return 1;

        // Recursive call
        return n * Factorial(n - 1);
    }

    static void Main()
```

```
    {
        int number = 5;
        int result = Factorial(number);
        Console.WriteLine($"Factorial of {number} is {result}");
    }
}
```

In this example, the Factorial function calls itself with decreasing values of n until n reaches 0 (the base case). The results are then combined as the recursion unwinds, eventually giving you the factorial of the input number.

Keep in mind that while recursion is elegant, it can be less efficient than iterative solutions for certain problems as each recursive call adds to the call stack, potentially leading to a stack overflow if the recursion goes too deep. However, many problems are naturally suited for recursive solutions, and they can be more concise and easier to understand in a functional programming context.

Now that we've finished our look into functional programming in C#, let's recap what we've just learned.

Summary

In this chapter, we covered various aspects of functional programming in C#. Functional programming is a programming paradigm that treats computation as the evaluation of mathematical functions and avoids mutable data and state changes. In C#, functional programming can be embraced using Lambda expressions, higher-order functions, immutability, and other functional concepts.

Key principles of functional programming include immutability (avoiding mutable data), pure functions (no side effects), higher-order functions (functions that take or return other functions), and first-class functions (functions treated as data).

Functional data transformation involves transforming data using pure functions to produce new data without modifying the original. Functional pipelines chain multiple data transformation operations together declaratively and concisely.

Functional programming provides techniques for handling errors more elegantly, such as Option types, the Maybe monad, and the Either monad. These structures allow for explicit representation of the absence of values and success/failure outcomes without relying on exceptions.

Functional pattern matching allows developers to express complex conditional logic in a more concise way using the switch statement with pattern-matching features. It enables matching against types, constant values, or custom patterns to execute specific code blocks based on the matched pattern.

Concurrency with functional programming in C# involves using immutable data, pure functions, and asynchronous programming to manage concurrent and parallel execution. It encourages handling concurrent operations independently without a shared mutable state to avoid race conditions and data corruption.

By applying functional programming techniques in C#, developers can create more expressive, modular, and maintainable code. The use of pure functions, immutability, functional data transformation, and error handling enhances the reliability and scalability of applications. Additionally, functional programming facilitates better concurrency management, ensuring safer and more responsive concurrent applications.

In the next chapter, we will look at cross-platform development with MAUI. But before we move on, answer the following questions to see how much knowledge you've retained.

Questions

Answer the following questions to test your knowledge of this chapter:

1. What is functional programming, and how does it differ from imperative programming?

2. How can functional data transformation be achieved in C#? Provide an example.

3. Explain the concept of functional error handling in C#. What are the benefits of using `Option` types and the `Maybe` monad?

4. Describe functional pattern matching in C# using the `switch` statement with pattern matching. Provide an example of how it can be used.

5. How does immutability contribute to functional programming in C#? What advantages does it offer in terms of concurrency and thread safety?

6. Discuss the role of higher-order functions in functional programming. How can they be used to create more modular and reusable code in C#?

7. Explain how concurrency with functional programming is managed in C#. How does the use of pure functions and asynchronous programming contribute to better concurrent applications?

Further reading

- *Functional Programming in C#: Classic Programming Techniques for Modern Projects*, by Oliver Sturm: This book provides a comprehensive guide to functional programming concepts in C#, covering topics such as immutability, higher-order functions, and functional data transformation

- *Functional Programming Principles in C#* (Pluralsight course): This online course offers in-depth explanations of functional programming principles in C# with practical examples and hands-on exercises

- *Real-World Functional Programming: With Examples in F# and C#*, by Tomas Petricek and Jon Skeet: Although focused on F# as the primary language, this book explores functional programming concepts that can be applied to C# as well

- *C# Functional Programming: Unleash the power of functional programming for your real-world applications*, by Oliver Sturm: This book delves into functional programming techniques specifically tailored for C# developers, emphasizing practical applications

- *Concurrency in C# Cookbook: Asynchronous, Parallel, and Multithreaded Programming*, by Stephen Cleary: This cookbook provides in-depth guidance on handling concurrency in C#, covering asynchronous programming and other techniques used in functional programming

- *Introduction to C# 7 Pattern Matching* (Microsoft documentation): The official documentation from Microsoft on the C# 7 pattern matching feature, including examples and usage guidelines

- *Introduction to Asynchronous Programming in C#* (Microsoft documentation): Official documentation from Microsoft on asynchronous programming using `async` and `await` in C#, a key component of functional concurrency

Remember that while C# supports functional programming concepts, it's essential to adapt them appropriately to your project's requirements and context. Exploring these resources can help you deepen your understanding of functional programming in C# and enable you to write more elegant, expressive, and maintainable code.

13

Cross-Platform Application Development with MAUI

Microsoft .NET MAUI is an application framework for developing cross-platform applications. You can develop applications using C# and XAML or you can develop them using Blazor. In this chapter, we will focus on C# and XAML.

When using MAUI to develop applications, you can target Windows, Android, Tizen, iOS, iPad-OS, and macOS. We will be developing a simple to-do list application using C# and XAML.

We will cover the following in this chapter:

- Project overview: We will look at the screenshots of the project we will be developing in this chapter for the following platforms:

  - Android

  - Windows

- Creating the project: We will be building up our project using the following:

  - The MVVM pattern

  - `CommunityToolkit.Mvvm`

Here's what you will learn:

- How to build a cross-platform that you can deploy to Android, Tizen, iOS, macOS, Linux, and Windows

- How to install and use `CommunityToolkit.Mvvm` to remove the need for boilerplate code

- How to implement the MVVM pattern

- How to deploy your application to Windows and an Android emulator

Technical requirements

You will need the latest version of Visual Studio with the MAUI workload installed to complete the project presented in this chapter. It will also help if you have an internet connection. The source code can be downloaded from https://github.com/PacktPublishing/Clean-Code-with-CSharp-Second-Edition/tree/main/CH13/CH13_MAUI.

Project overview

In this section, we'll review the application we will be building in MAUI. It is a simple to-do list. The application will run on all supported operating systems and devices. Let's run through the Windows screenshots.

Windows version

When you start the Windows version, you will see what's shown in *Figure 13.1*:

Figure 13.1: The to-do list home page

If you have an internet connection, type your task's name and click the **Add** button. Your task will be added to the screen, as shown in *Figure 13.2*:

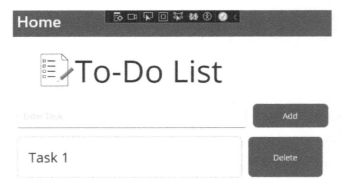

Figure 13.2: The to-do home page with a task added

As you can see, the task has been added with the option to delete the task once you have completed it. If you try and add a task without an internet connection, you will not be able to add the task and will be presented with the alert shown in *Figure 13.3*:

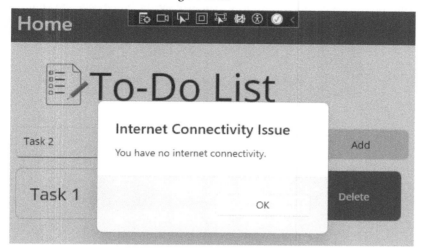

Figure 13.3: An alert showing that the user has no internet connectivity

The API that's used to check internet connectivity is the same across all platforms. However, it uses platform-specific code to check for network connectivity. Once a task has been added, you can click on the task to view its details, as shown in *Figure 13.4*:

Figure 13.4: The task's details page

The details page just displays the name of the task we clicked on. You could expand this page to edit the details and save them. There are also two back buttons. The first one is the default button in the top-left corner, while the second is the purple button that we added. Clicking either of these buttons will take you back to the main page. On the main page, when you click on the **Delete** button, it deletes the task from the item source and the main page.

Let's look at the same pages on Android.

Android version

For the following screenshots, we will be using Android Emulator for the Google Pixel 5 Android phone. When you run the application on Android, you will see the home page shown in *Figure 13.5*:

Figure 13.5: The to-do list home page on Android

Adding a test when you have internet connectivity will result in the task being added to the screen, as shown in *Figure 13.6*:

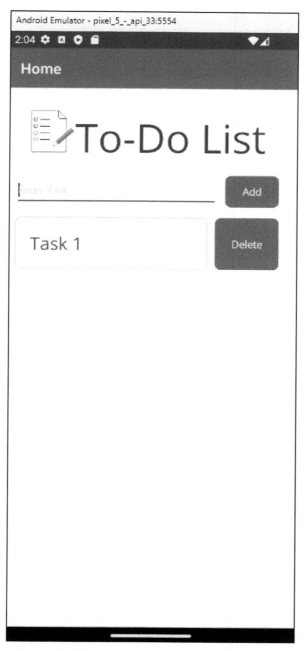

Figure 13.6: The to-do list with a task added to the list

As you can see, the task is added to the screen, along with a delete button. Tapping on the task will take you to the details screen, as shown in *Figure 13.7*:

Figure 13.7: The to-do details page

Again, just like in the Windows version, we have two buttons to go back to the main page. Once back on the main page, tapping the delete button will remove the task from the list and it will disappear from the screen.

If you try and add a task while the Android phone is in Airplane mode, then you will see the alert shown in *Figure 13.8*:

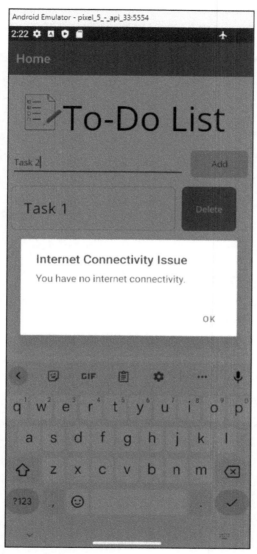

Figure 13.8: An alert regarding loss of internet connectivity

From the Windows and Android screenshots, it's clear that both versions of the app look identical despite their platform-specific layouts and features.

Now that you know what you will be building and how it will look on the different platforms, let's get to work and build the project.

Creating the project

In this section, we will build the application we have just walked through. Start by opening Visual Studio and creating a new project. From the list of available project templates, select **.NET MAUI App**, as shown in *Figure 13.9*. Then, click **Next**:

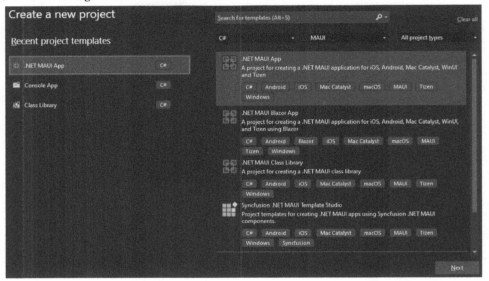

Figure 13.9: Visual Studio's Create a new project dialog

Call the project CH13_MAUI, as shown in *Figure 13.10*. Then, click **Next**:

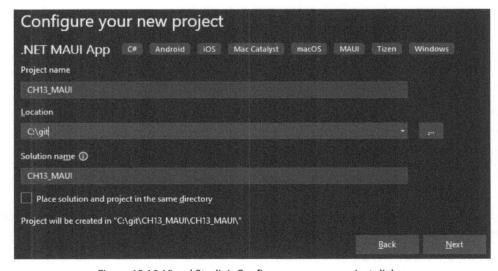

Figure 13.10: Visual Studio's Configure your new project dialog

Make sure that the version of .NET that's selected is **.NET 7.0 (Standard Term Support)**, as shown in *Figure 13.11*:

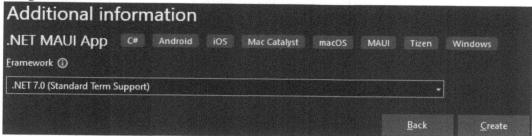

Figure 13.11: Visual Studio's Additional information dialog

Click on the **Create** button to create the solution. By default, Visual Studio will present a tabbed dialog with useful information on learning, building, integrating, and deploying MAUI applications, as shown in *Figure 13.12*:

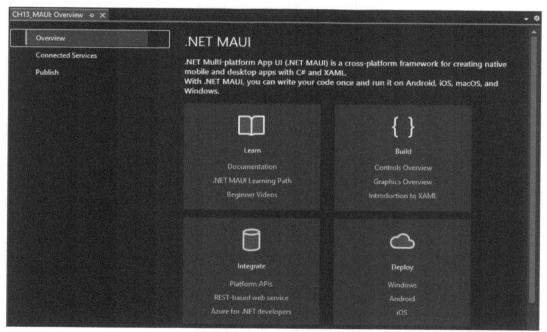

Figure 13.12: .NET MAUI's Help tab in Visual Studio

Running through these resources will help you learn and get the most out of developing applications while using the .NET MAUI cross-platform application framework. If you have a look at the **Solution Explorer** area, you will see the following items:

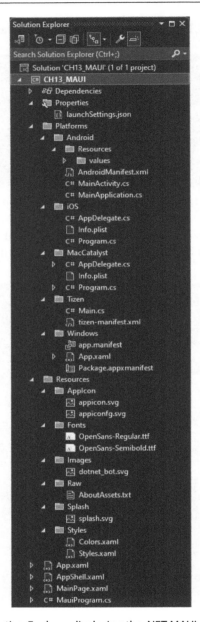

Figure 13.13: Solution Explorer displaying the .NET MAUI application items

As shown in *Figure 13.13*, we only have a single project in our solution that targets the Android, iOS, MacCatalyst, Tizen, and Windows platforms. Each platform has a folder that contains platform-specific items that we can use when targeting those specific platforms with platform-specific code and configurations.

In the **Properties** folder, you will find the `launchSettings.json` file. Use this to provide custom launch settings for when you build and run your project.

We group our resources in the **Resources** folder. This folder contains the following folders: **AppIcon**, **Fonts**, **Images**, **Raw**, **Splash**, and **Styles**. The preferred image format during development is SVG. When the application is being built, it will target a specific platform and will produce platform-specific PNGs from the SVGs during compilation time.

The **Raw** folder is used to store the assets that you want to include with your app when it is deployed to a target platform. Mark any assets that you put in this folder as **MauiAsset**.

You can use specific fonts within your application by placing font files (TTF files) in the **Fonts** folder.

To style the application, you can place XAML resource dictionaries in the **Styles** folder. We already have two resource dictionaries for colors and styles.

Finally, you will see the following four files:

- **App.xaml**: This file is part of the application's definition and is used for specifying application-level resources and styles, as well as defining the application life cycle. It typically contains XAML markup that declares resources such as styles, brushes, and other application-level elements. Additionally, you may specify the initial page or shell for your application in the **Application** tag.

- **AppShell.xaml**: In .NET MAUI, the concept of a *Shell* is introduced to define the structure of the application, including navigation and layout. `AppShell.xaml` is the main file where you define the structure of your application's user interface using the `Shell` class. Inside `AppShell.xaml`, you'll find the structure of your application, including tabs, flyout items, and other navigation-related elements. It essentially acts as a container for the main navigation structure of your app.

- **MainPage.xaml**: *MainPage.xaml* typically represents the main content of your application. It's the default page or view that is displayed when your app starts or when navigating to the root content. This file contains the user interface elements specific to the main content of your app. It's the starting point for the user experience and may include various controls, layouts, and views.

- **MauiProgram.cs**: In .NET MAUI, *MainProgram.cs* is the entry point for your application and is where the application is initialized and launched. It contains the `Main` method, which is the starting point of execution. The file typically includes code for initializing the application, setting up dependencies, and launching the main application instance. It may also contain platform-specific initialization code.

Understanding XAML structure

The MAUI XAML structure is similar to the `Xamarin.Forms` XAML, but there are some changes and enhancements to support the new .NET MAUI architecture. Keep in mind that details may have evolved since this book was published, so it's a good idea to check the official documentation or community resources for the latest information.

Here's a general overview of the MAUI XAML structure:

1. **Page element**: In .NET MAUI, UI layouts are defined within a *page*. A page represents a single screen or a UI component. The root element in a XAML file is typically `ContentPage`, which is a type of page that can contain a single view:

```
<ContentPage
    xmlns=http://schemas.microsoft.com/dotnet/2021/maui
    xmlns:x="http://schemas.microsoft.com/winfx/2009/xaml"
    x:Class="YourNamespace.MainPage">
        <!-- UI elements go here -->
</ContentPage>
```

2. **Layouts**: .NET MAUI provides a variety of layout containers to organize and structure the UI. Common layouts include `StackLayout`, `GridLayout`, and `FlexLayout`. These layouts help arrange child elements in a specific way on the screen:

```
<StackLayout>
    <Label Text="Hello, MAUI!" />
    <Button Text="Click Me" />
</StackLayout>
```

3. **Views and controls**: Inside the layouts, you can place various views and controls. Views represent visual elements such as labels, images, and buttons. Controls, on the other hand, are interactive elements such as buttons and text entry fields:

```
<Label Text="Hello, MAUI!" />
<Button Text="Click Me" />
```

4. **Data binding**: .NET MAUI supports data binding, allowing you to bind UI elements to data sources. This can simplify the process of updating the UI based on changes in your data:

```
<Label Text="{Binding MyData}" />
```

5. **Resource definitions**: You can define resources such as styles, colors, and templates in XAML. This promotes consistency and reusability across your application:

```
<ContentPage.Resources>
    <ResourceDictionary>
        <Color x:Key="PrimaryColor">#3498db</Color>
        <Style TargetType="Label">
            <Setter Property="TextColor" Value="{StaticResource
PrimaryColor}" />
        </Style>
    </ResourceDictionary>
</ContentPage.Resources>
```

This is a basic overview, and the structure can become more complex as your application grows. Remember to consult the official documentation and samples for the most up-to-date and detailed information on the .NET MAUI XAML structure.

- Now that we have created our project and understand how it is made up, let's start building up our to-do application.

The MVVM pattern

MVVM stands for **Model-View-ViewModel**, and it is a software architectural pattern that's used in the development of **graphical user interfaces (GUIs)**. MVVM is particularly popular in the context of frameworks such as **Windows Presentation Foundation** (**WPF**) and Xamarin, but its principles can be applied in various other environments as well:

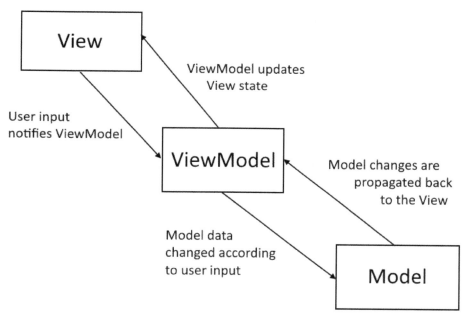

Figure 13.14: The MVVM pattern

Here's a breakdown of the MVVM pattern:

- **Model**: The **Model** represents the data and business logic of the application. It encapsulates the data and the rules for manipulating that data. It is independent of the user interface and does not directly communicate with the View.

- **View**: The **View** is responsible for presenting the data to the user and capturing user input. It is the visual representation of the data and the user interface. In MVVM, the View is kept as simple as possible, with minimal code-behind. It is primarily concerned with the presentation and layout.

- **ViewModel**: The **ViewModel** acts as an intermediary between the View and the Model. It contains the presentation logic and exposes data and commands that the View can bind to. It transforms the data from the Model into a form that can be easily displayed in the View, and it also handles user input from the View. The **ViewModel** doesn't have any knowledge of the View, ensuring separation of concerns.

There are three main concepts to the MVVM pattern:

1. **Data binding**: One of the key features of MVVM is data binding, which allows the View and ViewModel to be automatically synchronized. Changes in one are reflected in the other without explicit code to update the UI.

2. **Commands**: MVVM introduces the concept of commands to handle user interactions. A command in the ViewModel is bound to an action in the View, allowing the ViewModel to respond to user input.

3. **Dependency injection**: Dependency injection is often used to inject services or other dependencies into the ViewModel. This makes it easier to test and promotes a more modular and maintainable design.

The workflow for MVVM consists of four steps:

1. The View binds to properties and commands exposed by the ViewModel.

2. The ViewModel interacts with the Model to retrieve and manipulate data.

3. Changes in the Model are reflected in the ViewModel, which, in turn, updates the View through data binding.

4. User interactions in the View trigger commands in the ViewModel, which may update the Model or perform other actions.

MVVM promotes a clean separation of concerns, making the code base more modular, testable, and maintainable. It is widely used in applications where a clear distinction between the user interface and business logic is desired.

We will be using the MVVM pattern as we build up our application code.

Adding CommunityToolkit.Mvvm

To keep our code clean and succinct, we will be employing the use of the `CommunityToolkit.Mvvm` NuGet package, version *8.2.1*. So, before you continue, you will need to add this package to your MAUI project. To do this, follow these steps:

- Right-click on your solution and select **Manage NuGet Packages…**.

- Then, select the **Browse** page and search for `CommunityToolkit.Mvvm`.

- Now, select the toolkit and add it to your project.

- If you have successfully added it, it should appear in the **Solution Explorer** area under your project's dependencies grouping.

The `CommunityToolkit.Mvvm` NuGet package is a .NET MVVM library that provides useful helpers for developing .NET MAUI applications. Some of the advantages of using this package are as follows:

- It supports the **INotifyPropertyChanged**, **INotifyDataErrorInfo**, and **ICommand** interfaces, which are essential for implementing the MVVM pattern

- It offers two types of commands – `RelayCommand` and `AsyncRelayCommand` – that can execute synchronous or asynchronous actions and support cancellation

- It includes two messaging systems, **WeakReferenceMessenger** and **StrongReferenceMessenger**, which enable communication between different objects without creating strong references or memory leaks

- It provides an **IoC** helper class to configure dependency injection service containers, which can simplify the creation and management of dependencies

- It is compatible with various platforms, such as iOS, Android, macOS, Windows, Tizen, and more

- It is well-documented and has many samples and tutorials to help developers get started

You can find more information about the `CommunityToolkit.Mvvm` NuGet package on its official website, its GitHub repository, or its blog post. You can also check out a sample project that demonstrates how to use the package in a .NET MAUI application.

The models

Models can be primitive types or complex object types. For our to-do project, we will be keeping our model simple – it will be a string type. Therefore, we do not need to create model classes for our project.

But often, your projects will have multiple models that can be classes and/or structured, depending on your project needs. To keep things organized if you do create models, it is best to create a folder called `Model` and place your model classes and structures in it. If you have lots of models, you could create subfolders for the different areas of your project.

For reasons regarding data security and thread safety, it is always best to have your models be immutable so that once they're created, they cannot be modified. One way to do this would be to use constructor parameters with private setters and public getters.

The following code shows an immutable structure:

```
namespace CH13_MAUI.Models;

public struct ImmutableModel
```

```
{
    public int Id { get; private set; }
    public string Name { get; private set; }
    public string Description { get; private set; }

    public ImmutableModel(
        int id,
        string name,
        string description
    )
    {
        Id = id;
        Name = name;
        Description = description;
    }
}
```

As you can see, we have placed a `struct` type called `ImmutableModel` in our `Models` folder. This `struct` has public properties with private setters. The private setters are called during construction. These private setters use the constructor parameters to set the property values. Because we are using private setters during construction, once these properties have been set, they can no longer be modified.

Immutable structures and classes

When considering data security and thread safety in C#, choosing between immutable structs and immutable classes involves trade-offs. Let's explore the pros and cons of each:

- **Immutable structs**:

  - **Pros**:

    i.   **Thread safety**: Immutable structs are inherently thread-safe because their state cannot be modified after creation. They eliminate concerns about data races and concurrent modifications.

    ii. **Performance**: Structs are value types and creating them typically involves less overhead than creating classes. Memory is allocated on the stack rather than the heap, leading to potentially better performance.

    iii. **Copy-by-value semantics**: Immutable structs have copy-by-value semantics, which can simplify code and avoid unexpected side effects.

  - **Cons**:

    iv. **Limited size**: Structures are generally suitable for small, lightweight objects. For larger data, using structs may lead to performance issues due to increased copying.

v. **No inheritance**: Structures cannot inherit from other types, limiting their extensibility compared to classes.

vi. **Reference semantics for large structures**: When a large `struct` is passed as a method parameter, it's passed by reference, and the entire struct is copied if it's been modified within the method. This can lead to unexpected performance hits.

- **Immutable classes**:

  - **Pros**:

    vii. **Flexibility**: Classes support inheritance, making them more flexible for designing complex object hierarchies.

    viii. **Reference semantics**: Passing an immutable class by reference is more efficient than copying the entire object. Modifications to the object do not involve copying the entire dataset.

    ix. **Large data**: Classes are more suitable for large datasets as the cost of copying an object reference is much smaller than copying the entire dataset.

  - **Cons**:

    x. **Thread safety concerns**: While the class itself may be immutable, its properties might not be. Extra care is needed to ensure that all properties are also immutable to guarantee thread safety.

    xi. **Performance overhead**: Immutable classes may involve more memory allocations and heap usage compared to structs, leading to potential performance overhead.

    xii. **Complexity**: Classes may introduce more complexity due to inheritance and the potential for mutable properties.

When deciding whether to use structs or classes, you need to consider the following aspects:

- **Memory overhead**: Immutable classes typically involve more memory overhead due to heap allocations, while structs are allocated on the stack. This may impact memory usage and garbage collection.

- **Use case**: Choose based on the specific use case. For small, lightweight data structures, structs might be more suitable. For complex objects or large datasets, classes may be more appropriate.

- **Copying overhead**: Consider the cost of copying data when choosing between structs and classes. For large datasets, the overhead of copying a `struct` type might outweigh the benefits of immutability.

In conclusion, both immutable structs and immutable classes can be used to achieve thread safety and data security, but the choice depends on the specific requirements and characteristics of the data being modeled.

Now that we understand models and how they can affect data security, performance, and thread safety, we'll begin to create our ViewModels.

The ViewModels

In the context of C# and the MVVM architectural pattern, a ViewModel is a class that acts as an intermediary between the user interface (View) and the data model (Model). The main purpose of a ViewModel is to expose data and command objects to the View while keeping the underlying business logic and data access separate.

Here are the key aspects of a ViewModel in C#:

- **Data binding**: ViewModels are often used in conjunction with data binding frameworks, such as **Windows Presentation Foundation** (**WPF**) or Xamarin.Forms. Data binding allows you to establish a connection between the properties of the ViewModel and the controls in the UI.

- **Presentation logic**: The ViewModel contains the presentation logic and formatting required for the View. This includes formatting dates, numbers, and other data for display purposes.

- **Commands**: ViewModels define commands that are invoked in response to user actions in the View. These commands are typically implemented using the ICommand interface, and they encapsulate the logic that should be executed when a specific action is triggered.

- **Validation**: ViewModels may include validation logic to ensure that the data that's entered by the user is valid before it is sent to the Model. This can involve implementing validation rules for individual properties or the entire object.

- **Communication with the Model**: ViewModels interact with the Model to retrieve and update data. However, the ViewModel shields the View from the complexities of the underlying data source by providing a simplified interface.

- **INotifyPropertyChanged**: ViewModels often implement the INotifyPropertyChanged interface. This interface notifies the View when a property of the ViewModel changes, allowing the UI to automatically update itself in response to changes in the underlying data.

- **Testability**: ViewModels are designed to be testable. Since they encapsulate the application's logic, you can write unit tests to ensure that the ViewModel behaves as expected without the need for a GUI.

- **Separation of concerns**: MVVM promotes separation of concerns in your application. The ViewModel separates the presentation logic from the UI and the data access logic. This makes the code more maintainable and allows for easier testing and refactoring.

As an example, you could have a MainViewModel class that has a single property called UserName. The UserName property could be bound to TextBox in the View. MainViewModel could also have a command called SendGreeting that is bound to a button in the View. When the user clicks the button in the View, the command would check if the action to send a greeting can be executed, and if it can, then the user will be greeted with a message.

Remember that MVVM is just one architectural pattern, and the details may vary based on the specific framework or library you are using (for example, WPF or Xamarin.Forms). In our case, we are using MAUI.

Adding MainViewModel

In this section, we will be adding the ViewModel for our *MainPage*. It will check for internet connectivity and delete completed to-do items. It will also handle navigation to the details page.

Create a folder called `ViewModel` and add the `MainViewModel` class to it. Add the following using statements to the class:

```
using CommunityToolkit.Mvvm.ComponentModel;
using CommunityToolkit.Mvvm.Input;
using System.Collections.ObjectModel;
```

Make the class `partial` and make it inherit from `ObservableObject`:

```
public partial class MainViewModel : ObservableObject
{
}
```

The `ObservableObject` class from the `CommunityToolkit.Mvvm` NuGet package acts as a base class for objects whose properties must be observable, and it contains implementations for `INotifyPropertyChanged` and `INotifyPropertyChanging`.

By inheriting from the `ObservableObject` class, we don't have to implement `INotifyPropertyChanged`. Expand the class with the following code:

```
    readonly IConnectivity connectivity;

    public MainViewModel(IConnectivity connectivity)
    {
        Items = new();
        this.connectivity = connectivity;
    }

    [ObservableProperty]
    ObservableCollection<string> items;

    [ObservableProperty]
    string text;
```

Here, we are declaring an `IConnectivity` field that gets set in the constructor by the connectivity object that's passed into the constructor as a parameter. We are also declaring an observable property called `Items`. The `Item` property is a `CollectionsView` under the hood. This is initialized when the ViewModel is created. Plus, we have added an observable property called `Text`.

Now, we need to add our relay commands. Add the first `RelayCommand`, called `Add`:

```
[RelayCommand]
async Task Add()
{
    if (string.IsNullOrWhiteSpace(Text))
        return;

    if (connectivity.NetworkAccess != NetworkAccess.Internet)
    {
        await Shell.Current.DisplayAlert("Internet Connectivity
Issue", "You have no internet connectivity.", "OK");
        return;
    }

    Items.Add(Text);

    Text = string.Empty;
}
```

The `Add` method executes asynchronously. As `RelayCommand`, the `Add` method will not execute if the observable `Text` property is null or white space and if there is no internet connectivity. If we have no internet connectivity, then we will be presented with an alert message. If the checks pass, the text contained within the `Text` property is added to the `Items` collection, and the `Text` property is cleared.

Now, add the `Delete` command:

```
[RelayCommand]
private void Delete(string s)
{
    if (Items.Contains(s))
        Items.Remove(s);
}
```

Our `Delete` method takes a string, checks if it is contained within the `Items` collection, and then removes it from the collection. Finally, add our `Tap` command:

```
[RelayCommand]
async Task Tap(string s)
{
    await Shell.Current.GoToAsync($"{nameof(DetailPage)}?Text={s}");
}
```

This asynchronous command will execute when our button is clicked or tapped. It navigates us to `DetailPage`. That's it for our `MainViewModel` – now, let's add our details page ViewModel.

Adding DetailsViewModel

In the **ViewModel** folder, add the `partial class` property called `DetailsViewModel` that inherits from the `ObservableObject` class, and add the `QueryProperty` attribute. The class will have an observable property called `Text`, and a `RelayCommand` property called `GoBack()`:

```
[QueryProperty("Text", "Text")]
public partial class DetailViewModel : ObservableObject
{
    [ObservableProperty]
    string text;

    [RelayCommand]
    async Task GoBack()
    {
        await Shell.Current.GoToAsync("..");
    }
}
```

`DetailViewModel` will receive a string parameter that contains the string of the selected to-do item that we wish to view. The parameter can be obtained from `QueryProperty`, which has two string parameters for name and `id`. The `GoBack` method takes us back to our main page.

Now, we can start working on our views.

The views

In our project, we will have two views. The *MainPage* view will contain our text to add and remove tasks and to view them in a list. Clicking on the to-do item will take us to *DetailsPage*. This page allows us to view the detailed view of the to-do item. From the *DetailsPage* view, we can navigate backward to the *MainPage* view. Let's start by modifying the *MainPage* view.

Modifying the MainPage view

Our *MainPage* view will need to access `MainViewModel`, which we created earlier. We need to update the `ContentPage` tag in the XAML as follows:

```
<?xml version="1.0" encoding="utf-8" ?>
<ContentPage xmlns="http://schemas.microsoft.com/dotnet/2021/maui"
             xmlns:x="http://schemas.microsoft.com/winfx/2009/xaml"
             xmlns:vm="clr-namespace:CH13_MAUI.ViewModel"
             x:DataType="vm:MainViewModel"
             x:Class="CH13_MAUI.MainPage">
```

As you can see, we added the CH13_MAUI.ViewModel namespace with the vm: prefix. This lets the view know where to find our ViewModels. Then, we added the MainViewModel data type. This lets the View know which ViewModel to bind to.

Next, we need to start building the visual aspects of the page. We will use a grid to lay out our components on the screen:

```
<Grid RowDefinitions="100, Auto, *"
      ColumnDefinitions=".75*, .25*"
      Padding="10"
      RowSpacing="10"
      ColumnSpacing="10">
</Grid>
```

This XAML produces a grid with three rows and two columns. The first row's height is fixed at 100. The second row's height will be set to the height of the highest component. The last row will expand to fill the remaining space. The columns are set to 75% and 25%, respectively. To make our layout look nice, we must space the rows and columns by 10 and add padding within the cells of 10.

Now, we will add the banner section in between the grid tags:

```
<StackLayout Margin="20"
             Orientation="Horizontal"
             HorizontalOptions="Center">
    <Image Source="task_list.png"
           BackgroundColor="Transparent" />
    <Label Text="To-Do List"
           VerticalTextAlignment="Center"
           FontSize="55"/>
</StackLayout>
```

We use StackLayout with horizontal orientation and a margin of 20 to display our centered banner at the top of our screen. Within our stack panel is an image that contains our logo and a label that contains our banner text.

The next few items we need to add are our Entry for adding a task and a button to save it. We will add them after StackLayout:

```
<Entry Placeholder="Enter Task"
       Grid.Row="1"
       Text="{Binding Text}"/>
<Button Text="Add"
        Grid.Row="1"
        Grid.Column="1"
        Command="{Binding AddCommand}"/>
```

The **Entry** control has placeholder text to alert the user as to where they can enter the task text. It is bound to a property called `Text` and is placed on the second row in the first column. The button has the text `Add` and is placed in the second row and column, and it is bound to `AddCommand`.

We need somewhere to store our collection. For this, we'll use `CollectionView`, which we'll place after the button:

```
<CollectionView Grid.Row="2"
                Grid.ColumnSpan="2"
                ItemsSource="{Binding Items}"
                SelectionMode="None">
    <CollectionView.ItemTemplate>
        <DataTemplate x:DataType="{x:Type x:String}">
            <Grid Padding="0, 5" ColumnDefinitions=".75*, .25*" ColumnSpacing="10">
                <Frame>
                    <Frame.GestureRecognizers>
                        <TapGestureRecognizer Command="{Binding Source={RelativeSource AncestorType={x:Type vm:MainViewModel}}, Path=TapCommand}"
                                              CommandParameter="{Binding .}">
                        </TapGestureRecognizer>
                    </Frame.GestureRecognizers>
                    <Label Text="{Binding .}"
                           FontSize="24" />
                </Frame>
                <Button Text="Delete"
                        Grid.Column="2"
                        Command="{Binding Source={RelativeSource AncestorType={x:Type vm:MainViewModel}}, Path=DeleteCommand}"
                        CommandParameter="{Binding .}" />
            </Grid>
        </DataTemplate>
    </CollectionView.ItemTemplate>
</CollectionView>
```

The items we add will be stored and displayed within `CollectionView`. It binds to the `Items` property. Our `ItemTemplate` contains `DataTemplate`. Within `DataTemplate`, our view consists of a label to display our item text and a delete button to delete our to-do item that binds to `DeleteCommand`. We use `TapGestureRecognizer` to bind to our `TapCommand`, which will navigate to the details page.

That's our XAML sorted. Now, we need to add the code in the code-behind file:

```
using CH13_MAUI.ViewModel;

namespace CH13_MAUI;

public partial class MainPage : ContentPage
{
    public MainPage(MainViewModel vm)
    {
        InitializeComponent();
        BindingContext = vm;
    }
}
```

We reference our ViewModel namespace, inject `MainViewModel` into our view, and then bind `MainViewModel` to our `BindingContext`. This will need to be registered to work; we will do this later.

Now that we've completed the *MainView*, it is time to add and work on the *DetailPage* view.

Adding the DetailPage view

There is not much to our *DetailPage* view. All it does is display the selected to-do item and then navigate back to the *MainView* view. Start by adding the *DetailPage* view to the root of your project. Then, modify the XAML, as follows:

```
<?xml version="1.0" encoding="utf-8" ?>
<ContentPage xmlns="http://schemas.microsoft.com/dotnet/2021/maui"
             xmlns:x="http://schemas.microsoft.com/winfx/2009/xaml"
             xmlns:vm="clr-namespace:CH13_MAUI.ViewModel"
             x:DataType="vm:DetailViewModel"
             x:Class="CH13_MAUI.DetailPage"
             Title="DetailPage">
    <VerticalStackLayout>

        <Label
            Text="{Binding Text}"
            FontSize="25"
            VerticalOptions="Center"
            HorizontalOptions="Center" />

        <Button Text="Go Back"
                Command="{Binding GoBackCommand}" />
```

```
        </VerticalStackLayout>
    </ContentPage>
```

Here, we reference our ViewModel namespace and bind to `DetailViewModel`. Our UI uses `VerticalStackLayout` to display a label bound to the `Text` property and a button bound to `GoBackCommand`.

Now, let's update the code-behind, as follows:

```
using CH13_MAUI.ViewModel;

namespace CH13_MAUI;

public partial class DetailPage : ContentPage
{
    public DetailPage(DetailViewModel vm)
    {
        InitializeComponent();
        BindingContext = vm;
    }
}
```

Here, we are injecting `DetailViewModel` using constructor injection and assigning the ViewModel to `BindingContext`.

Now, all we need to do is configure our to-do application so that it works.

Configuring our to-do application

We need to ensure that we register our Views and ViewModels so that our `Connectivity` class, *MainPage*, and `MainPageViewModel` only use single instances. Our *DetailsPage* view and `DetailsViewModel` are transient, meaning they are created and destroyed each time we use them.

Update the `builder.services` section, as shown here:

```
builder.Services.AddSingleton<IConnectivity>(Connectivity.Current);
builder.Services.AddSingleton<MainPage>();
builder.Services.AddSingleton<MainViewModel>();
builder.Services.AddTransient<DetailPage>();
builder.Services.AddTransient<DetailViewModel>();
```

This code allows our ViewModels to be injected into the constructors of our Views. Our very last task is to register the route of our *DetailView* view. Add the following line to the `AppShell` constructor after the `InitailizeComponent` call:

```
Routing.RegisterRoute(nameof(DetailPage), typeof(DetailPage));
```

This line registers the route of the *DetailsView* view, enabling us to navigate to it from the *MainPage* view.

You should now be able to run the program and observe the same screens that you were shown earlier.

As a learning exercise, you could update the *DetailPage* view so that it has more items for the to-do that you can set and update against the `CollectionView` item.

That's it for this chapter, as well as this book. So, let's review what we have learned.

Summary

In this chapter, you learned how to write a single application in a single project that targets mobile devices such as phones and tablets, as well as desktops and laptops. You learned how to write one application and deploy it to multiple platforms and operating systems, such as Windows, Linux, macOS, Tizen, iOS, and Android. Now, using MAUI, you can write an application once and deploy it everywhere.

Then, we walked through the screens for our to-do application, which are written in MAUI for both Windows and Android. You saw how we can use Hot Reload to view changes to the UI while it is running on both Android and Windows, speeding up UI development.

We used the MVVM architecture to show how you can separate the View from the ViewModel and Model, binding to properties and commands to make the application responsive in real time.

Finally, you saw how easy it is to configure routes and services so that we can inject our ViewModels into the constructors of our Views, assigning them to `BindingContext`.

When coding, because we are using NuGet's `CommunityToolkit.MVVM` package, you saw how we were able to reduce the amount of boilerplate code we need by inheriting from `ObservableObject`, and how easy it was to create `ObservableProperty` and `RelayCommand`.

Going forward with your UI development, you are now knowledgeable of how to write an application using XAML and C# that targets multiple devices and multiple platforms with different operating systems.

Questions

Answer the following questions to test your knowledge of this chapter:

1. What is .NET MAUI?
2. What is the MVVM pattern and why should we use it with .NET MAUI?
3. What is `CommunityToolkit.Mvvm`, and what benefits does it bring in terms of clean coding in .NET MAUI?
4. How do we configure routes in .NET MAUI?
5. How do we register ViewModels to make them available for constructor injection?
6. What do we assign the ViewModel to in our View constructors?

7. What is `ObservableObject`?

8. What is `ObservableProperty`?

9. What is `RelayCommand`?

10. What is `CollectionView`?

11. What is `ObservableCollection`?

Further reading

To learn more about the topics that were covered in this chapter, take a look at the following resources:

- *Learn to Build Multi-Platform Apps with .NET MAUI*: This book guides C# developers through the process of creating cross-platform applications using .NET MAUI. You'll discover how to maintain consistent and beautiful user interfaces across various platforms, enhance your C# skills, and follow best practices for Microsoft's .NET MAUI. Starting with the basics, this book progresses to intermediate and advanced topics, covering page layout, navigation, data gathering, and the Model-View-ViewModel architecture. You'll also master unit testing using xUnit and NSubstitute. By the end, you'll be proficient in using .NET MAUI and creating a C# API for seamless interaction between your app and web frontends.

- .NET Multi-Platform App UI: `https://dotnet.microsoft.com/en-us/apps/maui`.

- MVVM Pattern on Microsoft Learn: `https://learn.microsoft.com/en-us/dotnet/architecture/maui/mvvm`.

- Enterprise Application Patterns Using .NET MAUI: `https://dotnet.microsoft.com/download/e-book/maui/pdf`..

14
Microservices

In this chapter, we'll cover microservices. Microservices are a modular architectural approach to building software applications where an application is developed as a collection of small, independent, and loosely coupled services that communicate with each other through well-defined APIs. This contrasts with traditional monolithic architectures, where the entire application is tightly integrated.

Microservices offer numerous benefits, including enhanced scalability, agility, and fault isolation, allowing organizations to develop, deploy, and maintain complex applications more efficiently. By breaking down applications into smaller, more manageable components, microservices enable teams to independently develop, test, deploy, and scale different parts of the application, fostering faster innovation and adaptability to evolving business needs.

In this chapter, we will be covering the following topics:

- What are microservices?
- Service registration and discovery
- Containerization and orchestration of microservices
- API gateways
- Event-driven communication
- Service resilience and fault tolerance
- Service monitoring and observability
- Security
- Scaling microservices
- Versioning and compatibility
- Microservice best practices and anti-patterns
- Case studies and real-world examples

By the end of this chapter, you will be able to do the following:

- Explain what microservices are and compare them to monoliths

- Understand the pros and cons of microservices

- Explain all the steps that are involved in designing microservices and managing their life cycle

- Explain what containerization and orchestration are and how they help to develop, deploy, and manage microservices at scale along with CI and CD

- Explain what API gateways are, why they are useful, and the benefits of using event-driven communication

- Explain how you can implement different forms of service monitoring and observability and the different ways you can handle security in microservices

- Explain how you can test, version, and scale your microservices and ensure compatibility between versions

- Understand and implement best practices while avoiding anti-patterns

- Explain how some companies used microservices to improve the delivery of their business models to clients

What are microservices?

As mentioned in the introduction, microservices are a software architectural style that structures an application as a collection of small, independent, and loosely coupled services, each running in its own process and communicating through well-defined APIs. The core idea behind microservices is to break down a complex application into smaller, more manageable components that can be developed, deployed, and scaled independently. This approach aims to improve agility, scalability, maintainability, and fault tolerance in large and complex systems.

Here's a more detailed, language-agnostic description of microservices and how they are used:

- **Decomposition**: In the initial phase, the monolithic application is decomposed into smaller, specialized services based on business capabilities. Each microservice focuses on performing a specific task or function within the application. This division allows developers to work on separate code bases, making it easier to understand and maintain the system.

- **Independence**: Microservices are designed to be loosely coupled, meaning they can function independently of one another. Each service has its own database (if necessary) and operates independently of the internal workings of other services. This isolation allows teams to develop, test, and deploy services separately, reducing the risk of impacting the entire system with changes to one service.

- **API-based communication**: Microservices communicate with each other through well-defined APIs, typically over lightweight protocols such as HTTP/REST or messaging systems such as Google GRPC, RabbitMQ, or Kafka. API contracts act as a contract between services, ensuring that they can interact without breaking each other.

- **Technology diversity**: Since microservices are independent, each service can be developed using different technologies, programming languages, and frameworks, so long as they adhere to the API specifications. This flexibility allows teams to choose the best tools for each specific service, enabling them to optimize performance and development speed.

- **Scalability**: Microservices enable horizontal scaling, allowing individual services to be replicated and deployed across multiple servers or containers. This way, resources can be allocated efficiently based on the specific needs of each service, ensuring optimal performance and resource utilization.

- **Resilience and fault tolerance**: Failure in one microservice does not bring down the entire system. Microservices are designed to handle failures gracefully and recover quickly, promoting overall system resilience.

- **Continuous deployment**: With microservices, it becomes easier to adopt continuous deployment practices. Changes in one service can be tested and deployed independently without impacting other parts of the application. This promotes faster development cycles and shorter time-to-market.

- **Team autonomy**: Microservices encourage organizational structure based on small, cross-functional teams, each responsible for one or more microservices. This autonomy allows teams to innovate and iterate faster, making decisions that best suit their specific service without being hindered by a centralized decision-making process.

- **Monitoring and observability**: With microservices, it is essential to have comprehensive monitoring and logging in place to track the performance and health of each service. Various tools and techniques can be employed to gain insights into system behavior and performance.

- **Complexity management**: While microservices offer numerous benefits, they also introduce some challenges, such as managing distributed systems, inter-service communication, and service discovery. Proper architectural and operational patterns must be employed to address these complexities effectively.

In summary, microservices are a powerful architectural approach that offers several advantages for building large, scalable, and maintainable applications. By breaking down complex systems into smaller, independent services, organizations can foster a more agile and resilient software development process, providing flexibility and better adaptability to rapidly changing business requirements. However, adopting microservices requires careful planning, architectural design, and the right organizational culture to achieve the full benefits while mitigating potential challenges.

The downsides of microservices, some gotchas experienced by microservices, and how they can be overcome and avoided

While microservices offer several advantages, they also come with their own set of challenges and downsides. Here are some common downsides and gotchas that are experienced by microservice developers, along with ways to overcome and avoid them:

- **Increased complexity**: Microservices introduce a higher level of complexity compared to monolithic architectures. Managing distributed systems, inter-service communication, and service discovery can be challenging. Additionally, handling eventual consistency across services can become more complex.

  - **Mitigation**: Proper architectural patterns, such as the use of API gateways, service meshes, and event-driven architectures, can help you manage the complexity. Adopting well-defined communication protocols, asynchronous messaging, and centralized logging and monitoring systems can make debugging and monitoring easier.

- **Operational overhead**: Running and managing multiple microservices requires more operational effort than managing a single monolithic application. Each service must be deployed, monitored, and maintained independently.

  - **Mitigation**: Embracing containerization technologies such as Docker and container orchestration platforms such as Kubernetes can help automate deployment and scaling tasks. CI/CD pipelines can streamline the release process and reduce manual overhead.

- **Data management complexity**: Data management becomes more complex when each microservice has its own database. Ensuring data consistency and handling distributed transactions can be challenging.

  - **Mitigation**: Consider using different data storage patterns, such as the Saga pattern, **Command Query Responsibility Segregation** (**CQRS**), and event sourcing, to manage data consistency across services. Also, explore the use of distributed databases or a combination of centralized and decentralized data management approaches.

- **Service dependencies and latency**: Microservices often rely on each other, leading to dependencies between services. This can introduce latency and increase the chances of cascading failures.

  - **Mitigation**: Strive for clear service boundaries and minimize direct synchronous dependencies. Implement caching mechanisms and consider asynchronous communication where possible. Implement circuit breakers and fallback mechanisms to handle service unavailability gracefully.

- **Testing challenges**: Testing microservices can be complex due to the need to set up and manage a network of interconnected services. Integration testing and end-to-end testing may require significant effort.

  - **Mitigation**: Adopt contract testing, where service interfaces are tested independently to ensure compatibility. Use mock services or test doubles during unit testing to isolate components and reduce dependencies. Embrace test automation to streamline the testing process.

- **Versioning and compatibility**: As microservices evolve independently, maintaining backward compatibility between services can become challenging. Changes in one service may break the functionality of dependent services.

  - **Mitigation**: Implement versioning in APIs and follow the principles of backward compatibility. Use API versioning techniques, such as URL versioning or versioning through custom request headers. Also, establish strong communication channels between teams to coordinate changes and align on API contracts.

- **Security concerns**: Securing microservices and managing access control can be more intricate, especially with numerous independently deployed services.

  - **Mitigation**: Implement security at various layers of the application, including communication channels (for example, SSL/TLS), authentication, and authorization mechanisms. Use API gateways with built-in security features, such as rate limiting and token validation. Regularly audit and update security measures to address emerging threats.

- **Resource management**: Microservices can lead to increased resource consumption, especially when each service is provisioned with its own resources.

  - **Mitigation**: Adopt resource monitoring and autoscaling strategies to optimize resource usage based on actual demand. Implement efficient resource allocation and utilization policies to prevent overprovisioning.

- **Organizational challenges**: Transitioning from a monolithic to a microservices-based architecture can lead to organizational challenges, such as creating and managing small, cross-functional teams and adopting DevOps practices.

  - **Mitigation**: Foster a culture of collaboration and communication between teams. Encourage knowledge sharing and invest in proper training for team members. Gradually transition from a monolithic approach to a microservices approach, allowing teams to adapt and learn along the way.

While microservices offer numerous benefits, their adoption comes with certain downsides and complexities that need to be managed carefully. By understanding these challenges and adopting appropriate architectural patterns and best practices, developers can overcome the gotchas associated with microservices and build scalable, resilient, and maintainable systems. It's crucial to strike a balance between the benefits and challenges of microservices and ensure that the chosen architecture aligns with the specific needs and constraints of the project and the organization.

Comparison between microservices and monoliths

Microservices and monoliths are two architectural patterns that are used in software development. Each has its strengths and weaknesses, and the choice between them depends on the specific requirements and complexities of a project. Let's compare microservices and monoliths in various aspects:

- **Architecture**:

  - **Monolith**: In a monolithic architecture, the entire application is built as a single, cohesive unit. All components and functionalities are tightly integrated, and the application typically runs on a single server or set of servers.

  - **Microservices**: In a microservices architecture, the application is broken down into small, independent services, each responsible for a specific business capability. These services can be developed, deployed, and scaled independently, communicating through APIs or message queues.

- **Scalability**:

  - **Monolith**: Scaling a monolithic application can be challenging since all components are tightly coupled. To scale the application, you often have to scale the entire monolith, which may not be cost-effective and might lead to resource wastage.

  - **Microservices**: Microservices can be scaled independently based on their requirements. This allows for more efficient resource utilization and the ability to handle varying workloads effectively.

- **Development and deployment**:

  - **Monolith**: In a monolith, development and deployment are relatively straightforward since the entire application is contained within a single codebase. However, this can lead to longer build times and more complex deployments, especially as the application grows.

  - **Microservices**: Microservices enable faster development and deployment cycles as each service can be worked on independently. This approach allows for smaller, more focused development teams and easier CI/CD practices.

- **Maintenance and updates**:

  - **Monolith**: Updating a monolithic application requires deploying the entire application, which can be risky if something goes wrong during the deployment process.

  - **Microservices**: In microservices, updating individual services is easier but comes with risks. Developers can update one service without affecting the others, allowing for more flexibility in maintaining and evolving the application. However, it is possible to break version compatibility.

- **Complexity and understanding**:

  - **Monolith**: A monolithic code base can become complex and challenging to understand as the application grows. It might be difficult for developers to isolate and comprehend specific functionalities.

  - **Microservices**: Microservices promote better code organization and encapsulation of functionalities. Each service has a clear purpose, making it easier for developers to understand and maintain their respective services.

- **Communication overhead**:

  - **Monolith**: In a monolithic architecture, components can communicate more efficiently since they are often within the same process. Direct function calls or method invocations are common.

  - **Microservices**: In microservices, inter-service communication usually occurs over the network through APIs or message brokers, which can introduce some communication overhead.

- **Fault isolation and resilience**:

  - **Monolith**: In a monolith, if one component fails, it can potentially bring down the entire application. If a single component goes rogue (such as using all the CPU), the entire application is affected. This is probably the most problematic issue with monoliths.

  - **Microservices**: Microservices offer better fault isolation as the failure of one service does not necessarily affect others. This enhances the overall resilience of the application.

Ultimately, the choice between microservices and monoliths depends on factors such as the size and complexity of the project, the development team's expertise, scalability requirements, and the level of modularity desired. Some projects might benefit from starting as a monolith and gradually transitioning to microservices as the application grows and demands more flexibility and scalability. Others might find microservices to be the preferred approach from the start, especially for complex and distributed systems.

The design process for building successful microservices

Designing successful microservices involves careful planning, architecture, and development. Here is a step-by-step guide to the design process for building successful microservices:

1. **Identify business goals**: Understand the business requirements and goals. Identify the functionalities that need to be broken down into separate services. Focus on the core competencies and domains that require microservices architecture.

2. **Decompose the monolith**: If you are migrating from a monolithic architecture, analyze the existing application and identify modules that can be decoupled into independent services. These modules can be good candidates for microservices.

3. **Domain-driven design (DDD)**: Apply DDD principles to divide your system into bounded contexts, each representing a specific domain. These bounded contexts will be the foundation for defining your microservices.

4. **Service boundaries**: Define clear boundaries for each microservice. Aim for high cohesion within each service and minimize coupling between services. This helps in maintaining autonomy and scalability.

5. **API design**: Design a well-defined and versioned API for each microservice. Keep the API contracts as simple and stable as possible to minimize dependencies on internal implementation details.

6. **Database per service**: Adopt the database-per-service pattern, where each microservice has its own dedicated database. This ensures data isolation and reduces the risk of data inconsistencies.

7. **Communication**: Decide how the microservices will communicate with each other. Use lightweight protocols such as RESTful APIs or message queues for asynchronous communication. Avoid direct database access between services to maintain independence.

8. **Security**: Implement robust security measures, including authentication and authorization, for each microservice. Consider using API gateways for centralized security management.

9. **Resilience**: Build resilience into your microservices by incorporating retries, timeouts, and circuit breakers. Handle failures gracefully and ensure the system can recover from faults.

10. **Monitoring and logging**: Implement comprehensive monitoring and logging mechanisms for each microservice. This enables better visibility into the system's health and helps in diagnosing issues.

11. **Scalability**: Design for horizontal scalability to accommodate changes in demand. Consider containerization with tools such as Docker and container orchestrators such as Kubernetes to manage scalability effectively.

12. **Testing strategy**: Develop a testing strategy that includes unit testing, integration testing, and end-to-end testing for the microservices. Automate tests to ensure consistency and reliability.

13. **Deployment and continuous delivery**: Set up a CI/CD pipeline to automate the deployment process. This ensures a smooth and efficient release of new features and bug fixes.

14. **Performance optimization**: Continuously monitor the performance of your microservices and optimize bottlenecks. Load testing and performance tuning are essential to handle real-world usage.

15. **Team structure and ownership**: Organize development teams around microservices to promote ownership and accountability. Each team should be responsible for the design, development, and maintenance of their respective microservices.

16. **Documentation and communication**: Document the architecture, APIs, and design decisions thoroughly. Effective communication between teams is crucial for successful collaboration.

17. **Evolution and adaptation**: Be prepared to adapt and evolve your microservices architecture as the system grows and requirements change. Embrace a culture of continuous improvement.

18. **Versioning: Application programming interface (API)** versioning is a crucial aspect of the design process that involves establishing a strategy to manage changes and updates to an API over time. During the design phase, developers need to carefully consider how the API will evolve to accommodate future enhancements, bug fixes, or changes in requirements without disrupting existing clients. There are various versioning approaches, such as URI versioning, header versioning, or query parameter versioning, each with its advantages and considerations. It's essential to choose a versioning strategy that aligns with the project's needs, provides backward compatibility, and communicates changes clearly to API consumers. Thoughtful API versioning ensures that developers can make improvements while maintaining a stable and predictable interface for those relying on the API, fostering long-term usability and minimizing disruptions during updates.

By following these steps and considering the specific needs of your project, you can design and build successful microservices that enable scalability, maintainability, and rapid development of complex applications.

The application life cycle management (ALM) of microservices

ALM in the context of microservices refers to the process of managing the entire life cycle of microservices-based applications, from their initial design and development to deployment, operation, and eventual decommissioning. ALM encompasses various stages and activities that ensure the smooth functioning and continuous improvement of the microservices architecture. Here's a breakdown of the microservices that ALM processes:

- **Design and development:**

  - In this stage, the microservices architecture is planned and designed based on the specific requirements of the application.

  - Services are defined, and their boundaries are established using DDD principles.

  - Development teams work on individual microservices, implementing them independently using the programming language and technology stack that suits each service best.

  - Collaboration among teams is crucial to ensure seamless integration and compatibility between services.

  - A mock version of the service should be created to provide a simple working version of the service for testing the API interface. A strict API reference is the key to success. A minimal implementation of that API (without any validation or real business logic) is the key to survival.

- **Testing and quality assurance**:

  - Each microservice is thoroughly tested at various levels: unit testing, integration testing, and end-to-end testing

  - Automated testing is emphasized to ensure quick and reliable feedback during continuous integration processes

  - Quality assurance teams validate the overall functionality and performance of the microservices application

- **Versioning and source control**:

  - The source code of each microservice is managed using version control systems such as Git

  - Proper versioning is maintained to track changes and ensure backward compatibility when updates are made

- **Containerization and orchestration**:

  - Microservices are containerized using technologies such as Docker, enabling them to be portable and scalable

  - Container orchestration platforms such as Kubernetes are used to manage and automate the deployment, scaling, and operation of containers

- **CI/CD**:

  - CI/CD pipelines are established to automate the build, testing, and deployment processes

  - Changes to microservices are automatically built, tested, and deployed to production environments, promoting a faster and more reliable release cycle

- **Monitoring and observability**:

  - Monitoring tools are set up to collect metrics, logs, and traces from microservices

  - Observability ensures that developers and operations teams can gain insights into the application's behavior and troubleshoot issues effectively

- **Scalability and load management**:

  - As the application grows, microservices can be horizontally scaled to handle increased traffic and load

  - Load balancing mechanisms distribute incoming requests evenly across multiple instances of services

- **Security and access control**:

  - Robust security measures are implemented to ensure secure communication between microservices

  - Access control and authentication mechanisms are enforced to prevent unauthorized access

- **Fault tolerance and resilience**:

  - Microservices are designed to be resilient in the face of failures

  - Techniques such as circuit breakers, retries, and graceful degradation are employed to handle faults and prevent cascading failures

- **Version upgrades and retirement**:

  - When a new version of a microservice is released, strategies such as blue-green deployments or canary deployments are used to minimize downtime and risks.

  - Microservices that are no longer needed are retired and decommissioned from the system.

  - For mission-critical microservices, the ability to run actual and future versions side by side is a real technical challenge but gives you a real lifesaver approach where you can deploy the Actual version +1, keep in parallel with the old version, redirect some of the calls on the new version, wait for everything to be ok, and then gradually redirect the call to the new application until no call is made to the Actual version. This can then be redirected and the Actual version is increased.

- **Continuous improvement**:

  - Feedback from users and monitoring data helps identify areas for improvement

  - Regular retrospectives and post-mortems enable teams to learn from incidents and enhance the system continuously

The ALM process in microservices is ongoing and iterative, ensuring that the application remains reliable, scalable, and maintainable throughout its life cycle. It requires collaboration between development, operations, and quality assurance teams, as well as the adoption of automation and DevOps practices to streamline the entire process.

Microservice architecture patterns

Microservices architecture is an approach to software development that structures an application as a collection of loosely coupled and independently deployable services. Each service in the system represents a specific business capability and can be developed, deployed, and scaled independently.

This architecture promotes flexibility, scalability, and easier maintenance of complex applications. To design and implement microservices effectively, developers commonly use various architectural patterns. Here are some of the most commonly used microservices architecture patterns:

- **Service registry and discovery**: In a microservices environment, services are often distributed across multiple servers. The service registry pattern involves a central service registry that maintains a list of available services and their locations (endpoints). Service instances register themselves with the registry, and other services can discover their locations dynamically using the registry. This pattern helps facilitate communication between services as each service doesn't need to know the exact location of others beforehand.

- **API gateway**: An API gateway acts as a single entry point for clients to access various microservices. It handles API requests and performs authentication, routing, load balancing, and other cross-cutting concerns. By centralizing these tasks, the API gateway simplifies the client-side interaction and reduces the complexity of microservices client implementations. When a team implements a microservice, they should not have the burden of implementing authentication, parsing input for security, and so on, and an API gateway allows you to isolate the caller from the real structure of the service behind the gateway.

- **Circuit Breaker**: The Circuit Breaker pattern is used to prevent cascading failures in a microservices system. When a service fails, the circuit breaker temporarily stops calling that service and returns an error response. This avoids overwhelming the failing service and allows it to recover. The circuit breaker monitors the service's status, and if it detects that the service is healthy again, it closes the circuit, enabling requests to flow through. The .NET Polly library is worth using in your microservices. For example, when calls to a database fail, Polly will retry the call many times until it either succeeds or decides to fail gracefully.

- **Event sourcing**: Event sourcing is a pattern where the state of a system is derived from a sequence of events rather than maintaining a current state. Events represent changes that have occurred in the system and are stored in an event log. This approach enables auditing, debugging, and reconstruction of past states, making it suitable for certain types of applications, such as financial systems. Event sourcing can be used with both microservices and monoliths.

- **CQRS**: CQRS separates the read and write operations of an application into two different models. The write model handles commands that change the state of the system, while the read model is optimized for querying and retrieving data. This pattern can improve performance and scalability as read and write operations have distinct and independent requirements. Event sourcing can be used with both microservices and monoliths.

- **Saga pattern**: The Saga pattern is used to manage distributed transactions in a microservices architecture. A distributed transaction involves multiple services cooperating to achieve a single business operation. Sagas are sequences of local transactions, each of which updates the database and publishes events or commands to trigger subsequent actions in other services. If something goes wrong during a saga, compensating actions can be triggered to undo the changes made so far.

- **Bulkhead pattern**: The Bulkhead pattern isolates different parts of a system to prevent failures in one component from affecting the entire system. It involves breaking the system into multiple isolated sections (bulkheads) with separate resources (threads, databases, and so on) to limit the impact of failures and improve fault tolerance.

- **Choreography and orchestration**: These patterns define how services interact and collaborate in a microservices ecosystem. Choreography implies that services communicate directly with each other using events or messages. Orchestration, on the other hand, involves a central service (orchestrator) that coordinates the interactions between services.

- **Polyglot Persistence**: In microservices, different services may have varying data storage requirements. The Polyglot Persistence pattern allows each service to choose the most appropriate data storage technology for its specific needs, enabling a diverse range of databases or storage systems in the overall architecture.

- **Feature Toggle**: The Feature Toggle pattern is used to enable or disable specific features in a microservices system without redeploying the entire application. It allows developers to release new features gradually or roll back features quickly if issues are discovered.

These are just a few examples of the many microservices architecture patterns available. Developers may choose different combinations of patterns based on the specific requirements and characteristics of their applications. The key is to design a system that is modular, scalable, and easy to maintain and update.

Service registration and discovery

Service discovery and registration are essential components of a microservices architecture that enable services to locate and communicate with each other in a dynamic and distributed environment. They facilitate the seamless interaction between services without the need for hardcoded configurations or static IP addresses. Let's dive deeper into each concept.

Service discovery

Service discovery is the process by which services within a microservices architecture can dynamically find and identify other services that they need to interact with. In a traditional monolithic application, service locations may be hardcoded or configured statically. However, in a microservices environment, where services can be added, removed, or scaled independently, this static approach becomes impractical.

Service discovery involves a central component known as the "Service Registry," which acts as a directory of available services and their network locations (IP addresses and ports). Each microservice registers itself with the Service Registry upon startup, indicating its presence, capabilities, and location. Likewise, services can deregister themselves when they shut down or become unavailable.

When a microservice needs to communicate with another service, instead of relying on fixed IP addresses or configuration files, it queries the Service Registry dynamically to obtain the location of the desired service. The Service Registry then provides the IP address and port information, enabling the requesting service to establish communication with the target service.

Service discovery allows the microservices architecture to be more flexible and scalable since services can be added or removed without requiring changes to other service configurations. It also promotes fault tolerance as the system can automatically adjust to changes in service availability.

Domain Name System (**DNS**) plays a crucial role in service discovery, providing an alternative to relying solely on IP addresses and ports for microservices communication. In this context, DNS can be leveraged to abstract away the underlying infrastructure details and enable a more dynamic and scalable service discovery mechanism. By assigning meaningful domain names to microservices, developers can use DNS to look up the locations of services within the network, reducing the need for hardcoding IP addresses or port numbers in the application code. This approach is especially valuable in distributed systems and microservices architectures where services may be deployed across multiple servers or containers. Service discovery via DNS simplifies the configuration, enhances scalability, and supports a more flexible and dynamic environment where microservices can be distributed across servers while still being easily discoverable through their DNS-resolvable names.

Service registration

Service registration is the process by which a microservice announces its existence and availability to the Service Registry. When a microservice starts up or becomes available, it registers itself with the Service Registry, providing relevant information such as its service name, network location (IP address and port), and any metadata that might be useful for other services (version, health status, and so on).

The act of service registration ensures that the Service Registry is up-to-date with the current status of all services within the architecture. If a service goes offline or becomes unavailable, it can deregister itself from the registry to reflect its unavailability accurately.

Service registration can be automatic or manual. In an automated approach, the service container or runtime environment may handle the registration process. For example, when a service is deployed in a containerized environment such as Kubernetes, the container can automatically register itself with the associated Service Registry. In a manual approach, the service may explicitly call an API provided by the Service Registry to register itself during startup.

Service discovery and registration play a crucial role in enabling the dynamic and flexible nature of microservices architectures. They provide a mechanism for services to locate each other, communicate effectively, and adapt to changes in the environment, making it easier to build and maintain complex distributed systems.

Containerization and orchestration of microservices

Containerization and orchestration are two critical aspects of managing microservices in a scalable, portable, and efficient manner. Let's explore each concept in detail.

Containerization

Containerization is a technology that allows you to package an application, including its dependencies, libraries, and configurations, into a single unit called a **container**. Containers provide a consistent and isolated runtime environment for applications, ensuring that they run reliably and consistently across different platforms, such as development, testing, and production environments.

The most popular containerization technology is Docker, but there are others, such as containerd, rkt, and Podman. Docker containers use operating system-level virtualization to create isolated environments that share the host operating system kernel. This approach makes containers lightweight and faster to start and stop compared to traditional virtual machines.

In the context of microservices, each microservice can be containerized independently, encapsulating all its dependencies, runtime, and configuration. This isolation ensures that each microservice can run without interference from other services, promoting modularity and scalability.

Here are some of the benefits of containerization for microservices:

- **Portability**: Containers can run consistently across different environments, from a developer's local machine to production servers, without worrying about dependency conflicts

- **Isolation**: Each microservice runs in its own container, preventing dependency clashes and ensuring that a failure in one service does not impact others

- **Scalability**: Containers can be easily replicated and scaled up or down based on demand and how code is written, providing efficient resource utilization

- **Easy deployment**: Container images can be versioned and deployed with ease, simplifying the CI/CD process

Orchestration

Orchestration refers to the automated management and coordination of containerized microservices at scale. As the number of microservices and containers grows, manually managing them becomes complex and error-prone. Orchestration tools help streamline this process by automating tasks such as container deployment, scaling, networking, service discovery, and load balancing.

Some popular container orchestration platforms are Kubernetes, Docker Swarm, and Amazon **Elastic Container Service** (**ECS**).

Kubernetes is widely used and one of the most feature-rich orchestration systems. It provides a set of abstractions for defining the desired state of the system, and it continuously works to ensure that the actual state matches the desired state. Here's how Kubernetes helps manage microservices:

- **Service deployment**: Kubernetes allows you to define how many instances of each microservice should be running, and it ensures the desired number is maintained.

- **Service discovery**: Kubernetes provides an internal DNS system that allows services to discover each other using their names. This eliminates the need for hardcoding IP addresses or service locations.

- **Load balancing**: Kubernetes automatically distributes incoming traffic across replicas of a service, ensuring even load distribution.

- **Auto-scaling**: Kubernetes can automatically scale the number of containers based on CPU utilization or other metrics, ensuring optimal resource utilization.

- **Rolling updates and rollbacks**: Kubernetes allows you to update microservices without downtime by gradually replacing old containers with new ones. It also supports rolling back to the previous version if issues arise; here, the code must be written with this pattern in mind. Rolling back can be complex, so it needs to be planned for before rollout begins.

- **Storage orchestration**: Kubernetes provides options for managing persistent data for stateful applications through persistent volumes and persistent volume claims.

Containerization and orchestration complement each other, making it easier to develop, deploy, and manage microservices at scale. Containerization provides a consistent environment for running microservices, while orchestration ensures that these containers are deployed, scaled, and managed efficiently and automatically. This combination empowers organizations to build robust and scalable microservices-based applications.

Serverless

Serverless computing is a significant aspect of the microservices landscape, offering a different paradigm for building and deploying applications. Serverless platforms, such as AWS Lambda, Azure Functions, and others, allow developers to focus on writing code without managing the underlying infrastructure. Here are some key points related to serverless computing in the context of microservices:

- **Event-driven architecture**: Serverless platforms excel in event-driven architectures, where functions (serverless units of code) are triggered by events such as HTTP requests, database changes, or file uploads. This aligns well with microservices, enabling the creation of independent, loosely coupled components that respond to specific events.

- **Scalability and cost efficiency**: Serverless platforms automatically scale functions based on demand, providing a cost-efficient model where you pay only for the actual compute resources consumed during execution. Microservices can benefit from this scalability, handling variable workloads without the need for manual intervention.

- **Simplified deployment**: Serverless platforms abstract away the deployment and management of servers, simplifying the deployment process for microservices. Developers can deploy individual functions without concerning themselves with the complexities of scaling and provisioning infrastructure.

- **Loose coupling**: Serverless architecture encourages loose coupling between functions, promoting the microservices principle of independence. Functions can be independently developed, deployed, and scaled, reducing dependencies and allowing for better maintainability.

- **Reduced operational overhead**: Serverless platforms handle operational tasks such as patching, maintenance, and server provisioning, freeing developers from low-level infrastructure concerns. This aligns with the microservices philosophy of offloading operational complexity to the platform.

- **Rapid development and iteration**: Serverless platforms facilitate rapid development and iteration, allowing developers to quickly deploy and test changes to individual functions. This agility aligns with the iterative and independent development approach of microservices.

While serverless computing complements the microservices approach, it's important to note that it may not be a one-size-fits-all solution. The choice between serverless and traditional microservices architecture depends on factors such as workload characteristics, execution time, and specific use case requirements. Combining the benefits of both approaches can lead to a powerful and flexible application architecture.

API gateways

An API gateway is a central component in a microservices architecture that acts as an intermediary between clients (such as web or mobile applications) and the backend microservices. It provides a single entry point for clients to access various microservices and is responsible for handling requests, routing, load balancing, security, and other cross-cutting concerns. The API gateway simplifies client-side interactions and improves the overall performance, security, and manageability of the microservices system.

Here are some key functions and benefits of an API gateway:

- **API aggregation**: In a microservices architecture, clients may need to interact with multiple microservices to fulfill a single request. The API gateway can aggregate the necessary data from multiple microservices and present it to the client as a single cohesive response, reducing the number of API calls the client needs to make.

- **Request routing**: The API gateway routes incoming requests from clients to the appropriate microservices based on the request's URL, headers, or other criteria. This allows for clean and logical URL structures on the client side while abstracting the complexities of the microservices' actual endpoints.

- **Load balancing**: To ensure high availability and even distribution of incoming requests, the API gateway can perform load balancing across multiple instances of the same microservice. This helps distribute the workload efficiently and prevents any one instance from being overwhelmed.

- **Caching**: The API gateway can implement caching strategies to store responses from microservices temporarily. This reduces the need for redundant calls to the same microservice for identical requests, improving the overall response time and reducing the load on backend services.

- **Security and authentication**: The API gateway can handle authentication and authorization for incoming requests. It can enforce authentication mechanisms such as API keys, OAuth, or JWT, and validate the client's credentials before forwarding the request to the appropriate microservices. This centralizes security concerns and simplifies the authentication process across the microservices.

- **Rate limiting**: To prevent abuse or excessive usage, the API gateway can enforce rate-limiting policies. It can restrict the number of requests a client can make within a specific time frame to maintain fair usage of resources and protect the backend services from overloading.

- **Transformation and response formatting**: The API gateway can transform and modify responses from microservices so that they match the expected format of the client. It can aggregate data, filter unnecessary information, or merge responses from different microservices into a cohesive format that suits the client's needs.

- **Monitoring and analytics**: An API gateway can log incoming requests and responses, providing valuable insights into usage patterns, error rates, and performance metrics. This information helps in monitoring the health of the microservices system and identifying potential issues.

- **Service versioning**: The API gateway can support multiple versions of microservices, allowing new versions to be rolled out without breaking backward compatibility for existing clients. This facilitates seamless updates and migrations.

By providing a unified entry point and encapsulating various cross-cutting concerns, an API gateway simplifies client-side development and improves the overall efficiency and reliability of microservices-based applications. It enables teams to focus on developing individual microservices while ensuring a consistent and secure experience for clients.

Event-driven communication

Event-driven communication is a messaging paradigm that's used in distributed systems, including microservices architectures, to enable asynchronous and loosely coupled communication between components. In this approach, components (services or applications) communicate by exchanging events, which are messages representing significant occurrences or state changes within the system. Event-driven communication promotes decoupling, scalability, and responsiveness in distributed systems.

Here are the key concepts and characteristics of event-driven communication:

- **Events**: Events are messages that carry information about specific occurrences or state changes within the system. Examples of events include "User Registered," "Order Placed," and "Payment Processed." Events are typically structured in a standardized format and contain relevant data about the event, such as event type, timestamp, and payload. In event sourcing, there is always confusion about what an event is. In event sourcing, the events *cannot* move outside the services; doing so is a recipe for disaster. Events that are used in event sourcing have the purpose of mutating the state of an aggregate. Events that you send outside the microservices have the purpose of telling if something interesting happens and are fatter.

- **Publish-subscribe pattern**: The most common pattern for event-driven communication is the publish-subscribe pattern. In this pattern, there are two main actors: publishers and subscribers. Publishers generate events and publish them to a central event broker or message queue. Subscribers express interest in specific types of events and receive copies of the events they are interested in from the event broker.

- **Event broker**: The event broker acts as an intermediary between publishers and subscribers. It receives events from publishers and distributes them to all relevant subscribers. The event broker allows decoupling between the event producer and the event consumer. Commonly used event brokers include Apache Kafka, RabbitMQ, and Amazon **Simple Notification Service (SNS)**.

- **Decoupling**: Event-driven communication fosters loose coupling between components. Publishers and subscribers are independent of each other, and they do not need to be aware of each other's existence. This allows services to evolve and scale independently without affecting others in the system – so long as you use event versioning to avoid having coupling.

- **Scalability**: Event-driven communication facilitates horizontal scalability because new instances of a service can subscribe to events and handle incoming messages without requiring coordination with other services. This makes it easier to distribute the processing load across multiple instances.

- **Asynchronous processing**: Event-driven communication is inherently asynchronous. When a component generates an event, it does not have to wait for a response from other components. Events are processed independently and at the convenience of each subscriber, enabling faster response times and better fault tolerance.

- **Event sourcing and CQRS**: Event-driven communication is often used in conjunction with event sourcing and CQRS patterns. Event sourcing involves persisting all state changes as a sequence of events, while CQRS separates read and write operations. Events are the source of truth for the state of the system, and different services can maintain their view of the data by subscribing to relevant events.

- **Distributed systems challenges**: While event-driven communication offers numerous benefits, it also introduces challenges in distributed systems. These include event ordering, event duplication, handling event failures, and ensuring eventual consistency across services.

Event-driven communication is a powerful approach for building scalable and loosely coupled distributed systems, particularly in the context of microservices architectures. It enables efficient, asynchronous, and event-based interactions between components, promoting flexibility and responsiveness in modern software applications.

Service resilience and fault tolerance

Service resilience and fault tolerance are two critical aspects of building robust and reliable software systems, particularly in the context of microservices architecture and distributed systems. Both concepts aim to ensure that the system can continue to function properly and provide essential services, even in the face of failures or adverse conditions. Let's explore each concept:

- **Service resilience**: Service resilience refers to the ability of a system or a service to remain responsive and operational in the presence of failures, errors, or unexpected conditions. Resilience is about gracefully handling failures and degradations, rather than trying to prevent failures entirely (which can be impractical or costly).

  The following are some key aspects of service resilience:

  - **Failure isolation**: Resilient services are designed to isolate failures, ensuring that a failure in one service does not propagate and affect other parts of the system. This involves using techniques such as fault domains and circuit breakers to contain the impact of failures. When implemented correctly, you can reduce the domino effect of services failing in response to a service going down.

  - **Graceful degradation**: Resilient services may degrade their functionality in response to failures but continue to provide essential services to clients. For example, if a non-critical component is unavailable, the service may still operate, albeit with reduced capabilities.

  - **Backpressure and throttling**: Resilient services implement mechanisms to manage incoming requests and prevent overload during times of high traffic or stress. Techniques such as backpressure and request throttling can help protect the system from being overwhelmed.

  - **Retries and timeouts**: Resilient services employ appropriate retry and timeout strategies to handle transient failures. For example, when a service call fails, the client may retry the request a few times before giving up or setting a timeout to avoid waiting indefinitely.

  - **Monitoring and alerting**: Service resilience often involves proactively monitoring the system's health and performance. Alerts are set up to notify operations teams when issues arise, allowing them to respond promptly to potential problems.

  - **Automatic healing**: In some cases, resilient services can automatically recover from certain types of failures or self-heal. For instance, a failed container in a container orchestration system such as Kubernetes may be automatically replaced.

- **Fault tolerance**: Fault tolerance is the ability of a system to continue operating properly even when one or more components fail. It involves designing the system in a way that mitigates the impact of failures and provides redundancy and backups to ensure continuity of service.

  Here are some key aspects of fault tolerance:

  - **Redundancy**: Fault-tolerant systems often have redundant components to take over when primary components fail. This redundancy ensures that critical services are still available even if some components become unavailable.

  - **Failover and replication**: Fault-tolerant systems implement failover mechanisms that allow secondary components to take over the responsibilities of failed components. Data replication may also be used to ensure that data remains available in case of failures.

  - **State management**: Fault-tolerant systems manage state and data in a way that can be easily recovered in case of failures. This could involve using distributed databases with replication or snapshotting mechanisms.

  - **High availability**: Fault-tolerant systems aim to achieve high availability by minimizing downtime and ensuring that services are accessible even during component failures.

  - **Distributed consistency**: In distributed systems, maintaining consistency across nodes is crucial for fault tolerance. Techniques such as distributed consensus protocols help achieve consensus on critical decisions and data.

By implementing service resilience and fault tolerance techniques, software systems can continue to operate effectively, even in the face of failures, thereby providing better reliability and improving the overall user experience. These principles are especially relevant in microservices architectures, where individual services must be able to handle failures independently and gracefully interact with other services in the system.

Service monitoring and observability

Service monitoring and observability are crucial practices in maintaining and understanding the health and performance of software systems, especially in the context of microservices architecture and distributed systems. They involve collecting, analyzing, and acting upon data to ensure the system's reliability, identify issues, and make informed decisions for improvement.

Service monitoring

Service monitoring involves the systematic collection and analysis of various metrics and logs from the software components and infrastructure to assess the system's health and performance. Monitoring provides real-time visibility into the system's behavior, enabling quick detection of anomalies and issues. Some key aspects of service monitoring are as follows:

- **Metrics collection**: Monitoring tools gather quantitative data, such as CPU usage, memory consumption, request rates, error rates, and response times, from various components and services. These metrics offer insights into resource utilization and system performance.

- **Logging**: Logging involves capturing and storing relevant events and information generated by the application or infrastructure. Logs provide a historical record of activities, errors, and other important events, facilitating post-mortem analysis and troubleshooting.

- **Alerting**: Monitoring systems are often configured to trigger alerts based on predefined thresholds or anomaly detection algorithms. When certain metrics exceed or fall below acceptable levels, alerts notify operations teams of potential issues requiring immediate attention.

- **Dashboarding**: Monitoring tools typically offer real-time dashboards that display key metrics in a visual and easily understandable format. Dashboards allow teams to quickly assess the overall health and performance of the system at a glance.

- **Long-term storage**: Some monitoring systems retain historical data for longer periods, enabling trend analysis, capacity planning, and retrospective investigations.

- **Integration with incident management**: Monitoring tools are often integrated with incident management systems. When alerts are triggered, incidents can be automatically created, tracked, and resolved in an organized manner.

Observability

Observability goes beyond traditional monitoring and focuses on providing insights into the system's internal behavior, making it easier to understand and debug complex distributed systems. Observability emphasizes understanding the system's overall behavior through the analysis of distributed traces, logs, and application-level events. Some key aspects of observability are as follows:

- **Distributed tracing**: Observability tools enable distributed tracing, which tracks requests as they flow through the microservices architecture. It provides a complete view of how requests propagate across services, helping identify performance bottlenecks and dependencies.

- **Contextual logging**: Observability often involves enriching logs with contextual information, such as request IDs and correlation IDs, to trace a request's path through the system effectively.

- **Metrics aggregation and correlation**: Observability tools can aggregate metrics across services to identify patterns and correlations. This helps in understanding how the system behaves as a whole and how changes in one service affect others.

- **Application-level events**: Observability tools capture application-level events and activities, providing deeper insights into the system's behavior beyond standard metrics.

- **Interactive exploration**: Observability platforms offer interactive exploration capabilities, allowing developers and operators to dive deeper into specific events, logs, or traces for detailed analysis.

By combining service monitoring and observability practices, development and operations teams can gain a comprehensive understanding of the system's behavior, troubleshoot issues more effectively, and make informed decisions to optimize the performance, scalability, and reliability of the software system.

Security

Microservices security is a critical aspect of designing and implementing microservices architectures. As microservices communicate over networks and interact with each other, securing the communication and data becomes paramount to protect against potential security threats and vulnerabilities. Here are some key considerations and best practices for microservices security:

- **Authentication and authorization**: Implement robust authentication mechanisms to ensure that only authorized users or services can access specific microservices. Use protocols such as OAuth, JWT, or API keys to authenticate users and services and grant them appropriate access rights based on their roles and permissions.

- **Secure communication**: Use secure communication protocols, such as HTTPS (TLS/SSL), to encrypt data transmitted between microservices. This ensures that sensitive information remains confidential and protected from eavesdropping and man-in-the-middle attacks.

- **Service-to-service communication**: Secure service-to-service communication using techniques such as **mutual TLS (mTLS)** authentication. This means that each service is both a client and a server, and they mutually authenticate each other during communication.

- **API gateway security**: If an API gateway is used to handle client requests and route them to microservices, secure the API gateway with proper authentication and access control mechanisms. The API gateway can also be a central point for implementing security policies, rate limiting, and throttling.

- **Input validation and sanitization**: Implement input validation and data sanitization at every entry point to microservices (for example, APIs and user interfaces) to prevent injection attacks and protect against malicious input.

- **Error handling:** Be cautious with error handling to avoid exposing sensitive information to attackers. Provide informative error messages to developers but limit the details that are exposed to end users.

- **Secrets management**: Store and manage secrets, such as API keys, passwords, and cryptographic keys, securely using tools such as Vault or **Key Management Service (KMS)**. Avoid hardcoding secrets in configuration files or source code.

- **Container security**: If microservices are containerized, ensure container images are built from trusted sources, and regularly update them to address security vulnerabilities. Apply container security best practices, such as restricting access to the host operating system and employing minimalistic base images.

- **Continuous security testing**: Implement continuous security testing practices, including static code analysis, dynamic security scanning, and vulnerability assessments, to identify and remediate security issues throughout the development and deployment process.

- **Logging and monitoring**: Implement comprehensive logging and monitoring to track activities and detect potential security breaches. Use centralized logging and monitoring tools to analyze logs and metrics from various microservices effectively.

- **Least privilege principle**: Follow the principle of least privilege, where each service should have the minimum permissions required to perform its tasks, reducing the potential impact of a security breach.

- **Regular security audits**: Conduct regular security audits and penetration testing to assess the security posture of the microservices architecture and identify potential vulnerabilities.

Remember that securing microservices is an ongoing process that requires a combination of secure coding practices, proper configuration, continuous monitoring, and a security-focused culture within the development and operations teams. By integrating security measures into the microservices architecture from the outset, you can significantly reduce the risk of security breaches and protect sensitive data and resources.

CI/CD

CI/CD is an essential practice in software development, and it becomes even more critical in the context of microservices architectures. CI/CD enables teams to automate and streamline the process of building, testing, and deploying microservices, ensuring faster and more reliable releases. Let's explore the use of CI/CD with microservices:

- **CI**: CI involves frequently integrating code changes from multiple developers into a shared repository. The goal is to detect integration issues early and ensure that the code base is continuously up-to-date and in a working state. With microservices, CI involves integrating changes from different teams working on individual services and ensuring that they work harmoniously together. The benefit of microservices is that the code base of a microservice is small, which allows the team to use trunk-based development or Gitflow with really short-lived branches. By leveraging Pull Requests and a series of automated testing in Pull requests, you can enforce versioning and other requirements.

Here are some key CI practices in a microservices context:

- **Automated builds**: Each microservice should have a build pipeline to automate the build process. This ensures that changes made to the microservice's code are automatically built and tested.

- **Unit and integration testing**: Automated testing is crucial to validate the functionality and integration of each microservice. Unit tests ensure that individual components work as expected, while integration tests validate the interaction between microservices.

- **Code reviews**: CI encourages frequent code reviews to maintain code quality and to ensure that changes meet the project's standards. Using Git, you can use Pull Requests to ensure that every modification is reviewed by the team. You can also run unit and integration tests automatically in Pull request code so that errors are caught before they reach the production branch.

- **Version control**: Microservices should be versioned in the code repository to enable proper management and tracking of changes.

- **CD**: CD involves automatically deploying changes to production once they've passed the automated tests. In a microservices architecture, CD becomes complex as each microservice may have its own deployment process. Coordinating the deployment of multiple microservices can be challenging.

Here are some key CD practices in a microservices context:

- **Deployment automation**: Automate the deployment of microservices to ensure consistency and reduce the risk of manual errors. Containerization (for example, Docker) and container orchestration (for example, Kubernetes) can facilitate this process.

- **Rollout strategies**: Implement different rollout strategies, such as blue-green deployments, canary releases, or feature toggles, to manage the gradual release of new versions and ensure smooth deployments with minimal disruption.

- **Service discovery**: Use service discovery mechanisms to enable newly deployed microservices to be discovered and accessed by other services seamlessly.

- **Monitoring and rollback**: Implement monitoring and alerting to track the health of microservices after deployment. In case of issues or performance degradation, CD pipelines should allow you to automatically roll back to the previous stable version.

- **Microservices-specific challenges**: While CI/CD is beneficial for microservices, it comes with some specific challenges:

- **Integration testing complexity**: Testing the integration of multiple microservices can be complex, especially when you're dealing with dependencies and communication between services. Each microservice team must give the other a simple mock version of their service. This mock is used during integration tests. Usually, the mock can randomly or programmatically fail.

- **Dependency management**: Microservices might have different release cycles and dependencies, making it essential to manage version compatibility and ensure smooth updates.

- **Data migrations**: Coordinating database schema changes and data migrations across microservices can be challenging.

- **Deployment orchestration**: Coordinating the deployment of multiple microservices with interdependencies requires careful planning and orchestration.

Despite these challenges, CI/CD is crucial for the success of microservices. It accelerates the development process, reduces manual errors, and allows teams to deliver new features and bug fixes more frequently, all while maintaining a reliable and stable system. As a result, CI/CD is a fundamental part of modern software development practices and plays a significant role in supporting microservices' agility and scalability.

Microservice testing

Microservice testing is a crucial aspect of developing robust and reliable microservices-based applications. As microservices are individual, independent services that interact with each other through APIs, they need to be thoroughly tested to ensure they function correctly both in isolation and when integrated with other services. Effective microservice testing involves a combination of unit testing, integration testing, and end-to-end testing to verify the functionality, performance, and stability of each service.

Here are the key types of microservice testing:

- **Unit testing**: Unit testing focuses on testing individual units or components of a microservice in isolation. It involves testing functions, methods, or classes to ensure they work as intended and produce the expected results. Unit tests are written to cover various scenarios and edge cases, providing quick feedback on the correctness of code implementations.

  In microservices, unit tests typically focus on testing the core business logic of each service independently. Since microservices are small and focused, unit testing can be highly effective in detecting bugs early in the development process.

- **Integration testing**: Integration testing verifies the interaction and communication between multiple microservices and their dependencies. The goal is to ensure that services work correctly when integrated with other services and external components, such as databases, message brokers, and third-party APIs.

  In microservices, integration testing may involve running tests against actual services, stubbing or mocking external dependencies, or using containerization and test environments to replicate the production environment more accurately.

- **Component testing**: Component testing aims to test a group of related microservices together as a cohesive unit. Instead of testing each microservice in isolation, component testing focuses on validating the interactions and collaborations between services that belong to the same functional area or domain.

Component tests provide a middle ground between unit tests and end-to-end tests, allowing developers to identify issues related to service integration without the complexity of end-to-end testing.

- **End-to-end testing**: End-to-end testing verifies the complete flow of a business process or user journey across multiple microservices. It aims to validate that the entire application works as expected, from the user interface to the backend services.

  End-to-end tests often simulate real user interactions and scenarios, helping to ensure that the microservices work harmoniously together. However, end-to-end testing can be more complex and time-consuming compared to other types of testing, so it's essential to strike a balance and focus on critical user journeys.

- **Performance testing**: Performance testing evaluates the responsiveness and stability of microservices under various load conditions. It helps identify performance bottlenecks, resource limitations, and potential scalability issues.

  Performance testing in microservices may involve stress testing, load testing, and capacity planning to ensure the services can handle the expected traffic and user demand.

- **Security testing**: Security testing focuses on identifying vulnerabilities and weaknesses in microservices that may lead to security breaches. It involves testing for common security issues, such as SQL injection, **cross-site scripting** (**XSS**), and unauthorized access.

  Security testing is crucial for microservices as a security vulnerability in one service can potentially compromise the entire system.

To effectively test microservices, automation is key. Automated testing enables rapid feedback, allows for continuous integration and deployment, and ensures that tests can be run consistently across different environments. Additionally, testing microservices in isolation, using mocking or stubbing for external dependencies, and adopting a **test-driven development** (**TDD**) approach, can contribute to building more resilient and maintainable microservices.

Scaling microservices

Microservice scaling refers to the process of adjusting the capacity and performance of individual microservices to meet the changing demands of a system. Scaling is essential in microservices architectures, where different services may have varying resource requirements and experience different levels of traffic at different times. By scaling microservices appropriately, you can ensure optimal resource utilization, high availability, and responsiveness. There are two main types of scaling – horizontal scaling and vertical scaling:

- **Horizontal scaling**: Horizontal scaling, also known as scaling out, involves adding more instances of a microservice to distribute the workload across multiple servers or containers. Each instance operates independently and can handle requests in parallel. Horizontal scaling is the preferred approach in microservices architectures as it allows for more flexible and granular resource allocation.

Here are some key aspects of horizontal scaling:

- **Load balancing**: To effectively distribute incoming requests across multiple instances of a microservice, a load balancer is used. This load balancer ensures that each instance receives a fair share of requests and prevents any single instance from becoming overloaded.

- **Statelessness**: For seamless horizontal scaling, microservices should be stateless, meaning that they do not rely on storing session or state information on the server. Instead, state is managed externally (for example, in databases or caches) to allow any instance to handle any request.

- **Container orchestration**: In containerized environments, horizontal scaling can be managed by container orchestration platforms such as Kubernetes or Docker Swarm. These platforms can automatically spin up new instances of a microservice based on predefined rules and policies.

- **Vertical scaling**: Vertical scaling, also known as scaling up, involves increasing the resources (such as CPU, memory, or storage) of a single instance of a microservice. In this approach, you upgrade the server or virtual machine where the microservice is running to handle increased demand or resource-intensive tasks.

Here are some key aspects of vertical scaling:

- **Resource allocation**: To vertically scale a microservice, you need to ensure that the server or virtual machine has sufficient resources to handle the expected workload. This may involve upgrading the server's CPU, adding more memory, or increasing storage capacity.

- **Limitations**: Vertical scaling has limitations as there is a maximum capacity that a single server or virtual machine can handle. Additionally, vertical scaling may cause temporary downtime during the upgrade process. Thanks to the cloud, vertical scaling is probably a cost problem. Horizontal scaling is something you need to take into account during development and is the preferred way to scale up cost-effectively. Scaling up has no linear cost, while horizontal scaling does.

In practice, a combination of horizontal and vertical scaling may be used to achieve the desired level of performance and resource optimization for a microservices architecture. Horizontal scaling is typically the preferred approach for handling dynamic workloads and ensuring high availability, while vertical scaling can be useful for addressing short-term spikes in resource demands.

Implementing effective microservice scaling requires closely monitoring performance metrics, resource utilization, and traffic patterns. Automated scaling solutions, such as auto-scaling in cloud environments, can dynamically adjust the number of instances based on predefined rules and performance thresholds, allowing the system to adapt to changing demands automatically. By scaling microservices appropriately, you can build flexible, resilient, and highly responsive applications that can handle varying workloads and ensure a positive user experience.

Versioning and compatibility

Microservice versioning and compatibility are essential considerations when working with microservices architectures. As microservices are developed and deployed independently, changes to their interfaces or behaviors can lead to compatibility issues between services. Proper versioning and compatibility management are crucial to ensure smooth communication and collaboration between microservices:

- **Microservice versioning**: Microservice versioning refers to the practice of assigning unique identifiers to different versions of a microservice's API, data structures, or contract. When a change is made to a microservice, the version is incremented, allowing clients and other microservices to know which version of the service they are interacting with.

  There are different approaches to versioning microservices:

  - **URL versioning**: In this approach, the version is included in the URL of the API endpoint. For example, "/v1/customers" and "/v2/customers" represent different versions of the "customers" API.

  - **Header versioning**: The version information is included in a request header. This keeps the URL clean but requires clients to explicitly specify the desired version in each request.

  - **Media type versioning**: The version is embedded in the media type or content type of the request or response payload.

  - **Semantic Versioning (SemVer)**: SemVer is a versioning convention that follows the "MAJOR. MINOR.PATCH" format, where each part represents significant changes, backward-compatible changes, and bug fixes, respectively.

  Proper versioning helps maintain backward compatibility while introducing changes to microservices, ensuring that existing clients can continue to communicate with older versions while new clients use the latest version.

- **Microservice compatibility**: Microservice compatibility refers to the ability of a microservice to interact and collaborate effectively with other services, regardless of the versions they are running. Maintaining compatibility is crucial to avoid breaking existing integrations and causing disruptions in the system.

  Some key aspects of microservice compatibility are as follows:

  - **Backward compatibility**: New versions of microservices should strive to be backward compatible, meaning they can handle requests and responses from older versions without issues. Existing clients should continue to work as expected when interacting with newer versions of the microservice.

  - **Forward compatibility**: Services should also be forward compatible, meaning they can handle requests from newer versions of clients. This allows clients to be updated independently without breaking the interaction with the microservice.

- **Graceful deprecation**: When deprecating older versions of a microservice, provide sufficient notice to clients and allow for a transition period. During this period, both the old and new versions should be supported.

- **API documentation**: Maintain up-to-date and detailed API documentation, including version information, to help clients understand changes and adapt their integrations accordingly.

- **Testing and version management**: Comprehensive testing and version management processes are essential to ensure that new versions of microservices work seamlessly with existing components.

- **Service discovery and registration**: Proper service discovery and registration mechanisms are crucial to allow clients to locate and interact with the appropriate versions of microservices dynamically.

By adopting effective versioning practices and ensuring compatibility, microservices can evolve and improve independently while maintaining smooth communication and collaboration across the system. This promotes a more agile and resilient microservices architecture, enabling faster development cycles and easier deployment of new features and updates.

Microservices best practices and anti-patterns

Microservices have become a popular architectural style for building modern, scalable, and maintainable applications. While microservices offer numerous benefits, it is essential to follow best practices and avoid common anti-patterns to maximize their advantages and mitigate potential challenges. Let's explore some key microservices best practices and anti-patterns.

Microservices best practices

These are as follows:

- **Single responsibility principle (SRP)**: Each microservice should have a single responsibility or business domain. This ensures that microservices are focused, maintainable, and loosely coupled.

- **Decentralized data management**: Each microservice should have its own database or data store, enabling independent scaling and isolation of data.

- **Service independence**: Microservices should be developed, deployed, and scaled independently. Avoid tight coupling between services to allow for flexible development and deployment.

- **Service contracts and APIs**: Define clear contracts and well-defined APIs for communication between microservices. This promotes consistency and avoids compatibility issues.

- **Containerization**: Use containerization (for example, Docker) to package microservices with their dependencies, ensuring consistency across development, testing, and production environments.

- **Container orchestration**: Use container orchestration platforms (for example, Kubernetes) to automate the deployment, scaling, and management of microservices.

- **Automated testing**: Implement comprehensive automated testing (unit, integration, and end-to-end) to ensure the correctness and reliability of microservices.

- **CI/CD**: Adopt CI/CD pipelines to automate the build, testing, and deployment of microservices for rapid and reliable releases.

- **Monitoring and observability**: Implement monitoring and observability practices to gain insights into the health and performance of microservices, facilitating troubleshooting and performance optimization.

- **Graceful degradation**: Design microservices to gracefully degrade functionality when facing partial failures or high loads, ensuring availability and responsiveness.

Microservices anti-patterns

The following are some crucial considerations when designing and implementing microservices architectures:

- **Monolithic communication**:

  - **Risk**: Synchronous and chatty communication patterns between microservices can lead to increased latency and performance bottlenecks.

  - **Long-term impact**: Such communication patterns can result in a tightly coupled system, limiting the benefits of microservices. Adopting asynchronous communication, such as message queues or event-driven patterns, can enhance scalability and maintainability.

- **Data sharing among microservices**:

  - **Risk**: Direct data sharing may cause tight coupling and jeopardize data consistency across microservices

  - **Long-term impact**: Asynchronous communication or event-driven patterns, such as publish-subscribe, allow microservices to exchange information without direct coupling, fostering autonomy and flexibility in development and deployment

- **Inadequate security**:

  - **Risk**: Insufficient security measures can expose vulnerabilities, risking data breaches and unauthorized access.

  - **Long-term impact**: Robust authentication, authorization, and encryption mechanisms are imperative for securing microservices. Regular security audits and updates are essential to protect against evolving threats.

- **Ignoring boundaries**:

  - **Risk**: Ill-defined boundaries between microservices can lead to overlapping functionality and reduced autonomy

  - **Long-term impact**: Clearly defining and enforcing boundaries ensures each microservice's independence and facilitates easier maintenance, updates, and scaling

- **Ignoring failure scenarios**:

  - **Risk**: Failing to plan for failure scenarios can result in cascading failures and system downtime

  - **Long-term impact**: Implementing fallback mechanisms, retry strategies, and effective error handling is critical for system resilience and minimizing the impact of failures

- **Microservices for all use cases**:

  - **Risk**: Applying microservices to every use case may introduce unnecessary complexity.

  - **Long-term impact**: Evaluate whether a monolithic or microservices architecture is more suitable for specific use cases. Striking a balance ensures optimal system architecture and development efficiency.

- **Microservices at early stages**:

  - **Risk**: Premature adoption of microservices can lead to complexity and hinder development progress.

  - **Long-term impact**: Start with a monolithic architecture and transition to microservices as the application's complexity and team capabilities evolve. Gradual adoption allows for more informed decisions.

- **Overlooking testing and deployment automation**:

  - **Risk**: Neglecting automated testing and deployment pipelines can result in errors and slow release cycles

  - **Long-term impact**: Investing in comprehensive testing suites, continuous integration, and deployment automation ensures consistent, error-free releases and accelerates development cycles

Incorporating these considerations into the microservices design process contributes to the long-term success, scalability, and maintainability of the overall system. Regular reassessment and adaptation are essential as the system evolves and requirements change.

Case studies and real-world examples

Here are some real-world examples and case studies of companies that have successfully adopted microservices architectures:

- **Netflix**: Netflix is one of the most well-known examples of a company that embraced microservices. They transitioned from a monolithic architecture to a microservices-based architecture to improve agility and scalability. By breaking down their application into hundreds of small, loosely coupled microservices, Netflix can innovate faster and release new features frequently. Each microservice is responsible for a specific aspect of the application, such as recommendation algorithms, user authentication, and video streaming.

- **Uber**: Uber also adopted a microservices architecture to handle its massive scale and dynamic demands. Microservices at Uber manage various functionalities, including user registration, trip management, payment processing, and geolocation services. This architecture allows Uber to independently scale services based on the specific demands of each component. It also supports the rapid development of new features and services to enhance the overall customer experience.

- **Amazon**: Amazon is another prominent company that employs microservices extensively. Amazon's retail platform is composed of a vast number of microservices, each responsible for specific tasks such as inventory management, order processing, product recommendations, and payment processing. This architecture enables Amazon to handle high traffic loads during peak shopping seasons and efficiently manage its large product catalog. The following article is worth reading: *Return of the Monolith: Amazon Dumps Microservices for Video Monitoring - The New Stack* (`https://thenewstack.io/return-of-the-monolith-amazon-dumps-microservices-for-video-monitoring/`). Sometimes, monoliths produce superior performance to services.

- **Etsy**: Etsy, an online marketplace for handmade and vintage products, shifted to a microservices architecture to improve scalability and developer productivity. By adopting microservices, Etsy's development teams gained autonomy over their services, enabling them to innovate faster and respond to user needs more effectively. The company also reported improved service reliability and faster deployments.

- **SoundCloud**: SoundCloud, a popular music streaming platform, re-architected its application using microservices to handle the growing number of users and media files. The microservices architecture allowed SoundCloud to scale different parts of their system independently, ensuring that services for uploading, processing, and streaming music could be individually optimized and scaled to meet the demands of the platform's users.

- **Zalando**: Zalando, a leading European fashion platform, adopted microservices to build a more flexible and scalable architecture. Their microservices architecture allows them to continuously deploy new features and services, supporting rapid growth and frequent changes to their platform.

These case studies demonstrate how microservices can help organizations achieve improved scalability, flexibility, and developer productivity. However, it's essential to keep in mind that adopting microservices is not without its challenges. The transition from monolithic architecture to microservices requires careful planning, investment in infrastructure, and a cultural shift within development teams. When implemented correctly, microservices can offer significant benefits for organizations aiming to build and maintain complex, scalable, and highly available applications.

Summary

Microservices is an architectural style for building software applications that focuses on breaking down the application into a collection of small, independent services, each running in its own process and communicating over lightweight protocols.

Microservices architecture emphasizes the principle of "divide and conquer" by breaking down complex applications into smaller, manageable, and loosely coupled services. Each microservice represents a specific business capability or domain, and they can be developed, deployed, and scaled independently.

Microservices offer numerous advantages, including improved scalability, flexibility, maintainability, and faster development cycles. They allow for granular scaling, independent service updates, and better isolation of failures. They also have several defining characteristics, including single responsibility, independence, decentralized data management, and communication through APIs.

Service discovery and registration mechanisms are essential for enabling microservices to locate and communicate with each other in a dynamic and distributed environment. Note that microservices need to be designed to handle failures gracefully and in a way that isolates failures to prevent cascading effects.

Containerization, such as using Docker, simplifies deployment and ensures consistency across various environments. Container orchestration platforms, such as Kubernetes, automate the management and scaling of containerized microservices.

API gateways act as central entry points for external clients and manage requests, load balancing, and communication with microservices.

Event-driven communication enables asynchronous and loosely coupled interactions between microservices through the exchange of events, promoting scalability and responsiveness.

Effective monitoring and observability practices are essential for gaining insights into the health and performance of microservices as they facilitate troubleshooting and performance optimization.

Proper versioning and compatibility management are crucial to ensure smooth communication and collaboration between microservices during updates.

Key best practices include adhering to the SRP, automated testing, continuous integration and deployment, and proper service contract definitions.

Common anti-patterns to avoid include monolithic communication, inadequate security, data sharing among microservices, and overusing microservices for all use cases.

Microservices offer a modern approach to building complex, scalable, and maintainable applications. However, adopting microservices requires careful planning, a cultural shift in development practices, and a focus on best practices to realize their full potential and achieve the desired benefits.

Questions

Answer the following questions to test your knowledge of this chapter:

1. What is microservices architecture?
2. What are the benefits of adopting microservices architecture?
3. How do microservices communicate with each other?
4. What is the role of service discovery in microservices?
5. How does containerization contribute to microservices architecture?
6. What are some key considerations for ensuring service resilience in microservices?
7. Why is automated testing important in microservices development?

Further reading

Here is a list of further reading resources on developing microservices in C#:

- *Building Microservices with ASP.NET Core*, by Kevin Hoffman, Chris Umbel, and Chris Richardson: This book explores microservices architecture using ASP.NET Core, providing practical examples and best practices for building microservices with C#.

- *Microservices in .NET Core: with examples in Nancy*, by Christian Horsdal Gammelgaard: This book delves into the fundamentals of microservices and demonstrates how to implement them using .NET Core, with a focus on the Nancy framework.

- *Microservices Architecture: Make the Architecture of a Software as Simple as Possible*, by Shahid Hussain: This book offers insights into microservices architecture, design principles, and C# implementation strategies, making it a valuable resource for C# developers.

- *Building Microservices with .NET Core 2.0 – Second Edition*, by Gaurav Kumar Aroraa: This book provides a comprehensive guide to building microservices with .NET Core, covering various aspects such as testing, containerization, and deployment.

- *Microservices in Action*, by Morgan Bruce and Paulo A. Pereira: Although not C#-specific, this book offers a practical guide to implementing microservices in various languages, including C#. It covers essential concepts and best practices for microservices development.

- *Designing Distributed Systems: Patterns and Paradigms for Scalable, Reliable Services*, by Brendan Burns and David Oppenheimer: While not C#-specific, this book provides valuable insights into the principles and patterns of designing distributed systems, which are fundamental to microservices architecture.

- *Learn Microservices with C#*, by Matt Parsons: This online course on Pluralsight provides a hands-on approach to building microservices using C# and .NET Core, covering topics such as API gateways, service discovery, and monitoring.

- *Microservices Fundamentals (Microsoft Docs)* (`https://docs.microsoft.com/en-us/dotnet/architecture/microservices/`): Microsoft's official documentation on microservices, specifically focused on C# and .NET Core, covers essential concepts and implementation guidelines.

These resources should provide a solid foundation and practical guidance for you to explore and implement microservices architecture in your projects.

Assessments

Chapter 1

1. Bad code refers to code that is difficult to understand, hard to maintain, prone to bugs, or inefficient. It violates coding principles, standards, or best practices and may cause problems in the software.

2. Good code is code that is easy to understand, maintainable, bug-free, and efficient. It adheres to coding principles, standards, or best practices and contributes to the software's stability and reliability.

3. Some common signs of bad code include long and complex functions or classes, unclear variable or function names, poor error handling, lack of comments or documentation, and inconsistent formatting or indentation.

4. Some common coding standards include naming conventions for variables, functions, and classes, consistent indentation and formatting, using comments to explain code or document its purpose, following design patterns, and avoiding hard-coded values.

5. Some coding principles include DRY, SOLID, YAGNI, and KISS.

6. Agile software development is an iterative and incremental approach to software development that values flexibility, collaboration, and continuous improvement. It involves breaking down the development process into smaller chunks called sprints, where the team delivers working software at the end of each sprint.

7. TDD is a software development process that involves writing automated tests before writing the code to pass those tests. The goal is to ensure that the code is functional and bug-free from the start and to promote a more thorough understanding of the requirements and design.

8. Refactoring is the process of improving the quality and maintainability of existing code without changing its behavior. It involves making small, incremental changes to the code to remove duplication, improve readability, or simplify complexity. Refactoring is an essential part of maintaining a healthy code base over time.

Chapter 2

1. The two roles in the peer code review are reviewer and reviewee.

2. The project manager agrees on the people that will be involved in the peer code review.

3. You can save your reviewer time and effort prior to requesting a peer code review by making sure your code and tests all work, that you perform code analysis on your project and fix any issues raised, and that your code adheres to the company coding guidelines.

4. When reviewing code, look out for naming, formatting, programming styles, potential bugs, correctness of code and tests, security, and performance issues.

5. The three categories of feedback are positive, optional, and critical.

Chapter 3

1. We can organize classes in C# using namespaces, which provide a way to group related classes and avoid naming conflicts.

2. A class should have a single responsibility, following the SRP from the SOLID principles.

3. To comment code for document generators, use XML comments starting with /// to provide documentation for classes, methods, and parameters.

4. Cohesion refers to how closely related the responsibilities of elements within a module (for example, a class) are. High cohesion means elements are closely related and focused on a single task.

5. Coupling refers to the degree of dependency between modules or classes. Loose coupling means classes are less dependent on each other.

6. Cohesion should be high, meaning that a class should have a single, well-defined responsibility.

7. Coupling should be loose, indicating that classes should be as independent as possible.

8. Mechanisms for designing for change include SOLID principles, DI, and design patterns such as the strategy pattern.

9. DI stands for dependency injection, a design pattern in which a class's dependencies are provided externally rather than created within the class.

10. IoC stands for inversion of control, a design principle that promotes decoupling and allows the control of the flow of a program to be shifted to external components.

11. One benefit of using immutable objects is that they are inherently thread-safe, simplifying multi-threading and concurrency issues.

12. Objects should hide their internal state and implementation details while showing a well-defined, public interface.

13. Structures should also hide their internal state and expose a clear, public interface.

Chapter 4

1. Methods with no parameters are called niladic methods.

2. Methods with only one parameter are called monadic methods.

3.   Methods with two parameters are called dyadic methods.

4.   Methods with three parameters are called triadic methods.

5.   Methods with more than three parameters are called polyadic methods.

6.   You should avoid duplicate code. It is not a productive way to program, can make programs unnecessarily large, and has the propensity to proliferate the same exception throughout your codebase.

7.   Functional programming is a software coding methodology that treats computations as the mathematical evaluation of computations that does not modify state.

8.   The advantages of functional programming include safe code in multithreaded applications and smaller, more meaningful methods that are easy to read and understand.

9.   Input and output can be a problem for functional programs as it relies on side-effects. Functional programming does not allow for side-effects.

10. WET code is the opposite of DRY in that code is written each time it is needed. This produces duplication, and the same exception can occur in multiple locations within a program, making maintenance and support more difficult.

11. DRY code is the opposite of WET in that code is only ever written once and is reused wherever it is needed. This reduces the code base and exception footprint, thus making programs easier to read and maintain.

12. You DRY out WET code by removing duplicate code using refactoring.

13. Long methods are cumbersome and prone to exceptions. The smaller they are, the easier they are to read and maintain. There is also less chance of the programmer introducing bugs, especially of a logical nature.

14. To avoid having to use try-catch blocks, you can write argument validators. You would then call the validators at the top of your method. If the parameters fail validation, then the appropriate exception is thrown, and the method is not executed.

Chapter 5

1.   The principle of handling exceptions as close to the source of the error as possible is known as "Exception Handling Locality." It is important for clean code because it promotes clarity and helps in understanding the context of errors, making the code more maintainable and readable.

2.   Making exception handling more specific involves catching more derived exception types before more generic ones. This approach allows for more targeted handling of specific issues and provides better information about the nature of the problem.

3.   A finally block in a try-catch-finally statement is a section of code that executes regardless of whether an exception occurs or not. It is essential for writing robust and maintainable code because it ensures that cleanup or resource release operations are performed, even in the presence of exceptions.

4. Using custom exception types allows you to create meaningful and specific exceptions for different error scenarios. This enhances the clarity of your code, provides more information to developers, and makes it easier to maintain and extend the codebase.

5. Best practices for logging and handling exceptions in multithreaded code include using thread-safe logging mechanisms, avoiding global state changes in catch blocks, and ensuring proper synchronization to prevent race conditions.

6. The global exception handler provides a centralized location to handle unhandled exceptions in an application. By hooking into this handler, you can log exceptions, perform cleanup operations, and gracefully terminate the application, enhancing overall reliability.

7. Testing exception handling is important to ensure that your code behaves correctly in error scenarios. Common approaches include writing unit tests for expected exceptions, testing boundary conditions, and simulating error conditions to validate the robustness of your exception-handling logic.

8. Common pitfalls to avoid in exception-handling code include catching overly broad exception types, swallowing exceptions without proper logging, and relying too heavily on global exception handlers. To ensure effectiveness and maintainability, focus on handling specific exceptions, logging relevant information, and considering the impact on system stability.

9. Exception handling can impact code readability and maintainability by introducing additional control flow and nesting. Striking the right balance involves handling exceptions at an appropriate level, using clear and concise error messages, and organizing exception-handling code to minimize complexity while maintaining a clear understanding of error-handling logic.

Chapter 6

1. Testing frameworks for C#:

    - **NUnit**: Widely used, supports parameterized tests, lacks some advanced features.

    - **xUnit**: Similar to NUnit but newer, promotes more modern testing practices, extensible.

    - **MSTest**: Integrated with Visual Studio, easy setup, but historically considered less flexible.

2. Best practices for unit tests in C#:

    - **Isolation**: Tests should be independent, not relying on the OOE.

    - **Readability**: Clearly express the intent of the test and use meaningful names.

    - **Speed**: Tests should run quickly, enabling frequent execution.

    - **Maintainability**: Regularly update tests to reflect changes in the code base.

3. Mocking data in unit tests:

- Use mocking frameworks such as Moq or NSubstitute to create fake objects.

- Mock external dependencies by providing controlled responses to method calls.

- Focus on testing specific code units in isolation without invoking actual external services.

4. Code coverage analysis in Visual Studio 2022:

- **Code coverage**: Measures the percentage of code lines executed during tests.

- In Visual Studio 2022, use the built-in code coverage tool.

- Identify untested code areas and improve test coverage for more robust testing.

5. Ensuring unit tests are exception-free:

- Use `try-catch` blocks within tests to catch exceptions.

- Log or report exceptions for analysis without affecting the test run.

- Ensure that assertions and verifications are appropriately handled to prevent false positives in case of exceptions.

Chapter 7

1. Security in a C# API can be ensured by implementing proper authentication and authorization mechanisms. Best practices include using HTTPS to encrypt data in transit, employing secure token-based authentication (for example, OAuth 2.0 or JWT), validating and sanitizing input data to prevent injection attacks, and implementing role-based access control to manage user permissions.

2. OWASP is a nonprofit organization dedicated to improving the security of software. It provides resources, tools, and best practices to help organizations develop and maintain secure web applications. OWASP is known for its "OWASP Top 10," a list of the most critical web application security risks. Its significance lies in promoting awareness and providing a framework for addressing common security challenges in web development.

3. OIDC is an identity layer built on top of OAuth 2.0, providing authentication services. While OAuth 2.0 is primarily an authorization framework, OIDC adds an authentication layer, allowing clients to verify the identity of end users based on the authentication performed by an authorization server. OIDC defines additional endpoints and ID tokens to facilitate identity verification. In contrast, OAuth 2.0 focuses on delegated authorization for resource access.

4. OAuth 2.0 involves three main roles: the Resource Owner, the Client, and the Authorization Server. The Resource Owner owns the protected resources, the Client is the application seeking access to those resources, and the Authorization Server authenticates the Resource Owner and issues access tokens. The typical OAuth 2.0 flow involves the Client obtaining authorization from the Resource Owner through the Authorization Server, after which the Client uses the authorization to request an access token, allowing it to access protected resources on behalf of the Resource Owner.

Chapter 8

1. Aspects of a software system that cut across multiple modules or components, affecting the behavior and functionality of the application as a whole.

2. They have a huge impact on the application.

3. They significantly impact the overall quality, maintainability, and performance of the application.

4. Logging, error handling, exception management, security and authorization, caching, performance optimization, transaction management, validation, auditing and compliance, localization and internationalization, logging, and monitoring.

Chapter 9

1. An aspect is a modular unit of cross-cutting concerns that can be applied to multiple parts of a software system. Using PostSharp, an aspect is applied as an attribute to the location where the code is to be weaved.

2. In C#, an attribute is a declarative tag or an annotation that provides additional information about various program elements such as classes, methods, properties, or parameters. Attributes can be used to add metadata, define behavior, or modify the way program elements are treated by the runtime environment. You place an attribute at the correct location surrounded by square brackets: [AnAttribute].

3. Aspects are added to source code as attributes. This helps the AOP framework identify an attribute that is to be weaved at compile time.

4. The AOP framework forms part of the build pipeline. When an aspect is identified via an attribute, it is weaved into the source code by the AOP framework.

Chapter 10

1. Code metrics are several source code measurements that enable us to identify how complex our software is, and how maintainable it is. Such measurements enable us to identify areas of code that can be made less complex and more maintainable through refactoring.

2. Cyclomatic complexity, maintainability index, depth of inheritance, class coupling, lines of source code, and lines of executable code.

3. Code analysis is the static analysis of source code with the intention of identifying design flaws, issues with globalization, security problems, issues with performance, and interoperability problems.

4. Quick actions are single commands identified by a screwdriver or lightbulb that will suppress warnings, add using statements, import missing libraries and add the using statements, correct errors, and implement language usage improvements aimed at simplifying code and reducing the number of lines in a method.

5. JetBrains' dotTrace utility is a profiling tool used for the purpose of profiling source code and compiled assemblies to identify potential issues with the software. With it you can perform sampling, tracing, line-by-line, and timeline profiling. You can profile execution time, thread time, real-time CPU instructions, and thread cycle time.

6. JetBrains' ReSharper utility is a code refactoring tool that helps developers identify and fix code issues and implement language features to improve and speed up the programmer's programming experience.

7. The decompilation of source code can be used to retrieve lost source code, generate PDBs for debugging, and for learning. You can also use the decompiler to see how well you have obfuscated your code to make it hard for hackers and other people to steal your code secrets.

Chapter 11

1. The three main categories of code smells are as follows:

    - **Structural code smells**: These are issues related to the structure of the code, such as excessive complexity, long methods, and large classes

    - **Functional code smells**: These relate to problems in how the code functions, including duplicated code, inappropriate comments, and magic numbers

    - **Architectural code smells**: These involve higher-level architectural issues, such as improper layering, tight coupling, and violation of SOLID principles

2. Different types of application-level code smells include the following:

    - Feature envy

    - Shotgun surgery

    - Parallel inheritance hierarchies

    - Blob

    - Swiss Army knife

3. Different types of class-level code smells include the following:

- Large class

- God class

- Data class

- Refused bequest

- Divergent change

4. Different types of method-level code smells include the following:

- Long method

- Nested method calls

- Too many parameters

- Primitive obsession

- Temporary field

5. Various refactoring techniques can be used to clean up code smells, including extract method, extract class, remove duplication, rename method, replace conditional with polymorphism, and more, depending on the specific code smell and its context.

6. Cyclomatic complexity is a software metric that measures the complexity of a program's control flow. It counts the number of linearly independent paths through a function or method. It helps in identifying the number of test cases required for comprehensive test coverage.

7. Cyclomatic complexity can be overcome by simplifying control flow, breaking down complex functions into smaller ones, and adhering to coding practices that reduce branching and decision points.

8. Contrived complexity refers to unnecessary complexity introduced into code due to overengineering or using overly complex solutions for simple problems.

9. To overcome contrived complexity, simplify the code by removing unnecessary abstractions, design patterns, or features that do not provide significant benefits.

10. Combinatorial explosion occurs when the number of possible combinations or states grows exponentially, making it impractical to handle all cases individually.

11. Combinatorial explosion can be overcome by using abstraction, simplification, or heuristic approaches to reduce the number of possible combinations or by finding more efficient algorithms.

12. Deodorant comments are comments that are added to explain or justify bad or smelly code instead of fixing it. When you find them, you should refactor the code to make it self-explanatory and remove the need for such comments.

13. When you have bad code but don't know how to fix it, you should seek help from colleagues, mentors, or online programming communities for guidance and code review.

14. Online programming forums, such as Stack Overflow, are good places to ask questions and get answers when you're facing programming issues.

15. A long parameter list can be reduced by using parameter objects, creating builder patterns, or grouping related parameters into structures or classes.

16. A large method can be refactored by breaking it into smaller, more focused methods that perform specific tasks. This improves readability and maintainability.

17. There is no fixed maximum length for a clean method, but a common guideline is to keep methods concise and focused, typically no more than a few dozen lines. However, readability and maintainability should be the primary considerations.

18. The ideal cyclomatic complexity for a program should generally be within a range of 1 to 10, although this can vary depending on the specific project and context.

19. The ideal depth of inheritance should be shallow, preferably limited to one or two levels. Deep inheritance hierarchies can lead to complex and tightly coupled code.

20. Speculative generality occurs when code includes unnecessary abstractions, such as interfaces or classes, that serve no current purpose. To address this, remove these unused abstractions.

21. If you encounter an oddball solution, consider refactoring it so that it conforms to established coding standards and best practices. It's essential to maintain consistency in the code base.

22. If you encounter a temporary field, you can refactor it by moving the field to a more appropriate scope, such as a local variable, or by reevaluating its necessity in the code.

23. A data clump is a code smell where the same group of data or parameters is frequently passed around together. To address it, you can create a new data structure (for example, a class or struct) to encapsulate the related data.

24. Refused bequest is a code smell that occurs when a subclass inherits from a base class but only uses a small portion of the inherited methods or properties. To address it, refactor the inheritance hierarchy so that it matches the needs of the subclass.

25. Message chains break the Law of Demeter, which states that an object should not have to navigate multiple other objects to access its dependencies. Message chains can be refactored by introducing intermediate objects or using encapsulation to hide the chain.

26. To refactor message chains, you can introduce methods in intermediate objects that delegate the calls, reducing the coupling between objects and adhering to the Law of Demeter.

27. Feature envy occurs when one class accesses the data or methods of another class excessively. It suggests that the code should be refactored to move the functionality to the class where it belongs.

28. To remove feature envy, you can use techniques such as the move method or extract class to relocate the code that's overly dependent on another class.

29. To replace `switch` statements that return objects, you can use the factory method or strategy design patterns to encapsulate the logic and provide a more flexible and maintainable solution.

30. `if` statements that return objects can be replaced by using polymorphism, such as creating subclasses or implementing interfaces, to handle different cases more elegantly and maintainably.

31. Solution sprawl refers to a code base with an excessive number of projects, classes, or files, making it challenging to manage. To tackle this, you can consolidate related code, eliminate redundancy, and simplify the architecture.

32. The Tell, Don't Ask principle suggests that code should instruct objects to perform actions rather than querying objects for their state and making decisions based on that state.

33. The Tell, Don't Ask principle gets broken when code excessively queries object state and makes decisions externally instead of delegating the behavior to the objects themselves.

34. Symptoms of shotgun surgery include making changes to one part of the code base, resulting in the need to make numerous changes in other parts. It can be addressed by refactoring to reduce interdependencies between classes.

35. Lost intent occurs when code no longer reflects the original design or intent due to numerous modifications. To address this, refactor the code to clarify its purpose and document changes.

36. Loops can be refactored by using higher-level abstractions such as LINQ queries, introducing helper methods, or employing recursion where appropriate. These refactorings improve readability and maintainability.

37. Divergent change is a code smell where a class is frequently modified for various reasons unrelated to its primary responsibility. To refactor it, you can extract the divergent parts into separate classes or modules to improve the separation of concerns.

Chapter 12

1. Functional programming is a programming paradigm that treats computation as the evaluation of mathematical functions and avoids mutable data and state changes. It differs from imperative programming, where programs are written as sequences of statements that change the program's state.

2. Functional data transformation in C# can be achieved using pure functions and LINQ. By using LINQ methods such as Select, Where, and Aggregate, developers can transform data without modifying the original data structure. For example, numbers.Select(x => x * 2) will create a new sequence with each element doubled.

3. Functional error handling in C# involves representing errors as data instead of using exceptions. Option types and the Maybe monad are data structures that are used for error handling. Option types represent the presence or absence of a value, while the Maybe monad represents the success or failure of an operation. Using these constructs, developers can handle errors explicitly and create more reliable and maintainable code.

4. Functional pattern matching in C# can be accomplished using the switch statement with pattern matching, which was introduced in C# 7.0. It allows developers to match against types, constant values, or custom patterns to execute specific code blocks based on the matched pattern. For example, in switch (shape) { case Circle circle: ... }, the code block will execute if shape is of the Circle type.

5. Immutability in functional programming means that data cannot be changed after creation. In C#, immutability is achieved using read-only properties, read-only fields, and immutable data structures. Immutability helps with concurrency and thread safety by eliminating the risk of data corruption and race conditions when multiple threads access the same data.

6. Higher-order functions in functional programming are functions that take other functions as arguments or return functions as results. In C#, they can be used to create more modular and reusable code by parameterizing behavior. For example, a higher-order function can take a sorting function as an argument to sort a collection in different ways.

7. Concurrency with functional programming in C# involves using immutable data, pure functions, and asynchronous programming with async and await. Immutable data ensures that concurrent operations don't interfere with shared state, pure functions prevent side effects, and asynchronous programming allows non-blocking concurrent execution, leading to more responsive and scalable applications.

Chapter 13

1. .NET MAUI, or .NET Multi-platform App UI, is an open-source framework for building native cross-platform mobile and desktop apps using C# and XAML. It's an evolution of Xamarin. Forms and allows developers to create apps that run on multiple platforms, including Android, iOS, macOS, and Windows, while sharing a single codebase. .NET MAUI provides a unified API and tooling, making it easier to build applications that work consistently across different devices and platforms.

2. **MVVM,** which stands for **Model-View-ViewModel,** is a design pattern used in software development to separate the user interface (View) from the application's logic and data (Model) by introducing an intermediary component called ViewModel. With .NET MAUI, using the MVVM pattern can lead to better code organization, maintainability, and testability. MVVM helps keep the user interface code (XAML) separate from the application's business logic, making it easier to manage and maintain. It also enables better support for unit testing, as the ViewModel can be tested independently of the UI.

3. The CommunityToolkit.Mvvm is a library provided by the .NET community that extends the MVVM capabilities in .NET MAUI. It offers various MVVM-related components, including RelayCommand, ObservableObject, and other utility classes. By using this toolkit, developers can achieve cleaner and more maintainable code in .NET MAUI applications. It simplifies common MVVM tasks and provides tools for implementing the MVVM pattern effectively.

4. You add the QueryProperty to a ViewModel that has a name and queryid argument that are both strings. This allows you to pass parameters into the ViewModel. In the AppShell constructor, you use Routing.RegisterRoute to register the route to your View. Then in your navigation command, you navigate to the View passing in the parameters.

5. We register ViewModels by adding them as Singletons or Transients to builder.Services in the MauiProgram.CreateBuilder method.

6. The BindingContext.

7. An ObservableObject is a base class often used in the Model-View-ViewModel (MVVM) architectural pattern. It typically implements the INotifyPropertyChanged interface. The purpose of an ObservableObject is to notify subscribers (often the user interface) when the properties of the object change. By doing so, it ensures that the user interface stays in sync with the underlying data. In .NET MAUI, ObservableObject classes are often used as base classes for ViewModels, enabling clean and efficient data binding and updates in the user interface.

8. An ObservableProperty is a property within an ObservableObject that is designed to notify subscribers when its value changes. It's commonly used in MVVM patterns to expose data in a ViewModel. When the value of an ObservableProperty changes, it triggers the PropertyChanged event (from the INotifyPropertyChanged interface), informing the UI that the property's value has been updated. This allows for automatic updates in the user interface when the bound property changes.

9. A RelayCommand is a class used to handle commands in MVVM-based applications. It encapsulates a method (an action) that can be executed in response to user interactions, like button clicks or gestures. The primary purpose of a RelayCommand is to enable clean and consistent command handling in the ViewModel layer. It's often used to bind user interface elements (e.g., buttons) to specific actions or behaviors, allowing the ViewModel to execute these actions when the user interacts with the UI.

10. A CollectionView is a user interface component in .NET MAUI designed for displaying collections of data in a user-friendly manner. It provides features for data binding, grouping, sorting, filtering, and presenting data in various layouts (e.g., lists or grids). CollectionView is commonly used to visualize data from ViewModel collections in a structured and customizable way, making it easier to create interactive and responsive user interfaces.

11. An ObservableCollection is a specialized collection class in .NET that is commonly used in MVVM scenarios, including .NET MAUI. It extends the standard .NET Collection classes by implementing the INotifyCollectionChanged interface. The key feature of an ObservableCollection is its ability to automatically notify the UI when items are added, removed, or modified within the collection. This automatic notification ensures that the user interface stays synchronized with the underlying data, making it a suitable choice for presenting data in MVVM-based applications, especially when the data can change dynamically.

Chapter 14

1. Microservices architecture is an architectural style where complex applications are broken down into small, independent services, each running in its own process and communicating over lightweight protocols.

2. Some benefits include improved scalability, flexibility, maintainability, faster development cycles, and better isolation of failures.

3. Microservices communicate with each other through APIs, often using lightweight protocols such as HTTP/REST or message brokers in an event-driven communication pattern.

4. Service discovery enables microservices to locate and communicate with other services dynamically in a distributed environment, where the locations of services may change frequently.

5. Containerization, such as using Docker, simplifies the deployment process, ensures consistency across various environments, and allows microservices to be packaged with their dependencies.

6. Service resilience involves isolating failures, using circuit breakers, implementing retries and timeouts, and monitoring service health for prompt responses to issues.

7. Automated testing, including unit, integration, and end-to-end testing, helps ensure the correctness and reliability of microservices, supporting frequent and safe deployments.

Index

`Packtpub.com`

Subscribe to our online digital library for full access to over 7,000 books and videos, as well as industry leading tools to help you plan your personal development and advance your career. For more information, please visit our website.

Why subscribe?

- Spend less time learning and more time coding with practical eBooks and Videos from over 4,000 industry professionals

- Improve your learning with Skill Plans built especially for you

- Get a free eBook or video every month

- Fully searchable for easy access to vital information

- Copy and paste, print, and bookmark content

Did you know that Packt offers eBook versions of every book published, with PDF and ePub files available? You can upgrade to the eBook version at `packtpub.com` and as a print book customer, you are entitled to a discount on the eBook copy. Get in touch with us at `customercare@packtpub.com` for more details.

At `www.packtpub.com`, you can also read a collection of free technical articles, sign up for a range of free newsletters, and receive exclusive discounts and offers on Packt books and eBooks.

Other Books You May Enjoy

If you enjoyed this book, you may be interested in these other books by Packt:

Real-World Implementation of C# Design Patterns

Bruce M. Van Horn II

ISBN: 978-1-80324-273-6

- Get to grips with patterns, and discover how to conceive and document them
- Explore common patterns that may come up in your everyday work
- Recognize common anti-patterns early in the process
- Use creational patterns to create flexible and robust object structures
- Enhance class designs with structural patterns
- Simplify object interaction and behavior with behavioral patterns

Refactoring with C#

Matt Eland

ISBN: 978-1-83508-998-9

- Understand technical debt, its causes and effects, and ways to prevent it
- Explore different ways of refactoring classes, methods, and lines of code
- Discover how to write effective unit tests supported by libraries such as Moq
- Understand SOLID principles and factors that lead to maintainable code
- Use AI to analyze, improve, and test code with the GitHub Copilot Chat
- Apply code analysis and custom Roslyn analyzers to ensure that code stays clean
- Communicate tech debt and code standards successfully in agile teams

Packt is searching for authors like you

If you're interested in becoming an author for Packt, please visit `authors.packtpub.com` and apply today. We have worked with thousands of developers and tech professionals, just like you, to help them share their insight with the global tech community. You can make a general application, apply for a specific hot topic that we are recruiting an author for, or submit your own idea.

Share Your Thoughts

Now you've finished *Clean Code with C#*, we'd love to hear your thoughts! Scan the QR code below to go straight to the Amazon review page for this book and share your feedback or leave a review on the site that you purchased it from.

`https://packt.link/r/1837635196`

Your review is important to us and the tech community and will help us make sure we're delivering excellent quality content.

Download a free PDF copy of this book

Thanks for purchasing this book!

Do you like to read on the go but are unable to carry your print books everywhere?

Is your eBook purchase not compatible with the device of your choice?

Don't worry, now with every Packt book you get a DRM-free PDF version of that book at no cost.

Read anywhere, any place, on any device. Search, copy, and paste code from your favorite technical books directly into your application.

The perks don't stop there, you can get exclusive access to discounts, newsletters, and great free content in your inbox daily

Follow these simple steps to get the benefits:

1. Scan the QR code or visit the link below

https://packt.link/free-ebook/9781837635191

2. Submit your proof of purchase

3. That's it! We'll send your free PDF and other benefits to your email directly

Milton Keynes UK
Ingram Content Group UK Ltd.
UKHW032219271223
435071UK00012B/996

9 781837 635191